QUEEN OF THE GYPSIES

The Life and Legend of
CARMEN AMAYA

FLAMENCO IN THE THEATER AGE: 1910-1960

Paco Sevilla

SEVILLA PRESS   •   SAN DIEGO, CALIFORNIA

QUEEN OF THE GYPSIES
The Life and Legend of Carmen Amaya

Published by:
Sevilla Press
P.O. Box 40331
San Diego, CA 92164

Copyright © 1999 by Paco Sevilla

ISBN: 0-9646374-1-3
Library of Congress Catalogue Card Number: 98-90943

TABLE OF CONTENTS

PREFACE

CHAPTER ONE SOMORROSTRO
Carmen Amaya: birth, early life. *Café Cantante*. The flamenco environment c.1920. Pastora Imperio. The "Generation of '98." The Bar de Manquet. *Farruca* and *Garrotín*. The fountain.

CHAPTER TWO DANCING VAGABOND
Carmen in Madrid. Pepe Marchena. Antonio Chacón. Los Gabrieles. Villa Rosa. Ramón Montoya. Guitarists in Madrid c.1925. Carmen in Madrid and Barcelona: El Teatro Español with José Cepero. Manuel Vallejo: *"La Copa Pavón," "La Llave de Oro." The Opera Flamenca*. The Villa Rosa in Barcelona. El Estampío: Salud Rodríguez, La Cuenca. El Sacromonte in Granada.

CHAPTER THREE THE FRENCH CONNECTION
The death of Antonio Chacón. Vicente Escudero: early life. Antonio de Bilbao. Escudero in France. Gabriel Ruiz and Vicente Escudero in Paris. Escudero's debut in Spain. The *cupletistas*. La Argentina: early life, Paris, New York. La Argentinita: early life, recordings. Raquel Meller. Carmen Amaya in Paris. Carlos Montoya. Gabriel Macandé. Carmen with Raquel Meller. La Argentina in 1929. Antonio Triana: early life. La Argentina returns to New York. La Argentinita's debut in New York: Ignacio Sánchez Mejías, Federico García Lorca, *Colección de canciones populares españolas*. La Argentina and *El Amor Brujo*.

CHAPTER FOUR CARMEN'S RETURN
Carmen's dancing: technique, footwork, male dress. Flamenco dance in 1930. The World Fair in Barcelona: Carmen's performance for Don Carlos de Borbón. Vicente Escudero in America. Pepe Marchena and the *cantes de ida y vuelta* (*guajiras, milonga, rumba, colombianas*). Manuel Torre (*tientos, tarantos, campanilleros, siguiriyas*).

CHAPTER FIVE SABICAS
Carmen Amaya, 1933. Sabicas: early life. Manolo de Huelva. La Niña de los Peines: La Serneta, *tangos, lorqueñas, marianas, bamberas, peteneras*, Currito el de la Jeroma, Pepe Pinto, Tomás Pavón. Niño Ricardo. Sabicas: recording and playing solo. The guitar soloist in flamenco: Paco el Barbero, Paco de Lucena, Javier Molina, Ramón Montoya. Sabicas and Carmen Amaya. Carmen in Madrid.

CHAPTER SIX EXILE

Las Calles de Cádiz, Death of Ignacio Sánchez Mejías, La Argentina in the USA (1930- 34). Carmen Amaya, 1935: with Luisita Esteso, La Hija de Juan Simón. Carmen in Sevilla, 1936. María de la O. Spanish politics leading up to the Civil War. Death of La Argentina. Carmen in Lisbon. Paris during the Spanish Civil War: Gabriel Ruiz, La Argentinita, Vicente Escudero, *siguiriyas* danced for the first time. Mario Escudero: early life. Ramón Montoya records in Paris. The war in Spain.

CHAPTER SEVEN AMERICA

The Amayas travel to Buenos Aires. Interviews with Carmen. Los Chavalillos de Sevilla. Ramón Montoya arrives in Buenos Aires. Sabicas in Buenos Aires. South American tours. Earthquake in Chile. Cuba, 1939. *El Embrujo del Fandango.* First meeting with Sol Hurok. La Argentinita in America, 1938-41. The Amayas in New York. The Beachcomber. Hotels and furs. With President Roosevelt. Los Chavalillos in New York. First recording for Decca. *Original Gypsy Dances.* Lola Montes. Carnegie Hall. Tour across America. Hollywood; *Panama Hattie.* Return to Carnegie Hall. Influence of La Argentinita on Spanish dance and Carmen Amaya.

CHAPTER EIGHT ACROSS THE FRUITED PLAIN

Second tour of the USA. Sabicas as a soloist. Third Carnegie Hall appearance in 1942. La Argentinita, 1943. José Greco. Carlos Montoya in New York; marriage. The Amayas on tour and in New York, 1943. Departure of Antonio Triana. Hollywood Bowl. Carmen's homes. *Follow the Boys:* footwork solo, admiration of film stars. Argentinita: illness and death.

CHAPTER NINE RETURN TO SPAIN

Pilar López and José Greco in Spain. Dance in America, 1945. Carlos Montoya as a soloist. *See My Lawyer* and other films. Carmen in Mexico. Sabicas and Carmen: love and breakup. Buenos Aires. Pepe Marchena. South American tours. Death of El Chino. Luisillo and Teresa. Return to Spain, 1947. Carmen and Antonio Mairena in the Teatro Fuencarral. Interview in Sevilla. Debut in Paris, 1948. Gypsy life in Paris. London. The José Greco Company. Additions to family and company. *Opera flamenca* in 1949. The death of Ramón Montoya: recollections by Rosa Montoya, Carlos Ramos; Ramón's guitars. Touring in 1950. Mario Escudero leaves the company. Juan Antonio Agüero. Carmen's marriage, 1951. *Flamencan Songs and Dances: Volumes 1 and 2.* Return to Somorrostro, 1951. Touring in Spain. José Greco in the USA. *Duende y Misterio del Arte Flamenco.* Portugal. London, 1952. Carmen in Spain, 1953.

CHAPTER TEN THE NEW GOLDEN AGE

La Zambra, 1954. The Hispavox Anthology. Vicente Escudero, 1946-55 (Decalogue). Antonio in New York. Escudero in New York. Carlos Montoya: solo career and recording. Carmen Amaya: South America, 1955. Lucero Tena. Carnegie Hall, 1955. *Queen of the Gypsies.* USA tours, 1955-57. La Chunga. *Flamenco! Carmen Amaya.* René Heredia. Return to Europe, 1958. New company. Carmen's fountain.

CHAPTER ELEVEN COMING HOME

Renaissance of gypsy flamenco. Carmen on tour in Great Britain, Spain, France, 1959. Plans for *Los Tarantos*. USA, 1961. Juan Maya "Marote" and Manolete. History of dance in the Sacromonte. Furia! Amaya. Gypsy flamenco in 1962: Mairena receives *La Llave del Oro, The Art of Flamenco* by Donn Pohren, Paco de Lucía. *Los Tarantos*. Tours in South America and USA. Party in New Jersey. Village Gate, 1962. Casa Madrid, Los Angeles. Mario Escudero. Illness and return to Bagur. Death of Carmen Amaya.

EPILOGUE
GLOSSARY
REFERENCES
INDEX

PHOTOGRAPHS

Carmen Amaya "Queen of the Gypsies" 10
Carmen dancing in the Sacramonte 49
La Argentina; La Argentinita 90
Niño Sabicas 128
The Amayas in the Decca Studio 242
The Amayas with Lola Montes 248
Preparing to tour, 1942 252
Hollywood Bowl, 1943 275
Fiercely elegant Amaya. 336
Portrait of Carmen in 1959 346
Carmen in fiesta in 1962 374

PREFACE

Carmen Amaya! Few names in the dance world have enjoyed such widespread recognition and respect. Among aficionados of Spanish dance her name inspires awe, and flamenco artists speak of her with reverence. Yet, if pressed for specifics about this legendary figure, few can respond with more than vague superlatives or some mythical anecdote. The little that has been written about her is often confused and contradictory.

Carmen Amaya belonged to a family of gypsies who did not write letters or keep journals, and during her early life she operated in a flamenco underworld that did not attract the attention of writers or newspaper reporters. Her birth and baptismal records were lost in a church fire (of which there have been many in politically tumultuous Barcelona). Interviews with her and her family have usually produced conflicting acounts. Age, place of birth, and early exploits were often altered and embellished with each telling. For years, Carmen lied about her place of birth. The details of her daily life changed with each observer: She never smoked; she smoked incessantly. She was illiterate and couldn't sign her name; she worked hard at her writing and handled all of her company's business affairs. She never learned English; she spoke English fluently. Even photographs of Carmen Amaya seem to portray different women—no two pictures are alike.

The lack of written history leaves the biographer with only a jumble of recollections by Carmen, her family, and her friends and acqaintances—all altered by the passage of time, fame, or gypsy embellishment. Add to that a series of popular anecdotes that sometimes reach mythical proportions and, inevitably, a biography of Carmen Amaya becomes a mixture of fact and fiction. But, given that Carmen was larger than life and a truly extraordinary figure in flamenco history, a biography that stretches reality is perhaps appropriate.

Carmen Amaya stunned the world with the fire and passion of her dance. Her technique may have been surpassed in recent times, but nobody has equaled her charisma or the presence and magnetism that held audiences spellbound for almost half a century. Add to her art the eccentricities and novelty of her very gypsy family and lifestyle and you have the makings of a legend. For these reasons I have chosen to call her story the *legend* of Carmen Amaya.

Carmen's life coincided with a very critical period in the development of Spanish dance and her story cannot be told independent of that history. Her career spanned three epochs: She was born at the end of flamenco's Golden Age, the period of the *café cantante*. She rose to the pinnacle of her art in the forty-year theatrical period of the *ópera flamenca*. And she finished her career in the early years of the renaissance of pure flamenco in the 1950s. In order to understand Carmen Amaya, it is necessary to be familiar with the circumstances that shaped her and the artists who influenced her. With that in mind I have included in-depth biographies of a number of important flamenco artists, many of whose stories have not been told before.

In order to compile this biography of Carmen Amaya, I have had to stand on the shoulders of those who came before me. Shortly after Carmen's death, Salvador Montañés published a short, highly anecdotal account of her life entitled *Carmen Amaya: la bailaora genial*. That book has been the source of much of the anecdotal material that has subsequently appeared in print. A lack of research, however, resulted in only a vague outline of Carmen's life. In 1994, French writer and flamenco aficionado, Mario Bois, published *Carmen Amaya o La Danza del Fuego*, a biography of Carmen that presents a great deal of new information about her life in France and reproduces valuable interviews with her in Buenos Aires. But many large gaps remained in her story. The following year, in *Carmen Amaya: Cuando duermo, sueño que estoy bailando,* Francisco Hidalgo Gómez brought to light the results of his intensive reasearch in Spain. Carmen's life began to take shape. Yet there still remained inconsistencies and large gaps, particularly when it came to the important ten years she spent in America and her subsequent return visits. Meira Goldberg began to fill those holes with her PhD. thesis, *Border Trespasses: The Gypsy Mask and Carmen Amaya's Flamenco Dance* (1995), in which she tackled the American period and was the first to extensively interview surviving family members and associates. I am very thankful to her for sharing with me her interviews with Sabicas's brother, Diego Castellón.

I have attempted, through exhaustive research in Spain and in the United States, to bring together what is known and to give the most complete picture of this unique dancer to date. I have many to thank for their assistance. I must give credit to the Spanish flamencologist José Blas Vega, whose many encyclopedic works on flamenco put so much historical information at the fingertips of researchers and writers. Without his efforts, my task would have been infinitely more difficult, if not impossible.

I have to thank Lola Montes for the time she spent with me talking of her days with Carmen Amaya. Luisa Triana, daughter of Antonio Triana, was extremely generous in her communications with me from her home in Sevilla and supplied me with vital information. As mentioned above, Meira Goldberg went far beyond courtesy in permitting me to use material from her interviews with Diego Castellón. It is to be hoped that she will publish the results of her extensive interviews with the Amaya family and others. New York writer Mona Molarsky was exceedingly generous in sharing with me her unpublished interview with Sabicas. Some of her work can be found in *Guitar Review* (No 82, Summer 1990). Others who took the time to provide me with invaluable information include Gary Lesker, Marilyn Perrine, Greg Case, Toño Portuguez, Paul Heffernan, and Thérèse Wassily Saba. I would particularly like to thank John Moore for lending me critical research materials. Mimette Wishart not only proofread, but kept me writing with her enthusiastic critiques and encouragement. Marysol Fuentes consistently came to the rescue when some obscure Spanish phrase seemed impossible to translate, and she was able to make sense of some particularly difficult recorded songs. Others who proofread and gave me important input and support were Mary Ellen Nolan and Dorothy Autry.

Carmen Amaya, "Queen of the Gypsies".

CHAPTER ONE

SOMORROSTRO

"The life of Carmen Amaya has been pure legend, and everyone should have seen her dance at least once."
—**Vicente Escudero** (*Sabado Gráfico*, 1963)

Peals of dark thunder shattered the night, howling their tormented lament with all the *rajo*[1] of an aged *cantaor* (flamenco singer). Torrential rain beat a steady, stacatto rhythm on the tin roof of a shanty in the gypsy barrio known as Somorrostro, while on the nearby beach, storm-driven waves crashed in rolling accompaniment to the tempestuous *juerga* (flamenco gathering). Inside the dwelling, a newborn infant squalled to the approval of shrill and harsh gypsy voices.

November 2, 1913, *El día de los difuntos* (The Day Of the Dead), and a thin, dark-skinned daughter had just been born to the gypsy dancer Micaela Amaya. Unwilling to give birth in the cold and wet of her own flooded hovel, Micaela had fled to the home of her husband's father in the Chinese nucleus known locally as *Pekín*. Since the birth of her first son when she was only fourteen, so many babies had died that it was with considerable anxiety that she looked down at her diminutive baby girl and, with unsuspecting premonition and good fortune, chose to call her Carmen.

An early biographer described the scene, based on the memories of family and friends:[2]

> An epidemic of flu, without regard for age or social class, mercilously attacks the families of Barcelona. In Barcelona, as in all of Spain, the *cuplé* [popular song done flamenco style] is all the rage, and the epidemic is baptized with the name of a *cuplé*: *"El soldadito de Napoleón"* ["Napoleon's Little Soldier"].
> In a shack in the Somorrostro of Barcelona, a thin, sallow-

---

[1] rajo: rough, raspy quality in a gypsy singer's voice.

[2] Montañés, Salvador, p. 5. This biography, published shortly after Carmen Amaya's death, is undocumented and contains some inaccuracies, but has been the major source of anecdotal information about the dancer's life.

skinned gypsy with oriental eyes and straight hair says, "This is all we needed!" Water leaks in through the cracks, and on a dirty mattress, Micaela writhes and moans...

Micaela Amaya, wife of *José*[1] Amaya "El Chino," is afraid, not for herself, but for the life that is calling out to be born. *José* "El Chino" makes a decision: "I will take you to grandfather's house, to the house of "Cagarrutas" ["The Dung"]; there you will be okay. You know that he has put a corrugated tin roof on his shack."

Micaela bites her lip and agrees. She is so afraid this time! Something tells her that the thing that is moving about inside her has a promise to fulfill. She says that her spirits tell her...that which is being born is more than a girl or a boy, that which is about to be born will be something important in the future...

The water, the rain, beats on the face and matted hair of "El Chino." Wrapped in a miserable shawl, Micaela protects her stomach the best she can. They arrive at the home of "El Cagarrutas " and within a few minutes the wind, and perhaps the sea, have calmed. The Somorrostro of Barcelona has a new inhabitant: it is a girl, dark and very small, with a large mouth and closed eyes, and she greets the world with a brazen cry. Micaela looks at her and feels tremendous anxiety, and the fingers of "El Chino" move restlessly, as if playing a guitar. "El Cagarrutas" breaks out a bottle of *aguardiente* [anise brandy] and in silence, in a solemn ceremony, serves a glass to "El Chino." The gypsies, without taking their eyes from the newborn, empty their glasses. The nearby sea has calmed and a solemn rain falls monotonously now, tranquil and constant.

This long-accepted version of Carmen Amaya's birth has recently been contested by biographer Meira Goldberg, who interviewed Carmen's younger sisters. Antonia and Leonor Amaya had been told in their youth that Carmen was born in the countryside, and that their mother had to take shelter from the rainstorm under a wagon. The implication is that the Amayas were itinerant gypsies and that Carmen learned to dance in a wagon. According to the sisters, it was only sometime after Carmen reached the age of five that José built a one-room house of mud and bricks in the Somorrostro.[2] There are some difficulties with this account: It doesn't fit with the father's skill as a flamenco guitarist and his need for stability in seeking work—there is no record of any nomadic gypsy achieving El Chino's level of skill and professionalism. Nor had anyone in the Amaya family ever hinted previously that they had at one time been wandering gyp-

[1]Montañés erroneously calls El Chino "Paco." For readability, I have corrected the name to "José" and placed it in italics.
[2]Goldberg, p. 175.

sies. However, nomadic gypsies were sometimes called *canasteros* (basket makers), and Carmen would mention on occasion that she had learned to make baskets as a child.

Information from the Amaya family can be problematic because their stories changed radically with each telling. As with many gypsies and other tribal peoples, the Amayas seem to have had a poor awareness of the passage of time. Their estimates of dates, ages, and time periods have been dramatically inconsistent. Throughout her life Carmen added or subtracted years, sometimes decades, from her age, depending upon the effect she wished to convey at the moment. She also changed her birthplace. However, even if Carmen was not born in the Somorrostro, it is clear that she was born not far away and had moved there by a very early age, probably long before the age of five.

The dancing talent in the Amaya family could be directly traced to Micaela's father, Juan Amaya Jiménez. Carmen's sisters said that their mother danced *tangos* and *bulerías* very well.[1] Carmen would later claim that her mother was never permitted to dance outside of the family circle because her father was too jealous.[2] Artistic tendencies in the family were further consolidated when Micaela married José Amaya, a guitarist recognized by gypsies as being the most "gypsy" among them. José's chocolate-colored skin bordered on black, and his deep slanted eyes and inscrutable expression had earned him the nickname "El Chino." By day, José el Chino sought to provide for his growing family by dealing in old clothes. Rough and illiterate, he transacted business with the wits and cunning of a wild animal. At night he wandered the streets of the miserable Barrio Chino with his guitar, mingling with drunks, prostitutes, thieves and smugglers, drinking bitter wine in cheap taverns that reeked of vomit, and finally staggering home at dawn with a few *pesetas*. José knew nothing of the formal rules of music. He played simply, by instinct and tradition, but he knew flamenco inside and out, far better than the majority of more polished guitarists. For him this complex and subtle music held no secrets.

It was only fitting that Carmen should be a direct descendent of two branches of the Amaya family, with ancient roots in the cave dwellings of the Sacromonte in Granada. Carmen Amaya Amaya was *gitana de los cuatro costaos*, pure gypsy on all sides, and clearly a true child of the bronze-skinned gypsies who had wandered into Spain from India centuries earlier. However, the Amaya family's link with the gypsies of Granada was tenuous at best, and evidence for it is based only on the fact that there are so many Amayas in Granada. Carmen's mother descended from gypsy families of the North—Aragón and Barcelona—while José had family roots in the Sevilla

[1]Goldberg, p. 171.
[2]Pohren, p. 233.

area in the South.[1] Carmen sometimes claimed to be from Granada, but she was, in fact, born in a slum on the outskirts of Barcelona, in the province of Cataluña. She would later admit that she was *"catalana* from head to foot" and that, although she never learned to speak *catalán,* she "understood it completely."[2]

Cataluña occupies Spain's northeast corner, bordered on the north by the Pyrenees and France and to the east by the Mediterranean Sea. The Catalonians have their own culture and language and have long sought to be an independent state. The result has been a history of unrest and rebellion. Barcelona is Cataluña's capital city and, at the turn-of-the-century, was Spain's most important industrial center and commercial port. It was a city of money and art. Picasso had just departed for France, Miró was painting, Dalí had begun his apprenticeship, and Gaudí had littered the city with the genius of his eccentric, often grotesque, structures. Tárrega and his students Miguel Llobet and Emilio Pujol dominated the classical guitar.

Barcelona was also a city in constant turmoil: Labor disputes and strikes, political protests and movements, and anti-church uprisings occurred with regularity, often bringing the city to a standstill. Thousands of immigrants flooded the city, coming from every corner of Spain to fill the labor needs of industry. As a consequence, construction was almost constant and the city grew out in all directions. But many newcomers settled in the colorful Barrio Chino, in the heart of old Barcelona. The densely packed buildings and narrow streets of Barrio Chino spread back from the docks along the lower end of the major social and commercial thoroughfare known as Las Ramblas. And beyond the Chinese section, on a dirty beach near the port, a motley and disorderly assemblege of wooden shacks housed the less fortunate. This was the feared Barrio Somorrostro, home to bohemians and gypsies, and a place outsiders were reluctant to enter and unlikely to leave unmolested. Against a backdrop of smoke-filled air, factory sirens, and the sounds of the docks, *gitanos* built their crude dwellings at the edge of the sea, on sand blackened by coal dust and littered with industrial debris. There were no sewers and only two distant fountains to supply water for thousands of desperate people. Every year, floods and epidemics of flu, dysentary, typhoid fever, cholera, and other illnesses killed hundreds. It was there, amid the squalor of Somorrostro, that Carmen Amaya Amaya spent her childhood.

Carmen was the second child to survive in her family. She had an older brother, Paco, and five years after her birth, Antonia would be born. Leonor would soon follow. The family would be completed much later with another brother, Antonio, and the youngest sister, María. Five other babies died at birth or shortly thereafter.

Carmen spent her infancy on the beach, where the rhythmic beating of the

[1] Goldberg, p. 170.
[2] Hidalgo, p. 37

waves rocked her to sleep and her first toys were the shells and rocks she found on the sand. Throughout her life, she would refer often to her relationship with the sea, claiming that it was her first dance teacher. Along with making baskets, she also learned to steal fish and fruit from the stands in the market. Years later, she would recount: "Tonio and Tonet, two young seamen, used to pursue her and the other gypsies in a vain attempt to recover a fistful of stolen fish... [On the other hand] Tonio and Tonet had also shared with her and her family many scanty, sparing meals, truly non-existent for those starving mouths."[1]

Among the little gypsy's chores was the long trek to get water from the fountain. Biographer Montañés tells us: "...often she left her band of ragamuffins to spend hours staring at the Mediterranean Sea, feeling her body agitated by strange tremors. The waves bathed the hem of her much mended skirt, calmly, as if caressing and blessing her. Carmen Amaya...dreamed of the future, until her brother Paco would shake her from her dreams with a distant shout: 'Carmela! Get the pot and lets go look for water...' And Carmen...takes up the copper pot and goes to the end of a long line of dirty children—children who are lice-ridden, starving, and cruel—at a fountain that is known by only one name in Barcelona: 'The Fountain of the Lice'."[2]

Barefoot and dressed in rags, Carmen appeared tiny and fragile, but her friends and family recognized that she was strong and lively, all nerve and muscle. She took after her father in appearance and build and had inherited his quick mind and musical ability. No one can be sure exactly when she began to dance, but in a family of gypsy performers flamenco music would be a part of daily life and Carmelilla would begin to absorb the rhythms and sounds from birth. With a mother and an aunt who danced, she would have been encouraged to dance even before she could walk. Carmen's earliest memories are of her obsession with dance. She said that, when her mother sent her on an errand, she would dance as she walked. Her father may have been responsible for her first formal instruction:

> Day after day, night after night, when El Chino returned from his "work," that is, from spending hours strumming his guitar in some run-down bar, he would sit on a bench facing the sea, pick up his guitar, and sing for Carmencita to dance. It wasn't necessary to call her; as soon as she heard the sound of the guitar and some *cante* [flamenco song], she began to dance. She may have been three years old, four at the most, but all the old women, on seeing her, would comment that she already knew everything about the *baile gitano* [gypsy dance]. The blood running through her veins turned to fire and had to be expressed before it burned her...

---

[1] Montañés, p. 43.
[2] Montañés, p. 8.

> "How well she dances, how that little girl can move!" "Infinitely better than the rest!" "She dances like a woman!" Her fragile body, her arms, her feet, her tragic expression, her knitted brow, her large and generous mouth that speaks of serious things, profound things, grandiose things, and expresses equally both sadness and joy. To see her dance is something more than a pleasure, it is a shock. El Chino, who is never wrong, perceives that she has exceptional gifts. He thinks to himself... "Might not she be the answer to so many problems?" The father didn't waste time and soon began to take her to the bars of Barcelona and exhibit her in the streets... He played and the little girl danced. One day, when they were on Las Ramblas, she danced so extraordinarily that El Chino said to her:
>
> "Pick up the money that is on the ground. You have earned it!"
>
> Carmelilla gathered the coins, looked at them, and replied, "I only want the *pesetas*, papa, the rest [smaller coins] are trash!"[1]

Carmen always said that the Mediterranean shore was her school of rhythm, the sea and its waves her first teachers. "She spent her childhood playing with the waves of the sea, as they would foam and curl up into the air, and then spill over and disappear on the burning sand. She loved to watch the fluttering of the blue sea, and during the night her restlessness was quieted by this measured pulsation of the sea. This gyration of the waves thrown into the air and the subduing of the foam on the sand, all these undulations and rhythms, suggest the esthetic elements that give life to the great flamenco dancers, and we could say that they were the ones who taught the brown and flexible body of Carmen the complicated mysteries of the dance."[2]

Carmen recalled what may have been the first time she danced in public: She was sleeping backstage in a Barcelona theater while her father performed. She awoke, wandered on stage and began to dance. The surprised audience broke into applause.[3]

The little dancer had a brief encounter with school:

> The time to go to school finally came to this little gypsy beachcomber; that was the first conflict for the little rebel. This vibrating child of nature could not submit herself to the ABC's and be a docile and attentive pupil. She lived her own inner life with passionate intensity. She was stirred by uncontrollable impulses from the demon of the *"jondo"* dance that wouldn't let her live in peace; that demon of which she'd always be a slave. Closing her

---

[1] Bois, p. 33
[2] Samperio, p.2
[3] Sugrue

slanted eyes she could see herself already transfigured into a magic dancer of flamenco. Her fingers on the desk would beat time to all sorts of rhythms, syncopated sounds and drums, impossible variations of tapping with heels and feet, and clicking noises of her tongue. A fine threading of sounds cascading into the air... Her frenzy caught like fire and spread over the school. The girls could not resist this whirlwind of dancing spirit and soon the school was like a music box full of beats and tapping sounds. Discipline had run amuck. The gypsy was dismissed from school before she could learn the alphabet.[1]

This description may seem a bit fanciful, but it is true that Carmen's rebelliousness and leadership among her schoolmates earned her the title *La Capitana*, a nickname that would follow her through life. Carmen claimed that, at age four, necessity forced her to work. Her infancy became a series of continuous and fatiguing rounds of the bars and cafes. From door to door they went, the father with his guitar under his arm and his tiny, ragged daughter following behind in her bare feet. At each stop, El Chino entered and began to play, and Carmelilla surprised the customers with the fire and arrogance of her dance. A few coins and on to the next establishment. Until the first light of dawn, when the exhausted pair would return to Somorrostro—with a few loaves of bread, some ham, and tomatoes, if the night's take had been sufficient.

In a plaza on the waterfront, where Las Ramblas ends at the docks, was the restaurant Las Siete Puertas. A favorite of the upper class, it was frequented by millionaires, shipping magnates, Nobel Laureates, artists of all sorts, and elegant women. The owner often permitted gypsies to perform at the tables, and it was there that Carmen first began to make a name for herself. On a tile floor, while dodging waiters as they came and went, Carmelilla danced in her bare feet, letting herself be carried by the rhythm of the guitar as if possessed by some internal torment, her eyes looking off into the distance, her hair falling over her glistening face, her mind in some other place, oblivious to the hustle and bustle of the busy salon. The customers paid her in dollars, francs, sterling pounds—money she hadn't the slightest idea how to use. While she danced, El Chino kept his eye on the door, watching for the Guardia Civil [police]. He knew that it could be very expensive for him if he were caught making a child work at night. "When she finishes her dance, Carmen Amaya, the daughter of El Chino, raffles off, at ten *céntimos* [cents] for each number, tickets for a drawing of two bottles of good Spanish wine that the owner of Las Siete Puertas gives to the Amayas each night. If some customer makes the mistake of giving a *peseta* [roughly equivalent to a dollar at that time], under the illusion that he will

[1] Samperio, p. 2

receive change, he is surprised to see that the little girl who dances as if in a trance has no change, or after a few mumbled words that the customer cannot understand, she says thank you for the gift of a *peseta*."[1]

The public cheered the pair with enthusiastic applause, and soon José Amaya was in demand throughout Barcelona. El Chino and his daughter became regulars in such taverns and cafes as El Chiringuito, El Cangrejo Flamenco, and Casa Escaño.

Carmen was born at the end of the period of the *café cantante*, sometimes referred to as the "Golden Age" of flamenco. This was a time, beginning about 1860, when the different folk elements of flamenco were brought together and formalized in the cafes of Andalucía (Spain's southernmost province and the birthplace of flamenco). The *café cantante*, a bar or restaurant with a stage to accomodate formal shows of song, dance, guitar, and other variety acts, became extremely popular in the last quarter of the 1800s. The *café cantante* brought together the two disparate elements of flamenco: the gypsy and the *payo* (non-gypsy).

The Andalusian folk music of the *payo* was based on centuries of cultural blending, the result of invasions by Phoenicians, Greeks, Romans, and Arabs, among others. In the small towns, this legacy led to the development of a rich variety of festive folk songs and dances, usually accompanied by primitive orchestras of string and percussion instruments.

The gypsies, on the other hand, faced constant persecution after their arrival in Spain in the late 1400s. Under constant threat of imprisonment, beating, banishment, and death, they developed a music tradition that was private, personal, and almost ritualistic. Songs and dances rooted in an Eastern heritage became an expression of suffering and a source of release from the fears and hardships of daily existence. Musical instruments were scarce among the gypsies and often their songs and dances were accompanied only by the clapping of hard hands or the rapping of knuckles on tabletops.

The *café cantante* revealed the music of the gypsies to the general public and, for the first time, *gitano* and *payo* artists appeared together on stage. The amalgamation of the two types of music produced new forms that are the staples of the flamenco repertoire today. It was during this period that the term "flamenco" first appeared. (In spite of numerous theories, there is no satisfactory explanation of how a word that means "Flemish" came to be associated with this Andalusian music.) Professional competition among the artists in the cafes led to the development of new styles, and encouraged a rapid development of technique in all areas of the art.

By 1910, the *café cantante* era had pretty much run its course. People

[1]Montañés, p. 10.

were interested in new forms of entertainment—slide shows, films, and demonstrations of electricity. Ballroom dancing was the rage and popular songs called *canciones* or *cuplés* had supplanted the *cante flamenco*. After a negro entertainer did an American dance called the cakewalk in Barcelona, nobody wanted anything but the cakewalk. In 1914 it was the Argentine tango. Toward the end, a typical evening's entertainment in a cafe would include an orchestra for dancing, a flamenco show, a magician, an animal act, a classical dance recital, and a number of singers of *canciones*. In some cabarets flamenco dancers were expected to take off their clothes. The singer/dancer La Chelito was a hit with her rendition of the very popular song, *La Pulga,* in which she removed her clothes piece by piece to search for a pesky flea. She claimed that this was not as scandalous as it sounded since she wore so many clothes to begin with, including pink tights.

Slowly the *café cantante* was replaced by the *varieté*—variety shows that took place in the larger cafes and in theaters. This represented a significant upscaling in venue and permitted women to join the audience for the first time. Juan Martínez, a dancer who lived and worked in this period, recalled the nightlife scene in the early 1920s:

> Who wasn't familiar with El Paralelo [another name for the Barrio Chino] in La Ciudad Condal [Barcelona] and certain variety showplaces like El As, El Royalty, La Gran Peña, and others, which the bosses had the nerve to call *varieté?* The police came often to those places, but couldn't stop them because the doormen warned everybody with their buzzers. In the programs at these places could be seen numbers of all colors. Even though there was *cante* and *baile*, almost everyone did the same thing—spicy songs and *rumbas*. The only thing that distinguished the performers was that the young and beautiful, those who were well-shaped and had good bearing, became stars. Those who danced Spanish dance, many only fifteen years old, had to compete with the brazen and frivolous popular dancers, or they had to do the same thing themselves if they wished to survive...that was the only way they could get a contract from the owners of those places (I don't want to call them impresarios because it would be an insult to those who truly were). Those owners were not concerned with dance. What they wanted was attractive girls. Art did not interest them at all, and male dancers even less!
>
> In Madrid we also had the same kinds of places, equal in quality, although not as many as in El Paralelo. Among others, there was Kursaal Magdalena, Eden Concert, La Cigal Parisien, and Terpsicore. With respect to art, the same thing happened as in other cities of Spain...I don't mean to imply that there weren't

still some places where the good artists could perform, such as theaters, clubs, cabarets, and a few *cafés cantantes*, but there weren't enough to provide a living to the many artists who were available. Many of the theaters and movie houses had variety shows only on Saturdays and Sundays, or, where they had shows daily they paid very little. All of the business went to the others, the frivolous variety shows.

The Spanish dancers, little by little, were mixing other types of dancing into the repertoire in order to be able to work. They would do Dutch, Russian, Italian (*la tarantela*), and American dances, and put Russian steps and acrobatic leaps into the Spanish dances. Others invented things, like walking on the tips of the shoes in the middle of a dance, or whenever they saw fit. [Martínez, himself, admits to responding to demands for an encore by tying his ankles together with a scarf and repeating his *zapateado*.] What is certain is that, day by day, the *chaquetilla corta* [the short jacket worn by *bailaores*] was disappearing, and he who insisted on wearing it ran the danger of working very little or not at all...

I have little doubt that an infinite number of dancers left Spain for foreign countries to look for a more favorable environment for their art...The public in Spain had a preference for little more than the beauty of the artist.[1]

The guitarist Diego Castellón gave a firsthand account of the difficulties faced by flamenco dancers in the Madrid of the 1920s:

There was one who used to dance in that environment in Madrid—Felipe de Triana, the brother of El Porras and the best there was. It was scary the way he could dance. And he sang better than he danced! There was another who used to dance well, El Peluzo, who used to say, "What is Felipe dancing the *bulerías* for, with all that he has here (in the throat)? What he does really well is sing."

That surprised me, with as well as that guy could dance, what he really did well was sing. And then I realized that the man had to change in order to live. A dancer was not needed in those rooms.[2]

A new breed of flamenco artist appeared, one who could perform solo and capture the public's imagination with something new. Many of the old gypsy singers could not make the change and were replaced by young *payos* who would become superstars—Manuel Vallejo, Pepe Marchena, José Cepero, and so many more. Although some variety shows continued to feature a

[1]Martínez, Juan, *"El Arte Flamenco," La Prensa*, 1941-42.
[2]Interview by Meira Goldberg with Diego Castellón, 1989.

cuadro flamenco (a flamenco group), many of the aging queens of the *café cantante* stage were replaced by a new generation of dancers with a greater range of ability and repertoire. Thus, dancers like La Macarrona and La Malena, who danced the pure flamenco and specialized in a few traditional styles such as *alegrías* and *tangos*, gave way to popular figures like La Argentina, La Argentinita, and Pastora Imperio—artists who could sing *canciones* (popular, non-flamenco songs) and dance a wide variety of styles, from the ballet-like classical Spanish dance with castanets (not used in flamenco at that time), to regional folk dances such as the *jota* of Northern Spain, and, almost as an afterthought, a bit of flamenco. In 1920, one writer commented, "Women who still know how to dance flamenco are sometimes one hundred and six years old!"

Pastora Imperio was the star of the early 1900s. Her gypsy mother, Rosario Monje "La Mejorana," had been born in Cádiz in 1862. La Mejorana had danced in the early *cafés cantantes* of Sevilla, creating a sensation when she became the first to raise her arms high overhead while dancing. Customers came early to see her, trying to get a seat near the stage where they might catch a glimpse of an ankle when she danced. It is said that when they went home at four in the morning they had not achieved their desired end. To the dismay of her followers, after only three years in the cafes, Rosario married Victor Rojas, a bullfighter's tailor, and retired from the stage. A year later, in 1889, Pastora was born. La Mejorana steadfastly refused to teach her dance to anyone, even her own daughter, so Pastora had to learn from others. That turned out to be a fortunate circumstance for Pastora, because she learned a wider variety of dances than she would have with her mother.

By age ten, Pastora was dancing regularly with youth groups. At twelve, using the name Pastora Monje, she began to perform professionally in Sevilla, and a year later, in 1902, she made her debut in the Salón Japonés in Madrid as part of a duo called Las Hermanas Imperio. The "Imperio" stuck and, as Pastora Imperio, the young dancer soon became the darling of Madrid. Within a few years she was known throughout Spain.

The great writer Ramón Pérez de Ayala witnessed one of Pastora's early performances: "I recall Pastora Imperio the first time I saw her, fifteen years ago. She was dancing in a little theater that was at the beginning of Calle Alcalá... She was just a young thing, almost a child, slight and nervous. She came out dressed in red: jacket, short pants, stockings, and shoes. Red flowers in her hair. Attention getting! She broke into a dance. It was all dizzying commotion, but at the same time rhythmic and measured. And at the center of that vortex of movement, an ecstatic focal point centered on two points of fascination, on two precious stones, two enormous and shining emeralds: the eyes of the dancer, the green eyes that captured and held the gaze of the spectator."[1]

[1] Quoted in the writings of Daniel Pineda Novo in the private collection of Emilio Díaz of Sevilla.

Pastora grew to be stunning in appearance, possessing great beauty of face and figure. Her deep green eyes, invariably described as "those two enormous and flaming emeralds," were softened by long dark lashes and gently curved eyebrows. A small nose, delicate pointed chin, and warm smile completed a serene and gentle face. Slender yet sensuously curvacious, her posture always gave the impression of dignity and elegance. Dressed in a formfitting white *bata de cola* (train dress) with a pastel fringed shawl wrapped about her body from shoulders to hips, she became a goddess when she raised her arms overhead and struck the arrogant pose she had inherited from her mother.

The guitarist Luis Maravilla said that Pastora was a great dancer from the waist up, but not much in the feet. "She would rise softly and subtly from her chair during the singer's *temple* [warm-up] with such style that the audience would begin to applaud." The author John Dos Passos saw her in Madrid in 1917 and was completely taken with her, describing in detail how she moved across the stage serenely and unhurridly, her brown hand held high, a half-smile on her golden face "...as if she were stifling a secret. She walks round the stage slowly, one hand at her waist, the shawl tightly wrapped over her elbow, her thighs lithe and restless... At the back of the stage she turns and suddenly advances; the snapping of her fingers gets loud, insistant...She is right at the footlights; her face, brows drawn together into a frown, has gone into shadows; the shawl flames, the maroon flower over her breast glows like a coal. The guitar is silent, her fingers go on snapping at intervals with dreadful foreboding. Then she draws herself up with a deep breath, the muscles of her belly go taut...She is off again, light, joyful..." Finally, the shawl falls loosely about her in disarray, the fringe fluttering about her, and walking slowly she disappears.[1]

In truth, flamenco played only a small role in Pastora's performances. She sang popular songs, recited poetry, and danced everything from folk dances like *la jota* and *el vito* to the *garrotín, tangos, alegrías,* and *soleares* that made up her flamenco repertoire. Everyone wanted to see her, as much for her celebrity and the stunning shawls and train dresses that she always wore, as for her artistic abilities. She was endlessly pursued by photographers, appeared on postcards, and inspired the work of painters and scuptors. Her adoring fans regaled her with gifts, including cars and emeralds, and her dressing room seldom lacked for orchids and other expensive flowers.

In 1911, after a whirlwind courtship, Pastora married the equally idolized eccentric bullfighter Rafael el Gallo. The couple became a permanent fixture on the front pages of the newspapers and the principle topic of conversation in theater and bullfight circles. Pastora quit dancing to fulfill her role as a wife, but only a year later she divorced her husband for reasons she never revealed—it may have had something to do with his jealousy and her forced

---
[1] Dos Passos, p. 15

retirement, or perhaps the rumors that circulated later regarding a prostitute's claim that El Gallo was impotent. In any case, the public rejoiced at Pastora's return to the stage.

In 1915, an early version of the Spanish ballet *El Amor Brujo* by Manuel de Falla opened in the Teatro Lara in Madrid. The work originated with Pastora Imperio's request for a song and dance from Falla and the well-known poet/dramatist, Gregorio Martínez Sierra. Inspiration for what would eventually become a full-fledged ballet came from Pastora's mother. La Mejorana sang *soleares, siguiriyas, polos,* and *martinetes* for Falla to note down, and recounted ancient gypsy legends and fables that Sierra would draw upon for the plot. The result, first billed as *"Gitanería,"* was a mixture of song, dance, and mime that portrayed the life of the gypsies in the caves of the Sacromonte in Granada. In the *"Danza ritual del fuego"* and *"La canción del fuego fátuo,"* Falla created the first orchestral renditions of flamenco forms. It was truly a family affair, with Pastora as the star and a cast that included Pastora's brother, the guitarist Victor Rojas, her sister-in-law, Agustina, and Agustina's daughter, who would later call herself María Albaicín. Critics came down hard on Falla, accusing him of "ostentatious orchestration" and calling the work an uninspired *"españolada"* (cliché). Some of this criticism grew out of the anti-flamenco environment that had been created by a group of young writers known as the "Generation of '98."

In April of 1898, two months after the American battleship *Maine* was sunk in the Havana Harbor, the United States had entered the war against Spain. The resulting catastrophic loss of men and ships by the Spanish army forced Spain to relinquish its colonies in Cuba, Puerto Rico, and the Philippines after only several months of fighting. The loss proved devastating to Spain. The Spanish people felt betrayed, for they had been kept in the dark about the seriousness of the Cuban revolt, the powerful resources of the enemy, and the lack of preparedness of their own army and navy. Spain seemed impotent in the eyes of the world, while at home chaos ruled: The constitution was flaunted with impunity, parliament appeared to be a joke, corruption was rampant, separatists threatened stability, and fighting in Spanish Morocco dragged on endlessly.

Young intellectuals rebelled. Led by Professor Francisco Giner de los Ríos, who had founded the Independent Institute of Education after he was expelled from the University of Madrid for refusing to take an oath of loyalty to the church and government, young writers lashed out at Spain's antiquated customs and position in the world. Miguel de Unamuno, Angel Ganivet, José Ortega y Gasset, and Valle Inclán felt that Spain had lost its character, and they vented their rage and frustration not only on the government and the *status quo,* but also on the clichés of the Spanish arts, on what they called *"españoladas,"* or "the Spain of Merimée (composer of the opera *Carmen*)," and "the Spain of the tambourine." Azorín, who coined the phrase the "Generation of

'98," called bullfighting "a cruel and stupid spectacle," while Pío Baroja wrote of a young girl dancing on a tabletop to the accompaniment of drunken handclapping, a dock worker singing about the cemetery and his dead mother, and a swaggering fat man marking time with his behind!

It is hard to be critical of these writers, for they did not know the true, intimate flamenco, but only the degenerate commercial flamenco of the time. At the turn-of-the-century, the frivolity, trivialization, and lack of authenticity of the *cante* made it an easy target. Flamenco was too often considered to be just an excuse for drinking and immoral behaviour, rather than a legitimate art form. The "Generation of '98" feared that these clichés would make Spain a joke in the eyes of the rest of Europe. The repercussions of their scathing attacks on flamenco would be felt for several decades.

In spite of the criticism of *El Amor Brujo*, the work enjoyed popular success—it couldn't fail with Pastora Imperio as the featured artist—and gypsies were the first to applaud the music. Pastora went on to make films, the first two being the silent films *La Danza Fatal* and *Gitana Cañí*, and toured widely throughout Europe and the Americas.

Pastora Imperio represented the popular image of flamenco in the second decade of this century. She was part of an environment in which Carmen Amaya would eventually have to compete. But in the bars and alleys of Barrio Chino in the early 1920s, little Carmen remained somewhat removed from the trends of Madrid.

Barcelona would seem an unlikely center for flamenco. Flamenco originated in Andalucía, and that is where it has always been most appreciated. Other regions have traditionally been patriotically devoted to their own music. Madrid has always been an exception. As the capital of the entertainment world in Spain, with a rich night life, it has been a place where flamenco artists could make a living. Flamencos consider it to be Andalucía's northernmost city. But why Barcelona? Part of the answer lies in Barcelona's large Andalusian population, the result of massive emmigrations from poverty stricken Andalucía in the 19th Century. Flamenco performers and gypsies followed these emmigrations and found a ready welcome among Barcelona's already large gypsy population. Add to this Barcelona's traditional support of the arts, a monied class in need of entertainment, a large shipping labor force far from home and in need of diversion, and a booming tourist trade after World War I, and you have the ingredients necessary to support a lively cabaret industry. There were more flamenco bars, cafes, and cabarets packed into District V, better known as Barrio Chino, than anywhere else in Spain. Even after these types of establishments began to decline in Madrid, they flourished along Barcelona's waterfront. In the words of Diego Castellón, "For the dance you had to go to Barcelona, where there were eight or nine *tablaos* [*cafés cantantes*]."[1]

[1] Goldberg interviews.

When Carmen Amaya was contracted by the Bar de Manquet in 1924, at age ten, she had only to be concerned with dancing for the working class customers who came to escape the daily grind with cheap drinks and good flamenco. Located in the heart of Barrio Chino, the Bar de Manquet was widely known as a place to go for flamenco, and aficionados often gathered there to listen to a large collection of flamenco records. But few tourists dared to enter that haven of dock workers and gypsies. Author Alfonso Puig describes what transpired:

> Those were happy times, when, for a *peseta*, in the Bar del Manquet in Atarazanas [the heart of Barrio Chino], they served us real coffee with three lumps of sugar as we sat among a motley crowd of dockworkers applauding an impressive *cuadro flamenco* that we felt would someday make its mark on history. It was made up of Carmen Amaya "La Capitana," her aunt, Juana la Faraona, an exemplary model of gypsy beauty and unmatched in her *zambras* and *farrucas*, La Romerito, unique in her more stylized *alegrías* and *sevillanas*, and El Gato, with his serious masculine demeanor, accompanied on guitar by El Chino (father of La Amaya) and Manolo Bulerías. A group that, for a few glasses of manzanilla wine, would treat us to some extra performances outside of the regular program and thank us for our faithful attendance.

> La Capitana, a stage name that the little Carmencita likes to use to present herself, is an exceptional case of "pure blood." When she dances, she vibrates from head to foot, contorts, and rises up with histrionic haughtiness, and her feet of steel pound with deafening fury, obsessed by the crescendo of the guitar, in an uncontrolled frenzy that is always closed by the final high of an explosive *desplante* [rhythmic variation].[1]

Carmen always insisted that she had no formal training, no teachers. But there can be no doubt that, once she began to dance in the *cuadros* of the cabarets and was exposed to a broad range of dance styles, she absorbed everything she saw and heard. In the Bar de Manquet, she observed the classical style of Andrea Romero "La Romerito" in *alegrías*, and she must have taken a great deal from the masculine dance of El Gato. Escudero el Gato, along with his brother, a guitarist from Madrid named El Pelao Viejo, belonged to a family that would create a dance dynasty in the next generation (Juan el Pelao, El Fati, Faíco, Toni el Pelao, Pelao Chico, etc.). El Gato achieved renown with his dance *por farruca*, which he often ended with the *media verónica*, a cape pass taken from the bullfight. Carmen Amaya would always remember him as the best in this dance.

[1] Puig, *El Ballet y el Baile español*

The *farruca* and another popular dance, the *garrotín*, had a parallel histories. Both originated as songs in northern provinces, outside the cradle of flamenco in Andalucía. When sailors from Asturias and Galicia settled in the port of Cádiz, Andalusians called them *"farrucos."* With that name, the songs of these immigrants entered the flamenco repertoire and were popularized in the early 1900s by singers like the great Manuel Torre. One source reported seeing the *farruca* danced for the first time in 1904, another in 1912. It is said to have been created by a dancer from Sevilla (with family roots in Cádiz) named Francisco Mendoza, better known as Faíco.[1] This handsome, elegant dancer looked more like a banker from New York than a flamenco performer. He learned from José Otero, the famous teacher of flamenco and classical school dances in Sevilla, so it is likely that he had a refined, academic technique. Faíco teamed up with the great guitarist Ramón Montoya to create the dance and music *por farruca*, employing the four-count rhythm of *tangos*, but giving it a unique, markedly pronounced cadence that brings out the best in the male dance. The dancer Vicente Escudero felt that the *farruca* had slavic qualities more typical of Eastern European gypsies than flamenco. Ramón used to play it in E-minor rather than the A-minor common today. The *farruca* reached the peak of its popularity in the period from 1910-30, but survived to modern times, generally without song accompaniment, having been given a big boost in the 1950s by José Greco.

The *garrotín* may also have roots in Asturias, but it is thought to have been developed by the gypsies of Lérida (about ninety miles west of Barcelona) and, later, Barcelona. If true, it would be the only flamenco song or dance form (other than the *rumba*) that developed outside of Andalucía. The *garrotín* really caught on when it was sung and recorded by La Niña de los Peines. It was Faíco, again, who recreated the *garrotín* and gave it the structure needed for dancing on stage. With its lively *tango* rhythm and major key, the *garrotín* enjoyed great popularity until it all but disappeared in the 1930s. Appropriately, it would be a *catalán* gypsy, Carmen Amaya, who would keep it alive and make possible its revival in the 1970s.

During the period of the Bar de Manquet, "...a fountain was inaugurated, a small fountain with a column of bricks supporting a lead spout. There were festivities and José joined in with his guitar and his daughter; the father, with his left foot resting on the bowl of the fountain, played, Carmen danced, and the people hurt their hands applauding."[2] Years later, Carmen recalled the installation of the small fountain in the embankment between the Somorrostro slum and the barrio known as the Barceloneta:

"I was seven years old when they first brought water to the

---

[1]Not to be confused with another Faíco, El Pelao's son, named in honor of this great dancer.
[2]Góngora.

Somorrostro."
Where did you live, exactly?
"In a shack, about twenty meters from the fountain. I would come home each day from work, about six o'clock in the morning, and go to bed."
Where did you work?
"In various places, in Casa de Manquet...I went from one place to the other. And, as I was saying, I got into bed and was asleep when Miguel Payo, the mayor of the *barrio*, who was crippled, came to wake me up. He said to me, 'Get up, you are our artist and you have to baptize the fountain!' My father got up too, took out his guitar, and we went. On the way, we bought a bottle of rotgut anise brandy from Señor Joaquín's bar, and then continued on to the fountain where there were children everywhere."
And what was the baptism like?
"I shattered the bottle against the fountain, my father played the guitar, and I danced *por bulerías*."
You didn't drink the anise?
"The fountain drank it. We drank water."[1]

---

[1] Interview reproduced by Hidalgo, p. 200, from an unnamed source.

CHAPTER TWO

DANCING VAGABOND

In 1925,[1] Carmen and her father were contracted to perform in a salon in the lower level of the Palacio de la Música in Madrid. The trip must have been a big adventure for the little girl. Travelers had to enter the Spanish capital by way of a bridge across the Manzanares River. One such traveler described the Manzanares as "a slimy shrunken stream almost hidden under the billowing underwear of all Madrid." The laundry of the city would be spread to dry on the banks of the river as far as the eye could see. From sun-up to sunset, hundreds of women knelt in the hot sun at water's edge, pounding and kneading the soiled clothes. They sang as they worked, creating a constant drone that sounded at a distance like a chorus of human frogs.

In spite of the antiquated laundry system, "La Villa" or "La Corte" (The Court), as Madrid was affectionately known, had become a bustling modern city with five-story buildings, wide streets and sidewalks, elegant hotels, electric trolleys and a subway system. The central plaza, La Puerta del Sol, was usually filled with a chaotic mix of clanging trolleys, horse-drawn carriages, donkeys, occasional honking cars, mounted police attempting to guide traffic with their whistles, yelling newsboys, and the hum of a throng of pedestrians going in every direction. Men still wore capes over their double-breasted suits, and women lacy *mantillas* when out for an afternoon stroll on one of the many tree-shaded avenues.

Flamenco had largely moved out of the cafes and become part of variety shows in large theaters with names like Novedades (Novelties), Olimpia (Olympic), Circo Price (Price Circus or Amphetheater) and Circo Paris. Movie theaters often featured a mediocre *cuadro flamenco* after the film to assure that the audience went home happy. A new generation of singers, largely non-gypsy, dominated "La Corte." At the head of the new movement in flamenco singing was the self-proclaimed "one and only king of the *cante*," Pepe Marchena.

Born José Tejada Martín in 1903 in Marchena (Sevilla), Pepe worked as a donkey driver, blacksmith's helper, and tavern boy until he began to sing

---

[1] Most dates during this period are only approximations, since there is so little documentation of Carmen's early life. The sequence of events surrounding this trip to Madrid leads me to place it in 1925.

professionally. Although he never went to school, his natural intelligence and good instincts insured that he would always be accepted as the equal of anyone, no matter how educated they might be. His curiosity and questioning of adults earned him the nickname *"La Vieja"* (the Old Lady). Pepe made his singing debut at age fourteen in Sevilla's Café Novedades, where he had gone to watch a *cuadro* that included the great dancer La Macarrona. During one of the breaks, friends encouraged Pepe and two other boys to go on stage and sing. The three who went up were destined to become leaders in the new *cante*: El Niño de Marchena, El Carbonerillo, and Pepe Pinto (future husband of La Niña de los Peines).

In 1921, El Niño de Marchena sang in Madrid for the first time and was an immediate success. In the ensuing years, he sweetened and softened the *cante*, emphasizing melody at the expense of *compás* (rhythm). He favored the non-gypsy *fandangos* family of *cantes* that includes the *granaínas*, *malagueñas*, *tarantas*, *cartageneras*, and a number of other styles of *fandangos*, altering the structure of their poetry at whim and extending the sung lines with endless operatic warbling in a falsetto voice. He also specialized in the Latin American flavored *"cantes de ida y vuelta,"*[1] the *guajira, milonga*, and *vidalita*. He single-handedly invented the *colombianas*, basing them on a Basque song. Marchena favored the *cuplé* (a pop song done in a flamenco rhythm), was the first to recite poetry in the middle of his songs, and the first to sing flamenco to orchestral accompaniment. Even his friends criticised him when he began to stand while singing—all *cantaores* before him had sung from a chair. Soon everyone imitated him.

Pepe Marchena did whatever he wished. Instead of using his abilities in the service of his art, he subjugated the art to his personality. His own words give a clear picture of the nature of his influence on flamenco during a period that would last for almost twenty-five years: "I was a *cantaor* starting at ten years of age. I had true *afición*. I was most attracted to the *tangos* and *farrucas*. The *bulerías* also appealed to me, but they didn't have enough personality...Very early on, I gave attention to the *fandango* because I felt it could become something important...I have made the essential technique of the *cante* more difficult than it was in the old times. I have added good taste and given more importance to melody than they did before...*Cante flamenco* is radically different from *cante gitano*. Let me clarify. On one hand you have *cante gitano*, on the other hand you have good singing, the true *cante flamenco*. I give no importance to those who make the *cante* into something gypsy; they are wrong and won't go anywhere."[2] On why he didn't sing for the true aficionados of the *cante*: "I know the taste of the public that pays to see Pepe Marchena. I am absolutely positive that in the hall are no more than

---

[1] *cantes de ida y vuelta:* songs of the round trip, that is, songs created by Spaniards in the New World and then returned to Spain to enter the flamenco repertoire.
[2] Climent, p.200.

ten aficionados of the *cante*...the rest, the majority, come to see the artist that I am!"[1] And finally: "Nobody can tolerate the *cante jondo*," and "There is no need for *compás* [rhythm] when there is art!"[2]

Pepe Marchena led the way, and others were forced by the public to follow—if not in the his excesses, at least in his emphasis on the non-gypsy *cantes* and the singing of *cuplés*. Among them: Manuel Centeno, Manuel Vallejo, Angelillo, José Cepero, Cojo de Málaga, El Mochuelo, and a host of *Niños* in what some have called the "age of the *Niños*" (age of the Boys)— Niño de Marchena, Niño de Jerez (Manuel Torre), Niño Gloria, Niño de Mairena (Antonio Mairena), Niño del Museo, Niño de Almadén, Niño de Tetuán, Niño de Linares, Niño de Madrid, Niña de los Peines, etc. Most of these singers acquired the *"Niño"* when they began to perform as children.

Among the old guard, the giants of *café cantante* period, some managed to hang on for a while, but the majority, especially the gypsies, were forced to return home to Andalucía, or eke out a living in private fiestas. Manuel Torre, the eccentric and brooding gypsy from Jerez, had been celebrated as a singer of *tangos* for some thirty years and remained active doing large shows and tours until a few years before his death in 1933. Francisco Lema "Fosforito" had driven crowds into a frenzy in the 1880s and '90s, but retired from the stage in 1923 to care for fighting cocks. The greatest of them all, *Don* (Sir) Antonio Chacón, continued to sing until shortly before his death in 1929, although at the end he was often poorly received by the public and even booed in his home town of Jerez. Juanito Valderrama, a follower of Pepe Marchena, once said, "Pepe Marchena made everything into easy *cante*, accessible to the masses. Chacón made everything difficult."[3]

There was little in Antonio Chacón's appearance to suggest a connection with the gypsy or the decadent night world of flamenco. In his fifties when Marchena first came to Madrid, Chacón dressed his heavy, pear-shaped body in elegant suits, usually topped off with a white bow tie. His round face, soft features, and bald head gave little hint of the flamenco within. The arrogance of his bearing and his elegant manners earned him the title of *Don* and permitted him to mix with high society.

But, in fact, Chacón had been a revolutionary in the *cante* since 1886. He created new forms of the *cantes libres* (free-rhythm songs like *granaínas*, *malagueñas*, *tarantas*, and *cartageneras*), practically invented some *cantes* that would later be used for dancing (*caracoles* and *mirabrás*), and revitalized and preserved the pure gypsy *cante jondo* (deep song). Some of his accomplishments paved the way for Pepe Marchena: Chacón was the first to give recitals in the theater. When he used a silver-tipped ebony *bastón* (cane) to beat out the rhythm while he sang, all the young singers abandoned the

---
[1] Rodríguez, R.
[2] Alvarez Caballero, p.190.
[3] Climent, Anselmo González. *Candil, No 6*, January-February, 1990. p. 307.

traditional *varita de estilo* (style stick) in favor of the cane. Chacón was the first to use a falsetto voice to create ornamental flourishes in the *cante*. He had such control of his tenor voice that he could go from a natural voice to falsetto without a break, and such power that he could be heard outdoors in a bullring without the benefit of a microphone. He developed the singer's warm-up, the *temple*, into an art form in itself, rather than just a brief testing of the voice. He was the first to sing flamenco in good Castillian Spanish, rather than in Andalusian dialect and gypsy jargon, believing it would increase the popularity of the *cante*. He even wrote his own verses, paying great attention to detail and believing that they were an important part of his success.

Don Antonio Chacón was a true musician and treated his art with great respect, almost as a religion, constantly studying the music and trying to improve it. He said: "In my early years I began by singing the *siguiriyas* [gypsy *cante jondo*]. With pain in my heart, I had to abandon them and follow the taste that was created by Juan Breva, El Canario, and El Mellizo [creators of the *malagueñas*]. And there I was, prisoner of the *malagueñas*. As much as the *malagueñas* may have given me, and they have given me many thousands, I really miss the old *cantes*."[1] In fact, Chacón became a master of the *malagueñas*, singing the more than fifteen different styles that he created, as well as those of others like Fosforito and La Trini.

Chacón broadened the horizons of the *cante jondo* and widened the *afición*, but he also opened the door to Pepe Marchena and others who did not have his respect for the traditional *cante*. He did not like *fandangos*, that is the new *fandango* derived from the *fandanguillo de Huelva*, and he never sang them, but he lived to see them dominate the flamenco world.

In spite of difficult times and declining health, Chacón remained before the public through most of the 1920s. However, it was in private fiestas that he reigned as the "giant of giants," the "Divo of the *cante*." Flamenco artists could be found in many bars and cafes each night waiting to be hired for private parties. But it was in two competing *colmaos* on the Plaza Santa Ana that the more prestigious artists went to look for work.

Chacón frequented the *colmao* Los Gabrieles in his early years in Madrid. This bar/restaurant opened in 1907 and was rebuilt into its present form in 1923. Ornately tiled rooms in the basement and on the second floor served as sites for fiestas in which a couple of singers and a guitarist might be hired for the night by some monied gentleman and his friends. At best, the *señoritos* would desire a night of fine food, expensive drink, and good *cante*. At worst, the flamencos would have to endure a night of orgy, complete with prostitutes and drunks who wanted to do the singing and dancing themselves. Artist's fees were traditionally not discussed, the flamencos accepting whatever they were offered at the end of the night. Even the artists pre-

[1] Blas Vega, *Vida y Cante de Don Antonio Chacón*, p.157

ferred this system. They felt that they might not give their best if they knew beforehand how much they would earn. After Chacón feuded with the management at *Los Grabieles*, as the flamencos called it, he moved across the plaza to the *colmao* Villa Rosa.

La Villa Rosa, which had opened around 1914 and began its period of greatest popularity with the arrival of Chacón in the early 1920s, has been described as a remembrance of Andalucía in Madrid. In the main room, multi-colored Moorish tiles ran halfway up the walls and plaster arabesques adorned the ceilings. Amid varnished casks of *amontillado* and other fine sherries, gleamed the massive polished bar, and behind it rose row upon row of bottles containing only classical wines of noble Spanish descent. Tapas of fried sardines, toasted hazel nuts, olives stuffed with anchovies, and slices of *jamón serrano*, were served on the house with each *chato* or *caña* of wine. In the rear were a series of ornately decorated private dining rooms, and up a wide staircase, more rooms for private gatherings. In the evenings, Villa Rosa filled with businessmen, bullfighters, politicians, and wealthy *señoritos*, along with shoeshine boys, lottery ticket vendors, flower sellers, and waiters. Flamenco artists, dressed in black, sat silent and expectant, with empty glasses in front of them, waiting for someone to emerge from the raucous, tobacco-smoking crowd and call for a *cantaor*. When that moment arrived, the chosen *cantaor* would signal a guitarist and the two would disappear into a *reservao*, followed by a waiter with a fresh rack of full sherry glasses.

The best of Madrid's flamencos assembled in the Villa Rosa each evening. If they didn't find work, they often performed for each other. Chacón is said to have spent a fortune listening to other singers, especially gypsies. A good fiesta might go on through the night and into the next day, or last for several days. The guitarist Luis Maravilla knew Chacón in his last years and gave the following picture of the maestro: "He would come down to a special room that the Villa Rosa had for artists, to test his voice. He had a pitch pipe to make sure of his tone and to give him confidence in his voice, and he would ask the guitarist to tune. He would say to me, '*Anda*, Luisito, tune your guitar, put the *cejilla* [capo] on three, and give me some rhythm.' If his voice was good, he stayed, if not, he went back to his room."[1]

Chacón could be generous to a fault, or a harsh critic. His feelings about the new trends in *cante* are made clear in the following two anecdotes:

Don Antonio did not care much for a fellow *jerezano*, thirty-seven-year-old José Cepero, known as "The Poet of the *Cante*" because he wrote his own lyrics. Cepero once bragged, "It took the Quinteros [famous playwrights] eight months of work to write a play, and I reduced it in minutes to a five-line verse!" When criticised for being too free in his composition and ignoring traditional structures, Cepero is said to have commented, "The line

[1] Maravilla, Luis. *Sevilla Flamenca*, No 68.

can be as long as the breath in your lungs!" A *payo*, like Chacón, Cepero knew the traditional *cante*, but felt drawn to the new styles and even created his own *fandango*. Once, he said of his singing: "The secret of my *cante* is to tune-up directly and rapidly in the *salida* [*temple*] and help the *cante* by tying the *salida* to the first line of song." To that he added, "Nobody can imitate me. Nobody in a *juerga* can sing after me because my singing is inspired!" Although he enjoyed great popularity and recorded extensively, his lack of personality kept him in the second rank of top artists. One night, in a fiesta, Chacón was explaining to some gentlemen about the *martinetes* (*cantes* of the gypsy blacksmiths), and Cepero dared to ask if he could sing some of them. When he had finished singing, Chacón said, "Everything you have just sung is truly crap!"[1] Cepero never forgave him.

On another occasion, shortly before his death, Chacón was in a gathering where Pepe Marchena was singing to the guitar of Pepe de Badajoz. When Marchena began to sing *por soleá* with his usual personal flair, Chacón stopped him, saying, "Don't go down unfamiliar paths where you don't belong! Stick to singing your own songs, those pretty little things for young damsels!"[2]

Chacón could indeed be patronizing. It is said that in 1925, when he sang before the royal family during the opening of the Patio Flamenco in Sevilla's prestigious Hotel Alfonso XIII, he performed his *granaínas* and *caracoles* so masterfully that he showed up all the others. Normally, Chacón would sing last, but on this occasion he asked another *cantaor*, Fernando *el Herrero* (the Blacksmith), if he could sing first. He said he was losing his voice from all the smoke. When Chacón had finished, El Herrero could not bring himself to sing. Later, the "blacksmith" went looking for Chacón. When he found the singer in a nearby bar, he berated him for the pompous demonstration of superiority he had given in front of the Spanish royalty. When Fernando had finished, Chacón merely replied, "Go on, go on, Fernando, get back to your tools!"

Chacón's favorite guitarist and companion throughout most of his career was the gypsy Ramón Montoya, *"El Emperaó de la Sonanta"* (The Emperor of the Guitar). Born in Madrid's gypsy Barrio de Lavapies, into a family of livestock dealers, Ramón began to play in the cafes when he was fourteen. Largely self-taught, he admits only to having learned a few *filigranas* by watching a guitarist named El Canito in the Café de La Marina, where he would eventually make his debut. But it is said that he took some lessons from Miguel Borrull, a gypsy from Valencia who probably helped him to master the *toques libres*, the free-rhythm styles of *tarantas* and *malagueñas* that were so prevalent in Eastern Andalucía.

Ramón was strongly influenced by the great Paco de Lucena, one of the

---
[1] Juarez, *Candil*, No 75, p. 698.
[2] Blas Vega, *Vida y Cante de Don Antonio Chacón*, p.133.

first guitarists to incorporate classical guitar techniques (scales, arpeggios and tremolo) into flamenco. Montoya would follow in Lucena's footsteps, learning from classical guitarists Miguel Llobet and Emilio Pujol, both students of Francisco Tárrega. The guitarist Carlos Ramos, who performed with Ramón, said, "I think that Emilio Pujol, a famous Catalonian guitarist of that time, had some influence on him. They were friends and Pujol helped him to some extent with his harmonizations. Ramón did not read or write music, but he had an incredible ear. I don't know exactly how Pujol helped him, but Ramón Montoya's harmonization was very good in everything he played, very well arranged. You never could detect a flaw in his style."[1] The result of these collaborations was a new kind of flamenco guitar playing, a music filled with technical complexities and rich harmonies.

Ramón soon dominated the guitar scene in Madrid. In 1912 he teamed up with Chacón to form one of flamenco's legendary duos, and the following year the two recorded together for the first time. In an interview, Montoya called Chacón the greatest singer Spain had known and a master of all the *cantes*. "He was capable of beginning to sing at eight o'clock in the evening and continuing until the same time the following day, with all the same enthusiasm and ability he had when he began, and outdo everyone—nobody could compete with him."[2] It was indeed true that nobody dared to sing after Chacón.

In 1918, Montoya began to record solos. By that time, he had created the guitar solo *por rondeñas* that required an altered guitar tuning. Miguel Borrull actually invented this *toque* (guitar form), but it was Ramón who refined it, recorded it, and made it into something that would endure in the flamenco repertoire. Clearly, Montoya did not develop his playing style in a vacuum. The top guitarists met often to exchange ideas in the guitar shops of José Ramírez II and, later, Santos Hernández. It was Santos Hernández who built Montoya's legendary guitar *"La Leona"* (The Lioness) in 1916, the faithful instrument that he played for over thirty years, and a second guitar, *"Pepita Jiménez,"* in 1924.

One source of inspiration for many of the younger guitarists was Rafael Marín, a professor of classical guitar. Marín, in his fifties, also played flamenco and had published the first known flamenco guitar method in 1902. A student of Paco de Lucena, he encouraged the younger guitarists to *"tirar p'abajo"*—to pick scales with their fingers instead of the thumb, thereby increasing speed and producing a more brilliant sound. He also taught them to pluck *all* of the notes rather than mixing in *ligados*, that is, unplucked notes played with the fretting hand. He probably passed on a number of other techniques from Lucena, as well as ideas from the classical guitar. In his guitar method, Marín gave an idea of the state of the flamenco guitar

---

[1]Chileno, El, *"Conversaciones con Carlos Ramos." Jaleo,* Vol V, No 6. February 1982.
[2]Interview in *La Nación*, Buenos Aires, May 11, 1937.

technique at the turn-of-the-century when he wrote, "...tremolo is not used much, and therefore it is hard to find anyone who does it well...The arpeggio is little used also, and he who knows more than one way to do it is an exception..."[1] In the arpeggio, a guitarist holds a fixed chord with the left hand while his right hand plucks an orderly sequence of notes, often repeatedly. By 1930, Ramón Montoya had incorporated at least seventeen distinct arpeggio patterns into his playing.

Luis Molina, another in the group, became the leading exponent of lightning *picado* (finger-picking) scales and used them to excess in his many recordings with top singers. Luis favored the use of chromatic[2] passages in his scales, a device borrowed by Montoya and, later, incorporated by Sabicas as one of his trademarks. The *cantaor* Pepe de la Matrona gave us a colorful picture of the two young giants, Montoya and Molina, in their formative years. Pepe had to go out to sing solo with the two guitarists when he began to work in the Café del Gato in 1907. He said:

> The two guitarists were Ramón Montoya and Luis Molina. The two would come out to play—two guitars that were real beasts, and it was when they were beginning and wanted to become known. They would begin, one after the other, to force the music more and more, and they would suffocate me. They killed me! And so I said to Montoya, 'Ramón, be careful, don't push so hard!'
>
> '*Pero Hombre*, it is my friend who is pushing—he wants to become known.'
>
> 'Well then, you two go out alone, because if you play for me that way, I will get up and leave you sitting there, you and your friend!'
>
> I sat down to sing. That night I had just gotten up from a tremendous drinking spree, in a room with a painter from Córdoba, that had ended at one in the afternoon. You go to bed, sleep two or three hours, and go out to sing with those two guitars...it suffocated me...
>
> '*Ea*, I won't sing any more!' I got up and left them sitting in their chairs. You wouldn't believe the commotion.[3]

Many considered Luis Molina to be as good as Montoya, if not better, and the two were close friends. Unfortunately, Luis died at the early age of thirty-six when his automobile hit a tree on a mountain road near Pamplona in 1919.

Montoya also took a great deal from Angel Baeza, a pioneer in the mod-

---

[1] Quoted by Blas Vega in "Ramón Montoya: La Guitarra Flamenca." *La Guitarra en la historia*, p. 71.
[2] Chromatic scales progress in half-tones, e.g. on the piano, all of the keys, both black and white.
[3] Ortiz Nuevo, *Pepe el de la Matrona*, p. 75.

ern technique that he and Molina built on and perfected. Ramón said that Baeza was the best dance accompanist he had ever seen. With these influences, and borrowing from the Tárrega school of classical guitar through Pujol and Llobet, Montoya developed his very lyrical and sophisticated style of playing. The guitarist Luis Maravilla described Montoya's playing as "like velvet. His music was so harmonious, with a quality of sound that was hard for others to achieve."

After Montoya started with Chacón, he became very much in demand among the politicians and nobility and was often charged with organizing their fiestas. His dignified bearing and gentlemanly manner eventually earned him the title of *"Don"* (Sir), previously unheard of for a gypsy performer. And his dedication to his art earned him the respect of his fellow performers. The singer Pericón de Cádiz said, "Ramón Montoya, with all that Montoya was, when we used to be in the Villa Rosa, he would pick up his guitar when it was time to eat and the dinner would sit there cold while he practiced and practiced, being what he was, a giant of the guitar!"[1] Ramón said that he practiced about four hours a day. Once, when asked what he was doing, he replied, "I'm here, getting pearls out of the guitar, which is how you have to play it, not like a drum!"

Many thought it odd that, unlike Chacón, Montoya was not offended by Pepe Marchena and began a long collaboration with him almost as soon as the singer became known. He considered Marchena to be in the lineage of the best flamenco tradition. Certainly, the two had something in common— a very lyrical and flowery approach to their music, a quality that would increase in Montoya's playing as he aged.

In 1925, when Carmen Amaya first came to Madrid, Don Ramón Montoya was the director of flamenco entertainment in a new cafe, the Kursaal Imperial. He brought all of the best artists to the cafe, including Pepe Marchena and Juana la Macarrona. La Macarrona had been the queen of the *cafés cantantes* in her day, and even at age sixty-five still commanded respect on stage. But Montoya wasn't the only guitarist to keep busy in Madrid that year. There was Angel Baeza and thirty-three year-old Luis Yance, a very popular soloist and accompanist of the top singers and dancers. Yance was a favorite of Marchena. A few years later, he would give concerts in several theaters in New York. Carlos Verdeal, another popular soloist and accompanist, would later commit suicide in Paris. Perico el del Lunar, thirty-one and heir to the Jerez style of playing of Javier Molina, often played for Chacón in the last years of the singer's life, after Chacón and Montoya had feuded and Montoya began to play for Marchena. Perico recorded with Chacón shortly before the singer's death. Niño Pérez, thirty-five and the son of Maestro Pérez, a guitarist who had dominated the *café cantante* period, had a reputation for his *bulerías* and became a favorite of

[1]Ortiz Nuevo, *Pericón de Cádiz*, p. 270

the singer Manuel Vallejo. Manolo and Pepe de Badajoz, two brothers from the town of Badajoz near the border with Portugal, had established themselves as fixtures in the Villa Rosa. Miguel Borrull's son, Miguelito Borrull was coming into his own, with originality and enviable rhythm in his playing. Unlike his father, who was extraordinary in the free rhythm *toques* but did not like to accompany dance, Miguelito was said to be superb in the dance. Young Carlos Montoya, nephew of Ramón Montoya, had just begun to make his presence felt when he had to go off for a two-year stint in the military.

Two guitarists based in Sevilla but often seen in the capital were twenty-one-year-old Niño Ricardo, who had already recorded with La Niña de los Peines and showed signs of the creativity that would establish him as a maestro to future generations of guitarists, and the legendary Manolo de Huelva. Manolo, at thirty-two, had created a hard-driving, powerful style of playing that influenced virtually every guitarist that came after him. One young guitarist to come under the spell of Manolo's playing was thirteen-year-old Niño Sabicas. In 1922, at age ten, Sabicas had made his debut wearing short pants in Madrid's El Dorado Theater, playing solo and accompanying the *cuplé* singer La Chelito (of "flea dance" fame). Now, only three years later, he had already become a fixture in Madrid, especially in the Villa Rosa. Even the grand old man of the guitar, Juan Gandulla "El Habichuela," remained active. He had begun his career in Cádiz and Sevilla during the 1870s, and continued to play until shortly before his death in 1927. These are only a few of the better known guitarists; there were so many others, like Luis Molina's brother Antonio, who didn't play nearly as well, and those with names like Petaca, El Tito, and El Quique. It was indeed a rich period in the history of the flamenco guitar.

In 1925, twelve-year-old Carmen Amaya was "contracted to work with her father, from whom she was never separated even for a moment, to perform in a salon located in the lower level of the Palacio de la Música in Madrid. The dream was short lived. After ten days, the impresario disappeared and father and daughter found themselves again in the street"[1] Carmen and El Chino left Madrid as they had entered, unheralded and unheeded.

Back in Barcelona, Carmen returned to familiar haunts. That same year, José Cepero *"El Poeta del Cante"* was contracted to appear as part of a series of Tuesday flamenco festivals in the Circo Barcelonés. While there, he accepted an offer to sing for Carmen in the Teatro Español. Montañés described what happened between the popular *cantaor* and the little gypsy girl with the hungry face and bold eyes:

Don José realized that with that little girl there was no room for

---
[1] Góngora

tricks nor foolishness. He had to sing seriously and well. There was a lot of *bailaora* [flamenco dancer] in that little body. During the rehearsal Carmen was bothered by her shoes—she could dance better without them. In the performances, Cepero, carried away, improvised verses when La Capitana, with great irritation, removed her shoes in a mechanical movement and her bare feet shook the floor of the stage, while the strings of Chino's guitar seemed as if they would shatter into a thousand pieces. The orchestra pit of the Teatro Español vibrated with electricity.[1]

"For the first time on the stage of a theater, she appeared in El Español, causing another near riot. The public applauded and screamed. The theater became a madhouse, and the police soon made their presence felt. The gypsy was not authorized to perform because of her very young age. There was a terrific battle between the police and the excited defenders of the little *'faraona.'* And during the fracas the gypsy, protected by the singer José Cepero, gained the safety of the street through the servant exit."[2]

Carmen loved to tell this story, adding, "My father ran for a taxi waiting at the stage door, and I ran backstage looking for a hiding place. You'll never guess where I hid—under the overcoat of the *cantaor* José Cepero! He was a big man and I a tiny tot, and he held me inside his coat while the police searched in vain... *Ozú!*"[3]

Carmen had barely settled into the cafe routine in Barcelona, when she received an invitation to tour with Manuel Vallejo. Thirty-four-year-old Vallejo, a *payo* like the majority of successful flamenco artists of the time, enjoyed the respect of both aficionados of the old *cante jondo* and a public that preferred the modern *cante flamenco* and the *fandangos*. Although a small and nervous man, Manuel had broad shoulders, a thick neck, and powerful lungs that enabled him to sing at length on a single breath. His clear tenor voice lacked *rajo*, the rough quality in the voice that is typical of gypsies and so desirable in flamenco, but he made up for it with technique, personality, feeling, and an extraordinary sense of rhythm. He sang and recorded with extraordinary *compás* [rhythm]—an exception to the rule that only gypsies had the *compás* needed for the *bulerías*. After La Niña de los Peines, Vallejo was the most important singer in creating the modern *bulerías*. At the turn-of-the-century, the *bulerías* were still in their infancy, and it was the younger artists like Vallejo who developed their complexity. Manuel was also a superb dancer of the *bulerías* and one of few to sing and dance them at the same time.

When it came to making records, Manuel Vallejo was the most prolific and encyclopedic *cantaor* in history. In the period before the Spanish Civil

[1] Montañés
[2] Sampero
[3] Pohren, p. 233

War, he recorded over three hundred songs—predominantly *fandangos* (including related forms like the *granaínas*, *malagueñas*, and *tarantas*), *bulerías*, and *saetas* (flamenco religious songs), but always with a sprinkling of the traditional *soleares*, *alegrías*, and *siguiriyas*. Recording helped to build Vallejo's popularity, but two events in 1925 and 1926 were instrumental in catapulting him to fame.

In 1925, Madrid celebrated the opening of the new Teatro Pavón. As a promotion, the management planned to award the *"Copa Pavón"* (The Pavón Cup) to the best artist of the *varieté*. Contests had been all the rage since 1922, when a group of intellectuals organized a contest of *cante* in Granada. Manuel de Falla, Federico García Lorca, and others, wanted to do something to counter both the damage done to flamenco by the "Generation of '98" and the trend away from the traditional gypsy *cante*. They were supported by a long list of well-known painters, musicians, sculptors, writers, and politicians, and the judging panel included Antonio Chacón, Andrés Segovia, and the popular guitarist Amalio Cuenca. But the contest only revealed a lack of good traditional singers and the fact that much of the old *cante* was indeed being forgotten. The surprising winners were seventy-two-year-old Diego Bermúdez *"El Tenazas de Morón"* and twelve-year-old Manolo Caracol, a gypsy descended from a long line of *cantaores* (Caracol would later take flamenco to unprecedented heights of commercialization on stage and in film). The organizers had failed to realize that by inviting only non-professional singers, hopefully untainted by commercialism and therefore "pure and authentic," they had eliminated all of those who were truly qualified. Flamenco had long ceased to be a music of amateurs; it required the dedication of professionals to do justice to its difficulties.

The Granada contest captured the imagination of the public, and soon other contests followed. Such was their popularity that even movie theaters held mini-contests after the films—two or three *cantaores* would be pitted against each other and the audience allowed to judge the winner. So it was that, in August of 1925, some of the best *cantaores* of the time convened in the Teatro Pavón to be judged by a panel headed by none other than Don Antonio Chacón. Among the older singers were Manuel Escacena, El Cojo de Málaga, and El Mochuelo, and the younger artists included Angelillo, Manuel Vallejo, and Pepe Marchena. The judges ended up divided between Marchena and Vallejo, but Chacón tipped the scale in favor of the latter. In a fiesta following the contest, Chacón told Vallejo, "I have given you the cup because you deserve it, but *La Vieja* [Marchena] will earn more money than you!"[1] Vallejo revered Chacón and always carried a photo of him. He said, "My *cante* was born under the influence of Don Antonio Chacón. My famous *granaína*, for example, I took directly from the personality of Chacón."[2]

[1] Blas Vega, *Vida y Cante de Don Antonio Chacón*, p. 107.
[2] Climent, A. G., Candil, No 67, p. 304.

The following year, the competition for the *"Copa Pavón"* was held again. Considerable contoversy resulted when Vallejo lost to Chacón imitator Manuel Centeno, a specialist in *saetas*, the religious songs of Holy Week. The decision may have been influenced by a jury dominated by Pastora Imperio, her guitarist brother Victor Rojas, and their good friend, the painter Julio Romero de Torres. Chacón had declined to be a judge because of the politics involved—the organizers felt that it would not be acceptable for the same singer to win two years in a row.

Flamencos felt that Vallejo had been cheated, and a week later, on the last day of an engagement that featured Vallejo singing in competition with the great gypsy singer Manuel Torre, a group of friends conspired to present Manuel Vallejo with the second *"Llave de Oro del Cante"* (The Gold Key for *Cante*). This *"Llave de Oro"* is perhaps the artistic world's strangest award. The first key had been presented spontaneously to the legendary *cantaor* Tomás el Nitri during a fiesta in the early 1860s. The second award went to Manuel Vallejo some sixty years later, in 1926, and there would not be another "Gold Key" until it was given to Antonio Mairena in Córdoba in 1962. With the passing of Mairena, the key would remain in limbo, awaiting another set of special circumstances.

After the *"Copa Pavón"* and the *"Llave de Oro,"* Vallejo's career took off and contracts poured in. Such was his success that he decided to go on his own and put together a touring company. Tours were something new, a phenomenon unto themselves. With the disappearance of most cafes by the 1920s, flamenco had no place to go and struggled to maintain a presence in music halls, movie theaters, variety shows, and *colmaos*. Then, in 1923, the impresario Carlos Vedrines began the idea of touring with flamenco *"troupes,"* as he called them, using big name artists to attract crowds to bullrings and large theaters. Venues with large seating capacity were necessary in order to meet the budgets of the huge spectacles. Within a few years, these flamenco spectaculars had multiplied in number under the management of *Espectáculos Vedrines, Exclusivas Vega, Circuitos Carcellés, Organizaciones Raval*, and others.

Vedrines had another idea that was to have long-term effects. It seems that cultural events such as orchestral concerts or operas paid a three percent entertainment tax, while the less prestigious variety shows had to pay *ten* percent. The ingenious Vedrines cleverly labeled his spectacles *"ópera flamenca,"* qualifying them for the lower tax.[1] Thus, the new trend in *cante*, away from the gypsy and toward the threatrical commercialization of the Andalusian *fandango* and the *cuplé*, acquired the name by which it would be henceforth be known. In the press, Vedrines attempted to conceal his motive for creating the flamenco opera, claiming, "The idea of the *ópera flamenca*

[1] The exact date that the term *"ópera flamenca"* came into use is not clear, but it appeared on posters at least as early as 1929.

was something that occurred to the mother of La Niña de los Peines [La Niña de los Peines was the top female singer of the time and one of the very best gypsy *cantaoras* of all time]. The phrase came to her one day during the excitement of a rehearsal in which her daughter was singing some *siguiriyas gitanas*. At the culminating moment in the *cante*, the mother, clapping enthusiastically, exclaimed suddenly, '*Olé*, and long live the *ópera flamenca!*'"[1]

With his newly acquired celebrity, Manuel Vallejo took to the road in 1926, attempting to go it alone, without an agent. His company included Bernardo el de los Lobitos, Juan Varea, Felipe de Triana, and eleven-year-old Carmen Amaya with her father and brother Paco on guitars. Little is known about this tour, but certainly one of the highlights would have been when Vallejo, fortified by the wine and aspirin he took to calm his nerves before every performance, came out dancing *por bulerías* with Felipe de Triana on one side and Tomás Chaqueta on the other. One account states that, during the tour little Carmen was seen dancing *bulerías* in a patio in Sevilla to the guitars of El Chino and Paco, and that all three of them were dressed in white.[2]

The following year, Vallejo abandoned the idea of heading his own company and returned to work with Vedrines. Carmen returned to Barcelona. But her world continued to expand when El Chino was contracted by the guitarist Miguel Borrull to work in his cafe.

In 1916, Borrull had taken over an existing cafe in Barcelona and renamed it Villa Rosa. The great esteem that Borrull enjoyed in flamenco circles enabled him to bring the very best artists from Madrid, and soon his cabaret rose to preeminence as the "Cathedral of Flamenco," and became a popular stop in the itinerary of the hordes of tourists that poured into Barcelona after World War I. Miguel's daughter Julia said in a newspaper interview, "The best [performers] of Barcelona and elsewhere have passed through the Villa Rosa…The best customers are the English and the Americans. The Englishman spends a lot and says nothing. The American also spends a lot, but he is *má juergista* [more of a party lover, more noisy]. The Frenchman spends little and criticizes a great deal. The German is always the most surprised."[3]

In the Villa Rosa—operated by the Borrull children after the death of their father in 1926—Carmen worked with and learned from the very best in flamenco. The house *cuadro* included Borrull's son, Miguel Jr., and his three daughters: Concha Borrull is said to have been the first to use castanets in the *alegrías* and later became famous in the United States; Julia was so beautiful that she inspired the central figure in Julio Romero de Torres'

[1] *Dígame*, Madrid, September 15, 1942.
[2] Bois, p. 37.
[3] *Mirador*, March 28, 1929 (quoted by Hidalgo, p. 50).

painting *"Alegrías;"* and Isabel had distinguished herself in the cafes of the time. Other regulars were four sisters who called themselves "Las Mendaña" and Rafaela Valverde "La Tanguera."

La Tanguera, a *paya* who looked more gypsy than most *gitanas* with her smoldering dark features, had appeared in the best cafes of Madrid, Sevilla, and Valencia before making her permanent home in Barcelona around 1920. She specialized in *tangos, farruca, garrotín,* and *bulerías,* relatively light dances that she imbued with captivating importance through her personality and inimitable rhythm. Another dancer in the Villa Rosa, La Joselito, gave a colorful portrait of La Tanguera, describing her as large and unattractive, with pockmarks. Apparently, La Joselito danced well during one performance in the Circo Barcelonés, and she says:

> ...The audience clapped like crazy. I was still so young, and when you're young and you do something well, it really makes an impression. Tanguera had to dance after me and they hardly took any notice of her. She was a great *farruca* dancer, but I couldn't help it if they liked me so well. When she finished, she raced backstage in a blinding rage and wham! wham! she boxed my ears so hard they bled. I was practically deaf for three months after that. You could hear my screams through the whole theater...But you have to hand it to her, she was a great *farruca* dancer. And I had danced her *farruca!* I copied it from her just like all my dances.[1]

There may have been some personal animosity between La Tanguera and La Joselito, for Tanguera's favorite guitarist, Juan *Relámpago* (Lightning), would later become La Joselito's husband. A 1919 poster for the cabaret Concert Sevilla, in Sevilla, had announced "El Niño de la Matrona, Tanguerita and her guitarist, Relámpago, and forty *suggestive and beautiful artists.*" As a friend of Carmen Amaya, La Tanguera certainly must have been a significant influence on the young dancer, with her *farruca* danced in pants, her *garrotín, tangos,* and *bulerías.*

Another regular in the Villa Rosa was El Batato, who danced only the *farruca* and *por chuflas* (comical dances, often done *por bulerías* or *tangos*) but with such acrobatic leaps that he was contracted by Diaghilev for the Russian Ballet, only to have the contract fall through because he was underage. Also in the *cuadro,* Concha la Chícharra, a dancer with undescribable *gracia* (wit, charm) in a playful Catalonian gypsy dance called *El Crispín,* to which she did a striptease down to her petticoat. El Mojigongo took the *farruca* to a new high, dancing it with passion and fury—some might say with demonic fury, for the dancer was tall and thin, with reddish skin, jet black hair that curled into two horns at his temples, bloodshot eyes, and a pointed chin. Manolillo de la Rosa, originally from Jerez, also excelled in

[1] Claus, p. 107

the *farruca*. Carmen Amaya called Manolillo and El Gato the best she had ever seen in the *farruca*.

The cream of flamenco alternated between Madrid and the Villa Rosa in Barcelona. Among the many singers, Chacón, Vallejo, Manuel Torre, La Niña de los Peines, and El Cojo de Málaga—a regular for many years. But it was the dancers who would have made the biggest impressions on Carmen. Juan Sánchez *"El Estampío"* (The Blast), from the gypsy barrio of Santiago in Jerez de la Frontera, would have been one of these, with his *zapateado* (dance of footwork) and *alegrías*. At first known as *"El Feo"* (The Ugly One), a nickname he acquired as a novice bullfighter and certainly inspired by his long face and jutting jaw, El Estampío had come to Madrid in 1912 where he fell under the spell of Salud Rodríguez.

Salud, the daughter of El Ciego, a blind gypsy guitarist from Sevilla, danced and dressed like a man—it was said that she didn't even know how to dress as a woman. She is thought to have been the first to put footwork into the *soleá*. They absolutely adored her in Madrid and she caused a furor wherever she went. The great dancer Antonio de Bilbao said of her, "Dressed up in the Jerez style and doing footwork, she was a monument to her race." Salud, in turn, had learned her dance from La Cuenca, the first woman to put on men's clothes and dance like a man. When La Cuenca put on a white ruffled shirt, short jacket, tight pants with a colorful sash, riding boots, and round cheese-shaped *calañés* hat, and came out with her blazing footwork, she became a sensation in the cafes of the 1880s. In *zapateado*, she dressed as a bullfighter and was the first to play out the acts of the bullfight, complete with cape, *banderillas, muleta*, and sword. La Cuenca passed her dance on to Salud Rodríguez, who, in turn, taught El Estampío.

El Estampío did not come by his skills easily. When he first went to Madrid to dance his *tango* in the Café Marina, he was fired after the first night. The following night he had better luck in the Café de la Magdalena with the comic *tango* he called *"El picaor"* ("The Picador"—a pantomime of the bullfight). After a stint in Málaga's Café de Chinitas he returned to Madrid, where he learned from Salud Rodríguez and began to acquire the reputation that would mark him as one of flamenco's great *bailaores*. Some attribute his graceful elegance and well developed arm technique to the fact that he had learned from a woman. His *alegrías* and *zapateado* were models to be copied by all, and the charm and humor of this gypsy dancer made him one of the important figures in the dance for more than fifty years. Later, Carmen Amaya would carry on some of the traditions that began with La Cuenca and continued with Salud Rodríguez and El Estampío.

It might be said that, for Carmen Amaya, the Villa Rosa was her academy of dance, the university that gave her the only formal dance education she would have. The newspaper critic Sebastián Gasch described Carmen at that time:

They called her La Capitana. She was a gypsy of pure stock, from the part in her hair to the heels that flew to the sound of her father's guitar. With the blood of pharoahs in the palms of her hands. She was barely fourteen years old. She stood little more than a meter in height. Seated in a chair on the stage, La Capitana remained impassive as a statue, arrogant and noble, with racial nobility beyond description, focused inward and oblivious to everything happening around her. Suddenly she leaped to her feet. And the *gitana* was dancing. Indescribable. Soul. Pure soul. Feeling in the flesh. The stage was vibrating with unheard of savageness and incredible precision. La Capitana was the unpolished product of Nature. Like all gypsies, she must have been born dancing. She represented the opposite of everything schooled, everything academic. Everything she knew, she must have known at birth.The spectator soon felt subjugated, dazed, and dominated by the energetic conviction on the face of La Capitana, by the fierce dislocations of her hips, by the bravura of her pirouettes and the ferocity of her *vueltas quebradas* [backbend turns], in which she matched animal heat with marvelous precision of execution...What created the most profound impression on seeing her dance was the nervous energy that drove her into dramatic contortions, her blood, her violence, and the wild impetuosity of a pureblooded *bailaora*.[1]

Montañés states that during this period, Carmen made her first trip to her ancestral home in Granada. Juana la Faraona, the sister of El Chino and aunt of Carmen Amaya, was well-known among gypsies and often called the daughter of the pharoah due to the arrogant bearing of her dance. When La Faraona was invited to Granada for a big celebration, she took her young niece with her.

After a two-day train trip in uncomfortable third class compartments, Carmen and her aunt would have been taken by carriage up out of the city streets, along Darro River. On the right, high above the river, the towering red fortress of the Alhambra loomed out of a forest of green. To the left, white houses and narrow stepped streets rose tier above tier in the Albaicín, the ancient and legendary Moorish barrio of the falconers. Further up the gorge, a mountainside appeared to suddenly come to life with teeming activity. This was the Sacromonte, the Sacred Mountain, home to gypsies for over four hundred years. A crisscross of narrow paths branched out in all directions, leading ever upward on a hillside honeycombed with cave dwellings. Each cave had been carved out of the dry, rocky soil and, in the majority of

---

[1] Gasch. This description appears with little variation in the Barcelona weekly *El Mirador* and in Gasch's book *El Molino*. However, in one case, Carmen is cited as being twelve years old, in the other fourteen. I selected the fourteen because it fits with the year she performed in the Villa Rosa.

them, doorways and windows appeared in the walls that sealed the openings. The fronts of the caves were whitewashed, making them stand out like bleached stains in the huge clusters of prickly pear and spiked aloe cactus. Many had only a flap of cloth for a door. Multicolored rags hung on the cactus clumps to dry and strings of bright red peppers dangling in whitewashed windows presented a festive appearance.

Everywhere, thin wisps of white smoke drifted up from irregular rows of chimneys that protruded from the red earth. With no bathrooms, walls and ravines served as latrines, and everywhere the smell of human waste hung in the air. All water came from distant public wells. Naked children laughed and played in the dust, amid bleating goats, gaunt dogs, ragged chickens, pigs, and lean, half-starved donkeys struggling up the steep paths with their milk cans or heavily laden baskets. Women, many with babies at their breasts, sat chattering in the doorways as they wove baskets or picked lice from each other's hair.

At the bottom of the mountain, where the paths were wide and formed terraces, large caves showed signs of prosperity. In many, three whitewashed rooms opened to the front, two with windows and the central living room with the doorway. A fourth chamber, dug back into the earth, served as a bedroom. On the red tile floors, wicker-seated chairs lined walls hung with highly polished copper pots and brass utensils, pictures of saints, and pots of cut flowers. Tiny stalagtites, formed by years of gathering moisture, covered the whitened ceilings like inverted miniature mountain ranges.

Some caves, hidden in immense cactus thickets, served as taverns, while others were host to tourists looking for authentic gypsy dance and music. Further up the hill, poorer caves might consist of only two or three rooms—the living room, a bedroom, and perhaps a room for the animals. Where there was no chimney, the family cooked outdoors or ate and slept in the smoke of the cooking fire. The highest caves were often no more than crumbling holes dug into the earth and not tall enough to permit standing. Whole families lived in these filthy burrows.

At night, the Sacred Mountain became a volcano of flaming furnaces as gypsy men pounded hot iron into ornate utensils and decorative window gratings in their smoke blackened smithies. Some of the poorer blacksmiths, working in open holes near the top, had only crude pieces of iron for anvils and piles of stones for furnaces. With this primitive equipment, they could do little more than turn out endless numbers of horseshoe nails.

In a time when the men of Barcelona sported three-piece suits, double-breasted jackets, and neckties, many of the gypsies of the Sacromonte clung to the fashion tastes of times past. The older men wore tight pants tied at the knee, high boots or spats, short jackets, and immense colored sashes tied about the waist. Mustaches, full bushy sideburns, and the cheese-shaped *calañés* hats, were still very much in style. Younger men adopted, to varying degrees, the European manner of dress.

Women invariably wore layers of full-length skirts, typically in polka-dot patterns and covered by an obligatory apron. A small fringed shawl crossed over the chest and tied at the waist in the back completed the outfit. Girls might go about barefoot, but older women favored cheap cloth slippers. The heavily greased hair might be pulled back in a bun or gathered in a loose pony tail. For special occasions each woman pasted trademark spit curls to her cheeks or forehead. The curls exhibited great variety in shape, from a single s-shaped curl in the center of the forehead, to wide flat curls at the temples, or thin sideburns that curled up against the cheeks or down as if to circle the ear. As a final festive touch, paper flowers perched jauntily on top of their heads.

The arrival of Carmen Amaya and La Faraona in the Sacromonte would have been an occasion of great festivity, with the *gitanos* coming down the hill decked out in their finest to greet the newcomers. Introductions all around. With so many Amayas, Mayas, Fajardos, Heredias, and Cortés making up the cave-dwelling families, there would be a seemingly endless number of aunts, uncles, nephews, and cousins to meet and hug warmly. Among the "relatives," guitarist Manolo Amaya and his mother Dolores la Capitana. The father, Juan Amaya, had created the first *zambra* in the Sacromonte. The gypsies of Granada called their fiestas *"zambras"* and by association the term also came to apply to the performing groups, to their *cuadros*. The *zambra* of Juan Amaya was so well-known that it had performed in Paris in 1900 and South America in 1913. After Juan's death, his wife Dolores became *La Capitana* of the *zambra* and inhabited the most luxurious cave on the mountain. In 1922, her son Manolo had taken the *zambra* to perform in Madrid.

Juana Amaya *"La Cagachina"* danced in the *zambra* of La Capitana. The daughter of singer El Cagachín and married to guitarist/singer Antonio Maya, her two young daughters, eight-year-old Tere Maya and five-year-old Rosario *"La Lili,"* already danced with a maturity far beyond their years. It is said in the Sacromonte that when babies are born they come out dancing. In truth, the *gitana* continues dancing when she is pregnant and, shortly after the baby is born, she begins to move it to the rhythm of the dance and work its arms. By one and a half years, the child beats time with its feet, and at two and a half is capable of full-length adult dances. After that, children may be forced to study long hours, but in reality they can dance without study. It is that lack of formal training, the natural spontaneity and passion, that characterizes the gypsy dance.

Little Carmen must have been overwhelmed by the presence of so many Amayas. From the Amaya-Fajardo family there was María la Gazpacha, a gifted singer about ten years older than Carmen, and her brothers and sisters, all dancers. Representing the Amaya-Cortés clan, the ancient María *la Golondrina* (The Swallow), who had danced to the *cante* of Don Antonio

Chacón in a fiesta during the 1922 contest in Granada, and her daughter, Carmen Amaya Cortés, also known as "La Golondrina." From the Maya-Cortés Family, La Cagachina's sister, the teenage María *"La Canastera"* (The Basketweaver) and her sister-in-law, María Maya, whose noble beauty earned her the nickname *"La Jardín"* (The Garden). Add to these performers an extensive array of parents, grandparents, brothers and sisters, and nieces and nephews, and it is easy to imagine that Carmen would feel bewildered, yet bask in a warm sense of home and extended family.

The fiesta would begin immediately and continue through the night, perhaps centered in the cave of Dolores la Capitana. Over the din created by hundreds of hands beating out the incessant rhythm and the cries of rough gypsy voices, the guitar and *cante* would be barely audible. And they would dance, one after the other, with fury and abandon, as only gypsies can do when they are dancing for themselves. La Cagachina, tall, dark, and beautiful *por alegrías*, Micaela la Faraona, intensity in her slanted Oriental eyes, *por tangos*, and *La Bizca* (The Cross-eyed), one of the better dancers, with bobbed curly reddish-blond hair, freckles sprinkled across her turned-up nose, and wearing a fashionable flapper dress complete with stockings rolled below the hem. There was La Filitú, La Salvaora, La Chata... And Carmen would see for the first time the dances of the Sacromonte.

The gypsies of Granada cultivated ancient dances not seen elsewhere in the flamenco world: *La cachucha*, a pantomine of the groom asking the pardon of the brides parents for having robbed them of their daughter, *el bolero gitano*, *la jota gitana* for four women and one man with a tambourine, and *el fandango del Albaicín*, or *fandangos de la Peza*, danced by a group of women. Unique to the Sacromonte were the many group and circle dances. In *las roás*, women formed a circle, while the men played tambourines and sang:

Decirme a mí que te orvíe	To tell me to forget you
es predicá en er desierto,	is like preaching in the desert,
machacá en jierro frío	trying to hammer cold iron,
platicá con los muertos.	or talking to the dead.
Tanto ha llovío,	It has rained so much,
tanto ha llovío,	it has rained so much,
la calabaza s'ha florecío.	the squash has flourished.

Women danced *la mosca* (the fly) in pairs, scratching themselves indecently, slapping their thighs, and shouting *"Mosca, mosca!"* while onlookers sang:

El demonio de esta mosca	This devil of a little fly,
donde se vino a poner?	where do you think he has landed?
Debajo del delantal,	Underneath my apron,
Cule, cule, cule,	Go, go, go,
búscala tú!	look for him, you!

Carmen Amaya dancing in the Sacromonte some time before 1936. Her father, El Chino, (right) accompanies her.

Salvador Montañés picks up the story:

One day the news spreads through the Sacromonte of Granada that Alfonso XIII, King of Spain, wants to attend a gypsy show. Important gentlemen with gray-flecked beards, clean, well-pressed suits, celluloid stays in their collars, and gray ties, warn the gypsies of the Sacromonte: "Let's have much seriousness, much respect; it is no less than the king who is going to listen to you!"

The gypsies of the Sacromonte rehearse and prepare. One night, Ana de Ronda [Ana Amaya Molina, about seventy-three years old at the time] takes up her guitar and intones, one after the other, all of the *soleares* that she knows, as well as those that she improvises at the moment, and her niece, or cousin, or granddaughter—nobody knows for sure—Carmen Amaya "La Capitana," the little Barcelona gypsy, dances amid the prickly pear cactus and whitewashed walls under an astonished moon, stepping on stones and stirring up dust, until the moon retires and it is the sun's turn to be surprised by that dream of feet and arms. There, in the highest part of the Sacromonte, hundreds of gypsies hold their breath while an old gypsy who has lost track of the years and a young Mediterranean gypsy who can't keep track of the days sing, dance, suffer, and cry. The miracle of flamenco, the inexplicable mystery, envelops them all. Finally, the little Barcelona gypsy collapses. Ana de Ronda holds her guitar a little tighter, and the sobbing gypsies return to their caves. Only one very old gypsy raises his withered arms to eyes that have been flooded by weeping and cries out, "Now I can die in peace! Nobody has danced like that!"

The night of the royal fiesta arrives. Alfonso XIII and his numerous court appear in the Sacromonte. The gypsies have dressed in their best regalia, their hair slicked down with oil, flowered blouses, bright dresses... The chief of protocol warns the gypsies: "As you have been told, above all, show much respect! Don't forget to dedicate your dances to His Majesty. Don't speak directly to the King under any circumstance. Only when you dedicate your dance can you say, 'For His Majesty!'"

The gypsies agree. The fiesta begins and each one shows off his art or inspiration. Alfonso applauds with pleasure. Suddenly, a little gypsy girl plants herself proudly and majestically in the center of the stage, bare feet together, skirt gathered in her left hand, her body arched tensely, and slowly raising her right hand she stares directly, face to face, at the King of Spain. With a facial expression that looks as if she is attempting to remember something, she looks like a frightened novice bullfighter. Alfonso XIII smiles and suddenly a hoarse but childish voice, trembling, is heard in that expectant silence: "This is for you, Señor King!" The guitar of Ana de Ronda sounds furiously and Carmen Amaya "La Capitana" beats the ground with her bare feet; her arms draw exorcisms and labyrinths in the Granada night.

The astonished royal court had fallen silent before that breech of protocol. The guitar stops, and the little gypsy girl, erect, tense, tragic, halts her dance. Then the King applauds enthusiastically and his retinue follows his lead in giving an ovation to the little girl.[1]

There are obvious errors in these accounts. Ana de Ronda, in her seventies at the time, did play the guitar and sing, and she was also famous for her *soleares*. But she lived all her life in Ronda, not Granada. And if she did visit Granada, she certainly would not have stayed in the highest cave in the Sacromonte, as Montañés described earlier in his account. The highest caves were the most decrepit and unfit for human habitation. Anilla de Ronda could never have played the kind of guitar needed for Carmen's dancing— she wouldn't have had the strength and very likely not the experience.

Carmen's age is given as eighteen, but she would have been barely seventeen when Alfonso XIII abdicated the throne and went into exile. It had to be earlier. Yet, in spite of these inaccuracies, there is probably a core of truth to this account. There are photographs of Carmen dancing in the Sacromonte before she left Spain in 1936, although they don't reveal her age, and she often told the story of dancing for the king. So, we are left with the likelihood that Carmen Amaya first visited the Sacromonte when she was fifteen or sixteen.

That evening resulted in five hundred *pesetas* for Juana la Faraona and her niece Carmen, allowing them to return to Barcelona and begin again their life, going from tavern to tavern, *colmao* to *colmao*, to El Manquet, La Criola, and the Villa Rosa of Borrull.

---

[1] Montañés, p. 18.

CHAPTER THREE

THE FRENCH CONNECTION

The year 1929, which would prove disastrous for so many, began on a somber note in the flamenco world. On January 21, Don Antonio Chacón passed away in Madrid, the victim of arteriosclerosis according to the death certificate. His death marked the closure of a glorious era in which he had reigned for forty years as the "Pope" of the *cante*. However, his last tour with Espectáculos Vedrines the previous summer had dramatically made clear the change in public taste. Vedrines had sought to outdo all previous efforts and had put together an imposing cast of artists for a tour that would play in bullrings of all the major cities of Andalucía. It proved to be a grueling schedule of travel, with performances about every third day.

A newspaper review of the Vedrines performances in Huelva and a poster for the event give some idea of the nature of the spectacle. The "Solemn Andalusian Fiesta," opened with the *cante* of Niño Sevilla, Bernardo el de los Lobitos, and El Chato de las Ventas, accompanied by the guitars of Luis Yance, and two regulars on the Vedrines tours, Manuel Martell, a young guitarist from Madrid, and Manuel Bonet, a twenty-seven-year-old student of Luis Molina. The first half closed with a "Grandiose *cuadro* of dance and *zambra gitana*" that featured almost twenty dancers, including El Estampío, "creator of the dance *'El Picaor'*," Frasquillo, "king of the *farrucas*," Carmen Vargas, "queen of the dances to the guitar," La Quica, "celebrated for her *alegrías*," Carmelita Borbolla (a great beauty, whose face and figure graced postcards sold to tourists in Sevilla) *"por alegrías,"* La Gabrielita *"por chuflas,"* El Tovalo, "surprising dancer," Acha Rovira, "the great serious/comic dancer," Lolita Almería, "noted dancer *por farrucas*," Manolita la Macarena *"por alegrías,"* and "The Six Little Gypsies from La Cava de Triana." (Triana is the gypsy barrio of Sevilla.)

After a ten-minute break, the second half opened with the *cante* of Guerrita, to the delight of the audience. But La Niña de los Peines was the highlight of the evening, driving the crowd into a frenzy with her *siguiriyas*. Handkerchiefs came out demanding that she be awarded an "ear!" José Cepero and Manuel Vallejo probably found La Niña a hard act to follow, accounting for the absence of comment by the press. "And, finally, the Pope:

Don Antonio Chacón. He sang only *caracoles*. And it was enough. It was a worthy finish to a pleasant Andalusian fiesta. The honorable figure of Don Antonio Chacón presided majestically over the fascinating chorus of esteemed artists."[1] This performance by Chacón must have been an exception, or the reporter extremely biased, for in most cities the crowds mocked the veteran *cantaor*, booing, whistling, and yelling for him to get off the stage. The young generation hadn't even heard of the aging maestro and wanted only the new *fandango*. There were rumors that some of Chacón's competitors had paid hecklers to stir up crowds against the singer, but in reality it was just a sign of the times. Antonio Mairena recalled: "I saw in the Reina Victoria Theater in Sevilla how they booed Antonio Chacón and La Niña de los Peines. My father covered his face with his hands, like a good aficionado, when he saw how the public reacted to such venerable artists, how they booed the knowledge of Chacón when he sang his *caracoles*. And the new singers, those just beginning, took advantage of the situation. I asked my father why the audience booed when these venerable artists sang and then went wild when someone sang two or three little things that were coming out then—flowery *fandangos* or one of the flowery *guajiras*...that genre that would last for fifty years."[2]

Chacón's passing was mourned throughout Spain. Flamencos attended his funeral en masse, and a huge crowd made up of all classes, from the waiters who had served him to the royalty who had admired his art, followed the funeral procession to the cemetery. All expenses were paid by the Duke of Medinaceli. In Barcelona, Pepe Marchena interrupted his performance with Luis Yance in the Olympia Theater to ask for a moment of silence "for the great *cantaor flamenco* Don Antonio Chacón, may he rest in peace." The audience assented to the request with great respect. And, in Barcelona, as Marchena bade farewell to a legendary figure in the *cante*, Carmen Amaya, a budding legend in the dance, prepared to leave Spain for the first time.

The controversial dancer Vicente Escudero takes credit for Carmen Amaya's first performance in France, in 1929. Carmen was again dancing in her familiar Barcelona haunts when, "one night Vicente Escudero happened to see her. He was just back from a resoundingly successful visit to Paris. He was overwhelmed and kept coming back night after night. Escudero perceived the true value of the precious jewel of flamenco dance, of which he was the acknowledged oracle."[3]

Vicente Escudero was certainly not an oracle—that title would not be bestowed upon him for several more decades, but he *was* beginning to estab-

[1] Blas Vega, *Vida y Cante de Don Antonio Chacón*, p. 132.
[2] Delgado, José, and A. Ramos Espejo, "I Was Strong as a Horse." *El Ideal*, November, 1981.
[3] Samperio

lish a reputation. Vicente was born in 1885, in Valladolid, the capital of Old Castile in northern Spain. In spite of the absence of gypsy blood in the family, or an artistic heritage, he felt the pull of flamenco at a very early age. He went against his father's wishes that he enter the printing business and spent much of his time hanging around the gypsy neighborhoods. The obsession he had for flamenco dance was something unheard of in that part of Spain. "The young Vicente's first heel beats were practiced on the metal manhole covers in the streets of Valladolid...When police chased him from manhole to manhole, he landed finally on the smooth surface of a tree trunk thrown across a river as an improvised bridge. Here he practiced on the resounding wood and, as it was narrow, he received many ablutions in the water below. In Vicente's own words, it was at this time that he established an unshakeable balance, for fear of being soaked again. This balance was to support him and secure the posture for which he was famous in his majestic style of dancing."[1]

By the age of nine, Vicente was dancing wherever he could, in town squares and at local fairs, earning money by passing the hat. At thirteen, he danced professionally for the first time, in a movie theater in his home town. Donn Pohren writes that Vicente "...consistently ran up against flamenco's big problem of old: secrecy. No one would teach him the fundamentals of the dance, such as the *compás*, *palmas*, etc."[2] Vicente called this not being *"enterao"* or "clued in." Frustrated, the teenage Escudero traveled to Granada to live with the gypsies, hoping to become *enterao*. Apparently it didn't work, for when he emerged from the caves of the Sacromonte six years later, at age twenty-two, and went to Madrid to debut in the Café de la Marina, he lasted only three days. According to his own confession, the other performers insisted on his dismissal because he couldn't do *palmas a compás* (clap in time). Vicente told of the first time he danced seriously with a guitarist. When the guitarist asked him if he was *"enterao,"* Vicente said yes. But a moment after he began to dance, the guitarist knew he had lied and said in front of the onlookers, "Young man, you have deceived me, you are nowhere near being *enterao!*"

No guitarist wanted to accompany Vicente, and he was dismissed by each cafe that gave him a tryout. This rejection resulted in a complex that he never got over. Discouraged, he headed north to work in Santander and Bilbao where artists and clientele would not be so demanding. There, he met the great dancer Antonio de Bilbao and his luck began to change.

Ramón Montoya tells the story of Antonio de Bilbao's appearance on the flamenco scene in 1906:

It was one of those memorable nights in Madrid's Café de la

---

[1] Niles, Doris, *"El Duende," Dance Perspectives 27*, Autumn, 1966.
[2] Pohren, p.190

Marina. After various artists had performed, Antonio, responding to the encouragement of his friends, appeared on the small stage and asked me to accompany him. The impression he made with his physique and dress gave no hint of the immense dancer within him. The beret perched on his head revealed his Basque origins. When I asked him what he wanted to dance, he said that he would do it *por alegrías*. I looked at him and thought it had to be a joke, and I decided to play it that way. But the man reacted and said to me with great self confidence, "No, play well, I know how to dance!"

And, sure enough, the man knew what he was doing, to such an extent that he overwhelmed all the other dancers that night, as well as the guitarists and the public. Such was the impression he made that the owner of the cafe came to me immediately and let me know that I should contract him—that duty was reserved for the official house guitarist, which at that time was me. I asked him what he wanted to earn, and he told me that he wanted twelve *pesetas*, at that time a good salary. But if he had asked for fifty, we would have given it to him. The only thing I can say about Antonio de Bilbao is that a short time later he was the head man in the Café de la Marina, and his name circulated through all of Spain in tones of awe.[1]

Antonio, the son of a guitarist/dancer from Sevilla, lived for a period in the Basque city of Bilbao and was thereafter called Antonio de Bilbao. While traveling with his father in Andalucía, he chanced to see a performance by Enrique *el Jorobao* (the Hunchback). Enrique, from Linares, was said to be quite ugly and deformed by two humps, but those defects seemed to disappear when he danced. He is considered to be the creator of *las campanas* (the church bells), a part of the *zapateado* footwork dance in which the dancer and the guitarist work together in unison, building from simple foot taps and bell-like guitar tones to rapid and complex steps on a repeated melodic theme. Antonio learned this *zapateado* from El Jorobao and improved upon it. El Jorobao also taught Salud Rodríguez, who passed the dance on to El Estampío. Antonio de Bilbao also claimed to have learned from *El Miracielos* (He who looks at the sky; a neck defect prevented him from looking down), the first known flamenco dancer and supposedly the first to dance to guitar accompaniment in the early 1800s. Antonio used to say that Miracielos taught him the *rosas*, a long-forgotten form of *alegrías*. However, since Miracielos died before Antonio was born, it is more likely his dance was passed down by one of his students, perhaps El Raspao, the teacher of El Jorobao.

In his early years, Antonio de Bilbao was always a surprise to those who

---

[1] Blas Vega, *Diccionario Enciclopédico del Flamenco*, p. 105

saw him for the first time. With his Northern accent, his small stocky stature, short arms and legs, and tiny feet, he seemed an unlikely prospect as a flamenco dancer. According to Pepe el de la Matrona, Antonio came into a cafe one night as they were closing, and went up on stage. With one quick footwork combination he caused chairs to fall off tables and startled everyone. He was, of course hired immediately. Donn Pohren writes that the first time Antonio performed in Sevilla, flamencos scoffed when they saw posters announcing Antonio and his guitarist Luis Molina, two *payos* from the North. They were prepared to laugh, but instead were astounded by Antonio's complex footwork and Molina's lightning *picado* scales.

By 1914, Antonio de Bilbao had begun to work a great deal outside of Spain, particularly in France. An early flamenco biographer, Fernando de Triana, wrote that Antonio de Bilbao "…was the best dancer in the execution of footwork. In *zapateado* and *alegrías* he was the greatest, but, just as there is no perfect happiness, it can be said about Antonio el de Bilbao that he was very uneven and had as much artistic indifference from the waist up as he had ability in his feet. If the placement of his arms had matched the execution of his feet, he would have been the greatest dancer to date."[1]

Vicente Escudero claimed that he met Antonio while working in Bilbao in 1907. He said that under the tutelage of the veteran dancer he soon became a bit more *enterao*, and after rehearsing a *farruca* and a comic *tanguillo*, he traveled throughout Spain working in movie theaters. This account may not be entirely accurate. Another great dancer, Antonio Triana, wrote: "May I tell you that Antonio de Bilbao, who was my good friend (as I danced with his wife, Julia Verdiales, on several occasions), never taught *anyone* his technique! He once told me, *'Yo no enseño ni a mi padre!'* [I teach no one, not even my father!].[2] On the other hand, Mercedes, daughter of the great *bailaora* La Quica, said that her future husband, Albano, studied with Antonio de Bilbao until his death, and then continued with Antonio Triana.[3]

Given Vicente Escudero's penchant for embellishing the truth, it remains uncertain whether he actually studied with Antonio de Bilbao. Perhaps he learned indirectly, or was given a few pointers. However, it is clear that his dancing improved and he began to travel around Spain with his *zapateado* and *tango*. The following year, 1908, Vicente fled to Portugal to escape the military draft. In Lisbon, he found his first real success as a dancer, performing for a public that did not understand him, but applauded and paid. He "…commenced his offbeat flamenco, first because he could not find a guitarist there who knew the rhythms, later because he began to enjoy the liberty gained by dropping the *compás*.

"Next stop, Paris, where Vicente was to build such a reputation for him-

---
[1]Triana, p. 164.
[2]Pohren, p. 369.
[3]Durbin, Paula Joann, "An Interview with Mercedes and Albano." *Jaleo*, October-November 1983

self that his name leapt the Pyrenees and became known throughout Spain. Shortly after Vicente's first Paris recital, in 1922, he became strongly influenced by the Dadaistic and surrealistic schools of painting, to such an extent that he took up painting himself and, what for us is more significant, began applying these concepts to his flamenco dancing. With an entire philosophy to back up his own instinctive feelings, Vicente really let himself go. He began to give concerts to the clashing of two orchestras going separate ways, or to the humming of dynamos set at different pitches. This, he states in his book, was the most delightfully creative period of his career. He went so far as to rent a little deserted theater in a Bohemian section of Paris in which to rehearse and give exhibitions of his surrealistic flamenco dance. That almost no one came to these recitals served only to delight him even further. Vicente feels that the doings of geniuses are never appreciated by contemporary generations; the gathering of crowds at his recitals would only have denoted failure."[1]

Escudero found himself at the center of a cult in the Paris of the 1920s. He hung out with intellectuals, musicians, and painters. Marc Chagall, Isadora Duncan, and the Russian dance impresario Diaghilev were his friends. He drew, painted, and designed unusual costumes with Picasso's help. A good description of his attitude at that time comes again from Donn Pohren, who wrote that Vicente did not respect imitation, that his dance was extremely creative and original. "One of the revered traditions scorned by Vicente was the *compás*. He could not stand to be confined within its well-defined structure, and he rebelled. He found accompanists who were willing to forego the *compás* and just follow his whims and fancies, thus setting the stage for widely varied opinions about his dance. The public in general did not know or care much about the *compás* as long as Vicente could produce his kind of dance. To flamenco artists, however, one who cannot, or does not, keep the *compás* is not even to be seriously considered. They also point out that at times Vicente employed many 'tricks' in his dance, such as the snapping and clicking of his fingernails, one white and one black boot, and so forth."[2]

Vicente enjoyed great success in Paris with Spanish dances set to the music of classical masters like Albéniz and Turina. In 1926, Manuel de Falla honored him by asking him to choreograph the dances for a new version of *El Amor Brujo*. Gabriel Ruiz, a guitarist who played for Vicente in Paris in the mid-1930s, says that Escudero "...contributed new ideas to the dress of the *bailarín* and *bailaor*. I still remember how he dressed for the *'Farruca del molinero'* of Falla: One leg sheathed in a stocking, the other bare, one arm with a rolled-up sleeve and the other bare. Often on stage he used to roll his fingernails strongly, imitating the sound of tiny *palillos* (castanets) as he retreated to one side of the stage, and when he did his exit, he used to tap on

[1] Pohren, p. 191.
[2] Pohren, p. 189.

the piano with his fingers and disappear amid thunderous applause. Of course, this happened in France, in Paris, where he had his headquarters and was famous."

Gabriel paints a colorful picture of Escudero, who affected gypsy dress and mannerisms in an attempt to pass himself off as one of them:

He lived at that time in a popular neighborhood and had rented the large basement floor of an old Parisian home. He lived with his wife Carmina and three or four young men—he told me they were his *sobrinos* [nephews], dance students and gypsies as well (I realized immediately that this was not true). There in his "basement" he had his studio. He told me he would be doing a benefit performance in the Salle Pleyel, one of the most important salons in the world in those times, and he wanted me to play the guitar. Frankly, I knew his manner of dancing, from what I had seen and been told by El Chileno, Relámpago [the guitarist from Barcelona who had been a favorite of La Tanguera until he married La Joselito and immigrated to Paris in the late 1920s], and everyone, and I told him that, although it would be a pleasure for me, I wasn't free at that time to make new artistic commitments. That was the truth, for I was then accompanying Emita Martínez [known today as Mariemma, Emita first studied flamenco dance in Paris with another expatriate, guitarist Amalio Cuenca], although I had complete freedom to play for anybody I wanted. But he insisted, assuring me that he could arrange it with Emita, since they were *paisanos*, both from Valladolid, and very good friends.

I knew well what Emita thought of Vicente and the type of "friendship" they had. But I said nothing and asked him what dances he was going to do. He replied that he was doing only one, a *tanguillo de Cádiz*, but that he would appear with the whole *cuadro* doing *palmas* [handclapping] for him. I figured that, with a dance as easy as the *tanguillo*, nobody could go wrong, so I said that I surely would be able to play for him, and that I would arrange it with Emita Martínez. He was delighted and said that, when I was able, we would rehearse. I answered, "But Vicente, a *tanguillo* needs no rehearsing. You dance, and when you want to finish, you let me know by saying, *'Ahí es,'* then call with a foot stomp, I give the *cierre* [closing], and it's over!"

"*Sí*, I know that! That's true. It is not for me, but for my *tribu* (he always enjoyed using gypsy terms), so that everything will come out well."

I returned a few days later. We rehearsed the *cuadro* and it was a disaster. His "nephews" knew nothing at all about rhythm and *compás*, and they only stomped the floor when it seemed like the right time to Vicente. Finally, with much patience—the whole thing truly amused me—we almost arranged the handclapping, with Escudero dancing a simple *tanguillo* and finishing in time with the guitar.

The night of the festival arrived, and the Salle Pleyel was filled with a select audience. There were various numbers, all good, with the best artists of different nationalities that were in Paris at that time. Argentinita, accompanied by her sister, Pilar López, and Antonio Triana, danced to the piano version of *"Danza No. 11"* by Albéniz with such success that they had to repeat it. I played a solo that was well received. Don Ramón Montoya played two solos, *"Romera"* and *"Gallegada,"* pieces that he used to like to play quite often and did as only he knew how [the solo based on Galician aires would be imitated by Sabicas and Carlos Montoya throughout their careers]. The *"Cuadro Flamenco"* of Vicente Escudero appeared in the second half. They were received by an imposing ovation, for, to the French in Paris, Vicente was the best. I began with the *tanguillo* and Carmina and the "tribe" began their *palmas*. Escudero began to sing and, at the end, rose from his chair and started his dance. I felt relaxed, for the *palmas* and the dance were going pretty well. After several minutes of dance, he said loudly to me, *"Ahí es, Gabrielillo!"*

When I heard the closing signal that he gave loudly with his foot, I quickly played the closing cadence, he stopped his dance, and I stopped the guitar. But, then, he immediately gave another loud foot stamp and I, not to be caught off-guard, hit the guitar strings immediately after. He gave another *taconazo*, and I followed with another strum on the guitar, then another stamp...The fifth or sixth time, I could take it no longer and, furious, I got up from my chair and exited to one side, saying in almost a shout, "You can just stay out there alone, Vicente," as I disappeared from the stage.

The audience began a loud ovation, while Vicente bowed with his company. He came looking for me and made me go out to bow with him. As we bent forward before the audience, I said to the famous Vicente Escudero, "If I hadn't done something, we would still be there going one-two, one-two, one-two...!" And Vicente laughed, saying, "That's true!"[1]

In 1929, Escudero returned to Spain for the first time in twenty years (the above incident actually took place a few years later). Gabriel Ruiz tells us how he was received:

---
[1] Ruiz, Gabriel, *"Algo sobre Vicente Escudero,"* Jaleo, March 1982.

Vicente Escudero was presented in Madrid, along with his wife and faithful companion, Carmina [Carmita García], an enchanting and tiny bailarina who was Vicente's equal in the dance. The rest of the company was irrevelant. Vicente was known a little in Spain, since, some time before, a film titled *El Bodegón* had premiered in Madrid with great pomp and propaganda. Since it was filmed in France, it was a true *españolada*, a cliché of "typical" Spanish themes. Vicente appeared as a dancer and had a minor acting role...The movie was assessed a hodgepodge and was shown for only a short time. Nevertheless, due to *El Bodegón*, the name of Vicente Escudero was known in Spain.

In those times there was a Madrid weekly called *Estampa* that had good reporting, good photos, and a boldness for the time. In that magazine there was a great deal of promotion for the presentation and debut of Vicente Escudero in the Cine Avenida. I remember that there were three or four pages of photographs of Escudero in *Estampa* that were unusual and aroused suspicion among the true flamencos. Above all, there was an exaggerated and preposterous promotion of Vicente and his dances. But it should be recognized that it was Vicente himself who told it all to the reporter. He said that they didn't know how to dance flamenco in Spain, that nobody was his equal in the dance, that he was the best in the world and would demonstrate it, etc. These statements left the Spaniards surprised and stunned, especially the flamencos, who couldn't get over their amazement at such boldness. This self-promotion was the topic of conversation in the artistic and taurine *tertulias* [conversation groups] that met in the cafeterias of that marvelous period in Madrid.

The night of Vicente Escudero's debut in the Cine Avenida arrived. The salon, converted into a theater for the occasion, was filled to capacity. I attended with my father and Pepe el de la Matrona, Juan Sanchéz "Estampío," Don Tomás *"El médico,"* and the dancer Filemón Merino (the first student of Estampío, who took lessons in the kitchen of my house)...Estampío and Pepe el de la Matrona were good friends of my father. They came often to our house and, as such, liked me and taught me *el paso castellana* [a part of the *alegrías* dance] for the guitar when accompanying the *cante* and the *baile*. As much as I could, I used to be with them in Los Gabrieles, Café Madrid, La Mezquita, or Casa Pololo...We also found with us Acha Rovira, a Basque *bailaor* who was good in *farruca* and whom El de la Matrona called "The English Rooster," perhaps because he was blond with light skin...In the hall were found all of the flamencos who had money that night (almost everybody was doing badly economically), anxious to see that which Vicente had said in the press—that he was the best! Among those who attended that night, I recall Perico el del Lunar, Luis Yance (a tremendous flamenco guitarist, technically), the *bailaor* Linares (very good in *chuflas*, comic dances), the dance teachers Pagán, Roig, and Reyes, many other flamenco dancers, and the fabulous and unforgettable Pastora Imperio.

The atmosphere and the expectation were incredible. One heard comments that were not kind to Vicente Escudero. We were seated near the stage in about the fifth or sixth row. Tension mounted with the passing of minutes until curtain time. I had observed that Estampío carried a small, brown paper bag in one hand. Intrigued, I asked him several times what was in it, and he always responded, with a malicious smile, "You will see very soon, boy...you will see, *Grabielito!*" I grew more curious with each minute.

The moment arrived. The front curtain lifted, then a second curtain opened. Vicente Escudero and his people appeared, and that "recital" of *baile flamenco* took place to the astonishment of all the flamencos and artists that were there. It all seemed absurd to us and, of course, was all out of *compás*; all of the dances were *"esparrabaos"* [gypsy jargon for "out of *compás*"]. Naturally, if the star performer was doing badly, imagine how the company would do!

Not many dances had passed when, to our astonishment, Juan Sánchez "Estampío" rose from his seat and, in his unmistakable, refined Andalusian voice, shouted, "*Señó* Escudero...you don't know how to dance, not in the slightest!" And with that, he took out a pair of flamenco boots from the paper bag that had been a mystery to me until that moment, threw them onto the stage, and continued shouting, "Put them on! They will teach you how to dance flamenco!"

It is not necessary to describe the uproar that occurred in that hall. Most of the people applauded Juan, but a few whistled and told him off. The "recital" continued, but in a confused manner, filled with mistakes. Many people left, including us, and said that Vicente Escudero was worthless. As it happened, Escudero, whom I believe had a contract for at least a month, did not complete two weeks with his show in the Cine Avenida before he returned to his "headquarters" in Paris, completely unsuccessful as a *bailaor* and speaking badly of the Madrid flamencos, swearing to get revenge some day.[1]

Escudero did not return to Paris immediately, but toured northern Spain with his company. In the next few years, he would enjoy great success

[1] Ruiz, Gabriel, "A Few Words About Vicente Escudero," *Jaleo*, January 1982.

throughout Europe and South America, ending with a triumphant tour of the United States. Vicente's celebrity in Paris and the fact that he was in Barcelona in 1929 lend credence to his claim that he helped to set up the circumstances leading to Carmen Amaya and her aunt going to France that year with Raquel Meller.

Forty-year-old Raquel Meller was the best-known *cupletista* of that time. A native of Aragón, she too had made Paris her base of operations. *Cupletistas* had enjoyed tremendous popularity for more that two decades with their very "Spanish" songs based on popular rhythms like the *pasodoble* and their highly varied dances. Some, like Pastora Imperio, had a background in flamenco. Teresita España sang, danced, played castanets, and accompanied herself on guitar. Her teacher, Juana la Macarrona, said of her, "The only one who has come out so well as a *bailaora*, and who I have taught, is Teresita España. *Vaya salero!*" The *cupletistas* generally possessed great beauty, a coquetish manner, and delighted audiences by dramatizing each song with scenery and sensational costumes. A typical costume might include a lacy *mantilla* draped over an exaggeratedly high Spanish comb and a brightly colored fringed shawl over a multi-ruffled train dress. By 1924, there were more than 1,400 established *cupletistas* and another 6,000 aspirants working in more than two thousand theaters of *variet*é in Spain. And, by that year, 145,360 *cuplés* had been copyrighted.[1] Among the many celebrated names—Amalia Molina (the first celebrated *cupletista*), Conchita Piquer, Imperio Argentina, Custodia Romero, Luisita Esteso, La Chelito, Antoñita Torres, Paquita Garzón, etc.—two stood out for the influence they would have on flamenco dance: La Argentina and La Argentinita.

Antonia Mercé y Luque was born in Buenos Aires in 1890. Her mother, from an aristocratic family in Córdoba, had danced in the Royal Theater of Madrid, while her father, a native of Valladolid, not only performed as first dancer for the Royal Theater, but also directed and did the choreography. Antonia's birth while her parents were on tour in South America gave her the stage name by which she would forever be known, "La Argentina." Upon returning to Madrid, the father opened a dance school and continued to direct the dance corps in the Royal Theater.

At age ten, Antonia began her training in the conservatory, maintaining a stormy and rebellious relationship with her father until his death in 1903. With the passing of Manuel Mercé, and despite the protests of a demanding mother who never in the course of her daughter's career could bring herself to give more praise than a "Not bad," the young adolescent quit the conservatory and began to work as a warm-up act in the Teatro Apolo and between films in the

---

[1]Bravo Morata, Federico, *Historia de Madrid, Vol. 5, Madrid.* 1985. p. 58

early movie theaters. In the Teatro Romea, the young Antonia first met guitarist Salvador Ballesteros, who would collaborate with her throughout her life. Salvador had been born in Madrid to parents who had always owned *colmaos* and, consequently, he grew up surrounded by flamenco. He began his career in the Teatro Romea, playing for Paca Aguilera, a singer whose beauty and skill in the *malagueñas* had captured the hearts of the public in Madrid. In a letter to Fernando de Triana, Salvador described this period:

> ...when I was young, I began to study for the priesthood. Imagine the contrast: In a *colmao* among that sort of people, and me playing the guitar, and then, later, attempting to say Mass! What had to happen, happened, and after four years they decided I was impossible, and I dedicated myself to the guitar, and that was when I worked with Paca...And, at that time, a young girl was also working in that theater and attracting great attention for her marvelous castanet playing and her way of dancing...Now I am with her and I drool with pleasure at the thought of her way of being, of the great friendship that has united us since she was ten or twelve years old, of how well she treats me, of the great artist that she is, and the joy I get from working with her, with the marvelous Antonia Mercé (La Argentina).[1]

Debuts in other theaters followed and soon La Argentina was alternating on stage with the major attractions of the day, with Amalia Molina, Pastora Imperio, La Fornarina, and Raquel Meller. She attracted the attention of a group of intellectuals, headed by the writer Valle-Inclán, who sponsored her recital in the Ateneo de Madrid, the first ever in that cultural center. A few years later, Manuel de Falla would become so enthralled with her that he would come nightly to see her in the Teatro Romea. At age sixteen Antonia left Spain for the first time, first performing in Lisbon and then traveling to Paris to appear in Le Jardin and the Moulin Rouge. By 1911, she had become a resident of Paris and in the following years performed widely throughout Europe and Russia. In 1914, she appeared with Antonio de Bilbao, Faíco, and the great teacher from Sevilla, Realito, in London's Alhambra Theatre. The program, entitled *Embrujo de Sevilla* (The Spell of Sevilla), included the first version of what would later become Falla's immortal ballet, *El Amor Brujo*. After appearing in the silent film *Flor de Otoño* in 1916, La Argentina embarked on a three-year tour of the Americas that included the New York debut of *"Goyescas"* by Granados..

La Argentina dominated the classical Andalusian dance that she had learned in her father's school, a style known variously as *escuela bolera*, *baile de palillos* [castanet dance], and school dance, and characterized by soft balletic postures, movements, and footwork, and the use of castanets,

---

[1] Triana, Fernando de, p. 241.

which were unheard of in flamenco at that time. The great teachers of this dance were Angel Pericet, Realito, and El Maestro Otero, all of Sevilla, who taught several generations to perform the intricate steps of the *"Bolero," "El Olé," "Malagueñas," "Panaderos," "Jaleo con peteneras,"* and *"Soleares de Arcas."* Some of the names of these dances may have a familiar ring to flamenco aficionados, but they bore little resemblence to flamenco dances of the same name. Otero had been the teacher of the early *cupletista*, Amalia Molina, a pioneer in using castanets to make music rather than primitive and noisy accompaniment to folk dances. Maestro Otero would be killed in a robbery attempt in 1934, when he was seventy-four years old. Angel Pericet began a dynasty of Pericets who would continue to teach the classical Andalusian dance, generation after generation, until the present day.

In 1911, when La Argentina moved to Paris, she began to experiment with setting Spanish dance choreographies to classical music. She would tour the world with dances to the music of Albéniz, Granados, Ravel, Grieg, Massenet, and others. This unprecedented move would eventually influence all of the major dancers who came after her.

To the classical dance, Argentina added a deep knowledge of regional dances, the folk dances of different provinces of Spain. She elevated simple peasant dances like the *jotas, valencianas, seguidillas manchegas, gallegadas*, and dances of Castilla, to a high technical level suitable for the stage. She continued the path begun by Amalia Molina and made the castanets, in reality just two simple pieces of wood, into an instrument capable of evoking the full gamut of emotions. It is said that she had large hands and long supple fingers that enabled her to control castanets that were nearly man-sized. And finally, her vocal training in the conservatory prepared her for success in the age of the *cuplé*.

After appearing in her last *varieté* in Barcelona in 1923, La Argentina began to dedicate herself exclusively to the dance. When Manuel de Falla asked her to prepare a new version of *El Amor Brujo*, she traveled to Granada to learn the dances of the gypsies of the Sacromonte. The results of her study were clearly evident in her interpretation of the "Firedance." The flamenco dancer La Joselito claims to have performed in the ballet and said that she taught La Argentina *alegrías* and *tanguillos* in exchange for lessons in playing the castanets.[1] Falla's work opened in Paris in 1925 to great critical acclaim, with La Argentina and Vicente Escudero as the stellar couple and more exhalted than ever in the public eye. Escudero said of La Argentina, "Antonia Mercé was the creator of a school of dance so original and genuine that all who wish to give universality to the dance have to start and stop with her...Her genius, however, reached its greatest expression with the castanets, which earned her the title, 'Queen of the Castanets.'"

A newspaper account described the Queen of the Castanets:

[1]Claus, p. 110

Argentina's castanets, as her dancing, stand untouched in either Europe or America. They are the product of long and arduous labor, dating back to a time when she was but three years of age and her father slipped a tiny pair of the instruments around her fingers. From that day she delighted in making the bits of wood talk to each other, and to her. They argue, they purr, they sing solos and warble duets, and to Argentina they are just as alive as her costumes, and just as essential in the scheme of things.

There is, perhaps, no one in the world as careful in choosing his instruments as Argentina in choosing her castanets. It is often necessary for her to sound through dozens of pairs before she can discover two halves whose tones are correct to be matched for the right hand, the "female castanet," and two whose tones are proper for the left hand or "male castanet." The "female," which is carried in the right hand, sings out the melody; the "male," in the left hand, accompanies and usually starts the arguments! The tones of the one are decidedly higher than those of the other.[1]

In an interview, Antonia testified to the fact that the castanets were an acquired taste: "Why, I disliked them at first," she said, "because they make a noise. My parents were professional dancers. I heard castanets day and night. They were a nuisance. Then I began to play them, and now I like them."[2]

On another occasion La Argentina elaborated on her quest for a musical sound in her castanets:

> I began a minute study of every means of drawing greater and greater tonal nuance from my bits of wood. I wanted to know the reason why castanets, instead of yielding to the touch, had up to that time resisted it with their heavy uniformity. Was it a matter of changing the thickness of the strings? Should there be an increase or decrease in the size of the hole through which the strings were passed? Or should the hollow itself be increased or decreased? It was this last problem that finally absorbed my attention.
>
> And so I ordered a whole scale of castanets with different concavities. The castanet maker became furious, asserting that it was not up to me to teach him his trade. I replied that he could sell his usual castanets to the whole world. But I wanted other ones. And that is how I arrived at my goal.[3]

La Argentina's name had spread around the world. In 1928, there was considerable excitement in the American press in anticipation of her upcoming

---

[1] Mayer, Mary, "Dance Art Demands All." *Los Angeles Times*, January 25, 1931
[2] Fried, Alexander, "Talent Alone Insufficient, Says Dancer." *San Francisco Chronicle*, February 22, 1932
[3] Argentina, *Dance Magazine*, December 1956

visit. The new dance critic for *The New York Times*, John Martin, wrote:

> The Spanish dance seems to be decidedly on the ascendant among us. Possibly because of the stirring rhythm of its music, it has for many years been an unfailing source of applause no matter how badly it might be performed, whether in vaudeville, picture theater, or M. Daghileff's ballet. Ito, Ted Shawn, and Doris Niles have all found it grist for their mills, though with varying response from native experts, ranging from warm praise to equally hearty damning. Carola Goya and Carlos de Vega have succeeded in filling the house for four programs in as many months, certainly no mean achievement for dancers hitherto unknown. And half a dozen other non-Spanish dancers have made a special feature of Spanish dancing.
>
> Of native exponents of the national art we have had the Cansinos [Eduardo Cansino, father of Rita Hayworth, ran the following ad in the *Los Angeles Times* in November of 1928: "Cansino Studio of Dancing announces morning and evening classes for women who wish to acquire poise and grace."], María Montero, Trini [sister of Raquel Meller], and many lesser artists; and now comes word that next fall we are to have also the great Argentina herself. Those who have seen her in Europe are extravagant in her praise. André Levinson, who contributes frequently and delightfully to *Theatre Arts Monthly*, wrote of her in the May, 1925, issue of the that magazine: "Today the ancient spirit of the opera of Madrid survives in the person of one single and possibly unique artist, Argentina, who began as a child to rebel against the devitalizing strictures of the traditional school. Since then she has imposed her own style of dancing on her surroundings. This is the style that organizes and completely realizes the plastic elements of the Andalusian improvisations, which modifies the ardors of the Moorish fancy by the discipline of Castillian decorum." This is high praise indeed from a conservative critic.
>
> If La Argentina has rebelled against the decadence of the the national dance in her own country, it is rather appalling to consider what her reactions will be to our American perversions of it. For certainly there is no type of dancing which offers so many inescapable pitfalls to those dancers unfortunate enough to have been born outside the Iberian Peninsula.[1]

La Argentina arrived in New York in November. Dance critic John Martin wrote:

---

[1] "The Dance: Spanish Forms." Copyright © *The New York Times*, March 11, 1928. Reprinted by permission.

When La Argentina sailed into the harbor aboard the *Paris* on Tuesday, she must undoubtedly have sensed the warmth of the welcome that awaits her when she makes her first appearance at Town Hall on Friday evening. American dancers and audiences were, figuratively speaking, assembled en masse at the dock to make sure that she had actually arrived and to send up a sigh of satisfaction which surely she must have heard when she put foot upon American soil. Not for many years—not, at any rate, since Nijinsky's first American visit—has there been such palpitating excitement over the advent of a dancer; indeed, great and glamorous dancers are not to be found more than once in a blue moon.

Strictly speaking, this is not La Argentina's first appearance in New York. Some seven or eight years ago, en route from South America to Europe, she stopped off for a brief period, danced quietly, and disappeared. Those who recall her performance at that time are so few as to constitute a negligible quantity, and the printed records are scant and elusive...

During the summer, press reports of her brilliant European season appeared at intervals and dancers drifting home from abroad have continued to spread the news. Paris was enthusiastic, and even Germany, which all but rejected the Diaghileff Ballet last year; Germany, the proud and jealous home of Mary Wigman [modern dancer], acclaimed Argentina herself and, even more remarkable, her ensemble as well. All of which has by no means dimmed the interest of New York...

What we are to expect from Argentina, then, is something quite removed from the representation of authentic peasant dances. It is an art, uniquely her own, built upon the themes of peasant dancing, but recreating them to her own ends, giving them form and meaning. The local color which we have become accustomed to look for when Spanish dancing is done, the atmosphere of the "Spanish gypsies of the Albaicín gotten up for the purpose of beguiling foreigners," is not the atmosphere of this artist, in whom alone survives "the ancient spirit of the opera of Madrid."[1]

Could La Argentina live up to this kind of exhalted praise and intense scrutiny? Here is what John Martin had to say after her debut:

The American season of La Argentina opened last night at Town Hall in a burst of brilliance. A distinguished audience, gathered to pay tribute to an internationally renowned artist, brought with it an atmosphere of anticipation which broke forth into cheering upon

[1] Martin, John, "The Dance: A Much Heralded Artist." Copyright © *The New York Times*, November 4, 1928. Reprinted by permission.

the dancer's first entrance and built steadily in the intensity of its enthusiasm until the fall of the final curtain.

Mme. Argentina's fear of American audiences must have been quickly dispelled by a response which would have done credit to a nation of Latins. Flowers were heaped at her feet, bravos were called in profusion, and applause of such spontaneous appreciation as is seldom heard in a concert hall, helped to mark the evening as an event of the first magnitude in the field of dance.

Much has been written of La Argentina's success abroad and expectation has run high; rarely has expectation been so far exceeded by realization. There can be no question of the superlative quality of her achievement. To rank her as second to Pavlova is to make an invidious comparison, for she is second to none in her own individual way. It is also something less than adequate to describe her as a Spanish dancer, for, although she bases her art on Spanish forms, it is universal in its character. Even the classic ballet itself is no more circumscribed by traditional limitations than is the Spanish dance, yet Argentina has molded it to her own will with a superb artistry that sacrifices nothing of the splendor of its tradition, but rather enlarges it to a wide significance. The composition of her dances is as free as their spirit, yet it is finished and balanced in its utilization of thematic material. Nothing escapes the design of the artist; even her heavily shadowed eyelids rise and fall in rhythm, and her magnetic smile spreads from her lips down through her arms and out into the castanets which accompany most of her movements. At no time, except by design, do the feet contradict the mood of the eyes or the temper of the castanet music. All the elements that are brought into play are animated by a unified impulse that is extraordinary in its clarity and effectiveness.

The sobriquet of "Queen of the Castanets" has been more than once applied to Argentina, but it is a pale description of her accomplishments along this line. She achieves not only a musical tone, but actually an emotional nuance with instruments that have heretofore been considered as minor percussion instruments. When she lays them aside, however, as for example in the fire dance from Falla's *El Amor Brujo*, there is still a running accompaniment of rhythmic sounds from her snapping fingers and strangely musical noises made with tongue and teeth. In this dance, which represents the exorcism of an evil spirit, the height of the program was attained, if it is possible to pick out any one item from a program which was, in every sense of the word, flawless...

If it is possible to translate music into movement, here is its supreme manifestation. Especially in the Granados "Dance No. 5" was this evident. Here was not only a sensitive response to rhythm and phrasing, but an actual transmutation of melodic line into physical form. Of the individual excellences of all the dances it is impossible to speak, but the "Bolero" [not that of Ravel, which had not yet been published] demands a special word of attention for its unusual vividness in the recreation of a lost period and of a lost art, the old Spanish theater dance of the eighteenth century, with its obvious contradictions and its almost ironic tawdriness.

An entrancing personal charm such as belongs to La Argentina is almost a danger to an art as subtle, as exquisitely conceived and performed, as hers; for, merely to enjoy the warmth and graciousness of her presence is sufficient, without consideration for the art that underlies it. Her moods flash and dissolve like light on water, never the same for two consecutive seconds, but luminous and brilliant at all times.[1]

Some worried that, after the excitement of the debut, flaws in Argentina's art might become apparent. But, after the second night, John Martin reported: "The audience filled every seat and stood rows deep in the back...Bravos and cheering were again the order of the day, and three numbers were repeated by insistent demand. The depth and subtle beauty of Mme. Argentina's art are revealed in even greater measure by a second contact, and her technical achievements only begin to take on their truly remarkable proportions." A week later, Martin continued this theme after seeing her for the second time:

With no little trepidation, one approached the second concert at the Gallo Theatre on Sunday afternoon. Perhaps with the glamour dulled, the new worn off, there might be disillusion ahead. But fears such as these proved unworthy and groundless, for an impression of greatness, of genius, indeed was strengthened upon second seeing.

In the clear light of day one marvels at La Argentina's technical accomplishments, both physical and mental. She has so unified the plans with which she works that her body reflects her mood from the crown of her head to the soles of her feet. The feet...execute intricate steps and are frequently the initiators of a rhythmic impulse which flows upward through the body and head. The ankles are as supple and controlled as those of a tap dancer. The tapping with the heels has an infinite amount of shading; sometimes it furnishes the predominant aural pattern; at other times it is so subtle and gentle that it all but escapes detection.

Her arms and hands are instruments of supreme eloquence, but they are also muscularly alive. When they rise above her head

---

[1]Martin, John, "Marvelous Dancer is La Argentina." Copyright © *The New York Times*, November 10, 1928. Reprinted by permission.

there is a stretch through the torso and legs as well; when they describe circular movements the impulse comes from the trunk. Such balance and lightness, such easy and effortless movement, are not the result of merely an astonishing talent; they are cultivated through applied technical labors.

Obviously La Argentina does not work on the inspiration of the moment, though the spontaneous enthusiasm with which she endows her dancing almost makes it appear that she did. Her dances are planned carefully in pattern and in mood, so that in repetition they are not only exact in outline but as fresh and alive as upon first performance. The very quality of high emotion which hangs in the air about each dance is built solidly and surely by a theatrical skill which in itself amounts to genius.

Her entrances and exits are masterfully contrived. There are a few bars of music on an empty stage, the curtains in the upper right-hand corner open slightly; a bit more music and sometimes the castanets begin to sound off stage; then suddenly the dancer stands forth. With a vigor not always physical, but at times, as in the exquisitely lyrical "Córdoba," with a pulsating inner energy. She compels an instantaneous response, frequently so strong that it expresses itself in audible "oh's" and "ah's…"

The quality of her castanet playing has been much spoken about, but much speaking reveals nothing of its true charm and finish. Occasionally she reproduces the rhythmic pattern of the music, but more frequently she provides a supplementary rhythm of unimaginable intricacy, in which castanets and heel tapping play in opposition to each other…Apart from their musical aspect, however, Mme. Argentina employs the castanets also as a means for speech. Her thought is conveyed more clearly, though perhaps less explicitly, through these bits of wood that seem to grow from the ends of her fingers than if she resorted to words…

There are volumes to be written on the art of this amazing woman… but perhaps the outstanding character of it all is its exhilaration, its gayety. Here is art in its most felicitous manifestations.[1]

Throughout November and December, La Argentina continued her performances in different theaters, including Carnegie Hall. She constantly refreshed the programs with new numbers, including a *garrotín* which, according to Martin, she danced as a "flirtatious gamin," *"Valenciana,"* and *"Cielo de Cuba,"* which she danced comically, "while creating a full-bodied impression of a living woman." Her farewell performance at Town Hall

---

[1] Martin, John, "The Dance: La Argentina." Copyright © *The New York Times*, November 18, 1928. Reprinted by permission.

on December 28 set a record unmatched by any other dancer—eighteen sold-out performances in less than two months! No other Spanish dancer before or since has evoked the universally high level of praise, the unembarrassed gushing of superlatives, that La Argentina encountered without exception in the American press.

From New York, La Argentina went to Chicago, then San Francisco, and on to Japan to begin a tour of the Orient. By May, 1929, she was back in Paris. Philip Carr wrote in *The New York Times*: "Argentina has returned to Paris and such is the international reputation that she now enjoys as a dancer that she, alone, dancing merely to piano, can fill the enormous Théâtre des Champs Elysées at top prices with a more fashionable audience than I have seen brought together since the Russian ballet."[1] She debuted a new dance, *"La Cariñosa,"* that she had brought back with her from the Philippines.

During this period, La Argentina presented the first "Spanish Dance Company" at the Opéra Comique in Paris. French critics called it a truly triumphant success and said that it had been a long time since that theater had resounded with such salvos of applause. The idea of presenting a group of dancers in a program dedicated to serious dance, rather than as part of a *varieté*, represented a true revolution in the Spanish dance. Over the next two decades touring "Spanish ballet" companies would multiply around the world. Eventually they would become a forum for pure flamenco and lead to their own demise. However, in spite of the success of her dance company, Argentina did not follow up on the idea and returned to solo performing as she prepared for a second season in America.

One of La Argentina's dance partners, Juan Martínez, wrote that Antonia Mercé did not necessarily have better technique than other dancers, nor more fluency, strength, or temperament. What she had was more knowledge of the dance. Her major strength as a dancer lay in her interpretation and a certain mystique in the use of her upper body. Her knowledge of armwork was so thorough that she could move her arms perfectly from any body position and she never used them the same way twice. Her use of castanets was magic, as were her hands in the gypsy styles. Her artistic presence was most evident when she stood still. Even her bows and encores were never the same and always in keeping with the mood of the dance she had just completed. It was not without reason that La Argentina was often called the Pavlova of Spanish dance.

Hard on the heels of La Argentina came La Argentinita. No sooner had Antonia "La Argentina" become established than she found herself imitated by a child prodigy. There would never be any love lost between these two.

---

[1] Carr, Philip, "The Palais Royal has a New Farce." *The New York Times*, May 19, 1929.

Encarnación López Júlvez, like her predecessor, was born in Buenos Aires, but eight years later, in 1898.[1] Her mother, Dominga Júlvez, from the northern province of Aragón, probably stimulated her early interest in the *jota*, while her father, Felix López, originally from Segovia (about fifty miles north of Madrid), ran a fabric store and played guitar in a *café cantante* in the Argentine capital. When Encarnación was about six, the family returned to Madrid where the little girl began her formal dance studies. At eight she made her professional debut in the Basque city of San Sebastián alongside the sultry *cupletista* La Fornarina. At that time, she performed primarily *jotas* and other regional dances to piano music.

The well-known impresario, Pardiñas, dubbed Encarnación "La Argentinita" and offered her a number of contracts in cities across the north—Zaragoza, Calatayud, Barcelona, and again in San Sebastián. Some contracts had to be cancelled due to the artist's young age, but eventually the father and daughter worked their way south to Valencia and, finally, Córdoba. Encarnación expanded her repertoire, so that when she appeared in Madrid for the first time, she included classical dances from the *escuela bolera* and the flamenco *tangos* and *bulerías*. She was applauded as a twelve-year-old wonder, and during the following ten years she consolidated her reputation in "La Corte."

An interesting photo appeared in the Madrid magazine *Nuevo Mundo* in 1911. The cast of a show called *"Mirando a la Alhambra"* ("Looking at the Alhambra") posed on the stage of the Príncipe Alfonso Theater, in a crude set portraying the Sacromonte in Granada, with the huge red Moorish fortress, the Alhambra, on a hill in the background. The artists were dressed in costume, mostly gypsy dress, but there was also a lady and gentleman, a soldier, and four young girls seated on the ground. The women in the picture include two of Miguel Borrull's daughters—Concha holding a tambourine and the other seated with a guitar—and Amalia Molina, the first celebrated *cupletista*. The tiny Amalia, with her large dark eyes and haughty manner, had been born in Sevilla's Macarena district and made her debut in Madrid in 1902. Just back from a tour of South America, her new *tango*, *"Lerele,"* had become a big hit.

And there, at center stage, in her unmistakeable classic pose, head held high, one hand raised behind her and the other curved gracefully in front, holding her ever-present castanets, a fresh-faced thirteen-year-old Encarnación "La Argentinita." There is no way to know the content of this program, but its mood predates by twenty-two years a 1933 production by La Argentinita that is usually considered to be the first presentation of flamenco with full stage scenery and child performers.[2]

---

[1] It has long been accepted that La Argentinita was born in 1895, but her family has recently confirmed the 1898 birthdate.

[2] Vela, Angela, *"Mirando a la Alhambra." Sevilla Flamenca, No. 87.* Morón, 1993. p. 44.

La Argentinita hit her peak of popularity with the Madrid public in 1914-15, when she appeared for two winter seasons in the Teatro Romea. With her fragile and refined thread of a voice, she sang a *canción* from Asturias that became an instant hit, and, following the example of La Argentina, she incorporated dances to the music of Albéniz and Granados. The young dancer continued to add to her knowledge, especially in flamenco, which she studied with La Macarrona and others in Sevilla and Granada. While in the student housing at the University of Madrid, she established a friendship with the poet/playwright Federico García Lorca that would endure until his untimely death some sixteen years later. It is likely that Encarna, as they called her, would have met others among Lorca's circle of friends in the university at that time, including poet Rafael Alberti, artist Salvador Dalí, and future film maker Luis Buñuel. She also belonged to an acting group created by the well-known playwright Gregorio Martínez Sierra. In March of 1920 she collaborated with Lorca in the ill-fated theatrical debut of his *El Maleficio de la Mariposa (The Charm of the Butterfly)*. The opening night was such a disaster that even Argentinita's dance of the butterfly could not save it. Later that year the dancer toured South America and then returned to Madrid to appear as a star attraction in the major theaters.

In about 1923, La Argentinita began to have competition from her younger sister, Pilar López. At only twelve years of age, Pilar began to appear with great regularity in Madrid's theaters, dancing, singing, and playing the piano. It would be many years before the two sisters would appear together on stage, and decades before Pilar would emerge from the shadow of her sister's fame. La Argentinita, in turn, had been able to escape from the shadow of Antonia la Argentina, whom she emulated in so many respects, by building a following in Spain, where she was considered to be the more "Spanish" of the two.

In 1924, La Argentinita retired from the stage to be with the bullfighter, Ignacio Sánchez Mejías. Perhaps she used this interlude to focus on her singing, for in early 1928 the Gramófono/Voz de su Amo Company began a series of forty-seven recordings of her songs and instrumentals that would be produced over the next five years. Previously, in 1916, this same company had recorded ten of her songs, but that was before the advent of electronic recording, when the artist had to practically stick her head inside a large acoustic horn and yell to mechanically record a sound impression in wax. After Bell Telepone and AT&T perfected the electronic recording system and the use of microphones in 1924, an artist could easily work with an entire orchestra. There had also been another twenty-nine recordings by the Odeón company between 1922 and 1925, under the title, "La Argentinita: The Greatest Marvel of Art and *Gracia.*" But it was on the records made between 1928 and 1933 that La Argentinita, singing and playing castanets to orchestral accompaniment, clearly displayed the qualities that had charmed her audiences and would soon captivate the world.

Encarnación had a high, pure voice, well-trained in the operatic style typical of the *culpetistas*. She often interrupted her songs with bits of monologue, speaking in local dialects. In *"Vaya cabeza,"* a song about a boy with a huge head, she speaks Andalusian—without a trace of Castillian *ceceo* (lisp)—saying *pare* and *conformao* (*padre* and *conformado*), *güeno* and *güerve* (*bueno* and *vuelve*), and *rueo y tó* (*ruedo y todo*). The personality that would be a constant in reviews of her work radiates from these recordings. Her warm sense of humor shines through when she cannot keep from laughing in the middle of a song.

Argentinita's ubiquitous castanets are played with a technical virtuosity that proves how far this instrument had come from its original use by peasants in their folk dances. Her castanets must have been quite large, for they produced a deep, rich tone. The footwork on these records would appear to indicate that Argentinita used only leather on the bottoms of her shoes, producing a dull sound—in contrast to the sharp taps generated by the nail-studded shoes of modern dancers.

Orchestra accompanied the various *cuplés* and such regional folk songs as *"Fandanguillo de Almería"* (*fandangos* in the typical Málaga style) and the *jota "De Alcañiz,"* but the accomplished guitar of Salvador Ballesteros was featured in *"Tango rosa,"* a traditional *tanguillo* with castanets meticulously choreographed to the guitar melodies, and *"Alegría solera,"* an *alegrías* played in A-major and accompanied by castanets and footwork.

The recordings of 1929 showcased La Argentinita's skills as an actress. In *"El couplet regional,"* she took the listener on a tour through the provinces, reproducing the songs and speech characteristics of Galicia, Valencia, Andalucía (singing a *taranta*-like *fandango*), and Madrid. In *"Mi viaje"* she imitated perfectly and charmingly the sing-song accent of Argentina, the typical sound of Chile, the authentic twang of Mexico, and the exaggerated broken Spanish of Cuba. The other recordings of this period consisted of a number of *canciones* and elaborate castanet accompaniments to music of Enrique Granados (*"Goyescas"* and *"Danza No. 5"*).

La Argentinita was away from Spain in 1930, but the following year she recorded her dance to Albéniz' *"Asturias"* (*"Leyenda"*), a prodigious display of footwork and castanet virtuosity. There was also a Cuban *rumba*, and a powerful *zambra* created and accompanied on guitar by Miguel Borrull. The next year, she recorded a *caracoles*, sung as a *pasodoble* accompanied by orchestra. Then, in 1933, it was *"Tango del escribano,"* a popular *tanguillo* that would become part of her landmark stage production of that year.

La Argentinita had clearly taken the art form created by her predecessor, Antonia "La Argentina," to new heights and in a direction that adhered more closely to its folk roots. By way of comparison, La Argentina would leave less than twenty recorded songs and a number of castanet accompaniments to orchestral pieces in her repertoire, while the world-renowned Raquel Meller would record more than 247 times.[1]

Of all the *cupletistas*, Raquel Meller enjoyed the greatest celebrity on an international scale. She was the first to sing in the language of each country she visited and to record in different languages. Although born in Zaragoza in 1889, she established her career in Paris. When she made her debut in Madrid in 1913, she was preceeded by her artistic reputation and an aura of intrigue surrounding her personal life. With her stunning face and figure, her charming Spanish accent, and a repertoire of songs that she popularized, including *"El Relicario"* and *"La Violetera,"* Raquel was adored by audiences everywhere. She became a talented actress, appearing in numerous films, and counted Charlie Chaplin as one of her close friends. To help finance her many homes, including a palace in Versailles, she permitted her name to be used to promote products from perfumes to ties.

In 1929, Raquel Meller was to sing in the Palais de Paris and she needed a *cuadro flamenco* to give her review a Spanish flavor. She contacted Juana la Faraona, perhaps through Vicente Escudero, and arrangements were made for the *bailaora* and her niece, Carmen, to join her in the French capital. It has never been made clear whether El Chino accompanied his daughter to Paris. However, given his possessive and controlling nature when it came to the affairs of his daughter, and the fact that the Amayas did some performing on their own in Paris, it can be assumed that he was there and might even have participated in Raquel Meller's show. However, Raquel already had a guitarist—none other than Ramón Montoya's nephew, Carlos Montoya.

There has always been a lack of agreement among historians concerning the date of Carmen Amaya's appearance with Raquel Meller, with estimates ranging from 1921 to 1933. Various facts point to the 1929 date, but the following account by the jazz guitarist Ivor Mairants, who published the first accurate flamenco guitar method outside of Spain, provides the strongest evidence:

> During 1929 I worked at the London Pavilion, playing in C.B. Cochrane's revue "Wake Up and Dream." The show featured many famous artists, one of whom was the international flamenco dancer Tina Meller, who was accompanied on stage by a flamenco guitarist. The guitarist used to practice incessantly, sitting on the stairs in front of our dressing room, and I would pass him every night on the way down to the stage but never spoke to him.

[1] Much of the technical data concerning La Argentinita's recording and the recording industry came from the booklet that accompanies the re-mastered collection, *La Argentinita: Duende y Figura* (Sonifolk 20062; 1995). The article, *"Discografía de La Argentinita...y algo más,"* was written by Antonio Massisimo.

The French Connection

I had later wondered who this terrific player was, and that is as far as it went. But [years later] as I unfolded this story to Carlos [Montoya], his face lit up. "That was me!" he exclaimed. "I was working with Tina Meller before I left to join 'La Argentina' for a European and American tour."[1]

Carlos García Montoya was born in Madrid in 1903, to Ramón Montoya's sister, Emilia Montoya "La Tula," and a livestock dealer. Carlos had a brother, Juanjo, who became a professional guitarist but died young, and another brother who spent most of his time with their father, going from fair to fair buying and selling mules and horses (this brother would later become the father of present day *bailaora* Rosa Montoya). Carlos was only two when his father died and his family went to live with Ramón Montoya. This would seem an ideal situation for the aspiring guitarists, but unfortunately Uncle Ramón refused to teach his nephews. He preferred to focus on his own son, also named Ramón, who, in spite of this attention, never amounted to much. One account says that, "Unfortunately for young Carlos, he not only had to follow in the footsteps of such an uncle and be compared to the established genius of the older man, but he also had to face the fact that his uncle had little or no interest in him and wished to teach another member of his family—on the grounds that young Carlos did not, in Uncle Ramón's eyes, have the ability to succeed to his mantle."[2] The situation created some feelings of jealousy in Carlos.

After the death of her husband, La Tula refused to play the guitar again. But when Carlitos was about eight she began to teach him chords and scales and oversee his practice. She always said that her son would make something of his life and be somebody.[3] When Emilia could teach her son no more, she sent him to study with a local barber (flamenco history is replete with guitar playing barbers). Pepe "El Barbero" would be Carlos' only formal teacher. Of course the young guitarist would learn from watching and listening to others. Later, he would single out Luis Molina as one he admired for his *"stacatos"* (*picados*) and thumbwork, and Angel Baeza, who was "very flamenco."

In later years, Carlos would often say, "One thing I want to make perfectly clear is that my own style was not influenced by that of my uncle, Ramón."[4] However, he must have been inspired by Ramón's playing, and he would later play occasional versions of Ramón's *falsetas* (melodies). But he would always assert that he felt fortunate not to have studied with his uncle, to have been free to develop his own manner of playing. There would be little similarity in playing style between the two guitarists, with Carlos favor-

[1] Mairants, Ivor, "Carlos Montoya: (1903-1993), A Personal Memoir." *Classical Guitar,* October, 1993.
[2] *Carlos Montoya Plays the Flamenco Fire Guitar* (album cover), Galaxy 4826.
[3] Delatiner, Barbara, "Montoya, 85, Playing Final Chords." *The New York Times,* August 6, 1989.
[4] D'Alessio, Gregorio, "Interview with Carlos Montoya." *Guitar Review, No. 19.* 1956.

ing *picado*, thumb, and *rasgueado* (strumming) over the elaborate arpeggio style of Ramón. It has been suggested that part of the difference between the playing of Ramón and Carlos came from their early careers. Ramón emphasized accompaniment of the *cante*, while Carlos would play for an impressive list of dancers. The result was a lyrical, melodic manner of playing for Ramón, with much *rubato* and bending of the *compás*, while Carlos would always play with emphasis on a well-marked rhythm.

During the year or so that he took lessons from El Barbero, Carlos said that he and his guitar-playing neighborhood friends often walked to other Madrid barrios and challenged the local boys to flamenco duels. He also began to frequent bars, where he bought drinks for the older singers and dancers, hoping they would teach him. These bars became his school of accompaniment, probably beginning with the occasional singer who would indulge the nine-year-old boy by singing for him. Carlos claimed that his first professional appearance came at age fifteen, when he played in a small town fiesta that lasted for three days. Shortly thereafter, he began to work in the *cafés cantantes* of Madrid. In El Brillante and La Incomienda he played for dancers like Gabriela *la Fea* (The Ugly), an aging *bailaora* known for her comic *garrotín* and *chuflas*, and Salud Rodríguez, whom Carlos said "danced like a man and was more powerful than Carmen Amaya."

The guitarist described his early years: "I joined the *cuadro flamenco*, where traditionally there are two guitarists in the center of the stage, dancers on either side, and on the ends, the singers..."[1] He went on to say that he usually played for two singers, one who sang *"atrás"* (behind) to accompany the dancers and one who sang *"p'alante"* (in front) as a soloist. He claimed to have accompanied some of the greats of the *cante*, including Antonio Chacón, Bernardo el de los Lobitos, and Manolo Pavón.

In spite of holding down a day job, first as a postal clerk and later as a court clerk, Carlos continued to progress and soon began to play in the renowned Kursaal de la Magdalena, Madrid's longest surviving cafe (dating back to 1885, it would close in 1935). There, he accompanied the top artists of the day, including the singers El Niño Gloria and El Cojo de Málaga, and dancers such as Antonio de Bilbao, El Estampío, La Macarrona, and La Camisona—the gypsy mother of guitarist Paco Aguilera.

In 1924 it looked like Carlos would have to put away his guitar, for he was drafted into the military and shipped off to fight Berber tribesmen in Morocco. However, the clever young man took his guitar with him and was soon accompanying singers in the North African city of Ceuta. It was there, or just across the water in Spain's border towns of La Linea and Algeciras that Carlos met and played for the eccentric *cantaor* Gabriel Macandé. The only known photograph of this singer shows a young Carlos, quite a small man, holding a guitar almost as large as himself and seated at the side of the

---

[1] Isaacs, Arlene, "Carlos Montoya: Flamenco Incarnate." *The News World*, Oct. 29, 1978.

even more diminutive and delicately featured Macandé.

Gabriel Macandé lived in a flamenco world unknown to audiences that filled the theaters of Madrid or Barcelona. He remained in relative obscurity in the bars of his native Cádiz and other towns along the southern coast, refusing to record or perform for the public. Yet, the very best in flamenco recognized his genius and originality. Pepe Marchena is said to have taken him to Madrid to learn from him, and then abandoned him—earning his everlasting enmity. Years later, after he was institutionalized, Macandé became enraged and destroyed one of Marchena's records when someone unwittingly played it in his presence. Antonio Chacón, deeply moved by Gabriel's singing, gave him money to buy a suit so that he could go to Madrid. Macandé counted La Niña de los Peines as a close friend and often stayed in her home on the Avenida de Hercules in Sevilla. But it was among the flamencos of Cádiz that Gabriel was best known.

A small, wiry man with an overabundance of nervous energy, Macandé suffered from progressive schizophrenia—*"Macandé"* is said to be a gypsy word meaning "crazy." After taking great care with his morning rituals of eating, dressing, and perhaps feeding his overly active imagination by reading the fantasies of his favorite author, Jules Verne, he would cook up a batch of carmel candy to sell in the afternoon. The candy vendor advertised his wares by singing fragments of *tangos*, *bulerías*, and *soleares*, or a song from Asturias that became his trademark.

At night, Macandé wandered the bars and cabarets, singing when he felt like it. He almost never accepted money and would refuse to sing if someone insisted on paying him. His inordinate pride led him to fight at any perceived slight, and some said that he was capable of killing a person who persisted in trying to pay him. On one occasion, Macandé attached two razor blades to a piece of wood and went looking for an imagined enemy. Unpredictable and moody, he might leave a fiesta at any moment to go outside, sit on the curb, and sing by himself for hours.

Yet Gabriel could also be entertaining, captivating his audience with superb dancing and a deep flamenco voice that emanated mysteriously from his tiny body. A prodigious drinker, he used to recover from a drunken stupor by downing a large glass of water, putting his finger in his belly button, and throwing up. That always left him refreshed and ready to continue drinking and singing.

In spite of an almost constant state of poverty, Macandé's generosity was legendary. On one occasion, a friend gave him a new pair of shoes. The next time the friend saw the singer, he was wearing one shoe and a slipper on the other foot. When asked what had happened, Macandé said that he had run into a crippled friend who had only one leg, so he gave him one of the shoes.

Although married to a mute woman and with two mute children, Macandé was usually romantically linked with prostitutes. In a number of his verses he declared his desire to save these women:

> *Tengo una hermana en la vía.*   I have a sister in the "life" ["profession"].
> *Siendo potente y con dinero,*   Being powerful and with money,
> *yo voy a devolverle*   I am going to return to her
> *la honra que tenía.*   the honor she once had.

Suffering from a deteriorating schizophrenia that made him hear voices and fear that people were following him, Macandé was also wracked by tuberculosis, syphilis, and trachoma that affected his vision. His drinking and the quantities of marijuana he consumed did not help his condition, and in 1935 he would be institutionalized in a psychiatric hospital in Cádiz and die there in 1947.[1]

With colorful singers like Macandé in Morocco and Spain's border towns, we can imagine that Carlos Montoya had a lively time with his guitar while in the military. In 1927, he returned to the flamenco scene in Madrid. And that is where Antonia Mercé "La Argentina" found him when she came looking for a guitarist in 1928. He would stay with her for three years. During that period, La Argentina spent a great deal of time touring the Americas and the Far East—without a guitarist. It is very likely that Raquel Meller met Carlos in Paris during one of those breaks and hired him for her revue. The guitarist would spend a number of years in Paris. He said that he worked for three years in the Casino de Paris with the singer Lolita Mas, earning up to four hundred dollars a day and living a life of luxury.[2] In 1932 he would tour with the company of Teresina, a dancer of the classical *bolera* school, and travel with her to the Far East and the United States. Later, with La Argentinita, he would make a number of return visits to America, where he would be stranded by World War II.

Raquel Meller's revue, "Paris-Madrid," opened in the Palais de Paris in 1929 to critical acclaim. A Paris correspondent for the Madrid paper *ABC* wrote: "Raquel Meller has not only triumphed as an artist, but as a woman, and as an elegant woman in this Paris of the most refined elegances, because 'Paris-Madrid' will remain a long time on the marquee of the Palais and will be like a beacon to attract the tourists who visit our beloved Paris."[3]

"Los Amaya," as the trio featuring Carmen, La Faraona, and Carlos Montoya was billed, were an immediate hit with the French, who had never seen anything like the explosive fury of the young girl and the statuesque grace of her aunt. Each night the enthusiasm for the group increased, until

---

[1] Much of this information on Macandé comes from *Pasión y Muerte de Gabriel Macandé*, by Eugenio Cobo. Ediciones Demofilo, SA. Madrid. 1977.
[2] Brooks, Michael. "Carlos Montoya," *Guitar Player* (date unknown).
[3] Hidalgo, p. 73.

they began to overshadow Raquel Meller. After six months, the personality clash between the proud and temperamental Raquel and the volatile gypsy, La Faraona, resulted in a confrontation between the two that, according to the aunt, "ended in blows, and I gave them all!"[1] The Amayas left the revue and worked in some cafes in Montmartre before returning to Barcelona.

Repercussions from the 1929 stock market crash in the United States were not immediately felt in Europe. The year proved to be significant for the Spanish dance. It is possible that Carmen Amaya witnessed the birth of the first Spanish ballet company when La Argentina presented a full program of dance in the Opéra Comique in Paris. Although most of the music was by classical Spanish composers such as Julián Bautista and Oscar Esplá, the company included the flamenco dancers Juan Martínez, Frasquillo (the flamenco/classical dance teacher from Sevilla, married to La Quica), El Viruta (a dancer from Madrid who would later tour with Carmen Amaya), and La Joselito.

La Joselito, who had performed previously with La Argentina in *El Amor Brujo*, hinted that the great dancer had a disagreeable side. She said that, after the Paris opening, the company toured Europe. Before a performance in Dresden, Germany, La Joselito received word that her father had died. Grief-stricken, she cried and danced her heart out. La Argentina, who didn't care for her and never complimented her, said to her that night, "You'll never again dance as well as you danced tonight!" La Joselito says that La Argentina was very jealous and often mean to her. The final blow came when La Joselito was not asked to join the company for an American tour later that year.[2]

La Argentina also revealed her professional jealousy when she refused to work with a young dancer from Sevilla named Antonio Triana because he had once performed with La Argentinita. Antonio García Matos "Antonio de Triana" was born in Sevilla in 1906 and grew up in the gypsy barrio of Triana. The youngest of four children, he began his artistic career by studying piano along with his older brother, Manuel. He detailed his start in the dance in a letter to biographer Donn Pohren:

> I was born in Sevilla (Barrio de la Macarena). Soon after, my father moved our family to Triana. I entered the Academy of Maestro Manuel Otero at age eight. He had previously refused to teach male dancers, but one day he caught me peering through a window at the beautiful young Sevillian dancers, and he invited me to join his class. He appreciated my daring, and he thought perhaps I could partner his more advanced pupils. La Quica was

[1] Montañés, p. 20.
[2] Claus, p. 110.

> by far his best pupil. We became partners and made our debut in the Salón Imperial. Otero taught a basic technique of heelwork and castanets that he himself described as *"bailes típicos andaluces y clásicos"* [typical classical and Andalusian dances—not flamenco]. That was all that was demanded of him. There was no cry for flamenco, as the average cafe dancer of the time earned a mere six *pesetas* a day. Through Quica, I became acquainted with her *novio*, Frasquillo, who instructed me in the rhythms of the *alegrías*, *farruca*, and *zapateado de Cádiz*, which were the only flamenco dances considered masculine.
>
> I was then hired to perform at the Café Novedades, to appear with La Malena, La Fernanda, La Sordita, Frasquillo, Malenita, El Tiznao, and Javier Molina. I was only fourteen years old, but they accepted me in their dance and I proceeded to learn and absorb from those wonderful surroundings.[1]

Francisca González, who would later become well-known as "La Quica," began her dance training in the academy of Frasquillo—her future husband. Quica was twelve when she and nine-year-old Antonio Triana first danced in the Salón Imperial as part of a program featuring La Argentinita. At age thirteen, Antonio made his debut in Sevilla, in the Teatro de Verano, along with the young *cantaor* Niño Medina (about whom we will learn more later). The poster for the event announced "Antoñito García, the brilliant artist of eccentric and flamenco dances."[2] A year later, in May of 1920, he began his apprenticeship in Café Novedades, where he was exposed to the greatest artists of the time.[3] Triana led an active life as a young man. He became the flyweight boxing champion of Andalucía and went to Madrid to learn to fly airplanes. In 1924, after attempting a number of odd jobs and seeing the futility of trying to survive as a flamenco artist, he signed on as cabin boy on a freighter heading for America. In New York he jumped ship and settled into the Spanish Quarter.

A banquet in honor of the Spanish Consul proved to be a turning point for the young man. Among the notables present were the celebrated Spanish artist, Ignacio Zuloaga, who exhibited his paintings, and the *cupletista* María Montero, who danced *sevillanas* with Triana. Apparently young Antonio impressed Montero, for she hired him on the spot for her vaudeville tour.

Life on the grinding circuit of three-a-days and cheap hotels was not easy and paid poorly, but it was an important time of learning for Antonio. Not only did he master English, but he picked up card tricks from Harry Blackstone and absorbed a number of different dance styles, including tap

---
[1] Pohren, p. 369
[2] Vega, p. 8.
[3] Vega, p. 9.

dancing. His last wife would later write: "Among Antonio's happiest memories was the time he spent with the great black American tap-dancer John Bubbles, of Buck and Bubbles, in the smoking car of a Pullman train. There the two compared and traded foot rhythms and wailed their sorrowful combination of blues and flamenco, as the speeding train carried them into the night."[1]

In mid-tour, Antonio deserted Montero to join the more prestigious company of *cupletista* Amalia Molina, at that time a big attraction on the vaudeville circuit. When he had tired of the poorly paid grind, he headed for Hollywood. There he found dance students and, based on his skill in the Argentine *tango*, performed in Grauman's Chinese Theater for the opening of the film *The Gaucho*, starring Douglas Fairbanks. That exposure earned him a dancing role in the first musical short to be filmed with sound, *La Mexicana*, where he again danced the *tango argentino*. In 1929, Antonio returned to Spain (one biography says that he abandoned his career in America due to some "impossible romances"[2]). There he found that his repertoire of foreign dances opened doors for him. He loved the *zapateado americano* (tap dance) and became close friends with a black man named Harry Flemming, a celebrated tap-dancer in Spain. Antonio' skill as a tap-dancer helped him to find extra work. He settled into working in revues in important theaters in Sevilla and Madrid. In 1930 he participated in a variety show in the Teatro del Duque in Sevilla, in a setting made to look like a cabaret in the Barcelona Exposition. *El Liberal* wrote:

> In that same cabaret, Antonio G. Triana made his presentation. A terrific dancer who dominates equally the *bailes exóticos* [dances from other countries] and the dances characteristic of this land. He had to repeat an Argentine *tango*, in which he was admirably accompanied by Anita Sevilla, who by the way achieved a new triumph last night, and afterward he danced an *alegrías* and a *tango cómico*, which is very difficult, if not impossible, to see these days. Antonio Triana's work satisfied completely and was awarded with the warmest applause.[3]

In October of 1929, Antonia Mercé "La Argentina" returned to New York. *The New York Times* wrote: "The hearty reception which greeted La Argentina last night in the Town Hall at the first recital of her second American season showed unmistakably the place she has made for herself, not only in the respect and admiration of the New York audiences, but in their affections as well...Neither familiarity nor the passing of time have served to diminish in the least the wonder of an art so exquisitely built from

---
[1] Vega, p. 68.
[2] Sent to me by Antonio's daughter, Luisa Triana.
[3] Review provided by the Triana Committee and Luisa Triana.

every formal standpoint, and yet so rich in sympathy and the qualities of human warmth..."[1]

Beginning November 14th, La Argentina gave three more recitals in Town Hall, debuting her Andalusian *tango*. She was forced by the public to repeat as many as four dances in their entirety. The following month she did another series of sold-out concerts in which she presented *"Seguidillas,"* danced without musical accompaniment other than her castanets. On December 16, Federico García Lorca, who was in New York for an extended visit, read some of the poems that he would publish the following year as *Poema del Cante Jondo* at a function in honor of La Argentina. Then the dancer began a tour across country and back. In Los Angeles, the critic wrote:

> Need one say aught more of her than that she is...exquisite?...La Argentina danced last night at Philharmonic Auditorium. She enchanted the multitude of rapt watchers, who were held under a spell by her idealization of Spain's rhythms and tunes...La Argentina exhibits a new creativity in dancing. I do not know that anyone indeed has been so evocative of rare and subtle impressions since Anna Pavlova came the way of the western world many, many years ago.
>
> One might say that she reminds of Raquel Meller in the realm of song. Perhaps, in fact, there is a certain kinship between the two. Truly they have a common meeting-place in what is magnetically elusive in their work. Both, too, limn [paint] strangely vivid pictures for the mind with the simplest of means.[2]

Similarly, the critics praised her performances in the Geary Theater of San Francisco, saying that, "Her personality is magnetic, her movements are lithe, if not immensely varied, and her conceptions in character and dress are brilliant." They also lauded the exceptional skill of her pianist, Miguel Berdion.

Back in New York in February, La Argentina attempted two farewell performances. She fell sick during the first, although she managed to get through it. But she was forced to cancel the second and postpone her return trip to Paris in order to undergo an operation for appendicitis.

It is easy to imagine that, as she recuperated in the Savoy Plaza Hotel, La Argentina was not overjoyed to read in the newspaper that her rival, La Argentinita, was about to appear in New York for the first time.

Encarnación López, La Argentinita, arrived in New York accompanied by her lover, the bullfighter/poet Ignacio Sánchez Mejías. Ignacio had many links to flamenco. He was born in Sevilla in 1891. After running away to New York as a youth and living with an older brother in Mexico, he returned

---
[1] Anonymous, *The New York Times*, October 15, 1929.
[2] Schallert, Edwin, "Subtle Dancer Exerts Allure." *Los Angeles Times*, January 10, 1930.

to Spain to pursue a bullfighting career. The Madrid newspaper *ABC* of June 21, 1913, reported on one of his early appearances as a *novillero* (apprentice bullfighter): "The *novillero*, who did superior work with the *capote* [large cape] and *muleta* [small red cape], was caught in the thigh on his second attempt at the kill, suffering a terrible goring, a fountain of blood impressing all who saw it." That would not be the last time Ignacio would be seriously gored.

When he was not fighting on his own, Ignacio worked as a *banderillero*, assisting the great bullfighters Rafael el Gallo (the husband of Pastora Imperio) and his brother, Joselito el Gallo, and Juan Belmonte. The much revered but very superstitious Rafael el Gallo was known to kill a bull quickly, without ceremony, if he thought it was bewitched. It is said that on one occasion he leaped over the barrier to escape a bull, saying to his equally famous brother, Joselito, "You kill it—it gave me the evil eye!"

Ignacio took his *alternativa* (initiation to become a matador) in 1920, with Joselito el Gallo as his sponsor. That same year, he would witness the death of his mentor, the idol of the bullfight world at that time. Joselito slipped in the bullring of Talavera de la Reina and was fatally gored. Ignacio married Lola Gómez Ortega, the gypsy sister of Joselito and Rafael el Gallo and the daughter of Gabriela Ortega, a noted *bailaora* in the early *cafés cantantes*.

As a bullfighter and a man Ignacio was considered to be without equal. He did not have great bullfighting technique and had difficulties with the kill— on one occasion his sword hit bone, springing out of the bull and into the stands where it narrowly missed a spectator. But he dominated the ring with his personality, and his bravery and impulsiveness were almost as pathological as the fear shown by his brother-in-law, Rafael el Gallo. He took many risks and performed suicidal passes with simplicity and a lack of concern. Over his twenty-year career this indifference to danger earned him numerous gorings, many of which should have killed him. He was an heroic figure, attracted to the most heroic profession of his day. Rafael once asked him, "What would you have done if there were no such thing as bullfighting?" Ignacio replied, "If there had been no bullfighting, I would have invented it!"[1]

Ignacio met La Argentinita, perhaps as early as 1914, while working as an assistant to Joselito. However, it was Joselito who first became romantically involved with the dancer, a liason that ended prematurely with the death of the matador in Talavera. Encarnación buried her grief in a flurry of activity that took her on tour through South America, Cuba, and Mexico—where she renewed her acquaintance with Sánchez Mejías. In the mid-1920s Encarnación stopped dancing to concentrate on her relationship with Ignacio, and then in 1927 the matador followed suit and retired from the ring. But by 1929 La Argentinita had returned to the stage, performing first

[1] Cossío, p. 294.

in Paris and Berlin. Shortly thereafter, she arrived in New York with Ignacio and the guitarist Luis Yance, whose guitar recitals were to be well received. Sánchez Mejías would give lectures on bullfighting, with his good friend, the poet Federico García Lorca, in attendance.

Sánchez Mejías and Lorca shared much in common: The matador fancied himself a poet and playwrite, while Federico thought of himself as a matador, dominating audiences and forcing them to applaud his work in spite of themselves. And they both enjoyed a close relationship with La Argentinita. Sánchez Mejías once made a long distance telephone call to Lorca to let him listen to Encarna's furious footwork during a *juerga* in his home.

If La Argentinita expected an easy conquest of New York, she would prove to be sadly mistaken. *The New York Times* gave the first hint of difficulties:

> Argentinita, the dancer whom Lew Leslie imported from Spain for his *International Review*, has retired from the cast of that musical show. According to Mr. Leslie's office yesterday, the dancer withdrew "by agreement between her and the producer." She appeared in seven performances of the revue. The office sent out the following statement, which was said to have been issued both by the dancer and producer:
>
> "Argentinita and Lew Leslie, considering that the time that can be allotted to her in the *International Revue* is entirely inadequate for a proper presentation of her artistry, have agreed to cancel their contract in order that subsequent appearances of Argentinita may be made at independent recitals, where she can properly present to the public her entire repertoire."
>
> Mr. Leslie first saw the dancer in Spain about four years ago and has endeavored several times since then to persuade her to appear in this country. By posting a bond of $10,000 and guaranteeing her a salary of $3,600 a week [c. $50,000 in 1990 dollars], the producer finally induced her to come to New York. Her departure from the show will cause Mr. Leslie to forfeit his bond, his attorney, Julius Kendler, said last night.
>
> Argentinita did not appear in the out-of-town performances of the revue, and on the opening night at the Majestic Theatre she came on so late in the show that few of the reviewers saw her specialty. She was not enthusiastically received by the audience.[1]

It is not surprising that New York audiences reacted negatively to La Argentinita's inflated publicity, her astronomical salary, and the similarity of name she shared with her predecessor. She appeared to be a pretentious imposter riding on the coattail of America's idol, La Argentina.

[1]"Argentinita Leaves 'International Revue.' Copyright © *The New York Times*, March 4, 1930.

Encarnación's friend, the ballet dancer Anton Dolin, gave his version of her introduction to New York:

> I knew her first when we both came to America in 1930 to make our New York debut in Lew Leslie's *International Revue*. She was a jealously guarded, beautiful creature of Spain, speaking not one word of English. Whenever I was allowed by her entourage, consisting of her husband [Sánchez Mejías] and faithful Spanish followers, I could and did interpret for her in French.
>
> Standing as I was in the wings of the Majestic Theatre on the opening night of *The International Review*, I saw a New York audience sit, watch, and listen to this great artist, and make no sound except that of disapproval, and finally walk out of the theater in dozens during her dance. The audience, uneducated in the art of the Spanish dance, could not understand or appreciate the genius of this true, authentic *artiste* of Spain...
>
> If ever exaggerated publicity hurt an artist, it did in Argentinita's case. The photographs that appeared day after day heralding her arrival and the stories of demands that she made when she reached New York were to be the means of hurting instead of helping her in the eyes of the American public. They expected so much more than she, in my opinion, could possibly have given or shown in her one appearance in this revue.
>
> She did ask for two dressing rooms, not because her clothes were so marvelous, but simply because her dresses had to be properly hung or they would have been spoiled. She did not ask for a carpet to be placed down for her to walk on to the stage, but merely for the carpet in her dressing room to be cleaned. The circulated story that *The International Revue* cast, including such stars as Gertrude Lawrence, Harry Richmond, and Jack Pearl, were locked out of the theater on the Sunday before the production because Argentinita would not rehearse with anyone there was certainly true, but only up to a point. What really happened was that she asked to be allowed to rehearse in the theater alone, which is a very natural thing—very few dancers care to rehearse with anyone around...To make matters worse, Argentinita's conductor could speak little English. The music was in bad order and difficult to read at such short notice.
>
> I remember standing in the wings with Lew Leslie. Argentinita had done her first dance. Imagine dancing a scene in a peasant dress which, although correct in every detail, was devoid of any effect that the average audience thinks is Spanish, against a fantastic background purporting to be Spain and showgirls in mar-

velous exotic Spanish dresses with trains yards in length, which were no more authentically Spanish, or meant to be, than the tango danced later in the same scene by Moss and Fontana. Once more her guitarist played [solo] and Leslie wanted him to stop, for by now Argentinita had changed again and the sooner it was over the better. The gamble was lost!

In accordance with Leslie's request, she flicked her fingers as a signal for her guitarist to stop playing. The audience heard this and a great number of them, I am sure, misunderstood her intention and thought she was only anxious for him to stop because he was getting more applause than she was. The end came soon now, and as she danced her last number they started to walk out. They hissed and booed. It was terrible and all a horrible mistake. And it need never have happened.

So much was written at the time about this unfortunate debut that was unkind and need never have been said. It is only necessary to say that two weeks after Argentinita retired from the cast of *The International Review* she gave a recital of Spanish songs, recitations, and dances one Sunday night at which I was present, and I can truthfully say that she was a triumph. I went round to see her in the dressing room after this performance. As she greeted me and I congratulated her on her great success, she only remarked: "I am so glad I have the opportunity of showing the public that Lew Leslie was not such a fool when he engaged me for New York."

...Following on this, she took a theater and gave a series of shows for a fortnight. They may have cost her a lot of money, but artistically they proved her worth and showed that she was a great artist. More than that, she is the personification of woman! Every gesture is feminine and beautiful, and to my mind she portrays everthing that is lovely and most desirable. She is the womanhood of Spain, warm, rich-blooded, wholesome. The night I saw her dance alone, in the proper surroundings, there were not enough hats in New York to throw at her feet to pay her the homage due her.[1]

But departure from the revue did not put an end to Argentinita's difficulties. Her first attempt to give a concert met with unexpected resistance:

> With plainclothes men in the audience and uniformed policemen outside The Playhouse on West Forty-eighth Street, Argentinita, billed as "The Idol of Spain," went through her program of interpretive dances last night. The Spanish danseuse appeared to be undisturbed by the warning from the New York Sabbath

[1] Dolin, Anton, "La Argentinita: A Tribute." *Dance*, November 1945.

Commission that the Sunday performance would be prevented. After the first series of dances, William A. Brady, owner of the theatre, appeared on the stage and, amid cheers and handclapping, challenged the police to arrest him..."I see," he said, "various plainclothes men distributed among this audience. They are here to take notes, to take evidence in order to enforce the threat to close up this show. Now, why is it a crime for this lady from Spain to dance here, when it is perfectly legal for her to do the same thing around the corner?"

The question was answered by general applause and laughter.

"We may be quite fed up," continued Mr. Brady, "with motion pictures and bicycle races and hockey and circuses and dangerous nightclubs who keep open and put on great shows in defiance of the law. It is a disgrace for this community, the greatest city in the world, that shows of this nature are not allowed on the legitimate theatre stages. They are not allowed by Mr. Whalen, by Mr. Walker, or by Mr. Roosevelt, so I challenge them all.

"I invite you policemen to arrest me. But I want no fake arrest. They will take me to the station house, and for the sake of principle, I will stay there all night. Policemen and plainclothes men—meet me at the back door."

But no one met him at the back door, and the show went on.[1]

A number of other performances had, indeed, been shut down on that Sunday. With an eye toward generating some much needed good publicity, Argentinita donated the proceeds from this concert to the St. Vincent de Paul Charity Fund. Critic John Martin described how Argentinita finally triumphed:

Such a "jinx" has pursued the American debut of Argentinita...that many an artist of weaker stuff would have given up in despair and sailed for home on the first boat. But Argentinita's mother came from the province of Aragon, where the people are notoriously determined and tenacious of purpose, and the daughter is, consequently, not one to admit to failure and leave under a cloud when she knew full well that circumstances and not any shortcomings of her own were to blame.

Her unfortunate experience in the "International Revue" is now generally known. Coming to the stage without a rehearsal; dancing numbers which she had not herself selected from repertoire; surrounded unfamiliarly by American chorus girls, in a setting which she had never beheld—these things would have been suffi-

---

[1] "Police are defied at Sunday Concert." Copyright © *The New York Times,* March 24, 1930. Reprinted by permission.

La Argentinita, 1943.

La Argentina, 1933.

cient trial for any much-heralded European artist in her first New York appearance. Add to this, however, the facts that the hour of this appearance was about 11:30, when the first-night audience was already weary and impatient, and that the style of the revue and that of the dancer were miles apart, and it is not difficult to understand both the rudeness of the audience on that occasion and the subsequent criticisms of the much-heralded artist...[1]

Clearly, many among the public resented the similarity of Argentinita's name with that of Argentina, feeling that she was attempting to benefit from the reputation of a superior artist. Given those conditions, it clear that Argentinita's debut was doomed to failure.

When Argentinita attempted to arrange her own performance, not only did she have to change theaters at the last moment, but then she was faced with the confrontation with the Sunday law. But that performance had to be considered a triumph, for people were turned away at the door due to lack of seating and it would lead to a week-long series of concerts in the Booth Theater. Billed as the "Idol of Spain," Argentinita vindicated herself in the eyes of the American public. John Martin reviewed the performance:

> Not within the memory of the present generation of concertgoers has there been any better Spanish dancing exhibited hereabouts. It is entirely without frills or pretentions, simply performed and offered for what it is worth. As it happens, it is worth a great deal. The heel tapping and the footwork in general are brilliant; the castanets are played excellently; the arms, the shoulders, the hips, are used elequently, but without that excess that frequently leads the less careful dancer into vulgarity...
>
> The addition of songs, largely of folk character though occasionally composed for comedy purposes, gives delightful flavor. They are sung as informally as the dances are danced, the two mediums growing easily and naturally out ot the same impulse...It is not even a bit of a surprise when spoken lines occur; when they are directed at the audience for the obvious purpose of eliciting response, instead of objecting, one finds one's self enjoying that intimacy between dancer and audience for which the Spanish dance is famous. Argentinita is an actress—it is not generally known that she was once the "first lady" in Martínez Sierra's "Art Theatre"—and her comedy is admirably timed and as skillful as her dancing.
>
> ...The orchestra of seven sits at the side of the stage and plays excellent accompaniments when they are called for, and pleasant,

---

[1]Martin, John, "The Dance: Argentinita." Copyright © *The New York Times*, March 30, 1930. Reprinted by permission.

informal entr'acts while the dancer is changing costume...The same thing applies to the guitarist, Luis Yance, whose music is extremely skillful and native in tang.

To compare Argentinita with La Argentina is to compare the incomparable. All they possess in common is a few externals: Both were born of Spanish parents in Buenos Aires; both returned to Spain in childhood and studied dancing; both chose stage names from the land of their nativity; both have been extraordinarily successful. There the similarity ends.

La Argentina took the Spanish dance as a basis for an art of her own creation. Upon it she built an exquisite superstructure with the spirit of the Spanish dance as the keynote, but with its body adapted to new usages. There is the formalism of the classic about it and the free eloquence of the modern; choreographic design of rare and lovely delicacy shares the field with musical nuance of almost unequaled subtlety; above all, there is the expression of an outstanding beautiful artistic individuality through a medium self-devised.

Argentinita, on the other hand, is much more of the soil. The blood of Spain courses though the veins of her dances. She has taken what she has found and has been well content to reproduce it with gayety and vitality, conscious that it wells from ancient springs and has substance in itself. Here is no great pioneering, no intellectual or esthetic searching—here is oneness with native origins, the body of the Spanish dance instead of its soul, a delight with things as they are. It is healthy, three-dimensional art with its feet solidly on the ground.[1]

The dancer La Meri wrote that Argentinita used to visit the New York dance studio of Juan Beaucaire Montalvo, a student of José Otero in Sevilla and former partner of Amalia Molina. She had some arguments there with Jerónimo Villarino, "a young stripling of a guitarist" who played for La Argentina. Always on the lookout for new ideas, she learned a *fandanguillo* from Montalvo at that time. Montalvo advertised classes in Spanish dancing, gypsy dancing, and castanet playing in his studio near Carnegie Hall, and years later one of his most promising students, La Trianita, would marry Carlos Montoya.[2]

Argentinita also saw Lorca frequently while in New York. Federico spent a year in the city, about which he said, "Nothing is so poetic and terrible at the same time as the struggle of the skyscrapers against the sky that covers them..." He studied, lectured, and lived at Columbia University, while com-

[1]Martin, John, "The Dance: Argentinita." Copyright © *The New York Times*, March 3, 1930. Reprinted by permission.
[2]Dance Magazine, January 1946.

posing a large body of poetry—surrealistic, condemning images of New York City, with its "extra-human architecture and furious rhythm...geometry and anguish."

Federico and Argentinita worked on harmonizing the folk songs the poet had been collecting for a number of years. Lorca had a passion for these songs of the people that he had begun to learn as a child in Granada. He used to say *"Soy el loquito de las canciones"* (I am the madman of the *canciones*). A skilled pianist, he enjoyed playing and singing for himself and close friends, but he felt that he did not have a good voice and was shy about singing in public. While in America he seemed less inhibited and taught the songs to students at the university and even led a choral group. Some of these folk songs, including *zorongo gitano*, *"Anda jaleo,"* *"Los cuatro muleros,"* and *"El Café de Chinitas,"* are familiar to flamencos today because Lorca rescued them from obscurity and recorded them in 1931 as *Colección de canciones populares españolas*.

The Spanish newspaper *El Sol* described the recordings: "In the catalogues for February and March appear two ten-inch records, the first of a series of six [only five would be released] to be recorded by La Argentinita. These records form a collection of *Canciones populares antiguas* that Federico García Lorca, as fine a musician as he is a great poet, gathered from the mouth of the people in some cases, and in others located them with keen instinct in a patchwork of songbooks where they reposed, their beauty unrecognized by the many eyes that passed over the pages... Sung by La Argentinita in a straightforward and natural manner, very much in the style of a young, small town girl, and accompanied by García Lorca on the piano in a strange way that makes the instrument sound like a typical family piano, or even a substitute for the guitar, the interpretation has a very special charm..."[1] Oddly, the version of *zorongo* recorded in this collection consists only of the *bulerías* verses and lacks the slow *"La luna es pozo chico..."* verse and melody that is associated with it today.

For her farewell performance in New York on April 6, Argentinita introduced some new numbers, including a comedy monologue by Martínez Sierra and a burlesque of a typical American song and dance act. The audience loved it and there were continuous spontaneous exchanges between spectators and artist. After returning to Spain, Encarnación and Sánchez Mejías began to collaborate on major projects that would bear fruit in 1932.

When La Argentina had recovered sufficiently from her appendicitis operation, she returned to Paris in early 1930. Ironically, as she began to prepare *El Amor Brujo* for performance in the Opéra Comique in June, two

---
[1] Salazar, Adolfo, *"Un Cancionero Viviente." El Sol*, March 13, 1931. Madrid. Reproduced in the brochure that accompanies the re-release of this collection by Sonifolk in 1994.

American dancers made their Spanish dance debuts in her city. La Meri gave her first European recital and Doris Niles joined the Raquel Meller revue (we can only be intrigued by the possible scenarios that led to the hiring of Doris Niles, an American Spanish dancer, so soon after Carmen Amaya had left the revue). La Argentina had performed *El Amor Brujo* some years before, but choreography on that scale was still relatively new to her. John Martin wrote of Argentina's shortcomings as a choreographer and gave interesting insights into the primitive state of choreography for ensemble Spanish dancing at that time:

> One may as well admit straightaway that Argentina the choreographer does not rank with Argentina the dancer. There is not the same perfection of detail, the same sureness and authority—not even, strangely enough, the same mastery of contrapuntal nuance. Musically she is never less than magnificent, but in the handling of ensemble scenes...[there is] on one hand, a certain degree of confusion when several dancers are differently engaged and, on the other hand, an unnecessary unison...
>
> Argentina's personal performance is a triumph. She provides for Candelas a glowing beauty which pierces through her distress...She is in every way superior to the atmosphere she has thrown about herself.
>
> This is in no sense to disparage her company of girls. Two of them are excellent in their own right—Madamoiselle Ibáñez, who is Lucía in the ballet, and Madamoiselle Joselito, who is billed simply as "une danseuse." They are both possessed of a fire and flavor essential to Spanish dance at its best. Both, it seems, were dancers of some accomplishments when they allied themselves with Argentina several years ago. When their services are not required by her, they still dance successfully by themselves.
>
> Indeed, it is inevitable that a Spanish ballet should be an aggregation of solo dancers, for the Spanish dance as it is practiced at present is exclusively a solo form. This probably accounts in large measure for the difficulty that presents itself so obviously in this valiant effort to create an ensemble. The corps de ballet must either be trained from raw material or recruited from those who have already accomplished something as individuals. Mme. Argentina employs both methods. The choreographer, likewise, must form the habit of thinking in terms of a group in a medium that has not heretofore found its expression in that direction at all.
>
> Argentina's attitude toward her little company is characteristically gracious. She is generous to a fault, providing Mlle. Joselito with an incidental solo which most stars would consider danger-

ous competition. In acknowledging applause she draws them all about her with much the solicitude of a mother for her family of youthful prodigies."[1]

This view of La Argentina's generosity conflicts with statements by La Joselito claiming that Argentina was jealous of her. La Joselito felt that she had been snubbed when she was not invited to go to America (although it is clear that La Argentina always performed alone on her American tours). When La Argentina returned to Paris, she sent word to La Joselito that she wished to speak with her. La Joselito described what happened:

> I was very suspicious because, after all, we'd had a complete falling out. I went, but I took my husband [the guitarist, Relámpago] along. I asked her what she wanted from me and she said she would like me to dance in a ballet based on Albéniz's music, *Triana*. My husband exploded. "First you complain about Carmen [La Joselito] in the opera and now you want her for your ballet!" And I said, "You ridiculed me in America and now you come to me only because you know your ballet won't make it unless I dance in it." Then she took me aside and said, "Listen, you have your whole life ahead of you, but I'm nearing the end. Pretty soon I won't be able to dance any more." But no sooner had I danced successfully in the ballet than she pulled a long face and said to me again, "Listen, I have a name to protect, leave the triumphs to me. You still have your whole career ahead of you, for me it's almost over, please try to understand!"[2]

---

[1] Martin, John, "The Dance: Argentina in Paris." Copyright © *The New York Times*, June 22, 1930. Reprinted by permission.

[2] All of this information about La Joselito is from Madeleine Claus' wonderful interview with her in the book *Flamenco*, edited by Claus Schreiner.

CHAPTER FOUR

CARMEN'S RETURN

When Carmen Amaya returned to Barcelona from France in 1929, she was not yet sixteen years old, but already had a lifetime's worth of dance experience. She had been dancing professionally for over ten years and, clearly, there had been strong influences molding her style and guiding the direction of her future work. Carmen had an inherent passion for the dance, a deeply-felt need to express herself in movement. The reckless abandon, at times approaching fury, with which she threw herself into the dance could not be taught. It would have been encouraged by her gypsy family and reinforced by the unschooled and spontaneous dance of the gypsies of the Sacromonte. The fire of her dance always made the biggest and most enduring impression on her audiences. However, one very respected dance teacher, the *bailaora* Teresa Martínez de la Peña, feels that Carmen's improvisational abilities have been exaggerated. She says:

> Written history says that Carmen's dance was intuitive, spontaneous, beyond any rules, that is, she more or less improvised when she came out on stage. That should be understood as a desire on the part of the writers to enhance her image and make her appear more enigmatic...For example, Sebastián Gasch used to say that Carmen was anti-school, anti-academic, forgetting that she had teachers in her home. She was raised among good flamencos who taught her. They say that her mother danced very well, although she couldn't dedicate herself because of the many children she had. Her aunt, La Faraona, definitely taught her to dance, and her father, El Chino, completed her education with very strenuous lessons that lasted up to six hours.
>
> When Carmencita went around to the *colmaos* of Barcelona with her father, she knew what she had to do, she had the dance well learned and then she added her temperament...
>
> First it was the family, then spending time with other dancers. Very early on, she had an intense professional life, relating with the best in her art. It is obvious that she was exposed to the work-

ings of the dance of that time. In her famous *alegrías*...the steps were the same as those done by Frasquillo and La Quica, the Pericets, Paco Reyes, Custodia Romero—her contemporaries, and later our teachers of the same choreography. She did the *campanas* [called the *silencio* today; a slow dramatic section in this otherwise lively dance], marked the *ida*[1]—the strummed transition to the *bulerías*—but then came out like a gunshot in her footwork for the first few *compases*, assisted by all the demons she had within her, and she didn't return to normal until she began the first *llamada* [rhythmic variation]. Strength and speed were the temperamental elements contained in her dance, and when she let them loose full-force, the rules were sent reeling.

It is not surprising that they speak of her intuitive dance. Where there used to be one turn, she did two, and violently; she doubled the footwork, and did it with an intensity unknown up to that time, not only in women, but also among the male dancers. She resolved the deliberate turns in slower music in a more decisive manner, with more than enough time to stop after the first turn, give a defiant glare, and then follow with the second turn.

It was an unusual dance, but she improvised nothing. She was accustomed to doing variations where she did strong footwork, at full speed, while her arms moved in relaxed curves at a different tempo. This, as difficult as it is, was no more than mastery of her profession. She had needed many hours of practice to be able to coordinate the two different rhythms in her tiny body. It was the exact opposite of improvisation.

In addition, she always did the same dances. Antonio, in his *Memorias*, commented on her dancing when he saw her in Buenos Aires in 1937, "...Carmen was a fabulous dancer, but limited; she danced two dances better than anyone else: the *alegrías* and the *fandanguillo*." She was not exactly that limited, she had other dances in her repertoire: *soleares*, *bulerías*, *siguiriyas*, and a *garrotín* that was like a tornado [not to mention her *farruca*, *tango*, *caña*, *zambra*, *zapateado*, and *rumba*]. The *garrotín* was a compendium of all her abilities in capital letters. She opened by beating out rhythm with her knuckles on a table top, a dry sound that filled the space around her. Then handclapping and footwork together at a frenetic speed. Her arms gestured feverishly, passing again and again in front of her face, double turns cut off sharply, with the following commotion of her skirt, and a look of fury on

---

[1] Up until the 1960s, the *alegrías* almost always ended with the *ida*, a set chord pattern strummed on the guitar and traditional steps. The modern *alegrías* transitions to the *bulerías* directly, without this intermediary sequence.

her face. There was room for nothing more, the dancer was pure energy and it seemed that, instead of being consumed by the dance, it revitalized her...

It was a dance created consciously, a complete physical effort, in keeping with her sense of responsibility; she gave all of her body and soul, and thereby earned the respect of the public. She was dignified, her movements were never grotesque, nor did her turns, which approached being acrobatic, evoke a look of disapproval in her audience. Her turns, technically perfect, finished in an absolutely precise stop, something never seen before.

She had much austerity, avoiding adornments or banalities. Neither sensual nor dramatic, hers was simply dance, without the need for anything more.[1]

Carmen's passion led directly to her inclination toward the male dance. Her body—small, wiry, and charged with nervous energy—was made for power and speed. Her figure never changed from its adolescent form, with slim hips, muscular legs, and tiny feet. Goldberg gives Carmen's height as four feet, ten inches, and her weight as ninety pounds.[2] Later in life, Carmen herself gave her weight as ninety-four pounds. She was fond of saying that she had so little bust and buttocks that it was hard to tell if she were coming or going.

Elements of the dance that were considered to be in the male domain—intense, often frenzied, movements of the arms and body, whiplike turns, and explosive footwork—allowed Carmen to express feelings that raged within her in a way that the soft, graceful movements of the traditional feminine dance could not. It is generally agreed that *bailaoras* in the *cafés cantantes* emphasized armwork, upper body carriage, and manipulation of the long trains on their *batas de cola*. One writer of the cafe period gives a good picture of this way of dancing in his description of the reigning *bailaora*, La Macarrona.

Juana Vargas inherited the stage name "La Macarrona" from her gypsy family in Jerez. She began to dance in the early cafes in 1868. Such was her dominance in the dance that, in the 1920s, when she was in her sixties, she still drew crowds as a headliner in the major cabarets of Sevilla and Madrid. Pablillo de Valladolid wrote: "She is a gypsy empress with a more exhalted lineage than Pastora [not clear which Pastora, but probably Pastora Imperio]. She rises from her chair with more majestic dignity than a Queen of Sheeba. Haughtily. Magnificently. She lifts her arms over her head as if she were blessing the world. They move like snakes, her hands weaving and adding to the shadows of her eyes...Slowly, with a religious cadence, her arms descend to curve at stomach level...In another unexpected rhythm, she poises one leg, scrapes the stage with the tip of her foot amid the graceful folds

[1] Martínez de la Peña, Teresa, *"El encuentro con Carmen Amaya, como bailaba, como vivió." La Caña, No. 1*, December 1991.
[2] Goldberg, p. 420.

of her underskirt that is lightly lifted by her right hand, while her left hand is held high, index finger pointed to the sky. Then, both arms arch overhead, like handles on an ancient Greek jar. She whirls. The ample starched ruffle of the great white train of her fine linen dress expands over the stage. She is like a peacock, white, magnificent, and arrogant..."[1] According to the Spanish press, the Shah of Persia is supposed to have said, after seeing La Macarrona dance in Paris, "That graceful serpent is capable of making me forget all of my 'wives' in Tehran!"[2]

Regarding the absence of footwork in the female dance, the guitarist Luis Maravilla went so far as to say that, in the early days, the men used to do the *redobles* and other complicated footwork from their seats to make it sound as if the women were doing it. Other sources support this claim and say that these men were referred to as *esquinaores* because they filled in the women's dances from their chairs at the corners (*esquinas*) of the stage.

However, the matter is not so clearcut. Apart from the obvious examples of La Cuenca and Salud Rodríguez, who dressed and danced like men, many of the top *bailaoras* employed considerable footwork in their dances. Returning to Pablillo de Valladolid's description of La Macarrona, we also find, "From the back of the stage she advances, doubling her heelwork on the floor, raising a cloud of dust that appears as if to lift the *bailaora* toward the ceiling...a carnation falls, yielding to the tremors of the final *redoble* by those feet clad in marvelous little red shoes, as if there were a pool of blood at her feet. The people are silent, holding their breaths with an almost religious fervor, while the feet of La Macarrona give rhythm to her dance. The chords of the guitar have little value now. Because La Macarrona dances to the *compás* of her own magnificent footwork."

Two of the most popular dances of the late 1920 were the *zapateado*, for men, and the *farruca*, which could be danced by either men or women. Both of these dances focused on viril displays of footwork. Carmen Amaya, who excelled in the *farruca*, clearly was not the first woman to employ footwork like a man in her dances. She had plenty of models to inspire her and she was surrounded by splendid dancers, both male and female, from whom she could learn. Her contribution would be in the technical virtuosity of her footwork, which reached a level that few men of her day could attain, and the application of her footwork to *all* of her dances, not just those that had traditionally served to display the feet.

Throughout her career, Carmen was criticized for wearing pants when she danced. It is not clear when she first adopted the high-waisted black or white pants that she wore with a matching vest and white shirt. Her sisters say that she had always danced her *alegrías* in pants as far back as they could

---

[1] Blas Vega, *Diccionario Enciclopédico Ilustrado del Flamenco*, p. 436.
[2] *Ibid.* p. 436.

remember.[1] In very early photos, she always wore a dress, although sometimes a tight-fitting adaptation of a ranch skirt that hugged her body and flared out at the knees. It is likely that she had tried pants by the mid-1930s. Many considered it scandalous that she should present herself that way, and later critics would blame her for the decline of the "feminine" dance.

For Carmen, the wearing of pants represented nothing more than a practical solution to the problem of making her feet visible when she danced. Why should she put out such effort if the audience couldn't see her feet! And certainly footwork in pants was considerably easier than when wearing a dress with five or more feet of heavy, starched train dragging behind or entangling the feet. Carmen was not the first woman to wear pants. La Cuenca and Salud Rodríguez set early examples, and La Tanguera was known to dance *farruca* in pants. However, Carmen Amaya would be the first to make widespread use of male dress, and the slender silhouette she presented in pants would become her trademark.

It was not only the male dance that made an impression on young Carmen. Her exposure to the *cupletistas* left an indelible mark that would follow her through life. Her father, El Chino, who always thought that Carmen was a better singer than a dancer, noted that the most successful performers were those who sang. No *bailaora*, no matter how talented and respected, had ever reached the heights of fame achieved by the *cupletistas*. While Carmen sang well, in a husky, throaty gypsy voice that she manipulated skillfully in such festive *cantes* as the *bulerías, tangos, rumbas,* and *garrotín*, she usually left the serious *cante jondo* to the *cantaores*. The highlight of her shows would always be her singing, dancing, and acting out of some popular *cuplé*. When she began to record some years later, it would most often be as a singer.

In the Spanish ballet companies of the *cupletistas* La Argentina and La Argentinita, who had begun to dedicate themselves to dance in the late 1920s, Carmen would find the format that she would follow with her own companies, particularly in the melding of flamenco with Spanish classical and regional music. The *cante* had all but disappeared from the dance. It had probably begun with the incursion of classical *bolera* dances and regional dances into the repertoire of the *cupletistas*. These dances had to be accompanied by piano, and it would be a natural evolution for the pianists to attempt the flamenco dances as well. And that, in fact, is what happened. Juan Martínez described the dances being done in the 1930s:

> The guitar acquired the following dance forms: *La Tana, soleares, alegrías gitanas, bulerías gitanas, zapateado, zapateado ilustrado de Cádiz, garrotín, zambria* or *tiempo moro* [zambra], *farruca, tangos, tangos por chufla,* and *sevillanas*.

[1]Goldberg, p. 176

On the piano we have the following: *pasodobles* (used by many flamencos as *farruca*), *"Moras, moritas, moras,"* *garrotín*, various *farrucas*—one of the first being *"Meu Meco"* by Maestro Pablo Onsalo, taken from the guitar music of Luis Molina. Then there was *"El baile salvaje,"* written by Quinito Valverde for the great Faíco, and the *"Alegrías,"* also by Maestro Valverde, written for Antonio de Bilbao and later popularized by La Argentina under the title, *"La Corrida."* Also, *"Soleares gitanas,"* one of the best compositions of Monreal, *"Alegrías gitanas"* that the Romero brothers transcribed so masterfully for the guitar, and *"Bulerías gitanas,"* the version by Vicente Romero being the most successful. There were many *tangos*, *zambras*, and *pasodobles*, thousands of musical pieces of this type, as well as the danceable *fandangos*, those of Huelva being the most popular, followed by those of Almería and others.[1]

 Martínez went on to explain that women had many more resources than men in the dance. Men and women might dance the *soleares* to piano, but only women could dance it to guitar. Men could dance *zapateado*, *alegrías*, *bulerías*, *tangos*, and *farrucas*. Women could dance anything, although they tended to specialize in one or two dances. Martínez listed some of the top dancers and their specialties, revealing that, just as in the modern *tablao*, two or three dances made up the preponderance of the repertoire: Antonio de Bilbao, *zapateado* and *alegrías*; El Estampío, *alegrías* and *"El picaor;"* Faíco, *baile salvaje* and *farruca por pasodoble*; El Mojigongo, *farruca por pasodoble*; Frasquillo, *farruca*, but dominating all dances; Niño de los Caireles, *farruca* and imitating a train; El Gato, *farruca*; Manolillo de la Rosa, *alegrías* and *farruca*; Acha Rovira, *farruca*; Ramírez of Sevilla, *farruca*; La Camisona, *alegrías*; La Malena, *alegrías*; La Macarrona, *alegrías*; La Joselito, *alegrías* and *farruca*; La Tanguera, *farruca*; Carmen Amaya, *farruca* and *tiempo moro*.

 For years, Carmen would continue to dance the *farruca* to piano accompaniment. With piano accompanying the dance, the *cantaor* became expendable and early dance companies seldom included a flamenco singer. When guitarists worked with the companies of La Argentina or La Argentinita, they often picked up the piano parts and included in their repertoires everything from classical compositions to *jotas* from Aragón. Decades later, guitarists Sabicas and Carlos Montoya would still have these compositions in their solo repertoires. Sabicas would play *"La Boda de Luis Alonso"* by Jerónimo Jiménez,[2] one of Carmen Amaya's favorites, *"Capriccio Espagnol"* by Rimsky-Korsakov, *"Czardas"* by Monti, *"Malagueña"* by

---

[1] *Martínez, La Prensa. 1942.*

[2] This dance has been called variously, *"Los Bailes y Bodas de Luis Alonso," "Los Bailes de Luis Alonso,"* and *"Las Bodas de Luis Alonso."*

Lecuona, and Tarrega's *"Gran Jota."* Carlos Montoya's solo playing would reveal the years he spent playing for La Argentina, Teresina, La Argentinita, Vicente Escudero, and others. His repertoire would include *"Andalucía"* and *"Malagueña"* by Lecuona, "Sacromonte" by Turina, *"Bolero," "El Vito," folías* from the Canary Islands, *jota* from Aragón, *sardana* from Cataluña, *"Rapsodía valenciana," "La Lagarterana"* from Old Castile, folk tunes from Asturias, Mallorca and Galicia, and "Madrid 1800," a medley of *tonadillas*—theater songs from the 18th and 19th Centuries that La Argentinita adapted to the dance.

Barcelona had been bidding for a World Fair for a number of years and finally succeeded in opening the Exposición Internacional in the summer of 1929. The whole city came to life for the fair. Along Las Ramblas and in the Barrio Chino, music halls, cafes, and bistros with names like El Gran Pay-Pay, Folies Bergere, Apolo, and Madrid-Paris, were animated day and night. Many never closed, and, in fact, some had no doors. Each night, after working in the fair, Carmen Amaya would go to the Barrio Chino looking for late night work.

The impresario Morell, who controlled practically all of the *cafés cantantes* of Barcelona, hired Carmen and her father for the *colmao* of Rosita Rodrigo in the Pueblo Español that had been erected for the fair. Carmen told of one late night experience:

> In the Pueblo Español, in the Exposition of Barcelona in 1929, I was sixteen, and we had to sing and dance for visitors who asked us. One night a gentleman came in, modestly dressed, or I should say, dressed in a very common manner. He asked us to come over. My companions refused, it didn't appeal to them to pay attention to that type. In spite of their teasing, I decided to appease the man. When I finished my performance, he seemed pleased and thanked me. Two hours later, you should have seen the faces of my friends! A messenger brought me an enormous basket full of hams, good wines, fruits, and sweets. It was splendid! It came with an envelope that contained five-hundred *pesetas* and a thank-you note signed by Don Carlos de Borbón, the brother of the King of Spain![1]

Miguel Borrull had a *tablao* in the Andalusian Pavilion where Carmen and many of her family worked alongside a dozen gypsies from the Sacromonte. Angel Zúñiga described his first contact with Carmen:

> I first met Carmen when she was young—she was still a child—

[1] Hidalgo, p. 76.

working in the Patio del Farolillo in the Exposition of Barcelona. Before that I had known of her wanderings...through the streets of Barcelona, dancing if they gave her a few cents, a ragamuffin full of life, insolence, and cunning. A precious thing with her uncombed mat of baby hair, [she danced] to the beat of a tambourine.

On those slow, sweet nights of the Patio del Farolillo, Carmen stood out like no other in the flamenco *cuadro* that built its excitement for the entertainment of travelers. At that time there were almost no tourists. I can see her now: She lifts her girlish arm majestically, fixes her gaze in the bewitched air—bewitched by her—and traces mysterious symbols, that unknowable cabbala in which the unknown is defined, a flask containing the perfume of a race that, in order to drown its sorrows, sings *por alegrías* [in joy].[1]

Over the course of the next year, many celebrated flamenco artists performed in conjunction with the Exposition, both in the fair and in theaters around the city. The ancient Anilla de Ronda came to perform with a *zambra* from the Sacromonte, along with La Golondrina and young Tere Maya. Maestro Realito, of Sevilla, brought a *cuadro* that included La Macarrona, La Malena, Frasquillo, the dancer Rafael Ortega (a relative of Caracol), and a trio that called itself *"ABC."*

After the Exposition, Carmen returned to dance for the next four years with the *cuadro* of the Bar de Manquet. The makeup of the *cuadro* had not changed much over the years, with her father and Manolo Bulerías on guitars, and the dancing of La Faraona, La Romerito, Escudero el Gato, María la Pescatera (said to be a first cousin to Carmen's mother[2]), and the *farruca* dancer Romero de Torres.

The Barcelona critic Sebastián Gasch wrote that, "one afternoon in June of 1931, Vicente Escudero, the guitarist El Chino, and myself were together in a room in the Hotel Oriente that belonged to the dancer from Valladolid. Vicente was writing to Ellis Gold, secretary to the impresario Sol Hurok, asking him if the daughter of El Chino, little Carmen Amaya, could work in the United States, in spite of her youth. Escudero wanted to take her with him to North America."[3]

El Chino did not relish the idea of the long trip across so much water, so Carmen would have to wait for her meeting with Sol Hurok. The famous ballerina Pavlova had asked Vicente to appear in the United States with her, but she had died before their plans could be realized. So Escudero went on his own in early 1932—after overcoming the dread of travel by sea that had

---
[1] Quoted in Hidalgo. p. 225.
[2] Goldberg, p. 172.
[3] Gasch, El Molino.

prevented him from accepting previous offers.

Sol Hurok presented Escudero in New York for the first time on January 17, 1932. In John Martin's review, we see Escudero through the eyes of the audience, rather than from the critical point of view of other flamenco artists:

> Vicente Escudero, the Spanish Gypsy dancer, proved in his American debut last night at Chanin's 46th Street Theatre that all the extravagant things said about him in his European appearances were well based in fact. One of the most brilliant audiences of the season crowded the theater from top to bottom and let him know in unmistakeable terms that he met with its approval.
>
> Señor Escudero is an astonishing personality. His approach to his art is elemental to the point of being brutal. He moves with the easy grace of a fine animal, his chest held high and his feet picking their way with the daintiness of a cat. For stagecraft he cares not a whit, and illusion has no meaning for him. The crude blue and white setting against which he dances, his casual wandering on and off with no effort whatsoever at making entrances and exits, his muttering and singing as he dances, all testify to the fact that he is interested only in the dances he is presenting and seems totally unaware that the theater is a sophisticated institution in which tricks are frequently employed. His attitude toward his audience is one of insolence. The same air is assumed toward his two charming partners, who meet it with the fiery response that is traditional of the primitive Latin woman toward the Latin male in his most elemental state.
>
> His dancing is a thing of amazing skill. There is an electric energy to it that transforms his body from the motionlessness of stone in an instant to a veritable dynamo of nervous activity. Apparently the designs of his dances are of least concern to him, for when he repeats them, they bear only the most general resemblance to their original forms. Almost invariably they are better the second time.
>
> Music is also not of great importance to him, though in its rhythms he takes his keenest delight. There is no music, however, to supply him with such patterns as he evolves in his unaccompanied dance entitled "Rhythms." Here he not only employs footwork which quite surpasses anything of the kind seen here before, both in brilliance and delicacy, but his snapping fingers, his clicking tongue, and even his fingernails, are all brought into use. The effect is quite as naive as such a description would indicate, but the excitement that he manages to achieve by these miscellaneous means is impossible to describe. He was compelled last night to

encore this item twice—always with different variations—and so far as the audience was concerned it could have gone on indefinitely. Indeed, the performance was lengthened to almost twice what the printed program offered by the insistence of a house which was highly entertained as well as intrigued by a rare novelty. Needless to say, the two girls, Carmita and Carmela, who dance with him and alone from time to time, do not measure up to his standard, for he is unique. They are nevertheless more than adequate, as are also the pianist and guitarist [Luis Mayoral] when allowance is made for the musical code of the performance. Only in the "Variations," which employs castanets of iron, silver, and aluminum, does the naivete of the style overstep itself and arrive nowhere.

If it is possible to select particular dances as having been of more than average excellence, perhaps the choice would fall upon the "Zapateado," the "Farruca," and the "Jota," not forgetting, of course, the "Rhythms" mentioned above.[1]

The influence of La Argentina on Escudero's repertoire is clear. His programs would include "Córdoba," "Sevilla," "Granada," and *"Seguidillas"* by Albéniz, *"Jota de Huesca"* and *"Jota de Navarra"* by Granados, and a variety of classical compositions by Falla and others. However, he differed from La Argentina in featuring more flamenco, including his *zapateado* and *farruca*, as well as an *alegrías* by Carmela and *sevillanas* danced by both women. John Martin makes it clear that in his staging he bore absolutely no resemblance to his female counterpart:

> For those who have been accustomed to the general desire among recitalists to make their perfomances as polished as possible, there was considerable shock during the first few minutes of Escudero's debut program. The rise of the curtain disclosed a garish blue and white background, lit without subtlety of atmosphere, and into this crude setting stepped a dark young woman who danced not too expertly, dropping pins and combs from her hair as she did so. There must have been many who asked themselves if this could possibly presage the famous gypsy whose art had caused so much excitement in Europe.
>
> But when Escudero himself came upon the stage, the situation cleared. His unconcern with theatrical pretense became evident as a matter of design and not of ineptitude. He fidgeted with his hat for the simple and natural reason that it was unsteady on his head; he adjusted his jacket for the same reason; he picked up the combs and pins with no apologies. When noises occurred off stage, he

---

[1] Martin, John, "Escudero, Dancer, in American Debut." Copyright © *The New York Times,* January 18, 1932. Reprinted by permission.

admitted frankly that he heard them; and he chatted with his partner when the spirit moved him.[1]

The Dancing Times of London had previously given a description of Escudero's unique approach to staging his dances: "The rising curtain discloses a bare stage with a plain backcloth, half black and half white. From the wings appears a rather diffident guitarist carrying a chair and his guitar. Having apologetically seated himself, he commences to strike chords on his instrument. From the opposite side, Escudero strolls in, completely unconcerned. He stops by the player and starts chatting to him. Soon he begins beating a rhythm with one foot while still leaning over his accompanist's chair. Then, apparently when the mood takes him and no sooner, he starts to dance." The same writer, Cyril Rice, added: "One can hardly say that Escudero dances to the guitar. It would be at least equally legitimate to say that the guitarist follows the dancer. United by some bond of sympathy, they so work together that they are always in perfect harmony...The flamenco dancer seems to be creating rhythms in collaboration with his guitarist. The sorcery that lies in Argentina's castanets, Escudero achieves with his feet."

John Martin gives us a picture of Escudero's stage personality and technique:

> Escudero has restored a great deal of the old and native charm of improvisation, where in Argentina's art is an exquisite and sophisticated formality... She is as utterly feminine as he is completely masculine, and that is perhaps as satisfactory an explanation as any for their difference... Considered strictly as a dancer, Escudero is as startling as when he is considered as a personality. He is equipped with everything that belongs to one who is obviously born to dance. He has great strength, which is offset by lightness and an almost unbelievable brilliance of movement. The speed of his footwork sets his whole frame aquiver, and the snapping of his fingers is almost too rapid for the ear to follow. His heels bite into the floor one minute and the next are touching it with the utmost delicacy. Such shading as Argentina accomplishes with her castanets, Escudero achieves with his heel-tapping. He springs from stony immobility into violent movement as by the application of an electric current, and relapses as suddenly into immobility... As a stage figure, he is not to be duplicated anywhere.[2]

Over the next two months, Escudero gave fifteen sold-out performances, billed as "Spain's Greatest Male Dancer." Often hundreds were turned away.

---
[1] Martin, John, "The Dance: Varied Spanish Program." Copyright © *The New York Times,* January 24, 1932. Reprinted by permission.

[2] Martin, John, "The Dance: Varied Spanish Program." Copyright © *The New York Times,* January 24, 1932. Reprinted by permission.

More often than not encores equaled the number of dances in the program as audiences demanded that he repeat his numbers time and again. Late in the season, he introduced the "Miller's Dance" from Falla's ballet, *The Three-cornered Hat*, in which he showed off "amazing virtuosity" in costumes by Pablo Picasso.

Escudero was so successful that, after a trip to Spain to be honored in his home town of Valladolid, he returned to America for a second tour later in the year. Reporters swarmed to the boat to meet him and trailed him to his hotel suite. Columns of copy began appearing about his fear of dying at sea and being thrown to the fish, the exploits of his pet cat, and other trivia. His arrogant disdain for the formal trappings of theater and his flair for improvisation captivated even the most conservative concert goers, and his American tours during the years from 1932 to 1935 covered as many as fifty-five cities each. In October of 1932, he was back in the Forty-sixth Street Theatre with all-new programs. He had studied in the Basque country while at home and incorporated a suite of Basque dances into his performances, along with a parody of the bullfight that ended with a "gypsy *bulerías*."

In November, Escudero's tour took him to the Memorial Opera House in San Francisco, where the reviewer, Alexander Fried, wrote: "Escudero's is an art that amuses or arouses admiration of its skill and trickery. It does not deal in deep ideas or seek to carry out elaborate expressive purpose... Frequently it has a gypsy energy made elegant by metropolitan culture. There are many surprising things about Escudero's dancing. In the midst of vivacious steps he may lapse into a careless walk. He may pick up props from the wings, sticks or swords to beat time. He may shout a little, or vary the patter of swift feet and castanets with the loud clicking of his fingernails."[1] By December, Vicente had returned to New York, where he was the first Spanish dancer to participate in the *International Dance Festival*.

Two years later, in October of 1934, Escudero performed as part of the *Continental Varieties* in the New York's Little Theater, and for the first time received negative reviews. The critics felt that he was lost on a large stage and consequently received few requests for encores. But, by the following year, he had corrected his deficiencies and presented the complete ballet, *El Amor Brujo*, in Radio City Music Hall. John Martin wrote:

> Vicente Escudero, known to New York heretofore only as a concert dancer, revealed himself in the new roles of ballet choreographer, director, and dancer... In all of those capacities he aquitted himself with distinction and, incidentally, bestowed no little of it upon the Music Hall, which has previously offered few if any dance productions of equal merit.

[1] Fried, Alexander, "Capacity House sees Escudero in Gay Dance." *San Francisco Chronicle*, November 17, 1932.

The story of the ballet, devised by Martínez Sierra, tells of the beautiful Candelas, who is haunted by the ghost of her dead lover and cannot break his spell when she falls in love with Carmelo, until her friend, Lucía, flirts with the exigent spirit and so torments him with love that he is destroyed. It is Candelas who is the central figure, and be it said that it is to the credit of Escudero's artistic integrity that he does not in any way change this accent for his own glorification.

Even in the vast ranges of the big theater, his sharp and incisive movement carries with complete clarity. His dances are admirable in the beauty of their movement and the complexity of their rhythmic patterns. As Candelas, Carmita plays charmingly and dances well. Hers is the unhappy problem of appearing in a role made famous by La Argentina, but she approaches it from so different a standpoint that the temptation to make comparisons does not arise...

There is the usual Music Hall overemphasis on spectacle, with bats, fireflies, a luminous crucifix, a great deal of colored spot lighting, and considerably more scenery than is necessary, though Vincent Minelli has done a good job of designing it.[1]

On May 3rd, the *San Francisco Chronicle* wrote:

With feet and fingertips tapping like telegraph keys, Vicente Escudero, greatest living exponent of Spanish dance, arrived in San Francisco yesterday to prepare for the ballet *El Amor Brujo* by Manuel de Falla, to be given in the Opera House May 15 to 18.

Accompanied by his vivacious and charming partner, Carmita, Escudero took over the William Taylor Hotel studio of his friend Adolph Bolm, and began immediate rehearsals for the ballet, to be presented here for the first time.

As the passionate music of the Spanish composer echoes through the hotel corridors, Escudero set forth his choreography for the ballet and during the brief intermissions expounded on his admiraton for streamlined American women. Speaking no English, the dancer turned to French to tell that he likes California very much indeed because it is like his native Spain; that he presented the Falla ballet first in Barcelona, dancing it with the incomparable Argentina; that he is toying with the idea of movie contracts; that his concerts in Los Angeles were tremendous successes...[2]

The review of the concert read: "Escudero appeared early in the program in a short divertissement, but his main contribution was Falla's *El Amor*

---

[1] Martin, John, Copyright © *The New York Times*, March 22, 1935. Reprinted by permission.
[2] Noted Spanish Gypsy Dancer Arrives Here." *San Francisco Chronicle*, May 4, 1935. .

Brujo, done with the assistance of his usual partner, Carmita, and with Guillermo del Oro, Maclovia Ruiz [both, residents of San Francisco], and a corps de ballet of other local dancers. The soloists, as could be expected, were perfection. Escudero himself is like a boxer's forearm, all muscle, tautness, strength, and grace."[1] Later in 1935, Escudero made his motion picture debut in *Here's to Romance*, and then planned to make his first Carnegie Hall appearance on October 15, with guitarist Jerónimo Villarino and pianist Emilio Osta. But he injured his back in a taxicab accident, forcing him to cancel the concert and return to Spain. In spite of this setback, Vicente Escudero had made his mark. For American audiences, as for audiences the world over, Escudero came to represent Spanish dance, in much the same way that Pavlova had come to represent ballet and Isadora Duncan the free dance. And he symbolized the gypsy, a facade he had not yet given up. In one of his last interviews in Los Angeles, Vicente told the reporter: "Each year I go back to my [gypsy] people, back to the soil that gave me all that I am. There I dance and drink with them, and spend my money on those who have so little. They do not give me importance. I like that, and I learn from the worst of them."

In 1931, Pepe Marchena did something curious that would directly effect Carmen Amaya. Marchena had become an absolute idol. His recordings sold like those of no other before him. In any small town, he could park his car, step out with his woman of the moment and a couple of subordinate *cantaores*, and within moments be surrounded by people whispering, "There's Pepe Marchena!... Look, it's Pepe Marchena!...It's him, Pepe Marchena!..." The crowd would grow until there wasn't room for them all in the town square. He thrived on the attention.

The singer Pericón de Cádiz described one occasion when Marchena didn't feel much like singing. He went out on stage, sang three *fandangos*, and left. The crowd yelled, pleading with the singer to come back, and the impresario went crazy with begging. But he wouldn't go. Then, on impulse, Marchena went back on stage and announced, "Respected public, I came out to sing when I shouldn't have, because I am sick. So that you can see that I tell the truth, I have my doctor with me, whom you shall meet now." And he grabbed Antonio el Mellizo [the eldest son of the legendary *cantaor*, Enrique el Mellizo], who was back stage, and brought him out. Poor Antonio, very old, with his glasses and cane, took Pepe's pulse there on the stage in front of the crowd, and the people gave him a standing ovation. Such was Pepe Marchena![2]

[1] Frankenstein, Alfred, "San Francisco Opera Ballet Scores With Bolm Program." *San Francisco Chronicle*, May 16, 1935

[2] Ortiz Nuevo, *Las mil y una historias de Pericón de Cádiz*. p. 41.

A noted womanizer and quite vain, Marchena dressed impeccably and took a great deal of care with his hair. He excused his frequent tardiness by saying, "But, how long do you think it takes Pepe Marchena to dress?" He often referred to himself in the third person and employed the formal *"usted"* in addressing even his friends. Marchena was said to own more than one hundred pairs of shoes, and he was a heavy user of cologne. He could be generous with his friends, but was very tight with money in business, complaining constantly that he "couldn't even afford tobacco." He spent lavishly and loved to gamble. "Coins are round so that they can roll! " he was fond of saying. He would buy out a street vender's complete supply of lottery tickets, and he won often. He was quoted as saying that, if he won big, he would buy himself a harem. But mostly he gambled away his earnings, even losing a ranch during one night's play. Unlike most flamencos, Marchena didn't smoke, drink, or stay up all night. He believed that he had to care for his voice and faithfully did breathing exercises.

Marchena's rise to fame was closely linked with the increasing popularity of the *fandangos personales*, personal *fandangos* that each singer customized to suit his whim. These *fandangos*, based on danceable folk songs called *fandanguillos*, from the province of Huelva (in Andalucía), had begun to take on a grander form at the hands of certain singers. A *cantaor* from La Linea named Rafael Pareja, a disciple of Chacón according to Pepe el de la Matrona, had created his own style and he passed it on to Pepe Marchena when they became friends in Sevilla. It was Pareja who convinced Marchena to go to Madrid, where Pepe would make his *fandango* famous throughout Spain a few years later. Pareja's *fandango* was preserved, more or less in its original form, by the singer El Gloria and is known today as *fandangos del Gloria*.

In Marchena's hands, the *fandango* became distorted into many forms, and the multitude of Marchena imitators confused them even further. Not only were these songs subjected to every possible indignity in their singing—falsetto voice, endless acrobatic warbling, and notes held to ridiculous lengths—but even the underlying poetic structure was not respected. Earlier in flamenco's history, illiterate singers instinctively followed unspoken rules of composition and all verses of the *fandangos* family of *cantes* (including the related *malagueñas, granaínas, tarantas,* etc.) had eight syllables in each of four or five lines of poetry (expanded to six lines of singing by repetition). The following early *fandango* composed by Pepe Marchena shows the beginning of the trend away from that structure (the number of syllables, given in parenthesis, is not entirely accurate, because they can be combined in singing to bring the total closer to eight):

Cuando una flor se marchita, (9)	When a flower withers,
es que le falta el calor; (8)	it is because it lacks warmth;
cuando un hombre se encuentra	when a man finds himself
aburrío, (13)	bored,
es que le falta el amor (8)	it is because he lacks the love
de una mujer que ha querío. (10)	of a woman he has loved.

The *fandangos* became something so trivial and without guidelines that anybody could sing them. The *cantaor* Aurelio de Cádiz said that they were a house without a foundation; Manuel Vallejo called them a *cante* within the reach of the whole neighborhood; El Niño de las Marianas (father of Luis Maravilla) said, "That which is sung by everybody is nothing!"

Pepe Marchena also played a major role in modifying what we call today the *cantes de ida y vuelta*, the songs of the round-trip. Spaniards took their music to the New World, where it was modified, and some of it then made the round trip back to Spain to enter into the flamenco repertoire. The oldest of these *cantes* is the *guajiras*.

In Cuba, white women, especially recently immigrated Spaniards, were called *guajiras*. The *cante por guajiras*, with its sensuous rhythm of alternating 6/8-3/4 measures, first appeared in flamenco as early as 1860—predating even one of flamenco's most basic forms, the *soleares*. Early guitar soloists included it in their programs in the 1860s and '70s, and it appeared among the earliest recordings, made in the 1890s by such singers as Juan Breva and El Mochuelo. Antonio Chacón sang the *guajiras* and probably enriched them, as he did everything he sang, but we cannot appreciate his contribution since he never recorded them. It was Pepe Marchena who elaborated the *guajiras* into their modern form, enlarging them and sweetening the melodies. Ramón Montoya had recorded a solo guitar version before 1920.

The *milonga*, a popular Argentinian song form since the mid-1800s, was brought into flamenco by the dynamic singer/dancer Pepa de Oro. Pepa had spent time in Argentina with her father, Paco de Oro, a modest bullfighter who coached her and pushed her, and she brought the *milonga* back with her to the *cafés cantantes* of the late 1880s. Dancing and singing the *milonga* in charismatic fashion, this *paya* who looked so gypsy became an attraction in Madrid around the turn-of-the-century, and the *milonga* began its rise in popularity, reaching a peak in the 1930s with the help of Pepe Marchena.

Antonio Chacón sang the *milonga* as Pepa de Oro had sung them, with a danceable *tango*-like rhythm. Years later, the guitarist Sabicas would record the *milonga* with a marked rhythm. But Marchena enhanced the mournful tone of the song by freeing it from rhythm and allowing the singer to exploit the melancholy melody to its fullest. He did the same with the *vidalita*, a melodic variation of the *milonga*, and mixed the two styles freely. The syrupy sweetness of the *milonga* and the *vidalita* was perfectly suited to the *ópera flamenca* period, but gradually these songs lost favor and all but disappeared from the flamenco repertoire. They have resisted modern-day attempts to revive them in the never-ending search for new material to feed the recording industry. This contrasts with the case of another *cante de ida y vuelta*, the *rumba flamenca*.

The *rumbita*, as it was often called in the early years, originated as a Cuban song and dance form that mixed Spanish music with African rhythmic and erotic influences. The word *"rumba"* is said to have referred to performing groups in poor Cuban neighborhoods, where wooden boxes, sticks, spoons, and pots and pans were used to create musical accompaniment. The *rumbita* had been a part of theatrical works in Spain during the 1800s, but when the loss of Cuba in 1898 inspired a nostalgia for all things Cuban, the *rumbita* began to enjoy popularity in the *varietés*. Around 1914, flamencos adopted the music as a closing number. Pepe el de la Matrona, Bernardo el de los Lobitos, La Niña de los Peines, and Manuel Vallejo recorded early versions. It appears that Pepe Marchena did not become much involved with the *rumba* and he did not record them. Perhaps he felt that an inconsequential bit of music used to end a flamenco show did not merit his attention. It would not be until the 1950s that the gypsies of Barcelona, including Carmen Amaya, would create the flamenco *rumba* style that would capture the attention of the world and eventually become an international music.

The guitarist Sabicas said that he used to hang out with Pepe Marchena, who was obsessed with changing the *cante*, with creating new styles and new ways of singing. He said that Marchena "used to go from bar to bar humming music, trying to develop new ideas and give them his own stamp." On one such occasion, Sabicas was surprised when he didn't recognize what Marchena was singing, and he asked what it was, confessing that he had never heard it. Marchena responded, "They are...*colombianas*."[1] And thus, the *colombianas* were born—with absolutely no connection to their namesake country of Colombia. Years later, when Sabicas created his first solo version of the *colombianas*, he entitled it *"Inspiración"* because it "had nothing of Colombia in it!"

The guitarist Rafael Nogales (known to many in San Francisco, California, as the revered maestro of guitar instructor Mariano Córdoba) adds further clarification. Nogales, then only a youngster of twenty-two, began to play for Marchena in 1932. He said that just before that, in 1931, Marchena created the *colombianas* from a Basque song called *"El pájaro carpintero"* (The woodpecker).[2] Nogales claims to have played on the first recording of these *colombianas*, in June of 1931, but there are some discrepancies in his account. The first recorded version did not include the words to *"El pájaro carpintero,"* and the guitarist is listed as Paco Aguilera, not Nogales. It is true that, on the first recording, entitled *"Mi colombiana,"* Marchena says to the

[1] Cobo, p. 58
[2] Cobo, p. 57.

guitarist, "This is the first time that we record *colombianas*!"

Such was the popular success of this song that the recording company, Gramófono, wanted another one quickly. In 1932, Marchena recorded a second version, this time including the verse *"El pájaro carpintero"* and giving the song the generic title *"Colombianas."* A new style of song had been born. For this rendition, Ramón Montoya created the music for the guitar, basing it on a *rumba* rhythm with the Latin *aire* of the *guajiras*. To add that final "Marchena" touch, the singer had his friend, El Niño de la Flor, sing harmony on the recording—something unheard of in traditional flamenco.

Other singers wasted no time in jumping on the bandwagon. Hot on the heels of Marchena, La Niña de los Peines and guitarist Niño Ricardo recorded an upbeat version of the *colombianas* for the Regal Company in 1932. Cleverly avoiding any mention of *colombianas*, they gave the song the title *"Mi inspiración,"* hoping to take credit for creating something original. The Gramófono Company responded to the competition by backing Marchena and Montoya with orchestra in an elaborate version that would become the definitive model for all that followed. The verse would become a classic:

Quisiera, cariño mío,	I hope, my darling,
que tú nunca me olvidaras,	that you will never forget me,
que tus labios con los míos	that your lips and mine
en un beso se juntaran,	will be united in a kiss,
y que no hubiera en er mundo	and that there will be nobody
nadie que los separara!	in the world who will separate them!
Oye mi voz!	Hear my voice!
Oye mi voz, colombiana!	Hear my voice, Colombian woman![1]

Carmen Amaya would learn this *colombiana* and, many years later, sing and dance it in her programs. Her recording of the *colombianas* would be the inspiration for the revival of the *cante* in the 1970s and lead to its inclusion in the modern flamenco repertoire. As for the origin of the name *"colombianas"* and its connection with the country of that name, there is no record of an explanation by Pepe Marchena, nor is there any record of his having visited Colombia. It appears to have been a fortuitous and inspired choice of name, and a unique case in flamenco of one man spontaneously inventing what would become an entire *palo* or branch of *cante*.[2]

---

[1] Much of this information about the origin of the *colombianas* came from the book *Flamenco de Ida y Vuelta* by Romualdo Molina and Miguel Espín, published in Sevilla in 1992 by Guadalquivir S.I. Ediciones. The authors, in turn, quote information from an article by Antonio Hita Maldonado.

[2] There have been a number of artists associated with the introduction of new flamenco forms, but seldom were they the creators of those forms. La Niña de los Peines based her *bamberas* on traditional folk music. Chacón took his *caracoles* from El Granaíno and others, elaborating them and creating new words. Marchena's *fandangos* were only the final step in an evolution begun by others. Ramón Montoya's *rondeñas* originated with Miguel Borrull. Etc.

On July 22, 1933, just hours before Marchena was about to perform with his company in Sevilla, Manuel Torre "El Niño de Jerez" died in the Red Cross Hospital there. Pepe, who had attended to Manuel in his last days, would pay all the funeral expenses and look after the family. If Antonio Chacón's death had ended an era, the passing of Manuel Torre put a final exclamation point to that ending.

Chacón and Torre shared a common beginning. Both were born in the gypsy barrio of San Miguel in Jerez de la Frontera, within blocks of each other, although nine years apart. Both had gone to Cádiz to learn from the *cantaor* of legend, Enrique el Mellizo. After serving apprenticeships in Jerez, each had made a name for himself in Sevilla. But that's where the similarity ends. Manuel was an illiterate, extravagant gypsy, an inconsistent *cantaor* who, when he was on, moved his listeners with power, passion, subtlety of shading and unforgettable soulfulness and echo. He was also an introverted man who buried his insecurity under endless obsessions. Chacón, a *payo*, achieved status as an elegant and cultured gentleman and could sing well under almost any circumstances, although, according to many, not with the same passion as his gypsy counterpart.

Manuel Soto Loreto was born in 1878 into a family of field workers. He acquired the nickname *"Torre"* (Tower) from his father, Juan Torre, who stood over six feet tall. Manuel was slightly shorter at five feet eleven, but in a time when the average height of men was a little over five feet, he was a veritable giant. Surrounded by masters of gypsy *cante* in his family and among his neighbors, and living in a barrio of gypsy blacksmiths, Manuel could not help but absorb the important styles of the *cante jondo*, the most profound gypsy songs, especially the *siguiriyas* and the *martinetes* (songs of the blacksmiths). While serving in the military in Cádiz he fell under the spell of Enrique el Mellizo. It is said that he became so emotional on listening to the old man sing that he took a bite out of a drinking glass, and on another occasion tried to throw himself off a balcony. It is also likely that he absorbed some of Enrique's eccentricity and hypochondria.

El Mellizo is credited with being the first to sing the normally festive *tango* in a slower, more profound manner. Some believe he got the idea from Diego el Marrurro, a professional *cantaor* who lived in a small room off the patio of the Torre home in Jerez. Regarding these slow *tangos*, La Niña de los Peines said that they had been sung for years in her family, and she recorded them sometime between 1905 and 1910 with the guitar of Luis Molina. Entitled *"Tangos de la tontona,"* they were pure *tientos* as we know them today, both in melody and the rhythm of the guitar, and included the well-known verse that begins *"Eres tontita e inocente..."* When Antonio Chacón began to sing the slow *tangos*, he improved them further, making them even more profound, and after recording them as *tangos* in 1910 and 1913 he began to call them *tientos*, possibly after a line of verse that went, *"Me tiraste unos tientos..."*

(You tempted me…). Another important branch of flamenco had been created. But it was Manuel Torre who first brought this slow *tango* of El Mellizo and El Marrurro to the public of Sevilla when he made his debut in Café Novedades in 1901. There is no record of that performance, but the following year he appeared in the Filarmónico-Oriente Concert Hall, where he was billed as "Manuel Soto (el Niño de Torres)—Singer of *Tangos.*" Sharing the program with him was a classical Spanish dance group, a comic song and dance group from Cádiz called *"Las Ranas"* (The Frogs), and a *cuadro flamenco* that included the cream of flamenco artists of the late 1800s: Dancing were Salud Rodríguez and her sister Lola, Juana la Sordita (the Deaf One), Juana and Fernanda Antúnez, Pepa de Oro (the *milonga* singer), and Josefa Molina. Interestingly, the singers were all women—unusual in that male dominated world: La Sordita's sister, La Serrana, one of the real giants of the *cante* at that time, Rita Ortega, and María Avila. On guitar were Salud's brother, Joaquín Rodríguez, and Juan Habichuela.

Manuel Torre must have made quite an impression with his height, his dark good looks, and his very gypsy way of dressing in a dark suit of raw silk, a white shirt with a white silk scarf tied about his neck, and a gold watch chain dangling from his vest pocket. It is possible that he sang this early and well-known *tango*:

Amparo, por Dios, amparo!	Help me, for God's sake, help me!
El enfermo busca el alivio;	The sick man seeks relief;
yo lo busco y no lo hallo.	I look for it, but don't find it.

And then there was the voice. Manuel's singing has been described variously as bewitching, black, hair-raising, spine-chilling, hypnotic… He lacked the gravelly vocal quality known as *afillá* (after a gypsy named El Fillo) that is normally desired in flamenco singing, and neither did he employ the typical nasal sound or sing with a constricted throat. Yet he still managed to produce a very flamenco sound, with just enough roughness to appeal to aficionados of the *cante*. He was the first important *cantaor* to sing with an open throat and and full lungs, which gave him tremendous power. The strength and passion of his singing won over the gypsies, while, at the same time, his clear tones appealed to the non-gypsy general public and contributed to his rapid rise to celebrity. The singer Pericón de Cádiz said that, "You got that sound of his in your ear and it stayed with you for weeks!"

The great singer of *soleares* from Alcalá de Guadaira, Joaquín de la Paula, told Antonio Mairena about a fiesta in Sevilla around 1920, given by Felipe Murube for some Galician friends. Although Murube considered Manuel Torre a good friend and was crazy about his singing, he was fed up with singer's difficult nature and didn't invite him. Among the guests was La Argentinita's lover, Ignacio Sánchez Mejías, and the invited artists included Antonio Chacón, La Niña de los Peines and her brother Arturo, Joaquín de la

Paula, Fosforito, Niño Medina, the dancers La Macarrona and La Malena, and the guitarists Habichuela and Manolo de Huelva. In spite of these great artists, by six o'clock in the morning the Galicians were bored and told Murube they wanted to leave:

> Murube said, "I have to call *Majareta* [The Crazy One, referring to Torre].
> Manuel Torre arrived at ten o'clock. Murube gave him a hug, and after chastizing him for his excesses, made him sit down and drink three or four large glasses of wine. Then he went to him and said, "Sing for these gentlemen, who say they don't like flamenco and are going to leave."
> Manuel Torre directed himself to Habichuela, saying, "Play *por siguiriyas!*"
> And he began to sing. And he sang such that, after the second or third verse of *siguiriyas*, one of the Galicians became so emotional that he kicked over a table. They picked up the table and Manuel continued singing. Then it was Ignacio Sánchez Mejías who knocked over the table and ripped his shirt to shreds. It appeared that Manuel had electrified everybody there and most of them were crying in the corners. After he had finished, nobody else wanted to sing. And that is when Joaquín el de la Paula gave Manuel Torre the nickname *"Acabareuniones* [He who puts an end to the fiesta]."[1]

For the most part, Manuel Torre did not invent *cantes*, but interpreted existing *cantes* in such a way as to make them into something new and memorable. In that way he established a number of *cantes* in the flamenco repertoire, *cantes* that might have disappeared without his contribution. For years he was much in demand as a singer of *farrucas* and the *peteneras* of La Niña de los Peines. He made the *tarantas*, the songs of the miners in Eastern Andalucía, into something more gypsy and, in the process, led to the creation of the modern *tarantos* that is such an important element in the dance of today. It has been suggested that he learned the *tarantos* from Concha la Cartagenera or from one of his early loves, Pepita la Murciana. His famous verse certainly supports the idea that he learned from a woman:

Ay! Que dónde andará mi muchacho?	Ay! Where can my man be?
Ay! Hace tres días que yo no lo veo!	Ay! I haven't seen him for three days!
Dime dónde andará mi muchacho	Tell me where he might be,
si estará bebiendo vino,	whether he is out drinking wine,
o andará por ahí borracho,	or wandering around drunk,
o una mujerzuela me lo ha comprometío.	or some slut has made him betray me.

[1] Mairena, p. 73.

Years later, Carmen Amaya would be among the first to dance the *tarantos*. Niño Ricardo told of the night he first heard Manuel sing the *campanilleros*, a marginal flamenco song derived from religious songs: Ricardo and friends were drinking in a bar in Sevilla, probably in the late 1920s, and decided to bring Torre to sing for them. "Manuel came and said, 'Put it on three for me...' [referring to the *cejilla* or capo placement on the guitar] and he sang those *campanilleros*, inspired by genius, that made your hair stand on end. But it could just as easily have been the opposite—we could have spent the whole night waiting for *cante* while Manuel did nothing more than stare at his lighter or his watch, two of his obsessions!"[1] Torre was the creator of the flamenco *campanilleros* and for many years the only one to record them.

Manuel is not normally associated with the dance—he became famous very early as a *cantaor "p'alante,"* a singer in the front of the stage, solo. But it is not surprising that he would excel in singing for the dance, for he came from Jerez, probably began by singing for dancers, and was linked romantically for many years with the superb and temperamental dancer, Antonia "La Gamba." In an early recording, he sang some *alegrías* for dancing that are remarkably precise and rhythmic.

Torre never succumbed to the *ópera flamenca*. He was unique among important *cantaores* of the opera period in refusing to sing *cuplés*. He sang *fandangos* and recorded a few, but it is said that he didn't like them. One of his original and profoundly moving verses goes:

Una paloma blanca yo te traigo.	I bring you a white dove.
Yo fui al nido y la cojí.	I went to the nest and took her out.
Quedó su mare llorando	But her mother was left there crying
como yo lloré por ti.	like I cried over you,
La solté y salió volando.	so I let her go and off she flew.

Manuel's more than fifty recordings—none of which are said to represent his true *cante*, because he couldn't produce on demand in a studio—are predominently of gypsy *cantes*, especially the *siguiriyas* and *soleares*. Manuel Torre is considered by many to be the greatest singer of *siguiriyas* who has ever lived. The soulful *siguiriya*, primitive and raw, is the most difficult of *cantes*, nurtured and perfected in the bosom of gypsy families in Jerez and Cádiz, out of earshot of *payos*. In Sevilla's gypsy barrio of Triana, the great singers of *siguiriyas* and *martinetes*, the Pelaos and Cagadchos, would not sing in the presence of *payos*. But gradually, in the time of the *cafés cantantes*, barriers came down and the *siguiriyas* could be sung in mixed company—although it remained more of a *cante* for the privacy of the fiesta rather than for the café or theater.

Manuel Torre knew more styles of *siguiriyas* than any of his professional

---
[1] Caballero, p. 168.

contemporaries, with the possible exception of Antonio Chacón. Chacón, with his organized mind, meticulous attention to detail, and the knowledge gleaned from a far-ranging search for new *cantes* in his youth, could accurately reproduce a wide variety of styles. Early pioneers in the *cante*, El Planeta, Silverio, Curro Dulce, El Nitri, and El Fillo, all had their own way of singing the *siguiriyas*. Later, other *cantaores* created their own variations: In Cádiz, Enrique Ortega, María Borrico, El Viejo de la Isla, Francisco la Perla, and Enrique el Mellizo; in Jerez, Manuel Molina, Paco la Luz, Loco Mateo, El Marrurro, and Joaquín la Serna; in Triana (Sevilla), Frasco el Colorao and Cagancho. Chacón sang these *siguiriyas* in his early years, but as he matured, he realized that his tenor voice was not suited to this type of *cante* and he preferred to listen to others. He used to go often to listen to Manuel Torre. Antonio Mairena related one such occasion:

> Salvaoriyo de Jerez told me that one time Chacón became so excited listening to the singing of El Niño de Jerez that he threw his hat and outer wear onto the stage. This must have happened around 1908, in Café Novedades of Sevilla, where the two *fenómenos* were alternating performances, that is, one day Chacón and the next, Manuel Torre. On the nights when it wasn't his turn, Don Antonio Chacón usually rented a box seat where he appeared surrounded by his court of the faithful, among them, his friend Salvaoriyo. Salvaoriyo, like the majority of those who surrounded Chacón, lived somewhat at the singer's expense and always praised him and told everybody that Chacón sang better than Manuel Torre.
>
> Well, on one of those nights when Manuel Torre was singing, Chacón became so excited that he jumped to his feet, yelling out in praise of the gypsy, and he went and threw onto the stage his hat, his cane, his cape, and who knows what else. Salvaoriyo, feeling he was being made to look like a fool because he always attacked Manuel and defended Chacón, threw his jacket over the singer and begged him to cease his outburst, saying that everybody was looking at them. But Chacón continued, as if beyond control, encouraging and cheering Manuel Torre until, at one point, he turned to the persistent Salvaoriyo and shouted, "Go to shit, *compadre!*"[1]

Another time, after an all night fiesta in Madrid, Chacón called to Sevilla for Manuel. Twelve hours later, when the singer arrived, the fiesta was still going. Torre downed two large glasses of wine and launched into a *taranta* that had the inebriated flamencos ripping their clothes, breaking bottles over their heads, and attempting to jump out the window.

[1] Mairena, p. 71.

The great respect that Chacón felt for Torre's *cante* is evident in the following account:

> They say that one day Manuel Torre, Don Antonio Chacón, and the brilliant guitarist Don Ramón Montoya were contracted for a flamenco *juerga*. Chacón sang with his natural ability and mastery. Montoya accompanied with his characteristic brilliance. But Manuel Torre was not in the mood and could only articulate this or that reason for being out of sorts. The hour arrived to collect their fees and Don Antonio, who was always the head of the group, was in charge. "For Montoya," he said, "twenty-five *pesetas*, and for Manuel and me, fifty *pesetas* each."
>
> "It seems fair to us," objected one of the *juerguistas*, "that you and Montoya should collect the agreed-upon amount, and even more. But Manuel Torre has not sung during the entire fiesta!"
>
> "And if he had sung?" pronounced Don Antonio. And with that the matter was closed.[1]

Like Chacón, Manuel Torre knew many forms of the *siguiriyas*, but with his spontaneous, impassioned, and anarchistic approach to the *cante*, he imposed his own style on them, shortening them and eliminating many of their complexities. In the process, he made them more accessible to the listener, more powerful and emotional, and easier for the next generation of *cantaores* to sing. Torre created no *siguiriyas* of his own, but some of his interpretations became so unique that they are are known today as *siguiriyas de Manuel Torre*. The best-known of these occurred spontaneously when Manuel mixed melodies from Curro Dulce and Cagancho of Triana and sang the powerful verse:

Era un día señalaíto	It was the Saint's Day
de Santiago y Santa Ana	of Santiago and Santa Ana
ay, ay, ayyy…	ay, ay, ayyy…
de Santiago y Santa Ana	of Santiago and Santa Ana
ay,ay, ayyy…	ay, ay, ayyy…
Le rogué yo a Dios que	I begged God to
aliviara las ducas	alleviate the suffering
al la mare de mi corazón.	of the mother of my heart.

Flamencologist Donn Pohren has written that this *siguiriya* was created in 1930, at a benefit performance for the ailing guitarist, Currito de la Jeroma. It was the eve of the Saint's days of Santiago and Santa Ana and Manuel had not been expected to sing, but he had given in to the insistence of the crowd and created the famous verse on the spot.[2]

This type of *cante* would not endear a *cantaor* to the general public in the

---

[1] Galindo, Pedro Camacho, *Los Payos también Cantan Flamenco*. Edidiciones Demófilo, Madrid. 1977. p. 128.
[2] Pohren, Donn, "La Alameda de Hercules." *Flamenco International*, Vol 1, No 1, January-March 1998.

age of the *fandango*. It was Manuel's *farrucas, malagueñas, tarantas, tangos, saetas*, and *peteneras*[1] that appeased the public and kept him working. But it was in private fiestas, where he could sing the *cante jondo*, that he established the reputation among flamencos that would make him a legend. And that reputation involved more than just his singing. Gypsies called Torre *"majareta"* (crazy). Chacón would say to him, *"Majareta*, when you sing you are like Castelar [a politician known for his oratory] when he speaks!" Torre masked his insecurities under a crippling array of obsessions. He had been a womanizer since a very young age. Oral tradition says that he had a serious affair with La Niña de los Peines before he became really famous and taught her a great deal of *cante*. His long relationship with the fiery *bailaora* from Sevilla, La Gamba, resulted in two of his known children. Later, he would father five more children with a second "wife," María Soto. The *cantaor* Antonio Mairena described the effect Manuel could have on women:

> Manuel Torre knew that his *cante* produced emotion in certain people, especially foreigners or those who knew little about the *cante*, who were there just to satisfy someone else. He had a magnetism in his voice that penetrated to one's insides and made them tremble, so that a person never forgot that unmistakable echo. Manuel used to focus on those people, especially if they were women, and might say to someone near him, "Watch and you will see how I make her cry!" And even if the woman had said that she didn't like the *cante* and appeared to be cold and indifferent, he would soon have her sobbing.[2]

Manuel functioned on animal instinct. He never learned how behave in society, how to be courteous or follow social customs. Yet he could be friendly and entertaining with his unique and often naive wit. In spite of not knowing how to read or write, he had a creative ability that resulted in many beautiful verses, often created on the spot. But it was his whims and compulsions that caused problems for those around him and cost him a great deal of money. He had an absolute mania for pocket watches and cigarette lighters. And nothing could come between him and the fighting cocks and greyhounds that usually shared his living quarters. Once, when interrupted while working with his roosters at home, he received a message asking him to come to the home of a duke to sing. He responded, "Your boss can be all the duke he wants, but my hounds and roosters come before him...and before the king!"[3]

Fernando de Triana spoke about Manuel and his donkeys in a 1933 inter-

---
[1] The gypsy superstition which held that performing the *petenera* brings bad luck did not exist at that time. Some of the most important interpreters were gypsies, including Manuel Torre (who was extremely superstitious) and La Niña de los Peines.

[2] Mairena, p. 75.

[3] Caballero, Angel A., p. 164.

view:

> His fondness for dogs and English roosters was his weakness. As soon as somebody told him that, in such and such a place, there was a good dog or a couple of roosters, he would get on his donkey, gypsy style (without a saddle, sitting over the hind legs) and he would go and pay whatever they asked for it. Now, in his dealings, he always preferred a trade. If he were going to buy a dog, he would take another and make the trade with money on top of it. The same thing would happened with donkeys and roosters. I recall one time when a *señorito* gave him a donkey that was worth at least three thousand *pesetas*, a magnificent specimen. He had barely arrived in his barrio, riding his precious donkey, when the dealers and go-betweens, who knew of his weakness, traded him for an inferior one, but a small one, the kind he liked. His brother didn't like the exchange and asked him very seriously, "Why did you trade it?" Manuel answered, "Because falls are shorter from this one!" And off went Manuel Torre on his small donkey, dragging his feet on the ground, as pleased as a horseman in the fair.[1]

Money meant little to Manuel. If conditions weren't to his liking, he wouldn't, or couldn't, sing well or at all. The great guitarist from Jerez, Javier Molina, describes one incident with Torre:

> They contracted us for a week in Huelva, and when we arrived, we saw that we were announced in very large letters. The night of our debut, the place was completely filled. We went out for the first number and my man sang like he was being condemned to jail. The people left speaking very badly of the singer. For the second show the audience had even less enthusiasm, and the next day was worse, and for six days it got worse each time.
>
> The last day of the contract arrives, and I have to say that he found himself completely hoarse, but he felt fine by the night. The boss had taken me aside to tell me, "Javier, I will pay you all the money I owe the singer, provided that he doesn't sing again!" But, as I said before, he felt good, with the voice very clear. And I, with sixty-four years as an artist, tell you that I have never heard better singing in my life. The boss of the place, after seeing everthing turn out so well, said to me, "What a shame it didn't begin like this!" The very scant audience made him sing again and again. The boss went crazy with enthusiasm for us and sent a case of González Byass wine up to the stage.
>
> And so, that was the way of Manuel Torre. He was the singer of

[1] Díaz, Emilio Jiménez, "Manuel Torre: On the Centennial of his Birth." *Nueva Andalucía,* July 21, 1978.

the *cante gitano* who has satisfied me the most.[1]

This was not an isolated incident, for those who knew Manuel have related many similar accounts. The singer was equally unpredictable in private fiestas. He might make an expectant group of aficionados wait through an entire night while he talked about the dogs he had brought with him or wandered in the garden, and not sing until dawn, or leave without singing at all. Walter Starkie, the student of gypsy lore and part-time gypsy himself, gave a colorful account of a typical night with Manuel Torre:

> He was a tall, gaunt figure of a man, with a bronzed face and flashing eyes. He had jet black hair, but with one white lock in the front. Capricious and moody, he would put guests off by the hour. Others would allow him to boast that his greyhounds were the best in the world. Still he would sit motionless, impervious to all tricks. The host would taunt him, begging him to sing *fandangos*, a form that Manuel despised as modern and degenerate. He would reply scornfully, *"Eso pa mi está en inglé!"* [That song is English to me!], that is, incomprehensible to him. At last, as the light of dawn appeared and guests were thinking of leaving, the other singers exhausted, Torre would begin tapping with his short style-stick, beads of perspiration would appear on his brow, and his copper face would glow with an inner demon. He would finally be possessed by the *duende* for which he had been waiting all evening. Then he would burst into the *siguiriya*, with its everlasting pessimism and tragic sense of life.[2]

Diego del Gastor called Manuel the greatest *cantaor* of all times:

> It was necessary to invite several singers to a *juerga* [fiesta] with him because, if he came at all, in the middle of it he might walk out and never come back, or he might just sit at the bar and drink all night. But the people at the *juerga* used to put up with it and waited for him to sing because he was Manuel Torre, and when it happened you never heard anything like it. And maybe then at six in the morning he would suddenly come in with a strange look, his face agitated. He would loosen his shirt collar—that was the signal—dash off his hat and stand there like a mountain in the middle of the room. *Put it on the fourth*, he would say to the guitarist. *I'm going to sing siguiriya*. Then he would sing one or two and everybody would cry and go on their knees. You couldn't take it. It was too intense. *Era argo bárbaro!* (It was barbaric, tremendous!)[3]

---

[1]Molina, Javier, *Javier Molina: Jerezano y Tocaor.* Edited by Augusto Butler. Jerez de la Frontera. 1964.
[2]Starkie, Walter. This account has been reproduced many times by the author and others. I believe it originated in *In Sara's Tents*, published in Munich in 1957.
[3]George, David, *The Flamenco Guitar.* p. 69.

People tried all kinds of tricks to get Manuel to sing. Donn Pohren writes that there was a half-crazy gypsy from Utrera named Araujo who imitated Manuel Torre badly. Torre would ask for Araujo to be invited to fiestas because the gypsy was so shameless that he would imitate Manuel in his presence, until Manuel could take it no longer and interrupted him, saying, "That's not how it goes, Araujo, it's like this!" And then Torre would launch into the *cante* as only he could do it.[1] In a fiesta thrown by the bullfighter Juan Bemonte, one of the frustrated *señoritos* (wealthy gentlemen) shot out a light bulb with a pistol, then pointed the pistol at Torre's chest and said, "Now let's see whether you sing well today or not!"[2]

One who knew how to deal with Manuel was the matador Ignacio Sánchez Mejías. Ignacio befriended the *cantaor* and looked after him financially, especially toward the end of his life. Torre was a frequent guest at Ignacio's ranch in Sevilla, a gathering place for the circle of poets that included Ignacio, Fernando Villalón, a bull breeder who dreamed of creating a bull with green eyes, the poet Rafael Alberti, who said that, although Torre could neither read nor write, his conciousness as a *cantaor* was perfect," and Federico García Lorca, who called Torre the "man with the most culture in his blood." Sánchez Mejías, being a good aficionado of the *cante*, knew better than to ask Manuel to sing. When the singer arrived, he gave him *aguardiente* (anis brandy, his favorite drink) or whatever he wanted, gave him a seat, and left him alone. Others would sing through the night until Manuel, dying to sing, would say to Ignacio, *"Hombre,* Ignacio, aren't you going to let me sing at least once? And Ignacio, *"Bueno, hombre,* if you want to sing, sing!" And Manuel would come out singing like a wild animal, crazy to sing, eating everybody alive![3]

Some of Torre's close friends have defended him, and it is only fair to point out that Manuel had a long and profitable career—something that would have been impossible if he were unfailingly difficult and irresponsible. Antonio Mairena's brother, Curro, when asked if Manuel Torre was crazy, responded, "Only someone who didn't know him would say that, because every time I heard him he was like a clock, and with more *duendes* than anyone!"

In those fiestas with the poets, Manuel would talk about his superstitious belief in *duendes*, little ghosts that inhabited homes and barns. He felt that those *duendes* were his source of inspiration, and he had to wait for them to possess him before he could sing. García Lorca latched on to the idea and developed his theory of *duende*. He would debate the subject with friends by the hour. The guitarist Manolo de Huelva once said, "Lorca used to come by

---

[1] Pohren, Donn, p. 313.

[2] Blas Vega, José and Fernando Quiñones, *"Toros y arte flamenco,"* in *Los Toros,* by José María de Cossio and Antonio Díaz-Cañabate. Espasa-Calpe, S.A., Madrid. 1982. p. 715.

[3] Ortiz Nuevo, *Las Mil y Una Historias de Pericón de Cádiz,* p. 254.

the house...and that fellow De Falla. They used to talk about *duende* and gypsies and all kinds of things. I never paid much attention... Lorca invented the term. He disregarded its true meaning and tried to apply it to flamenco. Lorca knew nothing about flamenco. He was a poet and I was a guitarist and we were friends. We understood each other. He was a good friend. He had his profession and I had mine and we got along. But when he wrote about *duende*, that was a little too much. Do you know what *duendes* really are? They are the name in Andalucía for those mischievous creatures who haunt a farm house. If the farmer has so much trouble that he has to move out, he blames it on the *duendes*."[1]

Manuel Torre fed off the discussions of those intellectuals. They validated his belief and gave it substance, and he became even more obsessive and difficult. The concept of *duende*, which had not existed in flamenco previously, caught on and came to signify that spark of inspiration in flamenco that allows a performer to go beyond his usual capacity, as if possessed, and transmit his passion to spectators in a profoundly felt manner.

At age fifty, Manuel retreated more and more into the shell of his compulsive behavior. Yet he still performed on occasion. In 1929, he appeared in at least one *varieté* in Madrid, and later that year toured with Manolo Caracol's *ópera flamenca* company. In Granada he was announced as "The maestro of maestros (the only one that nobody has been able to imitate), Manuel Torres (Niño de Jerez), THE AUTHENTIC ONE, 30 years of continuous success at the pinnacle of the *cante*; teacher of two generations of *cantaores*; The King of the *Cante Gitano*."

Antonio Mairena described an appearance in 1930. Antonio, then twenty-one, went to Sevilla to convince Torre to sing with him in a movie house in his hometown. He found the singer in the doorway of his humble home, with his donkey and English fighting roosters. After a few drinks in a local bar, Manuel agreed to sing for a fee of 150 *pesetas*—twenty to be paid in advance for the journey he would make on the back roads with his donkey and greyhounds. Mairena wrote:

> And that is how it was. On the afternoon of the indicated day, Manuel Torre entered Mairena with his little donkey and his greyhounds, accompanied by his oldest son, Tomás. A little later the show began. Since it would be a short show, he and I would sing two times each and, according to logic and the custom in these cases, I would sing first. Since what I sang came from his school of *cante*, as well as that of Joaquin de la Paula, and since I found myself in my home town surrounded by my people, I abused my innocence and dared to sing *por soleá* and *siguiriya*, while Manuel Torre encouraged me from behind the curtain. When I finished and it was his turn, he said to me, "*Finito*, bring me a big glass of

[1] George, David, The Flamenco Guitar. Society of Spanish Studies, Madrid. 1969. p. 109.

aguardiente!" (He called me *Finito* because I was so thin.) Manuel sat down to sing, the glass of *aguardiente* at his side...He had no sooner begun to warm up with the *medias granaínas* than the people, who filled the house completely, rose to their feet as if by magic—and they stayed that way the whole time Manuel was singing. From the *medias granaínas* he followed with the *soleá* of Enrique el Mellizo and of La Serneta. We all listened, electrified by that genius. To finish, he sang *por siguiriya*: "*A clavel y canela*," the *cante* of Joaquín la Serna, that of Diego el Marrurro, the "*Santiago y Santa Ana*" of Curro Dulce, and the *cabales* of Silverio. The audience threw their chairs and tore their shirts...I had never in my life heard anything like it, nor have I since.

When Manuel had finished, I had to go out to sing again, because there still remained the second half. I went out on stage. The audience waited for me to begin singing, but my artistic conscience stopped me and made me say, "Distinguished public. After the performance of Manuel Torre, it is impossible to sing again. The show is over!"[1]

But *Acabareuniones*, "He who puts an end to the gathering," was about to have his own fiesta ended by the tuberculosis that had been gradually stealing his vigor. In his last years, he spit up blood when he sang, and during the last eight months of his life, in 1933, he alternated between the Red Cross Hospital and the tiny room on Amapola Street that he shared with his daughters and his animals. A newspaper writer of the time wrote: "Lately, his gifted throat broken by the speechlessness of tuberculosis, he still used to make a ghostly appearance in the Europa [bar] where he saw so many dawns, and he never asked for anything, nor accepted anything from anyone."[2]

It is said that Ignacio Sánchez Mejías paid his medical expenses and visited him, but in this time of need, Manuel's eccentricities had cost him the two things he needed most—money and the many friends he hadn't known how to keep. Forty years after Manuel Torre's death, his daughters shared their memories of his last days:

"I was around eight years old," says María, "and Amparo five when my father died. I remember he would go to a corner of the coal shop and sit me on his knee, always humming a song. The greyhounds were his great obsession and he wouldn't allow anybody to touch them. I remember the last two he had, Andújar and Amapola, the best of his life and to which he gave very special pampering. Many times he would sit us on his knees so we would

---

[1] Mairena, p. 68.
[2] Galerín, *El Liberal*, Sevilla. August 9, 1933.

not touch them or play with them."

"Besides," adds Amparo, "we remember another habit he had when somebody came looking for him. 'Manuel,' we would say, 'there is a *señorito* looking for you.' And the first thing he would say was, 'Who is with him? What kind of wine is he drinking? What kind of cigarette does he smoke? What is he wearing?' And, based on what we told him, he knew beforehand who was waiting for him. If the person was of his pleasing, he would go. If not, he would stay in the little yard with his dogs and roosters, or stay sitting in his chair.

"At that time he was making a lot of money, but since he was a very strange man, he spent everything. He could have earned a lot more, but he would not sing until his money was gone, or if he enjoyed very much the friends he was with at the moment. The one anecdote we remember most about him took place when we were with him on the Calle de la Feria and he was carrying our sister Gabriela, the youngest one, in his arms. Since she would not stop crying, he started to sing a lullaby, and it was such a lullaby that he stopped the traffic of horse-drawn carriages and the few motorized cars that there were, and the whole street burst into an ovation...

"He died in his chair. At that time we girls were staying at the Red Cross of Capuchinos [charity hospital], but only in the morning, because he always wanted us to all sleep under the same roof. One day, when we arrived, we heard some yelling and running and somebody's voice telling us, 'Father is dead!' We were not allowed to see him. Later his brother, Pepe, came and got us. Since he could not support both his children and us, he took us, walking, to our mother in Utrera.

[After Manuel's death, the only one to help us was] "...a man who had a big heart and who organized a gigantic festival where much money was collected for our upkeep during the time we were with our uncle. That man was Pepe Marchena. Aside from him, nobody remembered Manuel Torre, as much as they said they loved him!"[1]

So, the new flamenco bade farewell to the old. Pepe Marchena assisted Manuel Torre in his last days, paid for his burial, and took care of his family. And in Barcelona, Carmen Amaya prepared to leave her old life and embark on a trip into the unknown.

---

[1] Rújula, Angel Marín, "Manuel Torre: A Interview with his Daughters." *Nueva Andalucía*, September 21, 1978.

Niño Sabicas with the *cupletista* Pepita Lláser, c. 1930.

CHAPTER FIVE

SABICAS

Barcelona, early 1933. The critic Sebastián Gasch wrote:

They told us that we were going to see the best flamenco *cuadro* on the peninsula. It may have been just that six months ago. Now, on the other hand, we don't dare to affirm that claim. The group in the Turó is, in effect, nothing more than the alumni of that terrific *cuadro flamenco* of the Bar de Manquet that we have spoken about on these pages. That amazing Gato who had no rival in the *farruca*, and that marvelous Romerito, queen of the *alegrías* and *sevillanas*, have been substituted by the insignificant Encarna and the gray Tobalo. In addition, we are sorry to have to report a considerable decline in the abilities of the tiny Carmen Amaya (La Capitana). Nothing, or almost nothing, remains of that energetic conviction in her facial expression, the amazing gyrations of her hips, that vigour and wild passion that surprised us with unexpected movements. They are ruining this young girl for us. Eager to make a profit, they make her perform three times each night: in the Bar de Manquet, in the Eden, and in Villa Rosa. These excesses fatally drain even the most robust constitution. And they are watering down her art. They make her sing "Manolo Reyes" and force her to use Russian, Negro, and Cuban steps in her dances, giving us a hybrid concoction. Without reserves and utterly exhausted, if this continues for long, soon there will be no Carmencita. But we don't want to jump to conclusions. We don't know if her father, El Chino, believing that she has to perform for an audience made up of pseudo-aristocrats, has imposed on her these concessions to popular taste. It has been some time since we have seen her work. We will withhold final judgement until after we have seen her in a warmer and purer atmosphere than that of the Turó.[1]

El Chino could see that the career of his young prodigy was stagnating.

[1] Gasch, Sebastián, *"Dos Mundos." El Mirador,* March 3, 1933. Barcelona

She seemed to be stuck in the cabarets of Barcelona. No longer a child, Carmen had to compete with the sensuous and coquetish beauties favored by the public. Her boyish figure and serious demeanor did not appeal to the tourists who paid to view the gyrations of seductive women. According to biographer Francisco Hidalgo Gómez, El Chino entertained the idea of having his daughter study dance in an academy in order to expand her possibilities, but Vicente Escudero and Sebastián Gasch talked him out of it. Feeling uncertain about the future, El Chino jumped at a suggestion from a young man working in the Villa Rosa, a gangly youth with enormous ears and an even larger reputation as a guitarist.

Agustín Castellón Campos came into the world on an unrecorded and unremembered date in 1912. "I was born in Pamplona," he says, "in northern Spain. Many of the people there regarded flamenco as that disreputable noise from the South. But I am a gypsy, and for the gypsies this is our music. My father played a little, and when I was five years old, I picked up the guitar, just to make noise. By the time I was eight, I had an audience."[1]

In spite of growing up in the north of Spain, Agustín had been surrounded by the flamenco atmosphere of his family. The facts of his early life are somewhat shrouded in mystery, both because he seemed to delight in embellishing accounts that he gave later in life and in confusing interviewers with conflicting versions. He also remained reluctant to grant interviews and did so on few occasions. In the most extensive of these, conceded to Mona Molarsky in New York shortly before his death in 1990, Agustín opened up for the first time.[2] He revealed that his father had been born in Zaragoza. "He was a good person, so nice that all the artists used to kiss and hug him. What he liked the most was tobacco...He always carried two packs of cigarettes, already rolled. He used to make them with a little machine. He spent all of his time giving cigarettes away. That is what he liked to do."

On another occasion, he said, "My father was never a great guitarist, but he liked it very much. I used to watch him and loved the way he played. An uncle of mine, who was not a guitarist but who knew a few positions, took the trouble to show them to me, and thus, my uncle became my first and only teacher. That was not enough for me. In about a week, I was strumming a small guitar they bought for me. I played tunes that I picked up from blind men in the streets. There I got started with flamenco and, according to people, I had some aptitude for this sort of thing, and for that reason I have been able to do something with the guitar, perhaps more than anyone else."[3]

The Castellón family did not live among gypsies in Pamplona. "After I was baptized, my parents bought a little house on Peralta Street. We lived

---

[1] Ericson, Raymond, "Sabicas in New York," *The New York Times*, October 19, 1979

[2] Agustín said to Mona: "You have succeeded in doing what no one else has done. You have brought me here to this interview. I would not have done it, even if forced to. I have done it gladly for you. I always do the things that I like, or I do not do them. I have been happy with you."

[3] Chileno, El Niño, *"Conversaciones con Sabicas." Jaleo: Vol IV No.8*, April, 1981

there for a few years...The gypsies that did live there, even though we were not very close, we used to see each other occasionally...We had a store. We used to sell fabrics for clothing..."[1]

Agustín acquired a nickname at a very early age. He was quite fond of the broad green stringbeans called *habas* in Spanish, and he carried them about in his pocket and ate them uncooked. When his mother returned from the market, the boy had the habit of begging for *las habicas*, which became in his childish lisp, *laS'abicas*. His family began to call him *Sabicas*.

Attempting to recall when he first began to play, Sabicas reflected, "I must have been very young. It was so many years ago. But I guess I picked up the guitar and put it down immediately, because it was too big for me. At that time I used to play just on the top part of the guitar, the fingerboard...I'm sure no one was able to sleep!"[2]

In 1935, Fernando de Triana published the story of Sabicas' early life, as the guitarist had related it to him:

> This child prodigy, as I believe they have called him since he first began to show his artistic abilities, is the unique case in the difficult art of the guitar. At five years of age he first conceived of the laborious apprenticeship—and it was even more unusual that this should happen in Pamplona, the city of his birth, where, unfortunately for Sabicas, there was no teacher of flamenco to show him the first *compases* of the *toque*, which was what pleased him the most from what he heard on the singing machine [record player].
>
> In front of Sabicas' house lived a man who used to spend hours and hours playing the guitar, but he always played the same thing. And as many hours as the man spent playing, the same amount of hours Sabicas spent listening—to the extent that the boy memorized everything his neighbor had more or less executed. "If I had a guitar," he would say, "I would play all of that and more!"
>
> One day, he went downtown with his parents to spend the afternoon in a cafe. Upon passing a music store, the boy spotted a tiny guitar, complete with six strings, among the instruments in the window. It was priced at seventeen *pesetas*. Sabicas begged his parents to buy him the tiny instrument, but since they thought the price was excessive for a toy, they tried to disuade him from his foolishness. Little Sabicas reached the point of saying that he would not leave until they bought him the guitar, at the same time promising that it wasn't for play, but to learn the many things he had memorized. The parents consulted, and what had to happen, happened. "Why upset him! Let's buy it for him!" They went in and acquired the diminutive instrument, which for the aspiring

[1] Molarsky interview
[2] Molarsky interview

guitarist represented a world of dreams. Finding himself in possession of the desired guitar, the boy lost his wish to go to the cafe, and he asked his mother for the key to the house, promising that he would allow nobody in. After he succeeded in his request, he headed off alone, while his parents continued on to the cafe for the afternoon. What a surprise when the parents returned home to find that Sabicas was getting sounds from the guitar that resembled the popular melody, *"La banderita española!"* By himself, he had learned to tune the guitar! In light of his boundless *afición*, the parents bought him a record player that he could play at slow speed [easy to do with the old wind-up players] and thereby begin to copy whatever he heard.

When Sabicas was seven, the military in Pamplona organized a fiesta in conjunction with a swearing-in ceremony in the Ballare Theater. A captain, whom people said could sing flamenco very well, would take part. But they ran into a difficulty—there was no one in Pamplona who could accompany him on the guitar. Somebody said there was a young boy, the son of a friend who played very well, so a commision set off to ask the father's permission for little Sabicas to take part in the festival as a guitarist. Only with great effort did they achieve their desired end—the parents felt that the boy would be frightened by the audience and wouldn't produce a single note that would fit with the *cante*. But it was just the opposite: whenever the captain sang that which he had learned from records, that which Sabicas had memorized, the number came out very well, and Sabicas, after receiving a fine gift, was congratulated by all those present, who had been enchanted.

This brilliant performance assured the parents of the diminutive guitarist that he was on the right road to becoming an artist, and they began to do whatever was necessary to help him…[1]

Sabicas did attend school—probably briefly. He said that he went to a religious school of the Marian Order when he was four or five.[2] At age eight, his mother thought that he should take lessons. Sabicas recalled, "She took me to the best teacher in Pamplona, and he asked me to play something. I did a scale, and the teacher became furious. He accused my mother of pulling his leg and threw us out of the house!" Sabicas does not make it clear why the teacher became so enraged. Did the man feel insulted to be asked to teach a youngster who played so badly? Or was he intimidated by the boy's skill? We can suspect the latter, for it is unlikely that a teacher would be angered by a youngster who played badly, and Sabicas would have been well on the

[1] Triana, Fernando de, p. 216
[2] Molarsky interview

way to possessing the technique that would surprise the flamencos of Madrid only a couple of years later.

Sabicas' parents encouraged him and gave him special privileges. He stayed up all night playing his guitar, slept late, and didn't have to have to help out in his father's store. "I used to wake up very late, pick up my guitar, and that is all I did!"[1] Sabicas admits to having been pampered to the end by his mother. She waited on him hand and foot. "My mother, poor dear, would say to me, 'Please, go to bed, it is already three o'clock in the morning!' I would reply, 'Yes, yes, Mama!' while still going *tram, tram, tram*, on the guitar. I loved it then and continued to do so all my life...When I was eight or nine years old [the general consensus is that he made his debut in Madrid in 1922, when he was ten], I went to Madrid with views toward becoming a professional artist. I took my entire family with me. I always took my father and brothers everywhere I went."[2]

It is very likely that Sabicas has been less than forthright when speaking of his relationship with his father. He always claimed to have learned on his own, and he said that he took his family with him to Madrid. It is more likely that a gypsy father would seek to exploit a young child's abilities and take him to Madrid for financial gain. A ten-year-old boy doesn't take his family anywhere. The father would certainly have guided the boy's early career. Guitarist Gabriel Ruiz has described being in Los Gabrieles with Sabicas and his father, also named Agustín, as well as Sabicas' younger brother "Dieguico."

An isolated comment by the blind singer La Niña de la Puebla adds credence to the idea that the senior Agustín may have played more guitar than his son ever let on. Dolores Jiménez, "La Niña de la Puebla," built her career on a single *cante*, the *campanilleros*. About that, she said, "I listened to the *campanilleros* of Manuel Torre, my father wrote a new lyric, and later I made my own creation. I know that Manuel Torre was first, as I have said many times, but he sang them his way, while I made a creation that became so popular and famous that I owe it everything—it made me an international figure. And don't believe that I am exaggerating. It was a revolution..." Concerning Sabicas, she said, "I met him when I first came to Madrid [1932]. His father and he did many tours with me—they were both guitarists..."[3]

According to Fernando de Triana, Sabicas opened in Madrid's El Dorado Theater at age ten, accompanying the well-known *cupletista* La Chelito and playing solos. The youngster performed in short pants and was an over-

---
[1] Molarsky interview.
[2] Chileno, El Niño, p. 6.
[3] Martín, Manuel Martín, "*La Niña de la Puebla: dulzura y luz del cante.*" *Candil No. 58*. July-August 1988. Jaén. p. 26

whelming success. "They made so much noise that I thought they were going to hit me!" Very early on, Sabicas recalled, "I won an award in the Teatro Novedades, a very beautiful theater in Madrid, and that is how I got started." In another interview, Sabicas said that he won first prize in a flamenco contest in the city's Monumental Cinema when he was eleven.[1]

It wasn't long before Sabicas could be found hanging out with the flamencos in the Villa Rosa and Los Gabrieles. His acceptance into the flamenco world of Madrid was truly extraordinary. It was not without just cause that, early in his career, he earned the nickname *"El Fenómeno"* (The Phenomenon). It is almost impossible for a person to learn flamenco in isolation, in a non-flamenco city like Pamplona, much less for a child with no teacher. Yet, no sooner had Sabicas arrived in Madrid than he began to accompany one of the best known *cupletistas* of the time, and within a couple of years he was working regularly, despite his youth. Between the ages of twelve and twenty-four he toured Spain as accompanist for La Niña de la Puebla (for the better part of a year), La Niña de los Peines, José Cepero, Estrellita Castro, and many other top figures in the *cante*. There is very little record of his work, but in 1925, at age thirteen, Niño Sabicas accompanied El Niño de Tetuán in the Teatro Romea. El Niño de Tetuán (Tetuán is a barrio in Madrid) was a one-man show, singing, dancing, juggling, and doing comedy. From the Romea, the two went to the Teatro Pavón to work alongside La Argentinita. For Sabicas to accomplish all of this so quickly, his talent and gift for creating music on the guitar had to be truly phenomenal.

Speaking of those who had inspired him during his eary development, Sabicas said, "There were two guitarists whom I enjoyed very much. They were the absolute best there was at that time: Ramón Montoya and El Niño de Huelva. One in the classical flamenco, the other in the gypsy form. I loved listening to them, their recordings. I used to say to myself, 'If only I could play like that!' I admired them very much. I listened, but I never copied from them. Ever since I started playing, I always did it my own way. I played whatever sounded right to me, and it seems that it also sounded right to others. Thus, I stayed with my own things and continued to study guitar. The guitar is, of course, very fickle, and you must be with it all the time, as much as you can, and even that is not enough. Sometimes, after you have been practicing a certain piece for hours, you still make mistakes. 'Why am I making a mistake?' you ask yourself. 'My fingers are all right. Why?' I have always found the guitar to be very difficult."[2]

Sabicas always claimed to be completely self-taught. With irrefutable gypsy logic, he said, "I never had a teacher in my life. The proof of that is the fact that I have a brother to whom I have never been able to teach a single melody. I don't know how to teach and therefore have never given

---
[1]Ericson, Raymond, "Sabicas in New York." The New York Times, October 19, 1979.
[2]Chileno, El Niño, p. 5.

lessons, because nobody ever showed me anything."[1]

In spite of Sabicas' claims to the contrary, it is clear that he took a lot from the guitarists around him, especially Ramón Montoya and Manolo de Huelva. Much of Sabicas' left-hand approach to the guitar and the use of lyrical arpeggios and tremolos can be traced to Montoya, while his thumbwork and many melodic passages are clearly taken more or less directly from Manolo de Huelva. According to Sabicas, "The one who created the most was Ramón Montoya. He was the best guitarist of his time. Nevertheless, not everything he played was his. He took some sixty or seventy percent from others and he contributed twenty or thirty percent of his own. For sure, he gave it his own *gracia*, his *sello* [stamp, personal style], his way of doing the arpeggio and tremolo, his *gusto*. His arpeggios and tremolos were marvelous. The man did not play in the pure gypsy style, but he did play very well and he was, of course, the best of his time."[2]

In discussing his early influences, Sabicas brought up the most enigmatic guitarist in flamenco's history—Manolo de Huelva. Manolo and Ramón Montoya are often mentioned in the same sentence, and the two are usually compared and contrasted, representing two parallel schools of guitar playing. Montoya was pure gypsy, while the man from Huelva had not a drop of gypsy blood. The irony is that the gypsy, Ramón, played a melodic, *payo* style of guitar that employed flowery adornments and a free rhythm to create a reposed and ornate music. He teamed up with the two top *payo singers* of the day, Antonio Chacón and the troubador, Pepe Marchena. Manolo de Huelva, on the other hand, came to represent the epitome of the hard driving, rhythmic gypsy style, and he was most often associated with the dark and unpredictable gypsy *cantaor*, Manuel Torre.

The two men couldn't have been more dissimilar. Ramón was extroverted, egotistical, and exhibitionistic. On at least one occasion, he left La Niña de los Peines with her mouth hanging open while he brought the crowd to its feet to applaud his private recital between the verses of her song. Manolo, introverted and reserved, always subjugated his guitar to the *cante*. Qualities they had in common included a great love for their music, pride in their abilities, a gift for composing music, and an elegant and gentlemanly demeanor that earned them the respect of all who knew them.

Manolo de Huelva, intelligent and handsome, with the presence of a school teacher, created a guitar style that influenced all guitarists who came after him, yet he left no school of playing. He was very secretive about his art and therefore did very little recording, refused to teach, and, as he got older, would not play in the presence of other guitarists. He went so far as to have a curtain placed in front of him for one public performance. But it was not always that way.

[1] Caballero, Angel, A., El Pais, July 7, 1984
[2] Chileno, El Niño, p. 10.

Manuel Gómez Vélez came into the blazing red world of Riotinto, Huelva, on November 16, 1892. He arrived, thin and weak, a half-hour before the birth of his robust twin brother, Aurelio. Manuel was not expected to live, but he hung on to grow up in sight of the monstrous open pit, the hell-hole that was the copper mine of Riotinto. Sulferous fumes enveloped the ragged copper mountain in a wreath of suffocating smoke, while the Río Tinto, the deadly poisoness Red River, flowed sluggishly past mountains of lava-like slag, staining and corroding everything it touched. At the age of eight, Manuel and his family escaped from the inferno to the capital city of Huelva.

Manuel had two years of school, during which he learned to read and to write in a neat, careful hand. He was apprenticed to a tailor and mastered the art of cutting fabric. Later in life he would always cut his own suits and never failed to be elegantly dressed. Once, he said to the guitarist Manuel Cano, "You see how well I play the guitar? I used to make jacket lapels even better!"[1]

By the time he was seven, Manuel had begun to accompany local singers in the many styles of *fandanguillos* that are associated with the province of Huelva. It is uncertain how he learned to play, but by the time he reached Sevilla in 1910, he was already a virtuoso. The following comments by Manolo indicate that he also had a profound knowledge of the *cante*:

> "The *polos* are the oldest songs. All the old men said this when I was young. I heard it first from the oldest singer I have known, Antonio Silva 'El Portugués,' a Spaniard from the province of Sevilla, although Silva is a Portuguese name. I met him in Huelva, where I had just finished learning to be a tailor. My father brought him to the house and Antonio came with his guitar. That was when I first heard the *polos*.
>
> "When I arrived in Sevilla in 1910 and became a professional guitarist, there were three Sevillan singers from the Triana district who sang *polos*. Their names were Pepe Villaba, Fernando el Herrero, and Rafael Pareja—none of them gypsies. Others who sang the *polos* were Antonio Chacón and Diego Antúnez, a gypsy singer from Sanlúcar de Barrameda. By playing for these older men I learned to accompany those *cantes* with their exacting rhythm. But after about 1920, the new generation of singers no longer sang the *polos*; they turned to different *cantes*."[2]

Manuel implies here that his father, a craftsman by trade, had a strong interest in flamenco—if not, why would a prestigious singer like El

---

[1]Cano, Manuel, *La Guitarra: Historia, Estudios, y Aportaciones al Arte Flamenco*. University of Córdoba. 1986.

[2]Zayas, Virginia de, "Origins of Flamenco Music and its Oldest songs." *Guitar Review No. 43, Spring 1978*

Portugués visit his home—and it is possible that he played guitar. The same year that Manuel arrived in Sevilla, the magazine *Nuevo Mundo* published his picture, showing a very handsome and impeccably dressed seventeen-year-old holding a guitar in the position used by classical guitarists: the instrument rests on his left thigh which he raised by use of a footstool. A further indication that Manuel was playing classical music at that time is the absence of a *cejilla* on the neck of the guitar. The caption under the photo read: "Manuel Gómez Vélez. Concert guitarist whose prodigious execution is being the object of warm praise by the public and the press of Sevilla, where he has given highly notable concerts."[1]

Clearly, Manolo had no reservation about playing solos in public at that age. He once claimed that he knew eighteen classical compositions. On another occasion, many years later, he said to the *cantaor* Luis Caballero, "Let's go downstairs. I want you to listen to me. I will take the guitar on some travels through Albéniz and Falla."[2] Manolo also played pieces by Bach and Scarlatti and "the tremolo by Tárrega (almost certainly the well-known *'Recuerdos de la Alhambra'* that calls for the classical three-fingered tremolo technique)."[3]

Sometime in 1913, before Manolo became really well-known, Aurelio de Cádiz, not yet a professional *cantaor*, said that a friend told him, "There is a young man here who plays the guitar very well...he plays with more *flamenco* style than your *puñetera alma* (damned soul)!"

"Who is it?"

"El Niño de Huelva."

"Well, let's go see him!"

Aurelio sang to Manolo's accompaniment and predicted that the young man would become a phenomenon.[4] Later, Aurelio always took his favorite guitarist, José Capinetti, with him everywhere *except* Sevilla, where he would use Manolo de Huelva. He didn't care for Ramón Montoya, whom he felt was too self-important. He said, "The best was Niño Huelva. Montoya played his own way. He was a *fenómeno* (phenomenon), but a *fenómeno* for himself!"

The historical record is vague concerning the next ten years of Manolo's life. He preferred to work in private fiestas, although he didn't shun public performances. He maintained a close relationship with La Niña de los Peines and her family, and became a favorite of Chacón and Manuel Torre as well. While performing in the Sevilla cafes Novedades and El Kursaal, he played for Antonio de Bilbao, calling him the best in footwork. His prestige continued to grow. The classical guitarist Andrés Segovia, while still a young

---

[1] Quoted in Blas Vega's *Diccionario Ilustrado*, p. 366.
[2] Caballero, Luis, *"Manolo de Huelva: Imagen y anécdota,"* Candil (date unknown).
[3] Blas Vega, José, *"Manolo de Huelva (1892-1976), el guitarrista que inspiró a Falla."*
[4] *Conversaciones con Aurelio de Cadiz*, p. 23

man, heard Manolo play and said, "The last time I heard him was with some friends during the opening of a small hotel in Alcalá de Guadaira, near Sevilla, and Manolo de Huelva was accompanying Manolo de Jerez [Torre]...who sang *siguiriyas* better than anyone, except for La Niña de los Peines...Manolo de Huelva played simply, very flamenco, as it should be...his *toque* simple, emotional, and expressive. He was a distinguished follower of Paco de Lucena. Yes, Manolo de Huelva was the best when I was young."[1]

During this period, Manolo met Manuel de Falla and inspired some of the music for the composer's ballet *El Sombrero de Tres Picos* (*The Three-cornered Hat*). One biographer asserts that Manolo's *farruca* can be heard in the *"farruca del molinero"* and that the *"Danza de la molinera"* is a *bulerías al golpe* in Manolo's style.[2] Apparently, Manolo did some solo recording at this time—an *alegrías* and a set of *sevillanas* are known—which may have predated the early solo recording efforts of Ramón Montoya.

In 1922, Manuel de Falla and García Lorca listened to Manolo play in Sevilla and invited him to the first Contest of *Cante Jondo* in Granada. There, he shared the limelight with Ramón Montoya and won a prize in the competition. Later that year, when he performed in the bullring of Huelva with Manuel Torre and Antonio Chacón, the crowd insisted he play solo and rewarded him with a standing ovation. The following year, he returned to Huelva with Torre and Pepe Marchena. That same year, 1923, he recorded for the first time as accompanist, with the singer Manuel Centeno. It is possible that Manolo was contracted because he was considered to be a specialist in the *fandanguillos* de Huelva. These *fandanguillos* had not been given much importance up to that time, and this series of recordings by Centeno may have been the first attempt at a primitive anthology of styles, with *fandanguillos* of Pérez de Gúzman and Juan María, and those of Alosno and Almonte, along with *fandangos de Lucena*, *malagueñas*, and *tarantas*. Manolo played these *fandanguillos* with a very modern *aire*, employing the descending phrygian cadence (A-min, G, F, E) in a time when many other guitarists were still using only two chords (F-E).[3] He may have been a major contributor to the development of this *toque*, in which he displayed lightning *picados*, the use of chromatic scales, and a very fast thumb.

Other recordings followed the debut with Centeno, although not many. With Canalejas de Puerto Real he recorded a number of *fandangos* and *bulerías*. By the time of his last recordings—ten cuts of mostly *fandangos* and *bulerías* with Manuel Vallejo—Manolo had become more secretive, and it is said that he purposely avoided showing too much on these records. In a

---

[1] Segovia, Andrés, *Guitar Review*, 1977.
[2] Blas Vega, *"Manolo de Huelva (1892-19⁻6) el guitarrista que inspiró a Falla."* p. 5.
[3] You can hear Carlos Montoya using the two-chord rhythm on the modern recording, *Festival Flamenco*, RCA LPM-1713. 1958.

tango style from Triana known today as *tango del Titi*, he cut loose with some very fast *picado* scales and melodies, and he displayed a wonderful sense of rhythm and shading in the *colombianas*-like accompaniment. In the *bulerías* sung by Vallejo, Manolo again employed his crystal-clear *picado* and gave a lesson in the use of subtle rhythmic accompaniment, complete with a lavish use of taps on the face of the guitar (*golpes*) that give this style its name—*bulerías al golpe*. Twenty years later, Sabicas would still play in this way, although modernized a bit. After 1926, Vallejo and Manolo became linked as a team and their *bulerías* were legendary. Vallejo always referred to his guitarist as "the most famous and complete of all flamenco players."[1]

Knowledge of Manolo de Huelva's technique comes from these few records and some private recordings that he made for a student in 1937. Classical playing aside, it is clear that Manolo based his playing on early guitar soloists like El Maestro Patiño, Paco Lucena, and Javier Molina. Manolo learned to play the *alegrías en sol* (in G-major and minor) invented by Javier Molina, and he would play it in a film made in 1938 with La Argentinita. According to Pepe el de la Matrona, Javier created the modern Jerez style of *bulerías* ("modern" is a relative term, meaning here "as it was played in the first half of the twentieth century"). If that is true, then Manolo de Huelva may have inherited the *bulerías* from Javier and improved them. The guitarist Luis Maravilla said that Manolo was the creator of the *bulerías al golpe* as it is played today. Before him, they played *bulería por soleá*.[2] Some guitarists of the time, most notably Ramón Montoya, never mastered the new *bulerías* and continued to play it as a fast *soleá*.

Biographer Donn Pohren wrote:

> Just what makes Manolo's playing so exceptional? To start with, he has the best thumb and left hand in the business. He is flamenco's most original and prolific creator. He has a vast knowledge of flamenco in general and of the *cante* in particular, which causes his *toque* to be unceasingly knowledgeable and flamenco. He is blessed with the same genius and *duende* for his art that separated Manuel Torre from the pack; as was the case with Torre, when Manolo de Huelva becomes inspired, his playing drives aficionados to near-frenzy, striking the deepest human chords with overwhelming direct force.
>
> As is so rarely the case, Manolo's playing, when he is fired up, is truly spontaneous; he plays from the heart, not the head. His *toque* is full of surprises, of the unexpected. His manipulations of the *compás* are fabulous, his lightning starts and stops at once profound and delightful. He is a guitarist *impossible to anticipate—*

---

[1] Blas Vega, José, *"Manolo de Huelva (1892-1976), el guitarrista que inspiró a Falla."* p. 5.
[2] Maravilla, Luis, *Sevilla Flamenca*, No 68.

his genius flows so spontaneously that often not even Manolo knows what is coming next.[1]

Pohren knew the Manolo of the 1950s, after he had gradually turned more to techniques of the thumb and notes played with the left hand alone (*ligados*). His student, Virginia de Zayas, knew him in the 1930s. She described his playing:

> Manolo de Huelva plays almost exclusively on the four center strings of his modern guitar. The first and sixth strings are rarely used except in the cadences of *falsetas* [melodic variations]...He is more inclined to the bass strings, and frequently composes very flamenco repetitious phrases. *"Cuando más monótonas son las falsetas, más flamencas son,"* says Manolo [the more monotonous the *falseta*, the more flamenco it is]. "Many times they are almost the same notes but with different values. These are the enchantments of the flamenco guitar." Manolo thinks that playing on the four middle strings is "more flamenco." Because he constantly uses the traditional flamenco technique of playing with the thumb, this concentration of playing on these four strings requires a precise and practiced thumb. In the *rasgueados* [strums] and accompaniments, he stops the high E string from sounding by holding his right fingers against it. This steadies his hand and permits greater rhythmic exactness. His four fingers are held straight, with his nails against the *tapa* (guitar top), where he has almost made the beginnings of a hole in his practice guitar...
>
> He has a lightning thumb, very long, with a strong nail, and bent backward. He said he would not take a million *pesetas* for his thumb. He must have practiced a lot when he was young to develop such a thumb. He is particularly outstanding in *siguiriyas*, with curious dissonant chords. In *bulerías* he has complete control of the very difficult rhythm, upon which he improvises rhythmically and melodically with tremendous variety and inspiration...
>
> Manolo thinks ahead as he plays or, perhaps, his hands act with muscular continuity, accustomed as they are to the sequences of positions on the fingerboard. His left hand forms the next chord almost before he has left the last one. He plays with fully formed chords even when only a couple of its notes are pulsated...From his early playing of classical guitar music he has retained command of the chords of the upper reaches of the fingerboard, and he is quick to transpose or to find the same chord in alternative positions. He also accentuates strongly, using these accentuated notes upon which to pivot the sequence. He will tell me: "These accen-

[1] Pohren, p. 279.

tuated notes, whether in the song or the guitar part, are what gives sense to the phrase...Accents make the music come alive."[1]

Several of Virginia de Zayas' recordings of Manolo were released in the late 1980s,[2] and give, perhaps, the best picture of his early *toque*. The best of these recordings are fragments of dance accompaniments. The first is a big surprise, a set of *sevillanas* played solo for the dance. It is astounding that a guitarist of Manolo's stature would consent to accompany *sevillanas*, a trivial folk music from Sevilla, much less play them solo! In flamenco's history, few guitarists have played *sevillanas* as solos. Manolo not only played them, but he used them to demonstrate his creativity and a very fast and forceful *picado*. A guitarist who heard Manolo in his prime, Manolo Carmona, commented on the strength of Manolo de Huelva's technique: "Manolo de Huelva was another phenomenal guitarist. He had a very hard style...with a very hard touch in his *picado*, with great strength..." Sabicas, who would be the first to take the simple *sevillanas* to the concert stage, may have been influenced by Manolo—some of Sabicas' melodies resemble those on this recording.

A *siguiriya*, accompanied by footwork, shows off Manolo's powerful thumb and a beautiful tremolo. This tremolo, in which the fingers play a sustained mandolin-like melody on the treble strings while the thumb accompanies in the bass, puts to rest any notion that Manolo de Huelva did not have complete control of the more flowery classical techniques. The *siguiriya* is not well-suited to the tremolo because of its mood and the unusual rhythm that incorporates three fast beats and two slow beats. For those reasons, such a tremolo has rarely been attempted. Manolo brilliantly accomplished the tremolo by using the standard four-finger tremolo in the three short beats and doubling the tremolo to give seven notes in the long beats. Very difficult and innovative. In a *soleá* he demonstrated a smooth tremolo, fast thumb *ligados*, and at least two melodies that Sabicas would later claim as his own.

It is said that Manolo was the first to do *picados* on all six strings, rather than just the three treble strings, and he may have been instrumental in popularizing the hard rest-stroke that characterized his scales. He also played a role in developing the thumb technique called *alzapúa* that Sabicas would employ so effectively.

Fernando de Triana, who knew Manolo in his early years, paid tribute to the guitarist:

> Supreme artist of the guitar; composer with the most delicate and whimsical palette; accompanist who limits himself to that which it should be—he says, and he is right, that between verses of song,

---

[1]Zayas, Virginia de, "Origins of Flamenco Music and its Oldest Songs." *Guitar Review No. 43, Spring 1978*
[2]Dial Discos 54.9317/18.

he who wishes can demonstrate his art, but when the singer begins, the flowers are finished. And, because this is a maxim of El Niño de Huelva, that is what has placed him in the front line of accompanists. As a soloist, his work is simply marvelous. What *soleares*! What *rosas*! What *siguiriyas*! What *malagueñas*! What *tarantas* and everything else he plays! And without a rough note nor separating himself even one atom from the most strict *compás*.[1]

Throughout the 1920s Manolo remained active in Sevilla, primarily playing for private fiestas in bars and *ventas* located outside town and in parties in the homes of Ignacio Sánchez Mejías or the Duke of Alba. Gradually he became more secretive about his playing and stopped recording. He made clear his feelings about other guitarists learning his *falsetas* (melodies) when he said, "I don't teach my *falsetas* because it would be like giving a butcher a knife and asking him to cut out a piece of my flesh from wherever he wished!"[2] But long before his mania for privacy became full-blown in the 1940s and '50s, he had left his mark on the next generation of guitarists—including the young Sabicas.

In the Villa Rosa, Sabicas mingled with the best. "All the great artists were there, Juanito Mojama, José Cepero, guitarists Perico el del Lunar, Manolo and Pepe de Badajoz, Antonio Pérez…Antonio Chacón was there too, although I never saw him, I just heard his records. Ramón Montoya was family of ours, on my mother's side. We grew up with him. I used to go to Villa Rosa and we played together. I knew him very well…"[3]

"In Sevilla I met Manuel Torre and La Niña de los Peines, whose husband, Pepe Pinto, engaged me for her company. There has been no greater singer than La Niña de los Peines, everybody loved her. She and her brother Tomás were both superb artists. They're remembered as the greatest in flamenco."

Pastora Pavón, "La Niña de los Peines," considered to be flamenco's most complete *cantaora*, is unique among flamenco's most notable historical figures in that her legend is based solely on her voice and her contributions to the *cante*, rather than on her personality and lifestyle. Consequently, very little has been recorded about her life. We know that she was born on February 10, 1890, at Calle Butrón No. 10 in the Sevillian barrio of Puerta Osario, and baptized María Pastora de la Santísima Trinidad Pavón Cruz. Many in her family sang. Pastora's much older brother, Arturo, sang in private fiestas and in local bars and cafes. An extremely knowlegeable *cantaor*, Arturo would be both a teacher and father figure to his little sister. He not only taught her

[1] Triana, Fernando de, p. 162.
[2] Blas Vega, *"Manolo de Huelva (1892-19⁻6) el guitarrista que inspiró a Falla."* p. 7.
[3] Magnussen.

the *cante*, but also the dance he had learned from their father. Arturo would marry Eloisa Albéniz, who had partnered Eduardo Cansino (father of actress Rita Hayworth), and later have a dance studio where Arturo often helped out. Arturo and Eloisa would have a son, the celebrated flamenco pianist Arturo Pavón. So the dance tradition was strong in the family and it is said that Pastora became a highly skilled dancer, but would only dance in private. Manolo Caracol said that she was a fantastic *bailaora* and could have been a star in the dance if she hadn't had such a good voice.

Pastora and her younger brother, Tomás, used to go often with their mother to the gypsy barrio of Triana, across the Guadalquivir River from Sevilla, to visit their uncle, José el Pelao. José, said to be a good singer of *soleares*, lived in a *corral* (the old-style housing complex built around a communal patio) on Calle Castilla[1] and had a blacksmith shop on Calle Alfarería. At night, they would go around the corner to the tavern Casa de Baldomero, where Pastora might earn a couple of *pesetas* singing her *tangos*—the authentic *tangos de Triana*, not the more widespread style of Cádiz. She said, "At seven I was already singing and dancing in order to live."[2] One source says that when she didn't want to sing, her uncle grabbed her by the hair and forced her. In Triana, Pastora would have begun her education in some of the oldest traditions of the *cante*—the *martinetes* of José's brother, Juan Pelao, and other blacksmiths, and the *soleares* and *siguiriyas* of the Cagancho dynasty of *cantaores*. She and her brother would become the most important proponents of this school of *cante* and preserve it through their recordings.

In the building where Pastora was born lived a singer from Jerez named José Rodríguez de la Rosa, better known as Medina, *hijo* (junior). Some of Pastora's contemporaries claimed that Medina's father, Medina *el Viejo* (the elder), taught her many *cantes* of Jerez and Cádiz. Aurelio de Cádiz said that Medina el Viejo taught Pastora *tangos*, *bulerías*, *alegrías*, and *peteneras*, but that he could not sing the more profound *cantes*. Pepe Marchena said that Medina el Viejo was the *payo* teacher of Pastora. One flamencologist wrote: "How could Pastora have known the *cantes* of Jerez and Cádiz if she hadn't grown up at the side of that phenomenal *payo cantaor* El Niño Medina, faithful follower of the school of his father, El Viejo Medina."[3] Pastora could have learned Medina's *cante* from the father, the son, and or even her brother Arturo, who often sang with the elder Medina in local bars.

A small clique of gypsy singers have tried to deny that Pastora learned from anybody, and certainly not from any *payo*. The *cantaor* Juan Talegas used to say that Medina taught her nothing, that she learned all of her *tan-*

---
[1] Calle Castilla: A major street in Triana, named for the castle of the Inquisition that, until recently, housed the open-air food market within its ruins.
[2] Caballero, Luis, *"Pastora Pavón." Candil*, No. 53, p. 37.
[3] Yerga Lancharro. M., *"Evocación de Pastora Pavón, Niña de los Peines." Candil*, No. 70.

gos and *bulerías* from Manuel Torre, her only teacher other than Arturo. He claimed that Manolo Caracol started the Medina rumor out of jealousy, trying to detract from Pastora. However, Pastora most likely knew *tangos* before meeting Torre. She did not become Torre's lover until long after she was famous for her *tangos* and she said, "I remember, as a child, how it [the slow *tango* of Cádiz] was sung by Mercedes la Serneta, my grandfather Tomás, and my aunt Rosario."[1] Again, Pastora affirmed the existence of a great deal of *cante* in her family history. And she contradicted Juan Talega's friend Antonio Mairena, who said that Pastora did not learn from Merced la Serneta and never even heard her sing, claiming that Merced always said, "I can't sing, I have something blocking my throat!" According to Pastora's friend Curro de Utrera, Pastora went often to Utrera as a child, to listen to La Serneta. On one occasion, the great singer said to the girl's mother, "This child is going to sing well!"[2]

Merced Fernández said in an interview that she had been nicknamed "La Serneta" because, as a child, she was small and lively like a little bird of that name. Others have refuted this, pointing out that Serna is a common nickname in certain families of Jerez. Well into her sixties and long retired when Pastora used to visit her flower-filled patio in the small town of Utrera, La Serneta subsisted by giving occasional guitar lessons. This unusually beautiful and spiritual woman had earned the respect of her contemporaries with the unique and moving *soleares* she created from the ancient *soleá* of Triana. These *soleares* would become the base of the *soleares* of Utrera, sung in modern times by Fernanda de Utrera. La Serneta had never been much of a public figure and lived primarily from private fiestas and by giving *cante* and guitar lessons to aristocrats. Antonio Chacón found her living in poverty and arranged for her to give a concert in Madrid, very likely her last public performance. Through the efforts of Chacón, Manuel Torre, and the Pavón Family, four or five variations of her subtle and hauntingly beautiful *soleares* were popularized and recorded.

Two other influences on Pastora Pavón would come a little later. It is believed that, in her teen years, she spent time in Málaga with the legendary singer of *malagueñas*, La Trini, who was often called the "female Chacón." Actually, it was Chacón who honored La Trini by including several of her creations *por malagueñas* in his repertoire. Pastora became one of the best interpreters of these *malagueñas*. Then, probably in her late teens, Pastora had an affair with Manuel Torre. It is said that Torre passed on a great deal of *cante* to her, broadening her knowledge of the *tangos* of Cádiz, the *bulerías*, and many styles of *siguiriyas* of Jerez. Such was Pastora's knowledge of *siguiriyas* that she is credited with preserving fifteen distinct styles in her recordings. According to Antonio Mairena, "With the arrival of

[1] *Ibid.*
[2] *Candil*, No. 75, p. 701.

Manuel Torre in Sevilla came the creation of the House of the Pavóns and, like a prodigy, arose what we can call today the Sevillian School." At a very early age, Pastora began to sing in the local cafes frequented by her older brother, the Café Ceferino and Café de San Agustín. At age eight she performed briefly in Madrid and then lived for an extended period in the northern city of Bilbao. Her formal debut came when she was about twelve[1], in Madrid's Café de la Marina. Accompanied on guitar by the great Angel Baeza, the precocious performer wore the only formal dress she owned—her first communion dress! Three days later she was considered a success and given something more appropriate to wear. Soon, she moved to the Café de la Marina, where Pastora Imperio first heard her. Imperio, not yet an artist, lived across the street and at every opportunity stationed herself in the open doorway of the cafe to listen to Pastora sing: "I managed to hear her sing the verse that she created, the one that was destined to give her her name..."[2]

Péinate tú con mis peines,   Comb your hair with my combs,
que mis peines son de canela.   for my combs are made of cinnamon.
La gachí que se peina con mis peines The *payo* woman who uses my combs
canela lleva de veras.   will truly become cinnamon-skinned
                                                                             [i.e. gypsy].

Péinate tú con mis peines,   Comb your hair with my combs,
que mis peines son de azúcar.   for my combs are made of sugar.
La gachí que se peina con mis peines The *payo* woman who uses my combs
hasta los dedos se chupa.   will taste sweet even to her fingers.[3]

When young Pastora came out singing these *tangos*, dressed in gypsy ruffles and wearing immense Spanish combs in her hair, she soon earned the name by which she would become famous, "La Niña de los Peines" ("The Girl of the Combs").

La Niña de los Peines was not an attractive young woman. Jet black hair, usually pulled back in a tight bun, added to the severity of pencil-thin eyebrows over almost oriental almond-shaped black eyes. A heavy, piggish nose, ghoulishly thin lips, and a thick neck, created the impression of a rather plain, even homely, woman. She was always a little heavy and appeared matronly at an early age.

But when Pastora sang, she became transformed into an angel. Her voice has been praised as the most beautiful and flamenco ever. It was a very gypsy voice, at times a little shrill and nasal, but very flexible, with great sustain, and capable of minute detail. Some of her notes were more felt than heard, so swiftly were they introduced into trills and arabesques. She

---
[1] Sources give her age as eleven or thirteen.
[2] Caballero, Angel A., p. 204.
[3] Personal letter from Antonio Mairena to Emilio Jiménez Díaz.

dazzled audiences with her vitality and presence, so evident in the following description by a foreigner who saw her in Café Novedades in 1920:

> She sat alone beside her guitarist on the vast stage. She had an easy, proud carriage in her shoulders, a haughty angle of the chin, dominating glances. Long suspense. Finally, she closed her fan and used it to beat a rhythm on the rung of her chair—the click could be heard in the last row of the farthest gallery. Prelude on the guitar, long series of *ayyys* in a rich contralto:
>
> | | |
> |---|---|
> | *Naquelo con Undebé,* | I speak with God, |
> | *y a Undebé le digo,* | and say to God, |
> | *"Que me paese mentira* | "It can't be true, |
> | *las cosas que hases conmigo!"* | the things that you are doing to me!"[1]

Pepe el de la Matrona called Pastora the best *cantaora* ever, for her instrument, her way of communication, making people feel, and her extensive encyclopedic knowledge. He said: "I like to listen to Pastora swear, and sometimes I taunt her just to hear her curse, to hear the metal of her voice."[2]

Aurelio de Cádiz said, "I heard her sing for the first time in a *café cantante* that was in Puerta Tierra, called Jardinera and owned by Diego Antúnez, who told me about her, although I didn't believe what he said nor, much less, that she could live up to her fame. At the beginning of this century, flamenco was in a serious crisis. It was withdrawing into the hometowns of Jerez and Cádiz, and everyone resisted the idea that a woman could triumph when there were so many good *cantaores* around. But she really did triumph. And in what a manner! She vanquished all the other singers of her time and stood alone, sharing her success with none other than Chacón and Torre. There has never been a woman like her!"

In 1935, Fernando de Triana elaborated on Pastora's unique position:

> Just when women began to decline in the *cante andaluz*, the reign of La Niña de los Peines began. Being such a good artist, she found herself almost alone. La Antequerana, Carmen la Trianera, Paca Aguilera, and some of the others who didn't make it to the time of the war [World War I], soon disappeared from the artistic map and Pastora found herself completely alone as a singer, without competitors other than Antonio Chacón and Manuel Torre—the first secure on his throne and the second with his ingenius and enigmatic classicism. What remained of the art, and it was substantial, was concentrated in the three of them. Then the two competitors died and now we have Pastora as the lone, exclusive representative of an art that could previously count on scores of con-

---

[1] Brown, Irving. Deep Song. Harper & Brothers, New York & London, 1929. p. 309.
[2] Caballero, Angel A.. p. 207.

sumate artists in all facets of the *cante*...[She is] the best *festera* to date, successfully imitated only by Manuel Vallejo. And do you know why La Niña de los Peines and Manuel Vallejo are the best singers? Well, it is because they are the ones who have the best *son* [rhythm], the indispensable requisite for good singing.[1]

On one occasion, Pepe Pinto (Pastora's future husband) found Antonio Chacón in a bad mood. They went to eat, and Pepe asked Chacón what was bothering him. "Nothing, *hijo*, nothing," replied Don Antonio, brimming with indignation despite his despondence. "We were in a fiesta and that gypsy, Pastora, began to sing... After that I couldn't even tune-up my voice. She's a wild woman, Pepe, there is no one who can compete with her!"[2]

On another occasion, after Pastora had been with Chacón, she came to Pepe and exclaimed in flustered disbelief, "He was kissing my hands...on his knees, he was kissing my hands!"

La Niña de los Peine's contributions to flamenco were extensive. She began at a young age with the *tangos* that gave her her artistic name, those of Triana. *Tangos* became the rage of the day, and she was never surpassed in the styles of Jerez and Cádiz that she learned from Medina and Torre. She could sing *tangos* for hours without repeating.

Surprisingly, crowds never let Pastora end a performance without singing *siguiriyas*—in spite of the general disdain for *cante jondo*. Equally astonishing is the fact that, in the time of the *cupletista* and the operatic *fandango*, La Niña de los Peines not only survived, but reigned as a goddess. Her voice and vitality were in such demand that she did not have to make concessions to the popular fads of the day. She recorded more than twenty-five *siguiriyas*, certainly more than any other *cantaor* before or after her. Together with the forty *soleares* she recorded, these two very profound and difficult *cantes* alone made up about twenty percent of her total output of three hundred and fifty recordings.

Promotors offered La Niña de los Peines money and fame if she would dedicate herself to the *cuplé*, the pseudo-flamenco of the time, but she flatly refused. She did, however, relax her adherance to the pure flamenco enough to sing *cuplés por bulerías* and popularize a number of minor *cantes*. Pastora, Niño Medina, and Pepe de la Matrona were the first to record *bulerías*, around 1910. In the *bulerías*, Pastora could give in a little to popular demand. Unequaled in this festive *cante*, which she may have learned from Manuel Torre, she gave her creativity free rein, singing all sorts of *cuplés* with inimitable rhythm and flavor. Her version of the Mexican song *"Cielito lindo"* was a tremendous hit. She used to get together with Federico García Lorca, whom she met through Manuel de Falla, in La Argentinita's home in Madrid. Federico would accompany her on the piano,

[1] Triana, Fernando, p. 229.
[2] Caballero, Angel A., p. 207.

and eventually they created *"lorqueñas"*—*bulerías* with verses written by Lorca. Among Lorca's verses was one inspired by a *sevillanas*:

Esquilones de plata,	Silver cowbells,
bueyes rumbones,	grand oxen,
eso sí son señas	these are, indeed, signs
de labradores.	of field workers.

To finish these *lorqueñas*, Pastora usually sang *"Anda jaleo,"* an old folksong from Lorca's collection.

Pastora has long been considered the first to record *sevillanas*. However, the prolific *cantaor* El Mochuelo had recorded them on little 3-inch one-sided disks as early as 1900. But the *sevillanas* recorded by Pastora between 1905 and 1910, with the guitar of Luis Molina, are marvels that have not been surpassed, sung in a rich flamenco contralto and full of subtle nuances.

La Niña de los Peines practically invented the *garrotín*, popularizing it with a lively *tango* rhythm. She gave gypsy flavor to the little-known *marianas*, a folk music put to a dirge-like *tango* rhythm. The father of guitarist Luis Maravilla was one of the few to cultivate this *cante*, earning him the nickname "El Niño de las Marianas." Luis said that his father heard the song for the first time around 1905, sung by a group of *húngaros* (non-Spanish gypsies) while their goat did tricks. *"Mariana"* is the name given to the trained goats or monkeys used by itinerant gypsies in their street performances. One verse goes:

Sube, Mariana, sube	Get up, Mariana, get up
por aquella montañita,	on that little mountain,
arriba, sube;	up, get up;
no pegarle más palitos a la Mariana	don't hit Mariana anymore
porque la pobrecita	because the poor thing
está manquita y coja!	is one-armed and lame!

Luis' father put the song to guitar, called it *marianas*, and made it so popular that, by the time he recorded it at age twenty (1910), it had already been recorded by three other singers. La Niña de los Peines sang the *marianas* until they went out of fashion, sometime before 1930. After that, even El Niño de las Marianas didn't sing them anymore. Luis said that his father was a skilled ventriloquist and more than once put this talent to good use:

> In a fiesta, he was being accompanied by Ramón Montoya *por granaínas*. He sang the line *"Viva el puente de genil!"* and immediately after used ventriloquism to say in a different voice, "Ramón, long live Granada, my homeland...MONTOYA!"
>
> Montoya went pale and began to sweat. The third or fourth time this happened, Montoya, very frightened, stopped playing and began to say, "My dead ancestors are calling me...!"

You can imagine the explosion of laughter from those around him.[1]

The *marianas*—in reality only a rather limited variation of the *tango*—did not survive into the modern repertoire, although a few singers have tried to resurrect it (José Menese, Curro Malena, Diego Clavel). But another of Pastora's *cantes* had a more successful future.

La Niña de los Peines created the celebrated *bamberas* from an obscure folksong. In some rural Andalusian towns the ancient pagan tradition of the *columpio* survived in conjunction with spring fairs and late summer harvests. Swings, called *bambas*, were erected out in the fields or in narrow streets where ropes could be tied to opposing balconies. Young men would swing the girls, hoping to get a glimpse of their legs, while singing compliments to them. The *columpio* offered young people a culturally acceptable way to express their sublimated romantic urges. As the *bamba* rose and fell, the crowd yelled, the girls screamed and shrieked as they rode higher and higher, and the boys improvised verses of love, frustration, and jealousy:

Ni los rayitos del sol,	Neither the rays of the sun
ni la estrella más bonita	nor the most beautiful star
tienen tanto resplandor	have the splendor
como el de mi morenita.	of my little dark-skinned one.

Originally sung without musical accompaniment or defined rhythm, La Niña de los Peines put these verses to a lively *soleá* rhythm (like the modern-day *soleá por bulerías*) and imbued them with her *compás* and sweetness, her *rajo* and sense of the profound. One of her early verses, which she recorded as *"Bamberas,"* says:

Entre sábanas de Holanda	Between Dutch sheets
y colcha de carmesí	and a red coverlet
está mi amante durmiendo	lies my lover sleeping
como un serafín.	like an angel.

The *bamberas* did not catch on until the 1970s, when young singers, perhaps responding to the demands of the always starved-for-new-material recording industry, revived Pastora's rendition and developed it into a genuine branch of the *cante*.

La Niña de los Peines' crowning achievement had to be the creation of the modern *peteneras*. This *cante* has long fascinated aficionados, both for its dramatic somber music and captivating lyrics as well as the aura of mystery that surrounds it. The song has a sinister connotation for many artists, who believe that performing it will bring on misfortune. Who was La Petenera, and why is her death remembered in song? What is the meaning

---

[1]Cenizo Jiménez, José, "Luis Maravilla." *Sevilla Flamenca, No. 88.* Morón, 1994. p. 38.

of the many Jewish references in the lyrics? And why the superstitious fear that performing or even mentioning the *petenera* will bring bad luck?

Theories abound considering the origin of the *petenera*. It has been suggested that it has Latin American roots, based on the rhythm it shares with only one other *cante*, the *guajiras*, the existence of an important Spanish colony in the Guatamalan region of Peten, and some similar songs scattered around the Americas. Nothing concrete supports this view, but it is possible that, in the distant past, some Spanish-American song migrated back to Spain and entered into the popular culture.

The claim of Jewish origin is based on little more than a single verse that begins "Where are you going beautiful Jewess..." Any connection with Sephardic Jews in Spain would have to date back to the 15th Century. The consensus is that the *petenera* is very old, dating back to at least the 1700s. It probably owes its name to a singer from the town of Paterna de la Ribera who was first called La Paternera and, later, through typical Andalusian deformation of language, La Petenera. Many early verses imply that La Petenera was extremely beautiful, perhaps a prostitute. One verse says: "Whoever called you Petenera didn't know how to name you; he should have called you the ruination of men!" Another: "La Petenera, damned be the one who brought you to this land; La Petenera is the reason men lose their way..." And yet another: "Petenera of my life, Petenera of my heart; you are the reason, Petenera, that I suffer so..."

So abundant were La Petenera's followers that the most well-known verse says:

La Petenera se ha muerto,	La Petenera has died,
y la llevan a enterrar,	and they are taking her to be buried,
y en el panteón no cabe	and in the mausoleum there is no room
la gente que va detrás...	for all of those in the procession...

This verse spawned many take-offs when the *petenera* became very popular in the 1870s. After the collapse of the First Spanish Republic in 1874, one *copla* began, *"La República se ha muerto..."* ("The Republic has died...") Another referred to *"El Cerandero,"* a daring dance of the 1700s:

El Cerandero se ha muerto,	El Cerandero has died,
lo llevan a enterrá;	they are taking it to be buried;
le han echo poca tierra	but they didn't cover it with enough dirt
y ha vuelto a resucitá!	and now it has come back to life!

About 1880, when the *petenera* was at its peak of popularity, Medina el Viejo appeared with a flamenco version, slowing the rhythm and giving it the flavor of *soleares* (there still exists a *cante* called *soleá petenera*). Antonio Chacón was the first to sing the *peteneras* of Medina. At the beginning of this century, the aging Juan Breva recorded a primitive *peteneras*, with the guitar of young Ramón Montoya. It is not clear whether this is an early version of Medina's *cante* or pre-dates him. The melody is essentially the same as that of the modern free-rhythm style, but it is sung in strict and unchanging *compás*. This way of singing *peteneras* has been completely lost, and its great beauty would be worthy of consideration by modern *cantaores*. Montoya's playing was quite modern sounding, but in a traditional rhythmic style.

A few years later Montoya again recorded the *petenera*, this time with Niño Medina. His introduction made clear that the *petenera* had changed, for he played more reposed, with loosely structured *falsetas* that were not always easily identifiable as *peteneras*. Medina sang the style of his father, as somebody made clear on the recording by saying in the background, "Let's see what you can do, Medina, this is your thing!" This version approaches the modern style, with the first line being repeated and the melodies extended and developed to the extent that the guitar has to leave the *compás* and wait for the singer. Again, it is not clear whether this is the pure *cante* of Medina, or had already felt the influence of La Niña de los Peines.

La Niña de los Peines learned the *petenera* from Medina, or from his son, and popularized it in a majestic and profound version. Her earliest recording, made before 1910, featured the playing of Luis Molina, who abandoned the traditional *toque* to play with the abstract *aire* of a *fandango*. In true *ópera* style, Pastora put rhythm aside in order to expand the melodies into complex and passion-filled cascades of arabesques, forcing her guitarist to wait in silence and join her at the end of each phrase. One of her magnificent verses, recorded in modern times by Camarón de la Isla with some word changes, says:

Soy como aquel fiel peregrino,	I am like that devout pilgrim,
que de penitencia andaré,	who will wander in penance
hasta yo encontrar el asesino	until I find the assassin
que me roba tu querer	who steals your love from me
como ladrón de caminos.	like a highway robber.

Inevitably, the *petenera* of La Niña de los Peines soon overshadowed that of Medina, who would be remembered only as her imitator.

Apparently there was considerable controversy among flamencos when Pastora abandoned the *compás* of the *petenera* in order to develop its melodies. Javier Molina believed that this *cante* should maintain its rhythm and structure. On one occasion he arrived at Los Gabrieles after accompanying Pastora in one of her rousing successes in a theater. He was fuming and said, "I would like to say to that audience, 'Son of the Great Whore! Why do you applaud her, when she doesn't know how to sing it, and you don't applaud me, the one who *does* know?'"[1] Manolo de Huelva, who accompanied Pastora

---

[1] Blas Vega, *Vida y Cante de Don Antonio Chacón*. Córdoba, 1986. p. 172.

often, confirmed that she sang out of time. Singers also complained that guitarists didn't know how to accompany this *cante* properly. Once, Chacón said to Manolo de Huelva, "Now that you are here I am going to sing the *petenera*, since my friend Montoya doesn't know how to play it."[1] Pastora had to depend upon Luis Molina, said to be the only one who could do justice to her difficult rendition of the *petenera*. In spite of resistance by some flamencos, Pastora's *peteneras* would become the definitive model for the future.

The older rhythmic style of *peteneras* did not die out completely, but survived as an accompaniment to the dance. The more free and profound *cante grande* of Pastora is preferred for listening, although in recent times it has become quite popular among dancers, who must interpret its loose rhythm in an abstract manner and usually resolve the dance in the older style.

Regarding the curse of bad luck associated with *peteneras*, La Niña de los Peines had this to say: "Look, anyone who doesn't want to sing *peteneras* does so because he doesn't know how to sing them!" In the early years, everybody sang *peteneras* without fear. The superstition appears to be a modern phenomenon, arising from an occurrence in 1945. In that year, a young dancer/singer from Aragón named Mari Paz was starring in the touring show *"Cabalgata."* A popular number, *"Gloria de la Petenera,"* played out the famous burial of the legendary Petenera. At the climax, all of the dancers hoisted Mari Paz up over their heads and carried her feet-first as in a funeral procession.

One night, according to the story, Mari Paz broke down and cried after this number, saying that she had a premonition that she was going to die. And sure enough, just as the show was about to leave for London, she came down with a chest infection and died shortly thereafter. Her funeral was as tumultuous and crowded as that of the mythical Petenera. The press played it to the hilt and created such superstition that no dancer would substitute for Mari Paz and the tour came to an end. After that, the *peteneras* was subject to blame for any misfortune or illness.[2]

However, not all modern artists succumb to the *petenera* superstition. José Greco, Manuela Vargas, and Carmen Mora performed it with dance companies that included mostly gypsy performers. Gypsy *cantaores* like Rafael Romero, Juan Talegas, Manuel Mairena, and Camarón de la Isla have all sung *peteneras*, while guitarists from Carlos Montoya to Paco de Lucía have played it.

---

[1]*Ibid.*
[2]This account is taken from *Flamenco de Ida y Vuelta* by Romualdo Molina and Miguel Espín. VII Bienal de Arte Flamenco, Sevilla, 1992. p. 116.

Although based in Sevilla, La Niña de los Peines became a frequent visitor to Madrid after 1920. When she first appeared there with her preferred guitarist, Juan Habichuela, she became the highest paid flamenco artist of the time. Year after year she packed the theaters of Madrid and toured the major cities. Eventually, Habichuela, well into his sixties, was replaced by Ramón Montoya, Niño Ricardo, and a young genius named Currito el de la Jeroma. Habichuela, whose thumb-driven playing created such emotion in his audience that it was said his notes became converted into tears, never recorded with Pastora.

The selection of guitarists for recording was usually in the hands of the recording companies, not the individual singers. Most of Pastora's early records were made with either Luis Molina or Ramón Montoya. But, around 1918, she recorded a wide range of *cantes* with a young guitarist from Sevilla named Currito el de la Jeroma. Currito, a small, wiry gypsy with chocolate-brown skin and a cocky manner, was born in Jerez to a guitarist father and the celebrated dancer La Jeroma. He learned from his father and Javier Molina and developed a prodigious thumb, due in part to the loss of use of one of his right-hand fingers from a knife accident, or, according to oral tradition, the bullet of a jealous husband. Currito's exploits with women were legendary, as was his capacity for alchohol consumption. He began performing as a *cantaor*, but that career was cut short by tuberculosis. He turned to the guitar and became such an accomplished accompanist that, it was said, he could make a *cantaor* sing well even if he didn't feel like singing. Manuel Torre's brother, Pepe, said that Currito was a genius and the best accompanist ever. The gypsy guitarist Melchor de Marchena ranked Currito among the top three guitarists, along with Manolo de Huelva and Javier Molina. Sabicas' brother, Diego, said, "Currito de la Jeróma was very handsome and very depraved, and invented some techniques for *bulerías*. Sabicas saw him several times in Sevilla, once in a fiesta with Ramón Montoya, in El Kursaal, where he [not clear who—probably Montoya] played for three or four hours and then Jeróma embarrassed him by playing so well."[1] Currito was also a brilliant dancer and the first to play flamenco solos on the piano. Unfortunately, the excesses of his bohemian lifestyle (most likely tuberculosis) would take his life at a young age, sometime in the mid-1930s.

In 1922, Pastora was invited to be part of the jury in the historic Contest of *Cante Jondo* in Granada. But she was a purely decorative figure and had no vote. Little did Falla, Lorca, and the other organizers realize that the very qualities they sought, and failed to find, in their misguided attempt to rescue the true *cante jondo*, were right under their noses in the person of La Niña de los Peines. A month after the contest, Pastora returned to Granada with Habichuela to perform in the bullring. Author Irving Brown wrote that he

[1]Goldberg interviews.

was present at a gathering in Granada with Pastora and Manuel Torre around that time. He described a rather poignant little incident: "All were mellow with drink. Half in jest, half in earnest, Manuel fell to his knees and declared his love for Pastora (he looked much older than she). As he finished his declaration, she bent and kissed him on the forehead. Two tears trickled down his cheeks..."[1]

In 1926, Pastora embarked on the first of many tours with Vedrines. She peformed often with Pepe Marchena, whom she admired greatly, and in 1928 toured with Chacón. In 1931[2], she married her longtime companion, Pepe Pinto, at the feet of the Virgen de la Macarena in Sevilla. Pepe, thirteen years younger than Pastora, had been one of the three fourteen-year-olds who had summoned up the nerve to sing in Café Novedades in 1917, the other two being Pepe Marchena and El Carbonerillo. Later, Pepe Pinto became a skilled roulette croupier, sought after by some of the best casinos in Europe. He earned tremendous amounts of money and spent much of it in *juergas* listening to the best *cantaores*, especially Antonio Chacón, whom he revered. When Spain prohibited gambling in 1923, Pepe turned to singing professionally and found success in the *ópera* style. Pastora always supported and encouraged his singing, and the two enjoyed a warm and deeply intimate marriage.

Pastora also shared a warm relationship with her brother Tomás, three years her junior. She always said that her favorite singers were Tomás and Pepe Marchena. And she was not alone in her view of Tomás Pavón. Antonio Mairena called him the "best singer of the century!" Gypsies in particular rate him highly. El Chocolate said, "Tomás Pavón carried on the music of Manuel Torre, but he sang better, with a profound echo." Tomás was, indeed, a singer's singer, but little known outside of his intimate circle of friends. Possessed of extraordinary faculties that included large lungs and a clear deep voice, he was a master of the *cante jondo*—*soleares*, *siguiriyas*, and the ancient *cantes* that are sung without guitar accompaniment, the *martinetes*, *tonás*, and *deblas*. He had no interest in the popular songs of the moment, the *farrucas*, *peteneras*, and *fandangos*, although he did excell in the *bulerías*, which he took as seriously as the more profound *cantes*.

Considered eccentric by those around him, Tomás was incapable of performing on-stage in front of a large audience. Unlike his extroverted sister, he needed an intimate environment, behind closed doors, surrounded by friends and knowledgeable aficionados. He was not a singer for the period of the *ópera flamenca* and largely depended on his sister for financial support. Pastora pushed him as much as she could and it was due to her prodding that he finally consented to record in 1927, with Niño Ricardo on guitar. On these few records that preserve for history the *cante* of a truly

---

[1] Brown, Irving, *Deep Song.* p. 313.
[2] Pastora's date of marriage is given as anywhere from 1930 to 1933.

exceptional *cantaor*, Pastora can be heard in the background maintaining an almost steady stream of encouragement.

Apart from his *soleares* and *siguiriyas* of Cádiz, Jerez, and Triana, Tomás Pavón's most celebrated legacy was his recreation of the *debla*. This ancient *cante*, done without musical accompaniment and said to be the most difficult *cante* to sing, had largely disappeared by the middle of the 1800s. Chacón is supposed to have known it, but did not sing it. Manolo de Huelva said he pried it out of Chacón and tried out fragments of it on other singers like Torre and Tomás, but they didn't know it. The *cantaor* Juan Talegas, who spent a great deal of time in Triana and knew well its *cante*, told how Tomás came to him one day and said, "I have made a *cante*, I have made the *debla*!"

Talegas, puzzled, replied, "You have made the *debla*? With who? Who has told you how it goes?" Talegas claimed that he had heard the *debla* at some point, but knew nothing about it, that he knew all of the gypsies in Triana and they did not know the *debla*. So he said to Tomás, "You have learned the *debla* from your father-in-law, haven't you?" His father-in-law was a gypsy from Triana called Antonio el Baboso who did not sing well.

Tomás could only answer, "Why do you have to argue with me about this in front of all these people, couldn't you have asked me about it later when we were alone?"[1]

Talegas went on to credit Tomás with resuscitating the *debla*, saying that the father-in-law was in with the Caganchos, who knew the *cante*, and he must have outlined it for Tomás, who then finished it by intuition. Manolo de Huelva claimed that the *debla* of Tomás Pavón is really a *martinete* of Triana with some *ays* of the *debla*. The only thing that is certain is that what is known of the *debla* today came from one source—Tomás Pavón.

The poet and flamencologist Ricardo Molina left a fitting tribute to La Niña de los Peines when he wrote: "This extraordinary woman is like a bottomless and endless ocean. By herself she represents the complete history of flamenco. She encompasses the whole mysterious legacy of our *cante*. We know little of what La Andonda, La Serrana, María Borrico, Merced la Serneta, and other famous *cantaoras* might have been in their time, but it seems impossible that any of them could have surpassed Pastora Pavón in the vastness of her repertoire, the freshness of her voice, or her gypsy *rajo* and contagious vitality."[2]

In 1932, Pastora toured with Vedrines, in a company that included Pepe Pinto, his good friend, El Cabonerillo, and José Cepero, and brought together the guitarists Sabicas and Niño Ricardo. Sabicas confirms that he met

[1] Caballero, Angel A., p. 202.
[2] Molina, Ricardo, Obra Flamenca. *Ediciones Demófilo*, Madrid. 1977. p. 160.

Niño Ricardo through La Niña de los Peines.
> They took me on tour. I was a young boy, so my father had to come along. We would go by car: El Pinto, El Niño Ricardo, La Niña de los Peines, my father, and I. Where did we go? Well, for instance, to Badajoz from Madrid. Three hours of singing *tientos*! My poor father, he would tear his suit off, his shirt, everything! I would say to him, *"Please*, Dad!" No one could resist that woman...
> We used to work and go on tours. She would ask me, and then we would go on tours for two or three months...We worked for many years. She was a good person, but people used to call her Herod because she killed the *niños* [children; young singers] when she sang. The young singers would come out, and when Pastora came out, people would say, "There is Herod."[1]

"Niño Ricardo and I practically grew up together. I met him when I was a child. The first time I saw Niña de los Peines, Ricardo was accompanying her. So, we discovered each other, and after that we were like brothers, always together. He was a great guitarist who always played very well, with tremendous feeling, and he was a marvelous person too."[2]

Manuel Serrapí Sánchez, better known as Niño de Ricardo (his father's name was Ricardo), was born in Sevilla in 1904. In his youth he worked at the dirty job of *carbonero*, making charcoal. His father, concerned about his son's obsession with the guitar, did what he could to dissuade the boy, even cutting his guitar strings one night as he slept. But Manolito persisted and took some lessons from the young virtuoso, Manuel Moreno, a featured attraction in Café Novedades. The director of flamenco in Novedades was Javier Molina, a guitarist of considerable renown.

Javier Molina had been a childhood chum of Antonio Chacón, and the two had traveled through Andalucía together in the 1870s in search of flamenco and adventure. Javier, after a great deal of classical and solo guitar playing, eventually developed what would become the Jerez school of *toque*, continued in modern times by the Morao and Parrilla families. He must have been impressed by the young Manolo Serrapí, who used to hang out at Novedades, for he put him to work in the house *cuadro* as second guitarist to the excellent accompanist, Antonio Moreno. Manolo's father heard about it and rushed to the cafe in anger, but relented when he saw the situation—on the condition that Manolo continue at his new job in a furniture company. Building furniture was hard on the boy's hands and the alcohol used in finishing softened his nails, but he persisted. His reward was to be asked to fill in for Javier during an illness. He did so well that Javier asked

[1] Molarsky interview.
[2] Magnussen.

him to join him as second guitarist. And that is how Manolo el Carbonero came to build the foundation of his playing style on that of Javier Molina. La Niña de los Peines was so impressed by the sixteen-year-old Manolo that she asked his father if she could take him with her to Madrid. The father refused to give permission. But, two years later he relented and Niño Ricardo went with La Niña and her brother Tomás to Madrid to perform in the Teatro Pavón. The year was 1922, the same year that Niño Sabicas arrived in the capital.

Niño Ricardo would assimilate some of the lyrical sweetness and the technique of Ramón Montoya, his arpeggios and tremolos. He would absorb the flavor, rhythm, and strength of Manolo de Huelva, especially in the new *bulerías* that Ramón never mastered, and go on to create a powerful and passionate style of guitar that would be the base for the ultra-modern playing that would arise some fifty years later.

Ricardo contributed many innovations to the guitar. He was unique in using all rest strokes in his arpeggios (the fingers pluck downward into the next string rather than up into the air). He used to say, "My ring finger is eighty percent of my arpeggio." He claimed that, after watching a classical guitarist, he invented a common arpeggio technique in which the thumb is followed by the ring and middle fingers together and then the index finger. Ramón Montoya once said to him, after noting his thick, clumsy fingers and weak, soft nails, "I don't know how you can play the guitar so well with those hands!" Ricardo replied, "Me either!"[1]

Ricardo's sense of humor is legendary, as the following anecdote confirms:

> One night, when Ricardo was working in a cafe in Sevilla, a wealthy rancher entered with one of his workhands who could sing. At an opportune moment, the rancher asked permission for his worker to go up on stage and sing a little something. "I made it my job to play for him," Ricardo tells us, "because I realized that there could be some fun in it. The fieldhand came up on stage without even removing his sheepskin jacket or his scarf, his cap pulled down to his nose and his boots full of mud. As soon as he sat down beside me he gave two big stomps on the stage and said 'Let's go!'
>
> "'What are you going to sing?'
>
> "And in the most resolved and confident manner, he said to me, *'Los pícaros tartaneros* [a difficult *cartageneras* popularized by Chacón].'
>
> "So, without asking him what key he sang in, I put the guitar in the clouds [clamped the *cejilla* or capo high up the guitar neck where the pitch would be impossibly high for singing]. But, since

[1] This quote and much of the other information comes from Niño Ricardo *"Rostro de un Maestro"* by Humberto J. Wilkes. Bienal de Arte Flamenco, Sevilla. 1990.

the hick had a good ear, he began the *cartagenera* perfectly in tune with the guitar, although with his voice strained to the breaking point. The verse was the one that says:

Un lunes por la mañana,	On a Monday morning,
los pícaros tartaneros	the roguish wagon drivers
les robaron las manzanas	stole apples from
a los pobres arrieros	the poor mule drivers
que venían de Totana.	that were coming from Totana.

"Only with extreme difficulty was he able to sing up to the point of *'los pícaros tartaneros.'* There he stopped and, looking at the audience with the same good nature that he had exhibited when he first sat down, he said in a speaking voice, 'Well, gentlemen.... to make a long story short, the wagon drivers stole apples from the poor mule drivers who were coming from Totana!' You can imagine the commotion that followed. Nevertheless, it was the best number of the night."[1]

In 1929, Pepe Marchena appeared in the first attempt at a flamenco musical play. *La Copla Andaluza*, by playwrites Antonio Quintero and Pascual Guillén, ran for over a year in Madrid. The script called for Marchena to compete in the *cante* with newcomer Jesús Perosanz, who was announced as a "revelation" and a "divo *por fandanguillos*." Inspired by the theater experience, Marchena took time off from *La Copla Andaluza* to write a script of his own. In November of 1929, his play, *En El Valle de la Pena* (In the Valley of Suffering), opened in the Maravillas Theater in Madrid. The press acclaimed the acting of Pepita Lláser, with whom Pepe had an affair, but little else. The play was, in reality, little more than a vehicle for the *cante* and was completely dependent upon the prestige of Pepe Marchena. A total failure, it closed after only three days. Undaunted, Marchena replaced Ramón Montoya with Pepe de Badajoz, Niño Ricardo, and Niño Sabicas for a performance in Córdoba that fared somewhat better. It is a measure of Sabicas' meteoric rise in his art that, at age sixteen, he appeared with Pepe Marchena, the maximum exponent of flamenco at that time.

Sabicas spoke of this period: "My father almost always came with me. We must have gone around Spain ten times, and I mean through cities and towns. We didn't just hop through the cities, we went to the small towns. I began to get hired in the year 1930-31. As soon as one contract was over with a company, another one would hire me."[2]

In spite of his youth and the absolute monopoly of the recording industry

---

[1]Caballero, Luis, Candil (date unknown).
[2]Molarsky interview.

by a few top guitarists—Montoya, Ricardo, Borrull, and Manolo de Badajoz—Niño Sabicas managed to break through and record with a number of popular singers. This would have been during the period 1932-36, for almost all of his recordings featured the *colombianas*, created by Pepe Marchena in 1931. It may be that Sabicas' manner of playing the *colombianas*, as a driving *rumba* rather than with the lyrical, *guajira*-like flavor of Montoya, made singers seek him out for recording this *cante*. With the very popular El Carbonerillo, Sabicas recorded *colombianas*, *soleares*, *medias granaínas*, and a number of *fandangos*. He also played *colombianas* and various types of *fandangos* for La Niña de la Puebla (with whom he also recorded *siguiriyas*, *soleares*, and *campanilleros* in the style of Manuel Torre). El Chato de las Ventas used him extensively for a variety of *guajiras* and *milongas*. On recordings with El Cojo de Madrid, El Chato de Jerez, and La Jerezana, Sabicas was asked to specialize in *fandangos*. With La Niña de Antequera, he was joined by orchestra for a *pasodoble-verdiales* in which he demonstrated a very fast and clean tremolo. Others who featured Sabicas on their records included José Nieto de Orellana and Juanito Valderrama.

About his solo playing, Sabicas said, "I was the first to play solo guitar. I was a boy when I started, but I saw the possibilities and knew that was what I wanted to do. They treated me rather as a joke at first, because flamenco guitar had never been played that way before. But I didn't care what they said. I was only nine or ten, but I kept at it." And on another occasion, "I played for all the good singers and dancers because that is the way it was done in those days. The flamenco guitar was never played solo. When I tried it, the artists would laugh at me. But I went ahead anyway. Sitting on my chair, I played whatever I thought I could play, wherever I could. And people liked it."[1]

Sabicas was not alone in claiming to be the first to play solos on the flamenco guitar. Ramón Montoya and Carlos Montoya headed a long list of those who made similar claims. But, in truth, guitarists had been giving flamenco guitar recitals for more than half a century. Julián Arcas, whose playing had inspired a young Francisco Tárrega, included flamenco solos in his guitar recitals as early as the 1860s.[2] The first true flamenco soloist is considered to be Francisco Sánchez, better known as Paco el Barbero. After a stellar career as an accompanist in the early *cafés cantantes*, El Barbero dedicated himself to giving concerts of "classical" and flamenco music. His classical repertoire consisted primarily of themes from popular operas and *zarzuelas*, the majority arranged by Julián Arcas. Two concerts given by El Barbero in Córdoba in 1885 included his flamenco arrangements of *guaji-*

---

[1] Chileno, El Niño, p. 5.
[2] Rioja, Eusebio, *Julián Arcas, o los albores del la guitarra flamenca*. Bienal de Arte Flamenco, Sevilla. 1990.

ras, peteneras, malagueñas, tangos, and *soleá*.

El Barbero may have been the first flamenco soloist, but a slightly younger contemporary, Paco de Lucena, would have the greatest influence on the next generation of guitarists. Paco began his training with a classical guitarist and developed a technique that was truly phenomenal for the period. He is credited with introducing into flamenco the *picado*, tremolo (the classical three-fingered tremolo), and arpeggios. Paco de Lucena had an ego to match his ability and was not beyond dazzling audiences with his prodigious technique while accompanying the very best singers and dancers of the *cafés cantantes*. Paco was married to the well-known *cantaora* La Parrala, and his career was most often linked with dancers and singers. There is no record of his playing recitals dedicated to the guitar, but the public usually demanded that he play solo and more often than not he obliged. During a benefit performance in Córdoba in 1879, held to raise funds to release draftees from their military obligation, Paco was enthusiastically applauded for his *guajiras, tangos, farruca, siguiriyas, malagueñas, rosas*, and other pieces.[1] Javier Molina, speaking of a time toward the end of the 1800s, said, "About this time, I met the great guitarist Paco el de Lucena—there was no one better. We gave a number of concerts with him in different towns. He played solo, and I played for the singer El Mezcle and the *cuadro flamenco*...About Paco el de Lucena I can say that he was a great artist, and we were like brothers. We were together until he went to Madrid."[2]

Around the turn-of-the-century, Javier Molina followed in Paco de Lucena's footsteps and decided to try his luck in Madrid. His friend, dancer Isabel Santos, spoke to the owner of a cafe located on the Calle del Gato, a tiny street that is little more than an ally, about the possiblity of a contract:

> "...the owner of the *café* told her that she already had two guitarists in the *cuadro*, and if I wanted to play in her place, it would have to be as a soloist, and she would give me a contract for one month.
>
> "Isabel Santos told me the conditions and I accepted. All the guitarists in Madrid at that time paraded through the Café del Gato to hear me. I played two times a night, and the repertoire that I performed was flamenco and classical.
>
> "That is when I met the great player Ramón Montoya, and the no less great Luis Molina. Each of them was playing in a cafe, and when they figured I was going to play, they came to listen to me, as did many others whose names I don't recall.
>
> "I fulfilled my contract, appreciative of the public and the professional guitarists, and shortly thereafter returned to Jerez."[3]

[1]Cano, Manuel, *La Guitarra: Historia, Estudios, y Aportaciones al Arte Flamenco*. The University of Córdoba, 1986. p. 89.
[2]Butler, p. 58.
[3]Butler, p. 51.

Back in Jerez, Javier teamed up with one of his students, Pepe Crévola, to play duets. He taught Pepe to play a number of pieces with him. When they could play exactly in unison, without mistakes, they took their *"número de varieté"* to the theaters, using an artistic name created by the combination of their last names—"Los Crevolina." After a brief attempt to launch their career as a novelty act, with varying degrees of success in Jerez, Córdoba, Ecija, and San Fernando, they abandoned the venture.

If even a dedicated accompanist like Javier Molina could work as a guitar soloist, it is clear that the concept of solo playing was not as alien to the flamenco world as Sabicas would have us believe. In 1910, Manolo de Huelva had given solo recitals in Sevilla. Although there is no record of Manolo's repertoire, it is very likely that he included some flamenco in his performances. And finally, Ramón Montoya.

Long before El Niño Sabicas arrived in Madrid, Ramón Montoya had recorded a substantial repertoire of guitar solos. In recordings made between 1910 and 1920 for two different companies, Montoya demonstrated that he had already developed most of the material he would record in Paris in 1937, for what has long been considered to be flamenco's first album of guitar solos. It is hard to believe that anybody was playing this well, with such a modern technique, at this early date. Ramón was a giant in the *toques libres* like the *rondeñas*, *mineras*, *murcianas*, *granaínas*, *tarantas*, and *malagueñas* he recorded at that time. In these free-rhythm numbers, he displayed crystalline tremolos, complex arpeggios, the new four-finger tremolo, and lush melodies. In the rhythmic *soleares* and *siguiriyas* he demonstrated a strong and virile thumb. The genius of his creativity shines in the *farruca*, *guaijiras*, *peteneras*, and *tangos* (which we would call *tientos* and *tanguillos* today). Ramón called his *alegrías* in E, *"Rosas,"* while his *alegrías* in A retained all the flavor of their ancestral *jotas* from northern Spain. Sabicas and Carlos Montoya would later record versions of this *jota*-style *alegrías*, but it is not clear if they imitated Montoya, or just played their versions of a style prevalent at the time.

In the years prior to 1936, Sabicas made a number of solo recordings that demonstrated the mature technique of the twenty-year-old guitarist. Much of the material would remain unchanged for the next two decades and appear on records made in the 1950s. The playing is much cleaner than that of Ramón Montoya or others of the time, with rich, pure tones and brilliant speed in the *picados*. Sabicas had brought the tremolo to a level of perfection that would not be surpassed for fifty years. The melody lines of his tremolos were complex, employing trills and difficult changes on the inner strings, and his bass-lines were equally innovative. And he could play tremolos very fast in an *alegrías*, *farruca*, or *verdiales*, with no loss of clarity. In numbers like the *soleá* he showed his mastery of the upper reaches of the guitar neck, made more difficult by his placement of the *cejilla* at the third fret for almost all solos.[1] Evident in these early recordings is the extensive use of tapping on the guitar face, a trademark of Sabicas' playing throughout his life.

Sabicas also showed an early interest in developing solo versions of some of the more trivial flamenco rhythms, those that other guitarists did not deem worthy of attention. In these first recordings, he created a *garrotín* that contains most of the melodies he would play for the rest of his life. Many credit Sabicas with changing the key of the *garrotín* to C-major, from the more typical A-major. But, in fact, Luis Molina had accompanied La Niña de los Peines in C as early as 1910. In the same category of trivial folk music developed into solos by Sabicas are his recordings of *campanilleros* and a *malagueñas* based on a *fandango* from the province of Almería. He also recorded *danza mora*, an arabic-flavored music that would become his specialty and that he would record in many different forms. Sabicas singlehandedly developed this Moorish dance for the guitar, but he did not invent it. Previously, Miguel Borrull had recorded *"Danza Arabe."*

Of his meeting with Carmen Amaya, Sabicas said, "We met when we were both children in Barcelona. I went to work there and I saw her dance one day—she was very young too. I became friends with her and her family."[2] "I met Carmen in a restaurant called Casa de Manquet. There on the dock, where all the sailors used to go. A singer took me there, telling me, 'Come, you'll see someone dance!' I went in. The flamenco atmosphere was great. There was Carmen, very young. I was stunned to see what she could do...her hands, her feet...She carried everyone."[3] "I saw her dance and it seemed like something supernatural to me...I never saw anyone dance like her. I don't know how she did it, I just don't know!"[4]

Sabicas had gone to Barcelona to record for the Parlophón Record Company. Apparently he spent considerable time there, probably in the Villa Rosa, for his brother, Diego, said that they tried to get him to marry one of the Borrull sisters. Seeing the potential in Carmen, Sabicas approached her frustrated father: "Look, Chino, you know that I have some understanding of these things. Your little girl has something very serious within her, but among these people who neither know nor care about this, she isn't going to do anything...You have to take her to Madrid. There are people there who know about all of this and they will know how to look at her!"[5]

[1] The *cejilla* or capo is clamped across the strings to raise or lower the pitch for a singer. It is sometimes used in solo playing to give a more brilliant sound and make the guitar play faster, but many modern players forgo the use of the *cejilla* in an attempt to facilitate the playing of high notes on the guitar.

[2] Magnussen, p. 19.
[3] Molarsky interview.
[4] Chileno, p. 6.
[5] Hidalgo, p. 87.

It didn't take much to convince El Chino, but, according to Sabicas, the father told him, "We can't afford to go!" To which Sabicas replied, "Don't worry about the money. Just go! I'll be there for you."[1] Shortly thereafter, El Chino and Carmen left the small family flat on Calle Nueva and headed to Madrid. In the capital, some small contracts came their way, enabling them to survive and even send a little money home to Barcelona. The two shared a room in run-down *pension* and went largely unnoticed in that big city. Many years later, Sabicas' brother, Diego Castellón, described this period in the only interview he ever granted. He told Meira Goldberg in 1989:

> Sabicas had advised Carmen's father that they should go to Madrid, that there would be more ability to understand her dance and more of a flamenco atmosphere in which she could earn more money, and she would stand out much more. And that is how it was. Some three or four weeks later they appeared in Madrid. Sabicas had told them not to worry about money—something would turn up...
>
> I met her in the Puerta del Sol. They were staring at me, they knew me by sight. El Chino greeted me, saying, "You are Diego, aren't you?"
>
> I said to him, *"Sí señor!"*
>
> "And your brother?"
>
> *"Tío*, I don't know. He's coming tomorrow."
>
> "My daughter, Carmen."
>
> "Pleased to meet you, *hija*!"
>
> I told them to come the following day to Café Madrid, which was where all the artists went, there in the Puerta del Sol. For sure they would see Sabicas when he arrived in the morning from his tour with La Niña de la Puebla...
>
> The next day—or perhaps that same day—Sabicas saw them and brought them home. He invited them to eat and offered them the necessities... Later, one night, he took them to Villa Rosa, the cathedral of flamenco, where there were all the great *cantaores*, the great guitarists. Father and daughter went, and everybody was in a private room in a *juerga*. Sabicas said, "Come in, come in! And the girl, too!" And he said, "This is a girl from Barcelona who dances very well."[2]

That night has become legendary. Here is the popular version, related by Salvador Montañés. He mistakenly placed it in Café Sevilla (more likely, Villa Rosa) where flamenco artists gathered before work. One evening,

---

[1] Molarsky interview.
[2] Goldberg interview, 1989.

Sabicas appeared in the cafe, greeted El Chino with a slap on the back and Carmen with a kiss on the cheek, and addressed those gathered there, "Look here, you have among you a *catalán* gypsy who does very well and knows all you could want to know about this business of dancing!"
Montañés continued:

> El Peluco hears Sabicas' remark. El Peluco is another of those who claim to know everything about flamenco. And it is true that El Peluco, a *cantaor* with knowledge and feeling, *"currela lo suyo en esto del flamenco"* [roughly, "knows what he is doing in this thing of flamenco"] as he himself says. But he is passionate, and upon hearing Sabicas, his guffaw is tremendous as he says, "A *catalana*? She has to be fraud!"
> Carmen is seated to the left of Sabicas, and at her side, El Chino. Peluco's comment does not sit well with Carmen. She rises abruptly, faces the *cantaor*, and says to him, "Fraud? Watch this…!"
> Carmen Amaya, the *catalán* gypsy, breaks into a dance, while Sabicas and El Chino hum some ancient verses of *soleares* under their breath and their hands beat on and caress the marble tabletop. El Peluco opens his eyes in amazement. Carmen is dancing for him! There is no sound of guitars, only an audience who knows about these things. Carmen improvises. Suddenly, El Peluco rises from his chair and, to the amazement of the rest, leans against a wall and, while beating his head forcefully against it, cries out wildly, "Fraud, fraud?…I called her a fraud! That is what it means to dance, girl!"
> Carmen, without stopping, comes close to El Peluco, corners him, drives him crazy… The spectators, astonished, stand on the chairs and tables in order to see the spectacle of El Peluco crying and bleeding from the wound in his forehead that he got from hitting the wall. The impassioned gypsy girl, such a little thing, has kicked off her shoes and is dancing, spitting fire from her eyes, all because they have called her a "fraud." Meanwhile, a voice sounds a *cante*, a profound *cante*, that speaks of passion, of mountains, sun, and bramble patches [*zarzales*]. Carmen Amaya, the *catalán* gypsy, dances to the rhythm of that *cante*. El Peluco shudders and continues singing. El Peluco sings for Carmen Amaya and Carmen Amaya dances. But now Carmen has forgotten that they had called her a "fraud," she has forgotten El Peluco, she has forgotten everything. Carmen Amaya now dances for herself. In reality, Carmen Amaya never has danced for anybody![1]

Now, thanks to Molarsky's interview of Sabicas and Goldberg's interviews with his brother, Diego, we have first-hand testimony concerning that

---
[1] Montañés, p. 23.

unforgettable night. Surprisingly, their accounts support many aspects of the popular legend:

> Sabicas: One day I was in a *juerga* with a group of gypsies in the Villa Rosa, and I saw her mother and father. I went over to the father and daughter and embraced them. I said, "What are you doing here?" I asked them to come in. Then I saw that Carmen was dancing in her chair. She wanted to dance. Two or three excellent *bailaoras* came out to dance, and then I gave my guitar to Carmen's father and said, "If it is okay with you?"
> And I said, "Now, Carmen Amaya, a *catalán* gypsy, is going to dance a little." And she went to the stage. She danced. One man hit himself against the wall and cracked his head open. The plates and tables were all over the place.[1]
>
> Diego: Sabicas said, "Come, *niña*, dance a little so these people can see you!" And when they saw her dance they were stunned and put their hands to their heads. She danced *por alegrías, por soleá*, and I don't know what..."How can this be? It is a miracle of God!"[2]
>
> Sabicas: Immediately everybody knew who she was. She was a star. She swept everybody away.

Soon, word spread through Madrid and of course everthing became distorted. They spoke of a wild *juerga*, a big fight, a drunken orgy. And, clearly, Carmen Amaya's name was on everybody's lips. Work began to come her way. Diego Castellón recalled: "There was a cabaret called El Alcázar where Carmen got her start. Everyone came to see her and everyone was talking about her. It was a cabaret, with *canción* singers and this and that, and then she did her thing...with her father playing for her, and later her brother Paco. And she always dressed in white pants. And her father also dressed in white."[3]

Before long, the impresario Juan Carcellé contacted El Chino.

---

[1] Molarsky interview.
[2] Goldberg interviews.
[3] Goldberg interviews.

CHAPTER SIX

EXILE

According to Antonio Triana, before Carmen went out on a tour of the provinces she learned some routines from him and performed in the Lido Club and the Casino de la Perla. He wrote:

> I was performing in Madrid when I was approached by the father of a young dancer who was about to make her debut. She danced only flamenco and her father asked me to teach her some routines that could be performed with orchestra. I proceeded to teach her my choreography to a *pasodoble* written by my brother [the pianist Manuel García Matos]. She responded admirably. Her father saw us as an ideal team and was intent on joining us. So it was that, in a casino in San Sebastián, Carmen Amaya and I danced together for the first time. Our paths soon separated, however, as I had other commitments.[1]

While Carmen Amaya alternated between tours of the provinces with the company of Carcellé and performances with her old *cuadro* in Barcelona, La Argentinita toured with her new show, *Las Calles de Cádiz* (The Streets of Cádiz).

In 1927, Ignacio Sánchez Mejías had joined La Argentinita in retirement, abandoning the bullring in order to dedicate himself to writing. In the Madrid home he shared with La Argentinita, the home she had built in the early 1920s, with its Sevillian-style patio adorned with colored tiles and potted plants, Ignacio wrote several plays that enjoyed moderate popular success. After returning from the trip to New York with Encarnación in 1930, he began to develop the script for a new dance work. In 1932, preparations for the first true theatrical presentation of flamenco began in earnest. Ignacio wrote the script, often attributed to Lorca, under the pseudonym Jiménez Chávarri. He also did the scenery, the promotion, the financing, and took on the task of casting the artists.

La Argentinita wanted *Las Calles de Cádiz* to bring authentic flamenco dancing to the stage in a natural setting, so Ignacio went to Cádiz to find

---
[1]Pohren, p. 368.

gypsies who had not been tainted by the *ópera flamenca*. He hoped to contract Ignacio Espeleta, an eccentric gypsy singer with a reputation for laziness. Although Espeleta occasionally worked in the slaughterhouse, he always bragged that his hands were virgins when it came to work. When his friends found him a job as a guard in the public park, it is said that he made a long whip in order to chase cats without having to get up from his park bench. But Espeleta was no slouch when it came to the *cante*. He had an extensive repertoire of Cádiz styles and excelled in the rhythmic *alegrías* and *bulerías*, in which he was the first to warm up with the *tarantrantrán*—a vocal imitation of the guitar. At first, Espeleta was reluctant to leave Cádiz, but he had such respect for Sánchez Mejías' love of the *cante* and his friendship with Lorca that he relented. Sánchez Mejías assured him that, in the role of the shoemaker, he only had to sing two times, *por alegrías* and *por tanguillos*.

In Cádiz, Sánchez Mejías also found El Churri, an old-time dancer of *tangos*, fifteen-year-old Adela Chaqueta, Pablito de Cádiz, who had worked with La Argentinita off and on for years, and his brother Curro Jiménez. Others who would serve in the chorus were Manolita de Maora, Paquita la del Morao, El Lillo (a popular dancer from Sevilla), and El Titi (possibly the singer from Triana who created a style of *tango*).

To head this cast, Ignacio selected the professional dancer Rafael Ortega and the very popular *cantaor* El Gloria. But the real stroke of genius was to bring three legendary dancers to the theater stage. La Macarrona, La Malena, and Fernanda Antúnez, all from Jerez de la Frontera—a breeding ground for good dancers—had established their careers during the heyday of the *cafés cantantes* in the last quarter of the 1800s. Juana Vargas "La Macarrona" had been the reigning queen of the flamenco dance for more than fifty years. She began to dance professionally at age eight and then went on to share the stage with two generations of flamenco's greatest artists. Now, at age seventy-two, she was asked to star in *Las Calles de Cádiz*. La Malena (aunt of the young guitarist, Eduardo de la Malena), renowned for her dark gypsy beauty and elegant and arrogant posture in the dance, had been a competitor of La Macarrona and joined La Argentinita at about age sixty. Fernanda Antúnez, age sixty-eight, had been a giant in her day, although often overshadowed by her more beautiful sister, Juana (by 1932, Juana had begun to go insane and would commit suicide a couple of years later by jumping off the roof of the charity hospital where she was confined).

It has long been accepted that Sánchez Mejías brought these dancers out of impoverished retirement to perform in *Las Calles de Cádiz*. However, the following comments by Antonio Mairena indicate that at least some of them were still quite active:

In 1930 [when Mairena was twenty-one], a close friend took me to Sevilla and introduced me in the Kursaal Internacional, which was a luxurious cabaret at that time and offered the attraction of a *cuadro flamenco*. After much begging, they let me perform one night, but without pay, as an audition. When my time came, I sang and the great guitarist Javier Molina, already quite old, played for me. He played in the *cuadro* they had, made up of La Malena, La Macarrona, La Sordilla, and some other gypsy women who were still around during those years. When it was my turn to sing, Javier Molina asked me, "What are you going to sing?"

Innocently, I said to him that I was going to sing *por soleares* and *por siguiriyas*. And Javier made a face, as if to say, "Those *cantes* are not for this time." And, in effect, they were not *cantes* for that time, nor for that audience...Nevertheless, I went over well that night, because some good aficionados happened to be there and they applauded me heartily, enough to get me a contract to perform additional nights.[1]

In June of 1933, before completing preparations for *Las Calles de Cádiz*, La Argentinita debuted a new version of *El Amor Brujo* in the Teatro Falla in Cádiz, dedicating the performance to García Lorca, who was in the audience. This work stressed the folkloric elements of the music and, as a result, was more "flamenco" than any previous version. On this occasion, La Argentinita danced for the first time with her sister, Pilar López. To provide the music, they engaged the Orquesta Bética de Cámara (Chamber Orchestra of Sevilla) which had been founded by Manuel de Falla. The oboist in that orchestra was none other than Manuel García Matos, the brother of Antonio Triana. When Matos discovered that Argentinita had not yet found a male dancer for the role of Carmelo, he recommended his brother and they sent for him in Madrid.

Antonio Triana described the experience: "[La Argentinita]...sent me a telegram in Madrid (where I was appearing in musicals) and I soon joined her and her sister Pilar for rehearsals in Sevilla. To give the ballet enormous authenticity, they contracted La Malena, La Macarrona, and La Fernanda for scenes in the gypsy caves. The choreography of the ballet itself was achieved though a mingling of ideas and improvisations on the part of Encarna, Pilar, Rafael Ortega (who was to play the ghost), and myself (as Carmelo). We had a triumphant opening night in Cádiz, the birthplace of De Falla. We then went on a complete tour of Spain...This was truly the birth of the '*Ballet Español.*'"[2]

Apparently *El Amor Brujo* was not considered sufficient for even one half of an evening's performance. When it played in the Teatro Español in

---
[1] Mairena, p. 78.
[2] Pohren, p. 368.

Madrid, it had to be prefaced by a suite of dances from Falla's *The Three-cornered Hat*. Then, after intermission, the second half consisted of what Antonio de Triana called *"conciertos de danza,"* brief scenarios, each based on a different musical theme: three dances to the music of Falla, others by Albéniz and Gamboa, two songs by Lorca, a *jota*, and *"Alegrías y Tango de Cádiz,"* accompanied on guitar by Manolo de Huelva. This would be the time described by Donn Pohren, when Manolo de Huelva was to appear in a version of *Las Calles de Cádiz* and insisted on having a special cage built that would hide him from the public. In spite of concessions to his desire for privacy, he walked out before the season finished.[1]

The Madrid newspaper, *El Sol*, wrote: "It must be said immediately that the clearest *españolismo* [love of things Spanish], with the toughest fiber and the sharpest, hardest, and most biting roots, was seen yesterday in the display of dances organized by La Argentinita. Equally true in both *El Amor Brujo* and in the splendid succession of assorted dances that followed in the second part of the program and finished up with something tremendous: the *'Alegrías'* of three old maestras of the dance: La Macarrona, La Malena, La Fernanda, along with Rafael Ortega..."[2]

Four months later, in October, *Las Calles de Cádiz* opened in the Teatro Español in Madrid. In this colorful hour-long program, each artist played a role—policeman, prostitute, waiter, shoemaker, drunk—and the streets of Cádiz were brought life on stage. In one scene, the curtain opened on the shoemaker (Ignacio Espeleta) as he sang a *tanguillo*. A child wandered out, joked with him, and tried to steal from his table. The shoemaker made attempts to hit the child, until the mother (La Macarrona) grabbed the boy by the neck and smacked him on the rear—all in perfect *compás*! Later, four *bailaoras* came out from four streets dancing *alegrías* in *batas de cola*, a true innovation at the time. According to Pilar López, it was the first time that full scenery had been used with flamenco and the first time that children had danced in a flamenco production. The program closed with everybody on stage for *"Nochebuena de Jerez,"* the singing of *villancicos* on Christmas Eve, accompanied by tambourines and *zambombas*.

The magazine *Ahora* reported on October 15: "Encarnación and her sister Pilar interpreted adaptations of Jiménez Chávarri, Falla, and Albéniz. They did a scene from Málaga entitled *'El Café de Chinitas'* by García Lorca, and finished with the debut of the poem *'Las Calles de Cádiz,'* by Chávarri. The titles of the scenes give an idea of their flavor: 'Song of the Chorus,' 'Dance Lesson,' *'Tangos,' 'Bulerías* of the Shrimp Vendor,' 'The Barrio Watchman,' *'Villancicos* of Christmas Eve in Jerez,' and 'The *Tango* of the Clerk.'"

The mention of music by Falla and Lorca in this article refers to other

---

[1] Pohren, p. 281.
[2] El Sol, June 16, 1933. Reproduced in the brochure that accompanies the re-issue of *Canciones Populares Españolas* by Sonifolk. Madrid, 1994.

parts of the program. *Las Calles de Cádiz* was only the second half of a massive evening's entertainment. La Argentinita began with a performance of the complete ballet, *El Amor Brujo,* and followed with a series of short dance scenarios: "Madrid 1890," "*Sevillanas* of the 18th Century," *"El Café de Chinitas"* (a *petenera* recorded by Argentinita and Lorca), "The *Romance* of the Pilgrims," and *"La romería de los cornudos"* ("The Pilgrimage of the Cuckholded").

The production took to the road. On October 16, the *Heraldo* of Madrid reported its debut in Cádiz: "The truly memorable was the second half of the program [*Las Calles de Cádiz*]... Alternating their performances, [Encarnación and Pilar] danced and sang with that art of theirs that is so much a part of them, that captivated and drew applause from even the coldest in the audience...Particular mention is deserved by those *archimaestras* of the gypsy dance, La Macarrona, La Malena, and La Fernanda, the pure essence of *el arte cañí* [the gypsy art]."

This was the first large theater experience for many of the artists, and it gave flamenco a new dimension, a dignity it hadn't known before. Antonia Mercé "La Argentina" had formed the first true Spanish dance company in 1929, and now La Argentinita had created the first theatrical Spanish ballet company. She called it *"La Compañía de Bailes Españoles."*

La Argentinita toured with her company through the year and into the next. In June, 1934, they reached Paris and performed on the 24th in the Théâtre des Ambassadeurs. By that time, Sánchez Mejías, age forty-three, had already decided to return to the bullring after seven years of retirement. His friends tried to dissuade him, and it is said that the gypsies in the Villa Rosa of Madrid had been warning him for a year that he smelled of death. It was not a good year for bullfighters—twelve men had already died on the horns of bulls and forty more had been seriously injured. On August 11, against the advice of friends and subordinates, he took the place of a matador who had just died in an automobile accident. In the bullring of Manzanares, a bull named *Granadino* trapped Ignacio against the barrier and gored him. He died of gangrene five days later.

It was a tremendous loss for Argentinita and for Ignacio's many friends. García Lorca expressed his grief in his most famous poem, *"Llanto por Ignacio Sánchez Mejías"* ("Lament for Ignacio Sánchez Mejías"), with its haunting, dirge-like refrain that is repeated over and over: *"A las cinco de la tarde..."* ("At five in the afternoon..."). In the last verse of this epic work, which he had dedicated to "My dear friend, Encarnación López Júlvez," Lorca lamented with more than casual affection:

> It will be a long time before there is born, if such a one is born,
> an Andaluz so clear, so rich in adventure.
> I sing the praise of your elegance with words that wail

and recall a sad breeze through the olive trees.

While La Argentinita conquered Europe with her new conception of Spanish dance, La Argentina continued her seduction of audiences worldwide. In October of 1930, she had arrived in New York aboard the *Paris*, along with pianists José Iturbi and Ignace Paderewiski and director Erich Von Stroheim. For her third American season she had prepared five new dances: "Andalusian Serenade" by Rucker, "Dance of Terror" from *El Amor Brujo*, a Cuban *"Habanera"* by Sarasate, a Mexican dance (*jarabe*), and "Iberian Dance," composed for her by Joaquín Nin. Of these, "Iberian Dance"—subtitled "a choreographic drama in three parts" and in reality a whole ballet compressed into a few minutes—was by far the most successful. For the first time, she used guitarists in her recitals: Jerónimo Villarino, who had settled in America, and Antonio Pérez, the son of the legendary guitarist of Sevilla, Maestro Pérez. She also brought a *canción* singer who performed standing by the piano on stage. La Argentina would give sixty performances during her five-month stay and tour from New York to Boston, throughout the South, and finish on the West Coast.

By early January, 1931, La Argentina was in San Francisco where the Geary Theater had "…an auduence crammed to the last corners of the house and applause echoing from the fascinating visitor's first appearance on the stage until well after her final encore." Following an appearance in Oakland, the dancer headed south. The *Los Angeles Times* wrote:

> It was last Monday that the artiste, who has taken the continent and America by storm, arrived in Los Angeles for her second season, wearing the ribbon of the French Legion of Honor and having the distinction of being the only Spanish woman ever awarded that decoration. Her last concert is scheduled for Tuesday night at the Philharmonic Auditorium. Thirty trunks, laden to overflowing with costumes, accompanied her, for La Argentina gives to her costumes the power of creating line and color for the dance.
>
> "Zee costume, he ees so important." Madame Argentina's accent proves a delightful mixture of French, Spanish, and English. She shrugged her shoulders in a true Parisian manner. "He should dance along weeth zee body. He should—what you say—carry out zee line and color of zee thought? He should follow evairy movement of zee danseur—whirl when she whirl, or fall een soft folds, n'est ce pas?"
>
> That a costume never be cut contrary to the line of the dance for which it is worn is almost a religion with Argentina. Together with some of Spain's finest painters she works out the lines and colors of her various gowns. Argentina chooses the materials, experi-

menting oftimes with as many as six or seven costumes for one number...

All of her compositions are inspired by music. She will select a composition and study it for as long as five months, or until she feels as intimate with its every intonation, every change of rhythm, as does its composer. Out of this grows the dance.[1]

From Los Angeles, La Argentina returned to Europe for recitals in Paris and Madrid and then set out on a tour of Asia. On December 3, 1931, the First Spanish Republic presented her with *La Cruz de Isabel la Católica* in honor of her "service in the interest of Spanish art in the Americas." This "Garland of Isabella the Catholic," given to Argentina by President Manuel Azaña, was the first award by the new republic. By the end of that month, La Argentina was back in New York for her fourth season. John Martin commented on some of her new dances:

> Among them two were outstanding, namely a classic bolero, *"Puerta de Tierra,"* by Albéniz, and the *"Charrada,"* an antique dance from Salamanca. This latter, it is said, has only recently been discovered by Mme. Argentina, who learned it in remote corner of Spain from an old man who is among the few who remember it. Certainly it never could have been danced by the peasants as it was danced last night, or they would not have allowed themselves to abandon it. It consists largely of extremely brilliant footwork, most of it done with a relaxed ankle, and quite apart in style from the conventional Spanish footwork...
>
> The "Shawl Dance" from Pittaluga's ballet, *La Romería de los Cornudos*, proved again that everything the dancer handles is turned to rhythm. By means of the shawl, which can become a troublesome property when unskillfully used, she extends the rhythm of her arms and torso at will and frequently makes use of it to establish an additional rhythm of its own...
>
> *"Malagueña,"* besides being an amusing and lively dance on its own, afforded the audience the pleasure of seeing the gracious Argentina play at being a fishwife. There was also the same type of pleasure to be found in watching the utterly feminine Argentina play at being a man in the "Miller's Dance" from Falla's *Three-cornered Hat*.[2]

While La Argentina was dancing in Town Hall, a number of modern dancers, following in the school of free dance created by Isadora Duncan, were performing in different theaters around New York City. Irma Duncan

---
[1]Mayer, Mary, "Dance Art Demands All." *Los Angeles Times*, January 25, 1931.
[2]Martin, John, "La Argentina's Art Again is Welcomed." Copyright © *The York Times*, December 30, 1931. Reprinted by permission.

and the Isadora Duncan Dancers were in Carnegie Hall, Doris Humphrey gave a recital, and Mary Wigman was a hit the same night in the Chanin Theatre with "Gypsy Moods." Martha Graham was also a frequent visitor to the city. La Argentina was asked her thoughts about this new type of dance:

> Her eyes stopped their gayety for a moment and she weighed a reply with manifest calculations of tact. "My conception of dance is different," was her response at last. "I believe that dancing should be all beauty—not necessarily personal beauty, mind you, but beauty of form, of line, of movement, of rhythm."
>
> Her own dances, she explained, are derived from Spanish folk dances. "But I have used the folk dances only as foundations upon which I have constructed idealized dance compositions. Still, I try to keep the folk spirit unspoiled."[1]

On another occasion she was not so tactful:

> "I think it's ugly!"
>
> And does La Argentina admit that the modernist dance in its way expresses something?
>
> Thrust number two: "I think it expresses ugliness."
>
> The Latin rapier look left La Argentina's dark eye in an instant. She waxed voluble and persuasive. Then she smiled her smile that has the Spanish hint of a wink about it. "There is room in the world for two ideas," she said. "The modernist dancers have their idea. I have mine... I think modernist theories of the dance are popular with dancers because modernist technique is so easy. It is no technique. One simply gets up on the stage and moves around."[2]

La Argentina left New York after a second performance on January 2nd, but returned after a short tour to continue the season. February found her in Los Angeles, where she spoke in Spanish at a luncheon given in her honor by the Dancing Teachers Business Association and the Dancer's Protective League of Southern California and then performed in the Philharmonic Auditorium in early March. In San Francisco, "Applause demanded the repetition of nearly every number in her repertoire. Occasionally she resisted the demand, often she yielded to it."

By March 20th she had completed her swing through the West and returned to New York for a farewell performance in Carnegie Hall—billed as "Spain's Glamorous Dancer." One of her new numbers was a Cuban *rumba*, in which, according to John Martin, "...she gave not the rumba but her opinion of the rumba and of the type of Cuban woman who is generally found dancing it."[3] In this concert, La Argentina also danced for the first

---

[1] Fried, Alexander, "Talent Alone Insufficient, Says Dancer." *San Francisco Chronicle*, February 22, 1932.

[2] "Noted Spanish Dancer Scores Modernists." *San Francisco Chronicle*, November 29, 1934.

[3] *The New York Times*, Frebruary 1, 1932.

time a number that would become a mainstay in the programs of future Spanish dance companies—*"Leyenda"* (*"Asturias"*) by Albéniz, in which she "...built rhythm upon rhythm in the most intricate contrapuntal designs." The Carnegie Hall appearance was Argentina's forty-eighth recital in New York. She would not be back for almost three years.

La Argentina continued to tour Europe and the Far East. In January of 1933 newspapers reported that she was in Montevideo, Uruguay, to vacation at the Carrasco bathing resort. Rumors were that she had gone there to divorce her Argentine husband, but she denied it, saying that she had come to found a dance school. In July of that year, she went to Buenos Aires for six performances in the Colón Theater, for which she was paid $14,000.

The November 20, 1934 issue of the *Los Angeles Times* told of La Argentina's return to North America after her long absence:

> La Argentina, volatile and at all times delightful, arrived in town yesterday from Mexico City, where forceful intervention was necessary before she was permitted to leave the enthusiastic populace. Radiant in the remembrance of her success there, where she went to give three programs and remained to dance seven, La Argentina spoke more staccato Spanish in one minute than anyone else could utter in five. The flash of her enormous black eyes and the "expresivo" of her large, mobile mouth is quicker and more alive than the eye or mind can catch.
>
> Mexico gave her her first inspiration and real appreciation in 1917 when she was unknown and unsung in the rest of America and again Mexico City has returned her to us with renewed enthusiasm...

A typical Argentina program was outlined in the *Los Angeles Times* after her concert on November 22:

> Her program last night began with a Spanish suite by Granados, played superlatively by the young Spanish pianist she brought with her, Luis Galve. After establishing the Spanish atmosphere on the high plane of Granados' music, Argentina made her first entrance in the Andalusian dance from "The Woman of Spain" by Joaquín Turina. It had an electric effect upon the audience. A dance from the opera *La Vida Breve*, by Falla, and the "Fire Ritual" from his *El Amor Brujo* followed in quick succession.
>
> An Andalusian Tango, the man-imitating "Zapateado," and the quaint charm of "Madrid in 1890" delighted her old admirers...The picturesque "Castilla" in the costume of Goya was a finished conception of the aristocrat of Spain and the emphatic "Jota from Aragon" presented another strata of Spanish life.
>
> Granados' slow rhythm of "Dance No. 5" gave a sinister beauty

to the program. The concert ended with the pictorial impressions of the bullfight to the music of Valverde, which was enchanting.[1]

The music for La Argentina's bullfight number, *"Corrida,"* was actually an *alegrías* composed on piano by Maestro Valverde for Antonio de Bilbao. La Argentina had become more interested in traditional flamenco and began to add flamenco dances to her repertoire. In time, she became a more complete *bailaora*, and when she returned to New York in December of 1934 for what would be her last concerts in America, she performed the *zapateado* to music by Granados, her *tango*, and a number listed in the program as *"Alegrais-Solera,"* which could have been a misprint of *"Alegrías-soleá"* or, more likely, *"Alegría solera"*—as Argentinita had recorded some years earlier. Fernando de Triana wrote: "Much has been said about Antonia Mercé, but they have omitted this: she is not only the first *bailarina* of the theater, but also the best *bailaora* of the *tablao* [flamenco nightclub]!" Perhaps an exaggeration, for La Argentina always kept her classical styling and lacked the primitive force needed for traditional flamenco.

Fernando de Triana, who had been a singer in the *café cantante* era, may have been prejudiced in Antonia's favor due to the help she gave him in 1935. When the dancer saw an impressive collection of photographs of flamenco artists that Fernando had painstakingly assembled, she proposed a benefit to raise money to publish them. The resulting evening, called "Exhaltation of the Art of Flamenco," took place in the Teatro Español of Madrid in June of that year and brought together an impressive list of artists. After a first half dedicated to poetry readings by such authors and actors as Manuel Machado, Antonio Quintero, José Ojeda, and six others, the second half of the program featured performances of *cante* and *baile*. The school dancer Angel Pericet performed with his company, as did the group of Frasquillo that included his wife, La Quica, their little daughter, Mercedes, and Rafael Cruz and El Estampío. Among the many singers were Bernardo el de los Lobitos and the very popular *fandango* singer, José Palanca. La Argentina arrived in the morning from Paris, danced *rosas* (*alegrías*), *soleares*, and *tangos* to the guitar of Salvador Ballesteros, and the following morning took the train to Brussels for another performance. Fernando's book, *Arte y Artistas Flamencos*, became the first collection of biographies of flamencos of the *café cantante* period, without which we would have little knowledge of that era.

It is not known whether Carmen Amaya ever had an opportunity to see La Argentina or La Argentinita's *Las Calles de Cádiz*. She was busy alternating between tours with Circuitos Carcellés and performances in Barcelona.

---

[1]"La Argentina Achieves Hit." *Los Angeles Times*, November 23, 1934.

Sebastián Gasch described Carmen's dancing in a benefit in Barcelona in February of 1935: "An unpolished product of the land, Carmen Amaya offered a magnificent display—magnificent and tempestuous—of temperament in its pure state. Rite, sexuality and symbol, wild negation of everything systematic, that little gypsy was a piece of living nature, struggling to get her impulses under control—her spasms of inner turmoil, her animal ferocity—without success."[1]

Carcellé, always on the lookout for ways to promote his new dancer, inserted Carmen between two numbers in an homage held for the actress Luisita Esteso and the *cupletista* Custodia Romero (also known as "The Bronze Venus") in the Fontalba Theater in Madrid. "When the tiny Carmen began to dance, nobody knew who she was. But ignorance was soon followed by astonishment, coldness by enthusiasm, and disinterest by curiosity. By the time the young girl finished, her name had been consecrated, and the following day, her triumph was so secure that the contract she was offered to work in the Coliseum only served to endorse it. Her fame quickly spread beyond the Capital."[2]

Luisita Esteso, the most famous comic actress of the time, must have been impressed by Carmen, for it wasn't long afterward that she presented the dancer in the Coliseum Theater of Madrid. On opening night, Luisita announced to the packed house, "It is an honor for me to present to you, Carmen Amaya!" She retired to the wing, while on the other side of the stage a nervous Carmen Amaya prepared to make her entrance. Once on stage, dancing furiously like a whirlwind, Carmen forgot her fears and soon had the audience on its feet yelling *"Olé!"* as if they were in a bullring. For weeks they came to see the tiny gypsy dance alone on stage to the accompaniment of ten guitars.

Other performances followed in Madrid's theaters, including sharing the stage with Conchita Piquer in the Teatro de la Zarzuela. Then, the young film maker Luis Buñuel asked Carmen to dance in his third film, *La Hija de Juan Simón*. Buñuel had achived notoriety with his first two films, most notably the surrealistic *Un Chien Andalou* that he made in France with Salvador Dalí. The melodramatic script of *La Hija de Juan Simón* was based on a *milonga* adapted by the *cantaor* Manuel Escacena from a Mexican song and sung in its most popular version by Angelillo—a Pepe Marchena imitator who carried the *ópera* style to an extreme with endless warbling in an impossibly high falsetto voice.

In the film, a young girl falls in love with an actor who comes to her village to make a movie. She goes off to Madrid with him, deserting the young man who dreamed of marrying her. Eventually, she returns home, disillusioned and sick. When she dies, her father, the town gravedigger, has to bury

[1] Hidalgo, p. 89.
[2] Góngora.

her. In the song, the townspeople ask, "Where are you coming from, Simón?" Simón replies, "I'm the gravedigger and I'm coming from burying my heart!"

The film received a great deal of publicity, but had a short life and its only real merits were the convincing performance of Angelillo and the dancing of Carmen Amaya, which was seen for the first time throughout Spain.

In early 1936, Carmen performed with the *cuadro* of Salón Variedades in Sevilla. Her first appearance in Sevilla became one of the great moments in her life:

> [The reason]…was the presence of two gypsy dancers, the most famous in the grand style of the *jondo* dance, who at the beginning of the century had inflamed the enthusiasm of the public. Both, full of years and infirmities, were present, basking in the admiration and homage of the Sevilla public that loved them dearly. They were La Macarrona and La Malena. They were waiting impatiently to see this new star beginning to shine in the magic circle of the flamenco art.
>
> After the first flourishes of the guitar, Carmen opened her dance with the *soleares*. The silence was impressive. Soon her demon took hold of her. And, 'Good Lord, what broke loose there!' La Macarrona and La Malena were on their feet, crying. It was a dream; they had come back to life in the person of Carmen. [Tradition has it that La Macarrona cried out, "You are the queen!"] The audience laughed and cried, encouraging the gypsy with rhythmical clapping. The two old gypsies were crying, and Carmen the beachcomber kept dancing, she too, full of tears…Here was the new *Faraona*, worthy to occupy the throne, for nearly thirty years empty.[1]

At another appearance there was a riot when hundreds became disgruntled because all of the seats were sold out. The *cantaor* Antonio Mairena recalled his experience with Carmen Amaya in Sevilla at that time:

> She was being presented in the Salón Variedades, today the Cine Trajano, where she performed for a few weeks in which she created a great excitement in artistic circles and, in general, among everyone involved in show business and flamenco. When Carmen finished her perfomances in Sevilla, she gave a fiesta for some friends and artists in the Venta de Antequera, and she invited me because she was interested in meeting me and listening to me.
>
> In that fiesta in the Venta de Antequera I pleased her with my singing, and she saw in me the *cantaor* she needed for her dance. Carmen was very gypsy in her ways, and it can be said that we agreed in everything. I pleased her so much that she told me she

---

[1] Samperio, José.

would call me to Barcelona to do the *cante* for a movie that was being filmed at that time, *María de la O*. My *cante* would appear to be sung by the actor Julio Peña. A few days later she called me from Barcelona and contracted me. I went to Barcelona...
During the recording that was done for the movie, everything went smoothly. Later, I spent with Carmen everything I had earned by appearing in the film. But a hopeful atmosphere had been formed for my artistic future. I returned to Sevilla...[1]

Carmen played the title role in the new film, that of María de la O, the gypsy daughter of a wealthy painter married to a gypsy woman who is killed because of her race. It is a measure of Carmen's growing status that her face was chosen to grace the posters for the movie. The film is a story of intrigue, romance, revenge, confused identities, and conflict between social classes. Again, the movie was based on a popular song—*"María de la O,"* by Valverde, León, and Quiroga. Many artists had recorded it, including Manuel Vallejo with *palmas* and *jaleo* by La Niña de los Peines, Juanito Mojama, and Bernardo el de los Lobitos. In the film, a jilted lover exacts his revenge by composing the song and putting the name of María de la O on everyone's lips. It is sung initially as a *zambra*, then as a *bulerías* by La Niña de Linares, and, finally, in a variety of popular rhythms by people in the street. Sometime later, Carmen would record it *por bulerías*, with her father and brother on guitars, singing:

Contri más te quiero yo,	The more I love you,
más mala eres pa mí.	the worse you treat me.
Explícame esa razón	Explain to me
porque juegas asín con esta corazón.	why you play with my heart this way.
Todo lo que me has pedío	Everything you have asked of me
yo siempre to lo di.	I have always given you.
Ahora, porque ves que	Now that you see
ya no tengo dinero,	I have no money,
te alejas de mí.	you run from me.
María de la O!	María de la O!
Viviendo juntitos con nuestro cariño	Living together with our love
nos sobra de tó.	we have more than enough.
Ya te puedes reir,	You can laugh,
pa que nadie te vea esos ojos moraos	so that nobody will see those eyes,
que tú tienes de tanto sufrí.	darkened by so much suffering.
Mardito parné!	Damned money!
Que tó la curpita de tó en este mundo	All the blame for everything in this world

[1] Mairena, p. 92.

es tan solo por él.	can be placed on it.
Bien lo sabe Dios!	As God well knows!
Bien lo sabe Dios!	As God well knows!
Que es la crucecita que llevas a cuesta,	For that is the cross you have to bear,
María de la O!	María de la O!

María de la O was the most expensive picture of its day, due in part to the high salaries paid to a cast that included the celebrated American actor Antonio Moreno, Spanish star Julio Peña, Pastora Imperio, and the flamenco singer Niña de Linares. Certainly costs went up when fire destroyed the Orphea Studios in Barcelona and filming had to move to Sevilla. Carmen had pleaded with the film makers to hire her entire family, insisting that each had an important talent to contribute. To placate her, they agreed to use a few and added some of her "relatives" from Granada—guitarist Manolo Amaya and *cantaora* María Amaya "La Gazpacha."

María de la O is the first opportunity we have to see Carmen Amaya in action. Twenty-two years old at the time, her face is that of a sweet young girl—very different from the intense, sculpted gypsy face that would become so familiar years later. Contrary to many press reports of the period, Carmen was quite attractive. Her figure in a tight-fitting dress reveals a small, well-proportioned bosom, but absolutely no hips—as straight as a boy. She had already developed quite muscular arms and legs (years later, Carmen's legs would be judged the best in Hollywood by an informal panel of celebrities). And her castanet playing shows that she was left-handed, something later confirmed by her sisters. She was very likely left-footed also.[1] In the film she portrays a sultry, sulky gypsy girl who smiles only once—when she is asked to dance—but that smile lights up the screen. Her acting is a little stiff at times, but she did manage to memorize her many lines.

Carmen first appears on screen as a young girl taking a dance lesson from her adopted mother (Pastora Imperio) in front of a cave in the Sacromonte. Pastora Imperio was no longer the svelt green-eyed beauty she had once been. At age forty-seven she had become a very heavy and matronly older woman with arms like Spanish hams. However, her dancing provides a glimpse into the past, into the *cafés cantantes* where women had emphasized the grace and majesty of the upper body and arms. Pastora used very natural hand movements, without the contortions of the fingers seen in more modern dancers—including Carmen Amaya. In contrast, Carmen's dancing exhibited a mixture of soft feminine dance and the intense, angular movement that would increasingly be associated with her. In the delightful *bulerías* lesson, mother and daughter accompany each other with singing

[1] Goldberg, p. 427.

and clapping. The *bulerías* seen throughout the film demonstrate clearly that many of the modern characteristics of the dance had been developed by 1936.

An *alegrías* danced by Carmen during a fiesta in the Sacromonte also contains much of the structure that would be seen in that dance fifty years later. There is an opening section done to guitar rhythm and the singing of María la Gazpacha. That is followed by a *silencio* (a quiet moment in the dance, free from footwork and accompanied by melodic guitar variations) and a *castellana* (a sequence of very exaggerated rhythm, done without singing in those days). The *escovilla* (extended footwork) follows and then a second *silencio* that leads to the *ida*—a stylized *desplante* sequence *por bulerías* that has a set, unvarying guitar accompaniment.[1] Carmen's powerful finger-snapping functions as castanets throughout much of the dance.

Carmen also dances *fandango por soleá*, that is, a *fandango* sung to the rhythm of *soleá*. She gives a taste of how she might have danced the *soleá*, but the *fandangos* gives it a lighter *aire* which she interprets with castanets and plunging leaps to the floor. Her family often performed *fandangos* to this rhythm and Carmen may have considered this dance to be more of a *fandango* than a *soleá*.

María de la O gives a glimpse of the unique flamenco history of the gypsies of the Sacromonte. The script is full of witty gypsy and Andalusian humor, as when the jilted lover says, "My heart is more broken than the Ten Commandments!" Only in Granada did the gypsies preserve some of the ancient circle dances typical of folk dances found throughout Spain. In *María de la O*, the women dance *fandangos del Albaicín* (sometimes called *fandangos de La Peza*) in circles and pairs, to the accompaniment of an authentic gypsy orchestra of guitars and mandolin-like *bandurrias*. Later, they perform another circle dance to the rhythm of the ancient *seguidillas*, which sound like *sevillanas*, but do not have the same structure.[2] Other points of musical interest are the traditional *sevillanas*, danced to some old and familiar melodies, and the film's title song, appearing to be sung by Julio Peña but actually dubbed by Antonio "El Niño de" Mairena and accompanied skillfully by El Chino as an impressive *zambra*. And finally, the role of Carmen's sister, Mary Cruz, is played by a girl named Rosario Imperio, very likely Pastora's daughter. She sings a *canción* in a rather thin voice.

With its star actors, its prestigious director and cinematographer, and a musical score by Maestro Quiroga, the movie was assured of success. The press was unanimous in its praise of Carmen Amaya and the authentic gypsy presence in the film. *María de la O* was a popular hit and circulated in Spain

---

[1] The *ida* disappeared from the *alegrías* in the 1960s.

[2] I don't know what name they give this dance, but it sounds like *sevillanas* (originally known as *seguidillas sevillanas*) without the structure of the modern *sevillanas*.

for a number of years.

With all of her success, Carmen was able to move her entire family, some twenty-five people, to a flat in Madrid. When she was asked to appear in the Teatro de la Zarzuela, she again thought first of her family and insisted that they be included. The impresario relented and contracted twelve of them. For Carmen, her family would always come first. She said on one occasion, "You don't love your family—you help them."[1] The size of her name on the billboard or the conditions of rehearsal and performance were of secondary importance. It is said that when she was paid, she divided the cash into as many piles as there were performers and family members, and divided the piles according to the needs of each family: one pile for herself, one for each single performer, four piles for an artist with a wife and two children, etc. This story may be part of her legend, for it has been generally agreed that El Chino controlled the family finances.

After the Zarzuela, it is said that Carmen decided to form her own company so that she could employ more of her family. In fact, few in her family were performers and most of them did not travel with her at that time. It is likely that she was accompanied by her father, brother, and the guitarist Sebastián Manzano Heredia, better known as El Pelao Viejo. El Pelao belonged to a family of dancers from Madrid that included his brother, "El Gato" (who had performed so often with Carmen in Barcelona, and whom she called "the best dancer of *farruca* she had ever seen"). Biographers have insisted that Carmen went out on her own, but the dancer stated in an interview that they went with Luisita Esteso: "Some months ago, I found myself in Valladolid with a group that had been formed by Luisa Esteso…"[2] It was mid-July, 1936, and Carmen was in Valladolid preparing to leave for Lisbon, Portugal, where she had a contract. It must have been a shock when the army comandeered her automobiles and left the company stranded.

Spain's modern political history has been a rocky succession of monarchies, democratic republics, and dictatorships. When Queen Isabel II, a weak and immoral ruler, was forced into exile in 1868, she left her country in chaos. Factions fought over the form the government should take and who should serve as king. Two years later, Isabel officially abdicated to make way for her thirteen-year-old son, Alfonso. While Alfonso studied in England, Spain went through a weak and unpopular king imported from Italy and a succession of four presidents in the First Republic. The country was in disarray, with provinces rebelling and seeking autonomy, bandits ruling in the backcountry, and Isabel plotting from Paris on the part of her son. On the other side of the Royal Family, the Carlists maintained their longstanding feud

---

[1] Hidalgo, p. 128.
[2] *La Nación*, Buenos Aires, December 1936.

with a series of bloody squirmishes. In 1876, Alfonso XII returned to Spain, formed a constitutional monarchy, and worked hard to improve industry, commerce and transportation. Alfonso was said to be a devotee of the guitar and on occasion he used to go out at night in disguise to visit the *cafés cantantes*.

In 1884, Juan Breva, the reigning patriarch of the *cante*, worked in three places in Madrid at the same time, earning unheard of amounts of money in each place—and all paid in gold, as stipulated in the contracts. The Café del Imparcial even supplied a house for his family. His friend, General Quesada, the Minister of War, arranged for Breva to sing in the Royal Palace for Alfonso and his wife, Doña María Cristina—an unprecedented event. Delighted by the performance, the King presented the *cantaor* with a tie-clip adorned with the royal crown and the King's initials and awarded him a pension. Years later, when the aged Breva was living in poverty in Málaga, he again performed for a king, this time Alfonso's son, and reminded him of the long-forgotten pension promised by his father. Alfonso XIII reinstated the pension, making life a little easier for the *cantaor*. After Breva's death in 1918, at age seventy-four, twelve tie-clips given to him by various members of the royal family were found among his possessions.

In 1885, Alfonso XII died of tuberculosis, leaving his pregnant wife, María Cristina, to serve as queen. During the reign of María Cristina, the Spanish fleet was crushed in Cuba and the Phillipines, and fighting grew more furious in the Spanish colony in Morocco. In 1902, sixteen-year-old Alfonso XIII took the oath as constitutional king. Four years later, he married Princess Ena of England, the wedding day marred by a bomb that damaged the royal carriage but left the newlyweds unhurt.

Alfonso XIII worked hard at modernizing his country, establishing telephone and electrical service throughout Spain. But he was surrounded by political unrest. Conservative and liberal factions jockied for power, as did those who desired a new republic and those who favored the monarchy. During a 1908 rebellion in Barcelona, mobs burned churches and libraries and fought the military for more than a week. Assassinations were commonplace. And the fighting in Morocco was almost a constant as Spain attempted to hold onto her last colony. Year after year thousands lost their lives in the unpopular war against Berber tribesmen under Abd-el-Krim. There was widespread opposition to military conscription. Mass protests in Barcelona against the draft led to three days of fighting, and in Málaga soldiers rebelled and refused to go to Morocco. Those who could afford it paid a fee to escape military duty.

According to Pepe el de al Matrona, the cafes of Madrid were full of aristocrats at that time—counts, dukes, marquis. Even the royal family was represented, by Alfonso before he married, and his brother, Enrique Borbón. Alfonso enjoyed going out incognito and palace guards were under orders not to acknowledge him when he went out at night. Among the flamencos invited to the palace by Alfonso XIII were Antonio Chacón and José Cepero. It is said that, during a fiesta where Chacón was singing for nobility, King Alfonso said, "How well you have sung, *Don* Antonio!" All the others followed his example and thereafter addressed the *cantaor* using the prestigious *"Don."*

When Chacón was asked how much money he had earned during his life, he is supposed to have answered, "If I say two million, I don't exaggerate. For singing in public I have received from the six *reales* [one and a half *pesetas*] they gave me for singing in a baptism when I was six years-old, to the five thousand *duros* [25,000 *pesetas*; perhaps $500—a huge sum at the time] for singing in a fiesta contracted by the king..."[1]

In another fiesta, the Count of Grisal gave Chacón twenty-five thousand *pesetas* in a wallet after listening to him sing all night. Later, when the singer saw how much it was, he felt it was excessive and that it had been an error. The following day he went to the count's home to return the money. The aristocrat insisted that he keep it all, but the *cantaor* would only accept a smaller amount.[2]

When Alfonso XIII held parties in his castle in Sevilla, he often invited Maestro Realito to bring his dancers. But by 1923 the King had little time for entertaining. With the post-World War I economic slump came union strikes, anarchist and communist terrorism, and executions of hundreds of businessmen. When General Primo de Rivera attempted a military coup while Alfonso was in Santander, the King decided to go along with it to save the country. He appointed Primo de Rivera dictator and went into exile.

People were jubilant. The new dictator immediately suspended the constitution, legally permitted for a three-month period. Later, when he extended the suspension indefinitely, nobody complained. He took power from the *caciques*, the large landholders who had controlled the voting of parliament and turned it into a joke. Under military dictatorship the change in Spain was dramatic. Lawlessness and violence subsided significantly as police and the courts regained control and criminals were tried and punished efficiently. With a stable government, the country became calm. In the next six years, Primo de Rivera accomplished twenty years of progress.

Stability and progress did not come without a price. Some personal freedoms were lost. In Madrid, it was prohibited for groups of people to talk in the street. If two or three people gathered at a tobacco stand, or to say goodbye outside a cafe, Civil Guards would come along and say, "Keep moving, keep moving!" That led to a popular joke: A man stops to ask another for a light, saying, "Can you give me a light...but quickly, please!"

Gambling was prohibited. And all cafes and bars had to close at 3:00 am,

[1]Caballero, Angel A., p. 156.
[2]Caballero, Angel A., p. 156.

presumably to get people home to sleep so they could work in the morning. The ruling proved to be a disaster for flamencos, who depended upon late night and early morning fiestas for their livelihood. Sometimes the law could be circumvented by continuing fiestas in private rooms after the cafes officially closed. *Ventas*, country inns located outside city limits, began to accomodate the flamencos late at night, allowing them to continue to work after city establishments closed down.

According to Pepe el de la Matrona, Primo de Rivera, a native of Jerez de la Frontera and a devoted aficionado of the *cante*, was a frequent visitor to the Villa Rosa. One night he was there with some foreign diplomats. At a quarter to three, he said, "Gentlemen, I'm out of here, because I don't let anyone kick me out of anywhere, and before they kick me out, I'm in the street. So, I'm going!"

Primo de Rivera, an intimate friend of Chacón, had a long-standing interest in flamenco, but that interest had to take back seat during the years he was in power. By 1926, the dictator began to fall out of favor. All of the improvements he had made in highways, railroads, and schools required high taxes—in a time when the value of the *peseta* was declining. In 1927, he had to step aside and permit Alfonso to head the government. One of his last accomplishments was to fulfill his promise to end the Moroccan wars by forcing the surrender of Abd-el-krim.

With more time to himself, Primo de Rivera involved himself more with flamenco and organized a number of festivals. In 1928, he spoke at a competition in the Zarzuela Theater in Madrid where his close friend, José Cepero, won the *"Copa Chacón"*—the "Gold Cup of *Cante.*" In that same contest, Primo de Rivera served on the judging panel and helped to select the winner of the *"Copa Montoya"* for best guitarist, saying, "I vote for that boy, *es una maravilla!* [he is a marvel!]" The guitarist was Luis López Tejera, who, based on the dictator's words, changed his name to Luis *Maravilla.*

In 1930, Primo de Rivera formally resigned and died in exile soon afterward. Alfonso XIII ruled for three difficult years. He came under attack for his luxurious lifestyle and apparent isolation from Spain's problems, as well as his lack of connection with the country's intellectuals. After three chaotic years of changes in leadership, failed military coups, increased repression and censorship, and an economy suffering repercussions from the Great Depression of 1929, the King found himself opposed by the youth, the intellectuals, the military, and the old politicians who had lost power. He agreed to an election.

Nationwide elections in April of 1931 resulted in a Republican landslide. Crowds poured into the streets of the major cities. People hugged, drank, danced, and climbed lamp posts and monuments to cheer. Spain exploded with joy at the arrival of democracy in the form of the Second Republic. After a number of assassination attempts, Alfonso abdicated and went to

France with his family.

The Second Republic went smoothly at first, with a constitutional assembly elected to create a new constitution. But again, flamencos suffered under a new government. Aristocrats, no longer in power, began to leave Madrid and there was less wealth in the cafes. When cafes began to close, flamenco was forced into other venues. La Argentinita took the old cafe artists on the road with *Las Calles de Cádiz*. Most of the other important artists were touring the provinces with the *ópera* companies and playing the major theaters. Sabicas recorded and toured with different companies, as did Niño Ricardo and Ramón Montoya. Carmen Amaya performed in theaters, toured, and made two films. The big dance companies, those of La Argentina, La Argentinita, and Vicente Escudero, performed primarily outside of Spain. This exodus from the cafes would define the course of flamenco during the next twenty years.

Under the freedom of the Republic, Spain's many political factions squabbled like never before. On the right, opposing the new Republican government, were the fascist *Falange*, the Roman Catholic Church, large landholders, big business, and the military. On the left, those who supported the government included intellectuals, artists, the educated middle class, workers, and the extremist socialists, communists, and anarchists. Inevitably, disturbances flared up. Anarchists burned churches—at least ten in Madrid and thirty-two in Málaga. Union strikes and fighting broke out in Valencia and across the North. Miners in Asturias took up arms, only to be forcibly surpressed by the army under General Francisco Franco.

The elections of 1936 were strongly opposed by parties of the right. In July, an uprising began in military towns, and soon the army had taken control of Spanish Morocco, the Canary Islands, Majorca, and many parts of the North. Fighting broke out everywhere as both sides attempted to consolidate territory.

According to the Spanish press, Antonia Mercé "La Argentina" was the first victim of the Civil War. They said that she died of a heart attack on July 18, moments after reading of the military uprising in Morocco. She was forty-six. The previous year, she had presented *El Amor Brujo* in the Teatro Español of Madrid, with Vicente Escudero as Carmelo, Pastora Imperio as Lucía, and herself as Candela. She had wanted to contrast two styles of dance—the gypsy flair of Pastora and her own stylized approach. Her last performance in Madrid, in June of 1935, had been in the festival to finance Fernando de Triana's book. In March of 1936, she had given several recitals in the Salle Pleyel in Paris, accompanied by the Paris Symphony Orchestra. That same month, she presented *El Amor Brujo* in the Opera Theater of Paris, with Vicente Escudero and his partner, Carmita García. This new version was completely redone into something abstract, filled with strong colors and violent movement.

Under doctor's orders to rest, Antonia retired to her villa in Bayona, France. On July 18, she attended a Basque dance festival held in her honor. When she returned home that evening, she heard about the military rebellion and died moments later, saying, "What is happening to me?" The Catalonian press wrote: "Last night, Antonia Mercé, the greatest theatrical Spanish dancer of all times, died in Bayona."

Federico García Lorca wrote in his *Elogio a Antonia Mercé, La Argentina*: "A Spanish dancer, or a *cantaor*, or a bullfighter, invents; they don't revive something, they create it. They create a unique art that disappears with each one of them, and nobody can imitate it."

Not long after La Argentina's death, Lorca, attempting to hide in the home of friends in Granada, was discovered by the rebel forces and executed in the night without a trial.

Carmen Amaya found herself in a predicament: Her company had been stranded in Valladolid when the military took her car. In an interview, she said, "We went through a terrible scare. At six in the morning, we all came up out of the basement of the theater."[1] She had a contract to work in Lisbon but no transportation to get there. According to Montañés, salvation came in the form of a local radio personality named Gerardo Esteban, who managed to locate a bus for them and get the papers needed to cross the border.

Upon arriving in Lisbon, the company moved into a luxurious hotel while Carmen went to see the impresario about her contract. To her dismay, she found that the contract had been cancelled. The impresario said that, when he had heard nothing from her, he gave up and replaced her with another company. When the Amaya company pooled its money, they found they hadn't enough to pay for even one hotel room. Somehow, all of the money they had earned had disappeared. With no money and no promise of work, the company moved into humble quarters in local *pensiones*. Antonio Triana's brother, Manuel García Matos, gave his version of what happened next.:

> Soon after, Anita Sevilla arrived in Lisbon, and a little later I met up with Carmen Amaya, who was there with her father and brother.
>
> One anecdote worthy of mention about those uncertain days was the way in which Carmen Amaya and I managed to introduce ourselves to the Café Arcadia, a very aristocratic gathering place in the center of Lisbon. In that cafe there was a quintet that cheered up the gatherings and played for the cafe-restaurant. I wanted to play there, but the boss didn't want it because, as we have said, he had his own quintet. But one day, without the knowledge of the boss, we got the waiters to let us perform. Carmen

[1] Hidalgo, p. 171.

Amaya put on her best dress and I accompanied her on the piano, such that, once on the platform, she began to sing and dance popular songs and I played *El Amor Brujo* by Falla. In that way, we were successful with the public and, at their insistence, the boss gave us a contract.[1]

Carmen was an overwhelming success, "without precedent," according to one critic, and in Carmen's words, *"Armamos un taco asín de grande!* [we caused a riot this big]" and "the room turned into *una olla de grillos* [pandemonium]."[2] Week after week, the cafe extended the contract. The troup was able to return to the luxurious hotel and live like kings. But Carmen missed the family members she had left behind in Madrid and wanted to return for them. Matos said he convinced her that she could not return to Spain and that the war could go on for thirty years. Then a tempting offer came in the form of a telegram from Buenos Aires, Argentina, proposing a contract of one million *pesetas* for three months of performing.

Carmen's agent paled when he saw the telegram—he desperately wanted to keep the dancer in Lisbon—but he generously said, "It is very little, what they are offering you, Carmen. If I had it, I would give you double!" Carmen decided to go, but not without a great deal of trepidation. In an interview, she responded to a question about the fear that gypsies have of traveling by sea:

> "It is more difficult to make a gypsy travel by sea than to find a bullfighter who is afraid. I have had proposals, a few years ago, to go to New York to dance in the company of Vicente Escudero, but when I found out there was no other way to get there except by water, I rejected them. Why don't they make a tunnel from Sevilla to New York? Don't they say that those Yankees can do anything...?"
>
> "What do you mean, anything!" replied El Pelao. I would like to see one of those Yankees sing flamenco!"
>
> "So it was yes and then no," continued Carmen, "and one day, closing our eyes, we went on board the ship."[3]

But Carmen couldn't go without her family. As she said on one occasion, "I don't know how to go through the world alone, and if I don't go with my people, I get nothing out of life." The majority of Carmen's biographers have stated that rest of the Amaya clan came to Lisbon for the trip to Buenos Aires, swelling the "company" to include her grandfather, Juan Amaya Jiménez, at one time a great dancer but now little more than the object of Carmen's tender affection, her father, José el Chino, her aunt, Juana la

---

[1] García Matos, Manuel, *Mi vida, mi obra y mis recuerdos.* Servicio Municipal de Publicaciones, Ayuntamiento de Alcalá de Guadaira (Sevilla). 1985.

[2] Montañés, p. 29.

[3] This quote resembles another that appeared in the magazine *Mundo Argentino* in November of 1936, but is slightly different and is taken from Hidalgo, p. 100.

Faraona, her diabetic mother, Micaela (Carmen took on the responsibility of daily insulin injections), her sisters, Antonia and Leonor, and assorted other relatives. However, in an interview with Antonia and Leonor, Goldberg learned that the sisters did not go to Argentina until almost a year later. They would receive a telegram from Carmen on Christmas of 1936 while staying in their grandfather's house in Barcelona. After arranging for false papers, they would go to Paris, then on to Marseilles and Buenos Aires, arriving in the middle of 1937.[1]

So it is unclear exactly who made that first trip on the boat to Buenos Aires. Brother Paco had just married Micaela *la Chata* (she of the upturned nose), who would eventually perform with the company and was said to be the only one who could keep straight rhythm with her handclapping (the Amaya sisters would usually lapse into countertime clapping). Along with Paco, the trio of guitarists included El Chino and El Pelao. Other recent additions to the group included García Matos and the *cuplé* singer Anita Sevilla. It is certain that Juana la Faraona did not make the trip and never performed in America. Those who may not have made the initial trip, including the mother and grandfather, would soon follow. In the fall of 1936, Carmen Amaya and her retinue boarded the steamship *Monte Pascoal* and embarked for the New World.

The Amayas were not the only flamenco artists to be stranded outside of Spain during the Spanish Civil War. Gabriel Ruiz picks up the story:

> I found myself in Oran with the *Compañía Teatral Alcoriza*, accompanying on guitar the *cantaores* Peña, *hijo*, and Florencio Castelló, and the *bailaor* Filemón Merino. Our company did not fare well and we were stranded [by the war]. I began to play, along with the guitarist Niño Posadas, for the very famous *cantaor*, Angelillo. In that same Moroccan city, fleeing from our cruel and horrible war, were La Argentinita, Pilar López, Luisita Esteso, some famous bullfighters, and other well-known names that I can't recall. Encarnación López "La Argentinita" offered me a contract with her company and then went to Paris to prepare some recitals for Europe. A short time later, I received money and my passage. I boarded in Oran and landed in Port Bou, from where I took an express to *"La Ville Lumière"* (The City of Light), the capital of France and, I believe, the capital of the whole world at that time...
>
> I arrived at the station that ended my trip. Above the station was the hotel, which I entered on a moving staircase—the first I had seen or stepped on in my young life. From the lobby, they took me

[1] Goldberg, p. 198.

to a luxurious and stupendous room that La Argentinita had reserved for me. I dove into an elegant, plush bed and fell asleep immediately, extremely tired from the long journey.

The telephone woke me, and I thought I had just fallen asleep. In reality, a number of hours had passed and I saw by my watch that it was ten o'clock in the morning. I was told that my breakfast was being brought up, since *Madame* Argentinita was expecting me for rehearsal at eleven o'clock. A few moments later, an impressive uniformed maid arrived with a fabulous breakfast—appropriate for a first-class hotel in those times. It all seemed like a fantastic dream to me. I ate the abundant and exquisite breakfast, bathed, dressed, and called a hotel servant who came immediately, very courteously, and took me to a new job in a new world.

It was a full *Parisienne* spring, fantastic in its beauty. We walked on the magnificent carpets of those elegant hallways in the hotel. The scent of the acacia trees that line all of the streets of Paris came in through open windows throughout the building, a fragrance I have never smelled again anywhere. At the same time, I heard, closer and closer as we walked, the soft and dream-like notes of a piano on which somebody was skillfully playing *"Sevilla."* Someone else was playing *palillos* [castanets] wonderfully in accompaniment to that famous music of the immortal Spanish composer Isaac Albéniz. At that moment, I lived and felt something that is not easy to explain, something sublime. It was something that one can never forget...Paris, springtime, *"Sevilla"* by Albéniz, and Argentinita playing *palillos* while she waited for me. And all of that in a luxurious hotel and in a world unknown to me until that moment...

We arrived in an impressive hall to find Argentinita, her sister Pilar López, and Antonio Triana, all in rehearsal clothes, and, seated at the piano, the great Spanish pianist, Miguel Elósequi. I greeted Encarnación and her sister, and was introduced to the pianist and Antonio Triana, whom I knew by name but had never met. Immediately we began to rehearse the *cosas flamencas* for some recitals in London. I recall that we did them without a *cantaor*.

Before the rehearsal had finished, El Chileno arrived. He was from Málaga, somewhat older than I, and *un bailaor a la antigua* [an old-style dancer] in both his personality and his dance. When we finished rehearsing, Argentinita put El Chileno in charge of finding lodging for me and the two of us went off together. We hit it off immediately and soon were good friends. He knew Paris well—he had lived there for many years—and it was not difficult for him to get me settled in a pretty good hotel on the Rue Pigalle, right in Montmartre and near to where he lived. El Chileno was both *bailarín* [classical dancer] and *bailaor* [flamenco dancer], very good in his "style." As a person, as a man and a friend, he was marvelous. He had a philosophy of life different from others, and he had unusually good luck in all aspects of life...When his luck was at its peak, he handled a great deal of money, was famous in Paris as a dancer, and had other domestic dealings as well. During his best period he maintained a stupendous automobile, a big and luxurious Spanish-Swiss make, parked in the Place Pigalle with uniformed chauffeur and a case of the best champagne inside—all at the disposal of any of his friends!

The following night, I entered for the first time the bar-restaurant Le Grand Duc, located on the Rue Pigalle right in front of the hotel where I was staying. This bar, which was quite small, never closed its doors, and the few flamencos that there were in Paris in those days used to stop in regularly. It was there that I met Relámpago, the veteran guitarist who was married to La Joselito—a well-known *bailaora* in those times. He played well for the dance. I also met Sabas Gómez, an Andalusian *señorito* who had fallen on hard times and lived there as a guitarist. And Carlos Montoya, who used to come in from time to time at night, since he was almost always playing in a *boite* called La Cabaña Cubana, located in the basement. I also met Fabián de Castro, Amalio Cuenca (both quite old), and a good classical guitarist named Gil, who was somewhat older than I.

Gil sweated all the time, like nobody else I have seen. El Chileno used Gil as a guitarist quite often, for his artistic tours, and when he played, the fingerboard of his guitar filled with sweat so that it seemed that water was pouring down the neck. He used to put enormous quantities of talcum powder on his hands and on the guitar, which created an ugly appearance in his recitals. Sometimes we all traveled together, since Emilio el Chileno used to pay me a salary when I didn't have a contract—just to accompany them on their tours. I used to laugh at some of their *cosas* [things they did].

It so happened that El Chileno had another use for Gil. When we traveled though central Europe, sometimes the trains were crowded with people and everybody in El Chileno's company had to stand in the passageways. Then Emilio would signal to Gil, who, being neither shy nor lazy, would take out from his valise a large piece of *bacalao*, a dried codfish that he enjoyed excessively and ate constantly both cooked or raw. He would find a spot in the passageway where he was conspicuous, sit on the floor, and remove his shoes. Instantly, an awful odor, terrible and nauseating, like rotten eggs, would permeate the air as it emanated from Gil's feet. I tell you sincerely that his feet gave off blue fumes...and, as El Chileno wished, in a short time we had all the seats we desired in the railroad car.

Carlitos Verdeal was a very good flamenco-classical guitarist from Madrid. He was twenty-some-odd years old and at that time used to acompany Goyito Herrero, a young, beautiful, and talented Spanish dancer who was having a great deal of success in Paris. I toured northern Europe with her some time later. One night, very late (we all came in after work), Verdeal arrived at the bar, looking very thin and nervous. He hardly greeted us, then had a *café con leche* and a cognac, and began to play the slot machines they had there. In a short time had lost all the money he had with him. About four o'clock in the morning he went back to his hotel, the same one that I stayed in, where he had a room near mine.

At noon the following day, I was horrified to learn that Verdeal had hanged himself in his room shortly after we saw him leave the Grand Duc. Carlitos Verdeal was a giant of a guitar player [very popular with singers in Madrid, where he had recorded with Pepe Marchena], although not a giant physically—he was very short, almost a dwarf, little taller than a guitar. He hung himself with a necktie tied to a tall heating radiator in his room. We were all very moved by his death, for he was a good person, polite and serious, and a great artist. We arrived at the conclusion that he had committed the act in desperation over the civil war in Spain, which had prevented him from receiving news about his family in Madrid. Perhaps the final blow was the large amount of money we saw him lose that night.

Sometimes Antonio Triana would come by. He was at the peak of his youth, art, and abilities, and he danced very well. His version of the *"Polo gitano"* by Albéniz has become part of the history of Spanish dance—nobody has equaled his interpretation, much less surpassed it. In the *alegrías*, in the middle of the dance where he closed for the *escovilla*, the audience would always applaud. In addition to his feet, he won over the public with his unique smile. In our debut in London he had to stop the dance, and I had to stop playing, in order to acknowledge many times the stolid, formally dressed English public who were applauding madly. On occasion I visited the house in Paris where he lived with his family, and I had the pleasure of holding in my arms a beautiful *señorita* named Luisita—today, Luisa Triana. I should make it clear that, at that time, Luisita was barely a few months old.[1]

One night, shortly after I began to go to the Grand Duc, Relámpago asked me *what* had happened to Vicente Escudero in Madrid. I, with the fervor of my youthful ignorance, told him about what happened in the movie house in the Spanish capital, adding loudly that Escudero was *un chalao*, crazy, and he didn't know what *compás* was. The husband of La Joselito told me that I should be very careful with Vicente, that he was a bully, *un gitano bravo*, and that he always carried a large knife and was capable of anything if he heard that I had said things like that. Much later, I found out that all of that had been a joke—Relámpago always liked jokes—but I took it seriously and began to curse myself for having such a big mouth, although my pride made me act the opposite.

I went on tour with Argentinita and her pianist, just the three of us, and we did a number of performances throughout Europe. Back in Paris, Encarnación offered me another contract, for Yugoslavia and, later, New York. I asked for more money, but she was a bit tight in these matters and we did not come to an agreement, even though she was insistent. In the end I stayed to live in Paris (which I loved) and Argentinita made immediate arrangements with Carlos Montoya, and he, therefore, came to the United States with her.

I worked a lot in those days. I was in the Moulin Rouge for one year as leader of the *Cuadro Español*, and at the same time, I performed in such fashionable *boites* as Bagatelle and La Vie Parisienne...Due to my work, I always arrived in the hotel around six o'clock in the morning. After the last show, which was very late, I would eat with other artists in the Grand Duc. One morning, shortly after I had gone to bed, the telephone rang. It was *la mamá*, as we called the good and courteous *señora* who was in charge of the reception desk, and she said, *"Mon petite* Gaby, *Monsieur* Vicente Escudero is here and he says he wants to talk to you about something very important...!"

All I know is the fear that went through me. The first thing that occurred to me was to escape through a window that led to the patio. But pride prevented it. I bolstered my courage by lighting a cigarette. Then I put on a suit over my pajamas, added a coat and hat, and prepared to leave. But when I opened the door of my room, I noticed that I was barefoot. I put on my shoes and went

---

[1] Luisa Triana went on to become an important dancer and teacher in the United States. She would have been about three years old in 1936. The most extensive biography of Antonio Triana, written by his second wife, makes no mention of Luisa or her mother.

out, "ready to die!"

To give myself more time, I took the stairs from the fourth floor, instead of the elevator, slowly, very slowly. When I lacked only a few stairs before reaching the small entrance hall of the hotel, I saw Vicente Escudero standing in the center of the hall. Without knowing why, I stopped and looked at him, while he did the same to me. I still remember him at that moment, wrapped in a gray overcoat, his hands in his pockets, his head covered by a gray hat with a wide brim. Over his forehead, protruding from under the brim of the hat, were some strands of hair, bangs of black hair, giving his face a certain fierce gypsy *aire*, while his small, sparkling and lively eyes looked at me with malice—or so I thought at the moment. Later, I learned that he had been using a toupee for some time, due to the small amount of hair he had in front, and I also learned that he was not a gypsy.

He spoke slowly. "You are Gabrielillo, *verdad?*"

"*Sí, señor,*" I answered.

"*Pues*, as I imagine you are a man, I have come to speak with you."

Slowly, I came down the few steps that separated me from him, as I answered, "Well, here I am, ready to talk about whatever you wish, *Señor* Escudero."

I had reached his side and stood there. He was a little taller than I. Then, to my astonishment, he put out his hand. At that moment I no longer felt fear, and I knew, I felt, that the man had not come to challenge me to a duel in the Forest of Bologna, nor anything like that—which filled me with enthusiasm and made me feel like a different person. Poor Vicente was not a bully, nor a gypsy, nor did he carry a big knife!

At his request, we headed off to the Grand Duc for coffee. Vicente told me that he knew I was a good *tocaor* [guitarist] and that he would like me to go to his home-studio someday. I have never been able to understand what impelled him to go looking for me at such an hour to tell me such things. Afterward, we talked for a long time, until noon, about his ideas and projects, and about how he saw *baile flamenco* and its future. It was then that I first admired him for his creative genius and imagination. In his conversation (I hardly spoke), he constantly mentioned the names of famous *cantaores*, *bailaores*, and *guitarristas* from the last century, as well as old and pure *cantes*. Surely he did it to show me that he knew well the history of flamenco, something that one could see was true. I supposed that he had read a great deal of what little was written on the subject, but that didn't

impress me in the least. Only his ideas about the dance were really worth something—although I knew that he would never be the perfect interpreter of that which he felt and desired for the *baile jondo...*
And that is how I met Vicente Escudero![1]

It was immediately after this meeting that Gabriel played the *tanguillo* that-didn't-want-to-end for Escudero. To complete this portrait, Gabriel tells us what happened a few days after the infamous *tanguillo*, and then takes us some five years into the future (c. 1940):

> Two days later, Escudero called me on the phone, telling me that, yes, he had made a mistake, and then he invited me again to his house. That night I told my friends at the Grand Duc about the new invitation and Relámpago again joked, "If you go this time, he will really kill you!"
> So I got together with Vicente on several afternoons, but not in his house. I asked him to meet me instead in the Bar de Pigalle. He asked me to teach him the *compás* for the *siguiriyas*, done with *palmas sordas* [muted handclaps]. He would buy me a *café con leche* and two croissants, and in a corner of the Grand Duc, we would do *"un, dos, tres...uno y dos...un, dos, tres...uno y dos* [the three fast and two slow beats of the *siguiriya*]."
> And so we were for a number of days. Later, life took us our separate ways and I didn't see him again for some time. When the civil war was over, I was in the Plaza de Toros Monumental in Madrid one afternoon, after the bullfight, when I heard somebody calling my name from some distant seats above mine, "Gabrielillo ...Gabrielillo!"
> I looked back, into the upper *tendidos*, and there was Vicente Escudero, unmistakeable, laughing and doing *compás* for me *por siguiriyas*. I waved to him cheerfully, and we made signals to meet at the exit of the bullring. But there was such a tremendous crowd that afternoon that it was impossible for us to find each other.
> I knew that Vicente lived in the Hotel Regina, right in the center of Madrid, since the newspapers frequently wrote about him. He was beginning to be an important star in Spain for many people, ever since he left France in 1939 at the outbreak of World War II and returned to his hometown, Valladolid. He did some dancing with Mariemma and then moved to Madrid with his wife. I believe that Vicente was dancing in *compás* by that time. But, in reality, I did nothing about trying to see him in those days, after our meet-

---

[1] Ruiz, Gabriel, "A Few Words about Vicente Escudero." *Jaleo, Vol 5, No 5,* December 1981, and *Vol 5, No 6,* February 1982.

ing in the Madrid bullring.

In 1940, Escudero became the first to dance the *siguriyas*, a *cante* long considered too profound, too sacred, and too esoteric to be danced. He said, "I created and presented it for the first time in 1940, in the Teatro Español in Madrid, where I was accompanied by the great guitarist Eugenio González. I studied this dance, which no one had attempted previously, for five years before presuming to present it on the stage. I was considered crazy by many because of my intense studies of its origins, but eventually others began to dance it too and now it is quite popular. But most often it is done erroneously, as a footwork dance, or with all sorts of fancy jumps and kicks which, to my mind, add nothing but vulgarity. I recently saw the *siguiriya* danced in a film by a horse and rider...it was unbearable!"[1]

It would appear that Escudero's interest in the *siguiriya* began at about the time he learned its *compás* from Gabriel Ruiz—although we cannot be certain whether Gabriel's explanation of the intricacies of the rhythm sparked that interest or Vicente sought out the guitarist specifically for the purpose of making himself *enterao* about that rhythm. We can be certain that the unusual nature of the *siguiriya* rhythm would delight Vicente and stimulate his creative impulse. He may have had difficulty learning about the specifics of the flamenco *compases*, but he never lacked for rhythmic ability. For some of his dances he provided his own musical accompaniment and became a one-man percussion machine. On that subject, he said, "There are some who are not even aware that before flamenco was danced to guitar, dancers themselves produced the rhythms to which they danced with whatever was at hand. Inspired by that period, in my dance *"Ritmos primitivos"* I produced rhythms with my fingernails. And if I drum with my fingers on a chair or whatever, it is because, since the birth of the first *tanguillo* until today, the true flamenco performer never hesitates to make his own accompaniment with his fingers on a table, chair, countertop, or whatever may be around him. One has to be very uninformed not to be acquainted with this tradition, and yet there are few professional dancers who have explored this intriguing avenue."[2]

Escudero took this adventure into dancing the most profound of *cantes* very seriously: "The gypsies originated in Hindustan," he wrote in a program for one of his recitals. "In this dance I try to evoke their origins and the odyssey of their wanderings and persecutions, their lamentations and rebelliousness, their crying out to Heaven and Earth. This is the most profound of all flamenco dances." "To dance the true *siguiriya gitana*, one must hold a dialogue with Death, with the Saints and with the Devils. One must address oneself to the Powers of Darkness and Sorcery, and evoke secrets of the past. The *siguiriya* should be reserved for the tragic tone which expresses itself in the gypsy

---

[1] Escudero, Vicente, "What is Flamenco Dance?" *Dance Magazine*, October 1955.
[2] *Ibid.*

odyssey throughout the ages. How much misunderstanding exists!"[1]

It took a rebel like Vicente Escudero to defy tradition and dance to a *cante* that "could not be danced." In doing so, he opened the door for others. It is not certain who was the first to dance *la caña*, an ancient *cante* with religious overtones and chant-like passages that have made it a popular vehicle for the *misa flamenca*—the Catholic Mass performed to flamenco music. *La caña* had all but disappeared by the twentieth century, but was partially revived after the Granada contest of 1922, when it was recorded by the contest winner, El Tenazas. According to some sources, Carmen Amaya claims to have created the dance in the 1930s, in collaboration with the musician Monreal and the guitarist Perico el del Lunar, based on the *cante* of Antonio Chacón. Of course Chacón was dead by that time. There is no corroberating evidence for this assertion, and *la caña* did not appear in Carmen's performances until the 1950s. Manolo de Huelva claimed that *la caña* was first danced by La Argentinita, in the 1940s. Considering that Argentinita did not dance in Spain in the 1940s and that *la caña* did not appear in her American repertoire, Manolo's claim would appear to be unfounded. The well-known dancer, Rosario—of Antonio y Rosario—had a slightly different view. In speaking of the dance *por taranto*, she said, "That dance was danced first in the history of flamenco by me, in the Teatro Fontalba, just as Pilar López did *la caña*, Antonio the *martinete*, and Vicente Escudero the *siguiriya*. I choreographed the *taranto*, and it had never been done before."[2]

Almost certainly, Pilar López was the first to dance *la caña*, in the late 1940s. It is a tribute to Carmen Amaya's creativity and desire to expand her repertoire that she would be performing all of these new dances within a few years of their first appearance.

The great Spanish dancer Antonio would become the first to dance to the *martinete*, a *cante* with much of the tragic passion and somber mood of the *siguiriya*. The traditional song of the blacksmiths, it had been considered undanceable due to its lack of rhythm and musical accompaniment. In 1952, Antonio danced the *martinete* in the film *Flamenco* (in Spain called, *"Duende y misterio del flamenco"*), against the magnificent backdrop of an arch of the bridge of the Tajo de Ronda and to the accompaniment of a hammer beating out the rhythm of the *siguiriyas* on an anvil. After that film, the *martinete* adopted the *compás* of the *siguiriya*, even when not danced.

It is ironic that Vicente Escudero would be critical of the new dance *por martinete*. Rebels often cannot tolerate innovations by others, and they tend to become more critical as they age. Vicente said: "Among the worst breaches of taste belongs to those who have dared to dance the *martinete* to the rhythm of the *siguiriya gitana*. All flamenco artists should know that the *martinete* is a song which has neither fixed music nor rhythm. Although, like

[1] *Ibid.*
[2] Verdu, p. 24.

the *siguiriya*, the *martinete* was born, through anguish and torment, around the blacksmith's forge to the beat of hammer, red-hot iron, and anvil, the first has quite different qualities—as expressed in regular rhythm and cadences— from the free form of the latter."[1]

Gabriel Ruiz concludes the tale of his meeting with Escudero after the encounter in the bullring:

> In the fall of that same year, I saw him again. I was coming out of the *metro* at the station of Alcalá and Peligros, important and central streets in Madrid, when I heard his voice calling "Gabrielillo!" Vicente Escudero opened his arms toward me and we embraced with joy. In reality, I appreciated Escudero for his genius and innovations, for all that he brought to the Spanish dance and flamenco. In that sense, I admired him. I felt proud that he called me his friend and that I had been the one to teach him something about our *compases*. He wore, as always, his colorful hat and the gypsy curls at his forehead. I noticed his small feet, now larger and heavier. Vicente was now *mayor* [older, elderly], but he looked good, *un buen tipo, fino y aflamencao* [in good shape, stylish and flamenco].
>
> Vicente was accompanied by a young man, very proper and likeable, about thirteen or fourteen years old. He introduced us: "*Mira*, Gabrielillo, I want to introduce you to a 'nephew' of mine who is beginning to play the guitar and already plays better than his father. His name is Mario Escudero."
>
> Turning to the youth, who greeted me with a smile, he said, "Gabriel is a very good guitarist, although he has lost a little because he is fighting bulls now under the name *El Chavalillo*." (That was true.)
>
> We continued talking and Vicente proposed that we go to the home of young Mario to hear him play. And so we did, walking between Calle Fuencarral and Calle Hortaleza to where the boy lived with his family. The fall afternoon was almost dark when we arrived at the house. Mario's father, somewhat of a friend of mine, was not at home, but Vicente introduced me to the rest of the Escudero family. We went into a large room that contained some beds and sat down on one of them. Young Mario took out his guitar and began to play. Immediately I realized that, if he continued to learn, he would be a great guitarist—*en él, había madera de sobra* [he had more than enough of the "right stuff"]. At the request of Vicente, I arranged some *soleares* for Mario—he was still a little green at that time.
>
> I believe that I returned two or three more times, always with

[1] Verdu, p. 24.

"Uncle" Escudero, and would have continued going, with pleasure, but I had to travel outside of Madrid and, later, outside of Spain, and would never see either of them again.[1]

Perhaps it is no coincidence that Mario Escudero, with the early influence of Vicente Escudero, would become one of the true revolutionaries of the guitar and be accused of a number of heresies. He would also become intimately involved with Carmen Amaya's family. In describing his early years, he said:

> The guitar was my toy when I was a child. I began by playing *with* it, rather than playing it, if you know what I mean. I was born in Alicante into a gypsy family [October 11, 1928]. My father [Jesús Escudero] played the guitar, as did an uncle of mine. My mother was a professional singer, not a *cantaora flamenca* but she sang *canciones* in the manner of Conchita Piquer or Sara Montiel. When the *movimientos* [war actions] began in Spain, we left and went to live in France, where I spent most of my childhood. We traveled all over France, Switzerland, and the Netherlands. As a child I spoke French with the other kids, in the street, in school, and even with my mother. When we went back to Spain, it was hard for me. I went to school a little, but not very much, because we were always moving.
>
> I was still a child when I was introduced to Vicente Escudero in France, where he had developed himself as a dancer and was considered an idol. When I was little, I would call him *Don* Vicente, or *Señor* Escudero. One day, he said to me, "I am neither *Don* Vicente, nor *Señor* Escudero...I am *El Tío* Vicente [Uncle Vicente]!"
>
> So, from that time on he became El Tío Vicente to me. He was not a gypsy, of course, but he admired the gypsy culture. Because we spent a great deal of time together and had the same name, people often thought we were related, but we had no blood ties. I am very indebted to him because he was the first to encourage me to go on stage with him, on the best stages in Europe, where he took our art with great dignity. He had an artistic dignity and a no-nonsense attitude toward our art that demanded respect. *Hombre*, artists are not gold coins that are admired equally by everybody. Some people like our art better than others. Some liked Vicente a great deal; others did not. But what we must recognize is the great work of that man with respect to the manner in which he presented his art. You can be a great dancer, a great artist, but if you do not present it with respect, with class, then it is something else.[2]

[1] Ruiz, Gabriel, "A Few Words about Vicente Escudero." *Jaleo, Vol V, No 7*. March 1982.
[2] Chileno, El, "Mario Escudero: Part II" *Jaleo, Vol VI, No 6*. December 1983.

In 1937, at the age of nine, Mario performed on stage for the first time, wearing the short pants of a schoolboy. His mother, father, and aunt were members of a large company assembled by the very popular French crooner, Maurice Chevalier. During a performance in the Cinema Galia in Bordeaux, Mario told his father he wanted to go on stage too. His father told him to be quiet, and the boy began to cry. Maurice Chevalier heard the commotion and asked, "What? What is wrong?"

"Oh, don't worry, Mister Chevalier, he wants to go on stage."

"Why not?"

He took the boy on stage and introduced him. Mario played a short song and received a standing ovation."[1]

After the war, Mario returned to Spain, to Madrid, where Vicente Escudero continued to guide him, and he met Ramón Montoya:

> I met Ramón Montoya in La Villa Rosa in Madrid...He had just returned to Spain. We owe Ramón Montoya almost everything. He was a pioneer. He may not have been the first, for there were others like El Gordillo de Linares, Luis Molina, Manolo de Huelva, and many other good guitarists. But Montoya was one of the first to explore, to search for new avenues for the guitar...the flamenco guitar has changed tremendously in technique. We are indebted to Ramón Montoya for much of that change...I don't think I am exaggerating when I call him a genius. But as extraordinary as he was, he would spend hours and days sitting around—just another guitarist.
>
> The truth is that I learned from *El Tío* Montoya by watching him. When there was no *juerga* I would sit like a monkey and watch him while he practiced in a room by himself. He may have taught me a couple of variations at most. I don't know that he had the patience to teach. You had to catch his variations like this [snaps his fingers]!
>
> He was influenced by the classical school of Francisco Tárrega, which is, of course, well known. The ideas of this school have been adapted to flamenco. I think this is good for the *flamenquistas*, the flamenco guitarists. Those techniques are good and useful to us...they are part of the instrument. The fact that, in the old times, the flamenco guitar was played like this [holds the guitar on his lap with the neck pointed straight up], doesn't necessarily mean that the style was more pure. Better techniques and ways of playing just were not known. Purity lies in the interpretation of what you are performing. I don't believe that because something is technically primitive it is necessarily more pure. This business

---

[1] Salazar, Guillermo, *"Gazpacho de Guillermo." Jaleo, Vol IV, No 10.* August 1983

of pure and impure often makes me laugh. If we go looking for purity, where will we find it? Maybe we should go to school to find it! For me, purity means preserving the basic structures, like two and two are four—they are now, always were, and will still be one thousand years from now. They will never add up to four and a half. The structure is there. If you know flamenco and its patterns, you can change the harmonies and enrich it. If we play up the fingerboard beyond the fourth fret, that is not impure.

To base your playing only on *pellizcos* [catchy little personal phrases]...well, *pellizcos* are all right, but there is more to it than that. And the so-called *duende*—the things that are done in the name of *duende!* Manuel Torre thought that up. If you don't see the *duende*, then *"vamos,"* you've had it! That was Manuel Torre's idea and García Lorca used it frequently in his *romances*. The term *"hay que tener duende"* originated among the common people and means that a person is very amusing. It is what we would normally call "inspiration." But you also have to have *duende* to play Bach, not only for flamenco. We need it for Bach, Mozart, or any form of expression. If, someday, the *Duende* really comes, it will eat two or three of us alive for how poorly we are performing!

So I passed through the flamenco *juergas*, the Villa Rosa and Los Grabieles, where Antonio Chacón, José Cepero, and other greats of the early 1900s had also gone. I call that the "flamenco university." There were many of us guitarists who used to hang around together in the cafes, or we would go to the shop of Santos Hernández, the guitar builder, where the classical and flamenco guitarists would get together. It was a very interesting *ambiente*. I met Daniel Fortea...he was the last student of Tárrega, and an older man when I met him. I also met Regino Sainz de la Maza.[1]

Mario developed a repertoire of classical pieces and always felt confident as a classical player. This facet of his playing would dominate his music and give a unique "classical" flavor to his flamenco. It certainly contributed to his superb sense of composition..

At age fourteen and using the name "El Niño de Alicante," Mario Escudero began his professional career with Vicente Escudero, touring the major cities of Europe. Soon after, he appeared with the popular singer, Estrellita Castro. He said that, in 1944, "I worked with Ramón Montoya in the Teatro Español in Madrid, along with Vicente Escudero. Don Ramón played solos, and I played for Vicente and the *cantaor* Jacinto Almadén."[2]

[1]Chileno, El, *"Mario Escudero."*
[2]Chileno, El, *"Mario Escudero."*

There followed an endless series of tours with *ópera flamenca* companies featuring big stars like La Niña de los Peines and José Cepero.

Ramón Montoya had been fortunate in encountering a set of circumstances that took him away from Spain for the duration of the civil war. In 1935, a group of aficionados and artists created the first flamenco *peña*, a club for the purpose of listening to and discussing the *cante*. Called *La Sociedad de Cante Flamenco*, it met in a *colmao*, and its members included Pepe el de la Matrona and Ramón Montoya. Through the president of the *peña*, Ramón was introduced to a graphic artist named Marius de Zayas, who became his guitar student. Zayas, who lived in Grenoble, France, proposed to Montoya the idea of recording an album of guitar solos, which he would finance and arrange with the French recording company BAM. Zayas' son, Rodrigo de Zayas described the events leading up to the recording:

> In March of 1936 my parents left Madrid with a crazy project in mind: to record Montoya as a soloist. The records would be large format disks, twelve inches, like those used for classical music, for performers such as Wanda Landowska, Pablo Casals, or Fritz Kreisler [flamenco had always been recorded on smaller disks]. The project was crazy because it had never been done before. But everything that is really new is crazy. Can you imagine? Folkmusic, and what kind of guitarist? Flamenco? A gypsy who can hardly read and write, and who has no idea what a musical score is? Yes, all of that is true. Montoya can write only with great difficulty and cannot tell the difference between an eighth note and a whole note. That is true, but you don't make records of writing, spelling, or the keys of G and F. What is recorded is living music, without which written music would not even exist. In this terrain, that of living music, Montoya was beyond compare. He is the best, by far the best. This conviction gave my father the strength to confront all difficulties and overcome them. In May he went to work, writing to Montoya to ask him if he would like to record as a soloist. On June 3rd, Montoya responded that he was interested and had fourteen pieces ready: *el polo, la caña, soleares, malagueña, granadina, taranta, bulerías, siguiriyas, guajira, farruca, rondeña, tango, minera*, and *la rosa*.
>
> A contract was drafted for six, or more, 12-inch records, to be recorded in Paris using the latest electronic recording techniques. To launch the operation Montoya had to first make a name for himself in France. They would begin with a concert in the Casino in Biarritz, under the management of the best impresario of the

time, Marcel de Valmalète. My father felt obliged to accompany Montoya on the journey to France. On Monday, June 20, he arrived in Port Bou, but there were no more trains to Barcelona. The next day the border was closed; the Civil War had begun...Passionately defended by her people, Madrid never gave in. Neither did my father. The concert, originally scheduled for July 9, would take place on September 7 at whatever cost. After a thousand and one difficulties, he managed to get Montoya and his wife, Mariana, out of Madrid...Spanish refugees [in Biarritz], who went to their gatherings in the cafes and talked of nothing but the tragedy being played out on the other side of the Bidasoa River, joined the French in rushing off to the Casino for the Montoya recital. It was a triumph...Everyone agreed. *La Gazette de Biarritz*, *Le Courrier*, *La Petit Gironde*, and even *La France* in Bordeaux were unanimous in their delirious enthusiasm: Montoya is a genius! They could now go forward, the road to Paris was open.[1]

Flamencologist José Blas Vega says that this concert had almost been cancelled because, "Ramón's wife, Mariana, convinced the guitarist to wear a toupee so that people wouldn't see how bald he was. When the curtain opened, the audience began to whistle [equivalent to booing in Spain] and yell. Ramón left the stage to ask what was going on. The management explained that the people didn't believe it was really Ramón Montoya, because they knew that he was bald. Montoya reappeared on stage without saying a word, and without the toupee. He played thirteen pieces and the success was overwhelming, with newspaper critics unanimous in their praise."[2] In an interview, Montoya said, "My art makes it so that people don't notice whether or not I have hair!"

Rodrigo de Zayas continued:

Ramón and Mariana Montoya arrived in Paris on September 23. Mariana wrote to us that they were staying "in a hotel costing ten *francs* a day, with cooking privileges." My father is more convinced than ever that Montoya should remain within classical circles. He managed to convince Lévy-Alvarez, the director of BAM records, to such an extent that the Montoya album is scheduled to be presented in the October catalogue, between Monteverdi's *"Orfeo"* and Bach's "Well-Tempered Clavier." But first the album had to be recorded. The 20th of October is spent getting Montoya

---

[1] This and the following descriptions of the recording in Paris are taken from the account by Rodrigo de Zayas in the pamphlet that accompanied the album *Arte Clásico Flamenco: Ramón Montoya*, published by the Government of Sevilla for the III Bienal de Arte Flamenco. 1984.

[2] Blas Vega, José, *"Ramón Montoya: La Guitarra Flamenca." La Guitarra en la Historia, Vol V*. Ediciones de la Posada, Córdoba. 1994.

psychologically ready. He is as tight as a bowstring. On Wednesday the 21st, they begin to record, and by the following night the master discs were finished. Montoya had given the best he had in him. My exhausted father wrote to my mother: "He poured his gypsy blood into it to the last drop." Everything had been recorded in two days, with no way of even the slightest editing. In those times there was no room for tricks: the masters were recorded directly.

Montoya was paid ten thousand *pesetas* for the recording[1]. Three weeks later the album *Arte Clásico Flamenco: Ramon Montoya* appeared on the market. It contained six 78-rpm records in the large twelve-inch size and included solo guitar versions of *soleá, la rosa, taranta, granadina, siguiriya, fandango, bulería, rondeña, guajira, tango, malagueña, minera, farruca,* and *alegría.* The album also included a pamphlet containing Montoya's biography and a commentary by Marius de Zayas' wife, Virginia Randolph, on Andalusian music and the styles played by Montoya, including some musical transcriptions.

Much of the music was similar to that on Montoya's earlier recordings, but the listener had to be impressed by the extremely clean technique, displayed here in amazing tremolos, innovative arpeggios, and flashy *picados*. In November of 1936, one reviewer wrote: "The most demanding critic recognized that the records contained pieces extraordinarily filled with subtle shadings, with some subtle rhythms that are absolutely bewildering. The technique of the flamenco style is extraordinarily complex...From a purely musicological point of view, this effort by Montoya represents, in itself, a true revelation."[2]

This first album of solo flamenco guitar would be a point of reference for decades, a source of inspiration and study for all aspiring soloists. A week after recording the album, Montoya intended to give a concert of the same material in the Salle Chopin in Paris. However, the demand for tickets was so great that the concert had to be moved from that small 500-seat hall, to the Salle Pleyel, which could accomodate 2,500. The French press praised the performance as innovative, captivating, and full of Spanish flavor. On the morning after the recital, Zayas had awaited the arrival of the *Excelsior*, whose classical music critic, Emile Vuillermoz, could make or break musical careers. He picked up the paper with trembling hands to read the verdict. Unbelievable! Vuillermoz was enthusiastic, unabashedly enthusiastic. Montoya and his guitar known as *La Leona* had become legend. Ramón had

---

[1] It is difficult to convert *pesetas* into dollars, given fluctuating exchange rates, the tail end of the depression, and the war years in Spain. Probably not more than $200 and perhaps around $1000 when converted to modern dollars.

[2] Quoted by Rodrigo de Zayas in the pamphlet accompanying the album *Ramón Montoya-Manolo de Huelva*, published by the Government of Sevilla for the III Bienal de Arte Flamenco. 1984.

a different memory of this recital, as he recalled for the press: "My first recital before people with a language and temperament different from the Spanish took place in the Salle Pleyel in Paris. And I recall the great scare the audience gave me, because when I finished playing the first part, everybody began shouting *'bis, bis!* [encore]' I thought they were kicking me out like a cat that has become a pest..."

The following month found Montoya back in the Salle Pleyel, in recitals with the dancer La Joselito. Although they appeared on posters together, the two artists actually performed separately and only came together for the closing *caracoles*. In December they returned for the "2nd Festival of the Flamenco Art," along with La Joselito's husband, Juan Relámpago and the guitarist Amalio Cuenca. Amalio, a skilled classical and flamenco guitarist, had been active as a soloist at the turn of the century. He moved to France, married an aristocrat, and opened the *colmao* La Feria in 1912. With the outbreak of World War I, he had to leave Paris and return to Spain, where he became artistic director of Sevilla's Kursaal Internacional and was on the jury for the 1922 Contest of *Cante* in Granada. Back in Paris by 1927, he helped the dancer Mariemma get started. It is unclear whether he and Ramón Montoya worked out duets specifically for the recital in the Salle Pleyel and recorded them later, or played together in the recital because they had already recorded the material. But we do know that they performed together and recorded duets *por soleares* and *siguiriyas*.

In early 1937 Montoya gave a number of concerts with La Argentinita in Brussels, London, Switzerland, and Paris. Then came a contract for Buenos Aires. Ramón had rejected offers before due to his fear of traveling by boat, but this time he accepted. On April 21, he set sail from Marseilles.

Toward the end of 1937, guitarist Manolo de Huelva arrived in Paris to work with La Argentinita. Antonio Triana confirms this, saying, "While in Paris, La Argentinita, Pilar, and I renewed our friendship and began rehearsing for our debut in the Salle Pleyel Theater. Manuel Infante was our pianist, and Manolo de Huelva, the guitarist."[1] During that time, in 1938, Manolo made a documentary film with La Argentinita in which he accompanied her *por alegrías*, playing the G-major style invented by Javier Molina.

Back in Spain, flamenco artists didn't fare so well during the Civil War. Opposing armies see-sawed back and forth in control of territory, leaving people confused and trapped. If people aided one side, they were subject to execution by the other, and if they didn't, the same fate. A minimum of 100,000 men were executed, murdered, or assassinated during three years of fighting. The rebels, who called themselves "Nationalists," were led by General Francisco Franco, head of the cruel and ruthless Moroccan forces.

[1]Pohren, p. 368

Franco began to assume more and more control and was eventually named head of state. The Nationalists had troops, tanks, and airplanes from Nazi Germany and Fascist Italy—these foreign powers using Spain as a testing ground for new equipment. Opposing this powerful force was the army of the established government, the Republicans, who also called themselves Loyalists. Although they received supplies from France, Mexico, and the Soviet Union, and were aided by an International Brigade of soldiers and back-up personnel from the United States and Europe, the Republicans were no match for the rebel forces.

Throughout most of the war, rebels held Madrid in a state of seige . Within the city, people lived without water or electricity and many lost their homes to bombing. Many flamenco artists fled, returning to their home towns to wait out the war. Those who entertained the military usually asked to be paid in food—money was worthless.

Antonio Triana's daughter, Luisa, related the circumstances of her family's escaped from Madrid: "We left Spain six months after the war began. We were living in Madrid, where my father had been performing and was well situated... The war was a bad time for everyone, but it was especially bad for artists. Besides that, one day they bombarded a house near ours and my father thought that we should go before it was our turn. I remember that we left at night, with my mother, my grandmother, and my two sisters, and we eventually reached Paris... Many Spanish artists who were fleeing the war got together in Paris at that time. My father began to perform there with Argentinita.[1]

In Paris Antonio Triana began to teach in a small studio in the Montmartre district, oblivious to the presence of Argentinita rehearsing in a hotel nearby. When the two finally made contact, Triana was already committed to perform in Budapest. Sometime later they began their collaboration with a performance in the Salle Pleyel and then a tour of France.

After three years of intense fighting and the death of one half to one million soldiers and unknown tens of thousands more who starved to death or died from war-related illnesses, a demolished Madrid fell in March of 1939. The Republicans surrendered and disbanded. General Francisco Franco outlawed all political parties and unions, except for the fascist Falange which became the official state party. His dictatorship would last for more than thirty-five years. The 1940s would be a time of near famine, rural poverty, a thriving black market, and brutal repression by the government.

It has been suggested that, under Franco, touristic spectacles—theater productions, dance companies, nightclubs—flourished, while individual expression was discouraged. It is true that most flamencos, especially gypsies, continued to fare poorly after the war, while the *ópera* companies resumed touring on a grand scale. The *cupletista* Conchita Piquer obtained

---
[1] Moreno, Gloria, *"La bailaora que vino de America."* *Diaro de Jerez*, November 21, 1992

the rights to *Las Calles de Cádiz* from La Argentinita and restaged it with integrity and good taste, even to the point of bringing La Malena and La Macarrona out of retirement at ages seventy and eighty to assume their original roles. The new cast included singers La Niña de los Peines, Pepe Pinto, and Pericón de Cádiz (as the shoemaker), dancers Rafael Ortega, La Ignacia, La Albaicín, and Mari Paz (the dancer whose death, after leaving this show, would lead to the *petenera* curse), and guitarists Niño Ricardo, Melchor de Marchena, and Esteban Sanlúcar—a young virtuoso who would soon abandon Spain for South America and become a legend as a composer. *Las Calles de Cádiz* would tour with great success for about five years, until 1945.

It is not clear whether the successes of large touring companies and the difficulties facing gypsy artists in the bars and cafes were directly due to the environment created by the Franco regime or merely coincident with it, but under Franco signs appeared for the first time in bars and taverns reading: *"Se prohibe el cante!"* [The Singing of Flamenco is Prohibited!]

CHAPTER SEVEN

AMERICA

Shortly after Carmen arrived in Buenos Aires in the fall of 1936, she described the trip from Lisbon in an interview:

"From the moment they gave us our tickets and we put them in our pockets, we began to be seasick—my father, my brother, El Pelao, even my handbag. I can't even begin to tell you...we found ourselves on the high sea, and continued that way for many days, until the first thing we saw was the Island of Fernando de Noronha—that really impressed me because it is there that they lock up men condemned to jail. The first port we entered was Pernambuco, and the following day the *Monte Pascoal* took us to Bahía and later Río de Janeiro. It is not for nothing that we gypsies are superstitious, and we are always right. A young man came on board in Lisbon, from Uruguay, I believe, and he wasn't in his right mind. *El tío* [the guy] was *majareta perdido!* [completely crazy], or as we say in Spain, *estaba mochales*. The man had a persecution paranoia and was saying that they wanted to kill him. One night, to scare us, he said he was determined to throw himself into the water, and without telling anybody, there went his body for the entertainment of the sharks. The ship stopped for eight hours to look for him before we gave him up for lost. Afterward, upon leaving Río Grande, the boat got held up in some place, and after a delay of several more hours arrived in Buenos Aires."[1]

El Pelao and Carmen commented on the trip in another interview:

They still hadn't gotten over the fright of the crossing. El Pelao commented: "Why does the ocean have to have so much water?"
Carmen recalls: "The first land we saw was the Island of Fernando de Noronha, where they take the prisoners..."
The gypsies have an ancestral hatred of prisons and the Guardia Civil [Spain's national police]. Carmen sympathized: *"Probesitos,*

---

[1] *La Nación,* Buenos Aires, December 1936.

> those poor prisoners, with the *civiles* inside and the sharks outside..."
>
> Because the other obsession of the gypsies is the sharks. When the ship ran aground, they blamed it on the sharks: "They knew that we were coming and they had their eye on us," interjected El Pelao.
>
> "Sometimes I practiced my dances on board," said Carmen Amaya, "and it left the Germans with their mouths hanging open, because I don't know what it is about us gypsies, but everybody likes us. It's just that we gypsies are *er cormo* [the ultimate]. What would the poor *payos* do if there were no gypsies in the world? But the Germans on board were *unos tíos* with no enthusiasm, who didn't know how to say *'Olé'* and only yelled *'brr'* with more *erres* than *una carretera* [with more *r's* than the word 'highway']. I was tired of hearing so many *'Bravos'* and I said to one of those redheads, *'Bravo* will be the bull that catches you, tedious one!"[1]

After ten days on the open sea, the gypsies arrived at their destination. When Carmen was asked what had impressed her most about the trip, she replied with typical gypsy *gracia*, "Knowing that Columbus also got seasick!"

While the ship was made fast to the dock in Buenos Aires and the gangplank put in place, the Amaya company was surprised to see a cloud of photographers, reporters, and curious onlookers crowding the dock. Carmen's fame had crossed the ocean without her knowledge. Montañés described the arrival:

> Nobody knows who was more surprised, Carmen and her people on seeing the mob of people waiting for them, or the expectant crowd on watching the dazed group of dark-skinned gypsies descend the gangplank, loaded down with strange goods and bundles held together with string. The Amaya clan have dressed in their best regalia for the occasion and it is precisely that regalia that has left the reporters, photographers, aficionados, and the merely curious with their mouths hanging open: garishly colored shirts and blouses, mops of hair slicked down with oil or butter, the men with sideburns reaching halfway down their cheeks, the women with their dark hair knotted in the back into huge buns. In their hands, cardboard suitcases and bundles of herbs tied with scarves...
>
> From the dock someone calls out "Amaya!" and about twenty heads turn in that direction. The same voice says, "But who is Amaya?" And twenty voices respond, "I am."
>
> Cameras flash one after the other, like a single lightning flash.

---

[1]*Mundo Argentino*, November 1936.

Now all of the Amayas stand on Argentine soil. The impresario who had contracted the *"Gran Compañía de Baile Español de Carmen Amaya"*—as it read on the posters—elbows his way through the crowd to confront the gypsies. "But, is it possible to know which one of you is Carmen Amaya?"

The impresario opens his eyes as wide as dinner plates when he sees that tiny woman who barely reaches the height of his shoulders. She says to him, "I'm Carmen Amaya." And that wisp of a woman continues, "And who are you?"

"I'm the impresario who brought you here. Isn't that enough?"

"Bueno, you pay and we'll dance—each to his own!"[1]

The following account explains why the impresario of the Maravillas Theater had been so anxious to meet his new attraction:

> The season was going from bad to worse and he was counting on the famous gypsy to straighten out his desperate financial situation. The businessman did not want to believe that the young girl before him was the famous artist upon whom the survival of the theater depended. He refused to attend the opening and they had to get him out of bed the following day to attend the exhaltation of Carmen. Also the following day, police and firemen with water hoses tried to contain a rioting crowd that wanted to get in to applaud the gypsy.
>
> Three months of performances in Buenos Aires, later Rio de Janeiro, back again to Buenos Aires, and always enthusiastic audiences applauding Carmen Amaya.[2]

The press described Carmen's triumphant debut:

> She made her presentation last night in the Teatro Maravillas, before a room filled to capacity by an expressive and enthusiastic audience. Above all, I have to point out that the gypsy dancer and singer, Carmen Amaya, offers all the merits of an exponent of art in the truest sense of the word. Tiny, agile, delicate, her art as a dancer of the purest gypsy style, offers dazzling contrasts that go from the softest sentimental note to a passionate theme with something wild and erotic at the same time. Our city has seen many dancers parade on our stage, but last night the one presented in the Maravillas was extraordinary. Blessed with a physique that might even be called unpleasant, a tiny figure, the expression of her dances contains the charm of her turns, as varied as they are daring in the rapid spins, and with something of the contortionist as

[1] Montañés, p. 31.
[2] Góngora.

she closes each dance. Frequently, Carmen Amaya appears awkward, putting her legs through athletic *desplantes* [variations], precise in her footwork, perfectly rhythmic in the rapid fire of her finger snaps. Regarding her arms, they stood out for their expressive and harmonious placement above her tiny body.

She began by offering a brilliant interpretation of *fandanguillo de Almería*, highlighted frequently by postures from the bullfight; then she offered a *canción* to the music of *farruca*; that was followed by a particularly splended dance *por soleares*, and finally, accompanied by three guitarists, she presented a *zambra gitana* that ended with the collaboration of one of the guitarists and was one of the most complete expressions of her art.[1]

The pianist García Matos, who had prepared a number of compositions for Anita Sevilla and Carmen during the boat trip, confirmed that the guitarists often got up from playing the guitar to do a few steps of dance, and it always came out well.

From that moment, Carmen never stopped. If she wasn't dancing, she was looking after the needs of the family, arranging papers, salaries, hotels, rehearsals, costumes, interviews, photo shoots, official receptions and dinners. That is when she began to drink her ten cups of coffee a day and smoke two packs of cigarettes. But, no matter how tired she might be, she never gave less than all she had in her dance. This ability to hold nothing back in her performances became her trademark. She often said, "The only thing I need is to dance!"

In an interview, Carmen felt the need to hide the fact of her birthplace. She hadn't forgotten being called a fraud because she had not been born in Andalucía:

> Carmen sees the new sofa that they had just placed in her dressing room, a sofa upholstered in purple that she feels will bring bad luck: "Get this piece of junk out of here, it looks like a coffin!"
>
> El Pelao comes in.
>
> "This is my father's cousin. But I don't call him *tío* because he is my uncle, only because he is old."
>
> ...Carmen recalls:
>
> "I was born in the Seven Caves, in the Sacromonte of Granada. I made my debut, that which they call a debut, at four years old. But dance, what they call dance, I danced before I was born. But from four years of age the Englishmen applauded me in the Sacromonte. At twelve years of age I began to grow and, at thirteen, I stopped. That's why I am such a *güena moza* [big girl]. We were several years in Mallorca, dancing between the sky and the

---

[1] Quoted in Hidalgo Gómez, p. 104.

water. I danced in Barcelona, in Sevilla, in Madrid, and in almost all of the important cities in Spain. And I was in Paris, where I worked with Raquel Meller. Also in Berlin, in Nice, and other large cities.

"Here in Buenos Aires, just after arriving, a mirror fell on my head and left me dazed. It was a mirror that must have been possessed, because they couldn't get it off me. Besides, it had looked at me with a pain and malice that scared me. It took a while to get me free of it. It was one of those days when *something* had to happen to me...It wounded me here. They wanted to sew the skin, but when they began to talk about stitches, the pain, and even the fear, went away. In spite of everything, when I finished dancing that night, my head was covered with blood."

How do you prepare your dances, Carmen?

"Well, I don't know. I let myself be carried by the music and I dance what comes out. I know how to begin the dance and how to end it. But I don't know what happens in the middle!"

And that is the impression that Carmen Amaya gives. Everything that she does is improvisation: an art of race, intuition, spontaneity, and perfection all at once. Each dance, or to be more exact, each interpretation that she does of the same dance, is a creation that is equal to, but different from, the previous. She dances as if in a trance, as if she were letting herself be carried by the inspiration of the instant, but always managing herself, controlling herself, according to internal guidelines. El Pelao confirms these impressions:

"I also know how to dance, but when I am with Carmen, I forget everything I know!" And not being able to explain himself better, he adds, "This girl is a phenomenon..."

Someone praises El Pelao's abilities as a dancer and a guitarist. He answers with a mixture of modesty and pride: *"Sí, sí,* I'm okay at that...but what I really do well is shear a donkey [a traditional gypsy occupation]..."

El Pelao is truly a picturesque and pure *gitano.* "The ugliest in all of Granada," Carmen says to him in a parody of the song, *"Manolo Reyes."*

"I could have been a great bullfighter," he says, "if I weren't so afraid..."

And while she dances, he encourages her in a deep voice that sounds as if it were coming out of the tomb of a pharoah: *"Olé*...Long live Egypt!"

She herself has said it: "I only know how to begin and end a dance." The rest is some sort of religious frenzy danced to the *compás* of her own music, because she creates her own rhythm, her own orchestra. She must not hear the guitarists, nor, perhaps, the orchestra that accompanies her. Perhaps she hears the rhythm of her blood, and to that rhythm beats her hands and makes the sound of castanets with her fingers. I have never heard such a loud sound of handclapping as that which she gets out of her small hands.

Why do you do clown around when you dance?

"*Hijo*, to rest," she says, to justify herself.

Nevertheless, you shouldn't do it, your dance is something very serious!

Convinced, she agrees, "Yes, I know. I won't do it again..." But, given her temperament, she just has to add, "Well, look, to make it more serious I will put on a mustache like a Guardia Civil—that is the most serious thing in the world..."[1]

Less than a month later, Carmen elaborated further on the fictitious details of her birth and early life:

"I am Andalusian, from Granada, or to be more exact, from the Sacromonte, and to be even more clear—although my skin won't allow it [a pun on the word *clara* which means both 'clear' and 'light-skinned']—I am from that idiocy of a place stuck between cactus and rocks that is called The Seven Caves, which is more or less the capital of the gypsy race."

Have you danced since you were very young?

"I believe I was born dancing, which is the mark of gypsy women. Now, of course I don't remember this because I was very small when I was born. Imagine how small I must have been, if now that I am somewhat older I hardly reach a *cuarto* from the ground...When I was just four, and dressed in many colors, I began to dance in the Sacromonte, before Englishmen, who are the best audience for the gypsy art—although they don't understand anything about it. I have seen some Englishmen, with faces like grilled red mullet, yelling *'Olé!'* in such a way as to make me believe they were gypsies. I still don't what it is about us, what we have that pleases people everywhere, even when they speak badly about our race. They say we are this, or that, but in the end, they all come looking for us, for the talent of the *raza cañí* [gypsy race]. And, just as I began my life, I continued throught the passage of the years, pounding my feet and doing *palmas* and snapping my fingers, and all thanks to the fact that I never grew and people couldn't see my age—I'm older than a parrot. You can

[1] *Mundo Argentino*, Buenos Aires, November 1936.

guess anywhere from sixteen to forty and you won't be wrong!"
Tell us something about your artistic career, your performances in Europe.

"Let me tell you. When they got tired of making me dance in front of the Englishmen for a few pennies, the day came when they decided to take me away from Granada. I was very afraid they were going to make me into one of those dancers with the *figura de paloma* [meaning not clear; perhaps refers to heavily busted *cupletistas*]" At this point Carmen got to her feet and took a comic posture to illustrate her point. "But, happily, it wasn't that way, and I continued to do my thing, *lo cañí*, that of the gypsy, the flamenco. And on the stage of the Teatro España [Español] in Barcelona, in *El Paralelo* [Barrio Chino], I performed for the first time outside of Andalucía."

And what did the Catalonians say?

"The Catalonians are the most flamenco *tíos* in the world. People have said to me many times that to dance *soleares* or *bulerías* in Cataluña is like wanting to win an argument with a tree, but I can say that I performed a miracle. What they told me and praised in Barcelona is something I cannot put into words. Then I traveled all over Spain and, later, I went to Paris to dance in the Palais Theater, with Raquel Meller. After a few years, I returned to work again in Paris, in the Alahambra Theater, and I can say without bragging that I pleased them more than the time before. I also worked in Berlin, in Nice, and in many other cities."

And how were they able to understand you in Germany?

"I made them understand, without, of course, speaking their language—which is more difficult than eating with a fork! To say that I wanted to eat, I closed the fingers of one hand and moved it toward my mouth, and those *tíos* understood me. If I wanted to ask for coffee, it was easier, because I always carried a few leaves of coffee in my purse and when I showed them to the *gachó* [*payo*] in the restaurant, he understood me immediately."

...And what do you like best about Buenos Aires?

"*Pues*, everything I have seen: Calle Corrientes, where I live, La Avenida de Mayo, and the obelisk [a towering stone monument]. And don't think that this admiration for the obelisk is due to some rivalry I feel because of my height. I don't want to grow that much, I'm fine the way I am, and besides, so that I never have to go on the ocean again, I'm staying here—even if I have to sell chestnuts to do it!"[1]

---
[1] *La Nación*, Buenos Aires, December 1936.

In February of 1937, a new act arrived to join Carmen in the Maravillas. The two diminutive dancers known as Los Chavalillos de Sevilla (The Kids from Sevilla) had been preceded by news of the furor they had been creating in Europe. Antonio Ruiz Soler was almost sixteen, while his cousin and partner, Florencia Pérez Padilla, had reached the ripe old age of eighteen, but for years to come they would be called "kids." Antonio, the youngest in a large Sevillian family, had abandoned his dream of becoming a bullfighter and entered the dance academy of Maestro Realito at age six. Florencia, also from Sevilla and better known by the family nickname "Rosario," had joined Antonio in the dance school of Realito, where the two of them learned the classical Andalusian dance. Later they studied regional folk dances with José Otero and the ballet-like *escuela bolera* with Maestro Pericet. For flamenco, Antonio went to Frasquillo, while Rosario learned from La Macarrona. They began to take part in dance recitals in the Teatro del Duque in Sevilla when Antonio was only seven. Their professional careers began a couple of years later, when they danced in the International Exposition in Liege (Brussels), Belgium. The following year, the city of Madrid dubbed little Rosario and Antonio "Los Chavalillos de Sevilla." Vedrines booked them for three years of touring.

The Spanish Civil War caught Los Chavalillos in Barcelona. They fled to France, where the impresario Marquesi contracted them for Buenos Aires, for the show called *"Las Maravillas de Maravillas"* ["The Marvels of the Maravillas Theater"]. Rosario described her first meeting with Carmen Amaya:

> I met her in Barcelona. She was performing in the Taberna de Manquet and we couldn't see her dance because Antonio and I were very young and they wouldn't let us into the Manquet. We waited in the street to be able to see her. Some flamencologists say that we worked with Carmen in Madrid, but that is completely untrue. I never performed with Carmen in Madrid...Much later, when the impresario Carcellé presented her in the Cine Capitol, dancing alone to ten guitars, then Antonio and I did see her.
>
> We met up in Buenos Aires. When the war began, she went to Portugal and Argentina, and we were in Marseilles as part of a tour of France when a contract came our way for work in the Argentine capital, and it was there that we came together...
>
> Her very personal style of dance was not very feminine. She danced like a boy, but there has been no man who could do footwork at Carmen's speed...not one! What she did was to sing with *mucha gracia* [much charm] and she sang some *cantiñas* that she embellished with her train dress, but her strength lay in what she did wearing pants...She didn't need [scenery nor choreography],

she was everything and needed nothing. The artists that were with her were secondary; Carmen Amaya was the show.[1]

The press gave an account of the debut of Los Chavalillos in Buenos Aires:

> The company of flamenco art that is performing in the Maravillas rennovated its cast last night. The hall was full, with no more room for even a hat, all booths and boxes were occupied, and even the uppermost sections were impressive, with the atmosphere of a blacksmith shop, not only due to the prevailing temperature, but as a result of all the shouting by the assembly. The pair of Andalusian dancers, Los Chavalillos *gitanos*, made their presentation, both very young, very likeable, and, although they do not exactly have *gracia*, they stand out for their dexterity, the precision of their steps, their rhythm, their expressions, their confident feel for the dance and how they evoke a cordial and youthful impression. As the conclusion of a strong presentation, Carmen Amaya offered, with her usual mastery, several gypsy dances, some of them new in her repertoire, in which the soul of her race appeared on her face and in her glistening eyes. In her steps, she displayed her extraordinary agility...this tiny dancer, one of the greatest interpreters of her race, rebellious and courageous, drew endless ovations from the hall, as she always does.[2]

Two months later, the newspapers reported a change in the program: "The dancer Carmen Amaya, accompanied by the guitarists Francisco and José Amaya and El Pelao, will debut an evocation of the flavor of Jerez entitled *'Gitanos contrabandistas'* ['Gypsy Smugglers']; the new production will feature the return of the *cancionista española*, Ana de Sevilla, who has been away from this hall for some weeks and will offer the songs, *'Arenal de Sevilla,' 'Placita de Doña Elvira,'* and *'Vete con los tuyos.'* For their part, Los Chavalillos Sevillanos will present the dances *'Seguidilla gitana,' 'La leyenda del beso,'* and *'Sevilla'* by Albéniz."[3]

Los Chavalillos became a mainstay in the Maravillas and remained in charge when Carmen took off on tour. Eventually they would conquer all of the Americas and rise to such prominence that they would be known by their first names alone: "Rosario and Antonio." Not long after arriving in Buenos Aires, Rosario fell in love with the music director of their show, Silvio Masciarelli, a native Argentinian. They soon married and had a son not long afterward. Silvio played piano, did the musical arrangements, and conducted the orchestra wherever Los Chavalillos performed.

Antonio, who never grew very tall and always wore platform boots when

[1] Verdu, p. 24.
[2] *La Nación*, February 18, 1937. Buenos Aires.
[3] *La Nación*, April 21, 1937. Buenos Aires.

he danced, would go on to become Spain's most celebrated male dancer, usually referred to as "The Great Antonio." Classical and regional folk dances dominated his repertoire, but many believe he was also one of the finest *bailaores* of flamenco, standing out for his passion and superb technique.

Carmen Amaya continued to perform to sell-out crowds. She performed throughout Argentina, then in neighboring Uruguay, and in Mexico enthusiastic crowds carried her out of the theater on their shoulders. In Rio de Janeiro, she made $10,000 a week and purchased a ranch. Later, she would go to Columbia and Venezuela.[1]

García Matos wrote: "While we were having this tremendous success, we met Ramón Montoya, the famous flamenco guitarist from Madrid, one of the best we have had in Spain. We spoke with him and agreed that he would join our show, making it more complete and insuring a complete success. We were in the same theater for no less than two years, that is, all of 1937 and 1938."

An interview with Montoya appeared in a Buenos Aires newspaper on May 11, 1937:

> In the early morning hours yesterday, the celebrated Spanish guitarist considered to be the most complete interpreter of the popular music of Andalucía arrived in our metropolis aboard the steamship *Campana*, which had come from Marseilles. The artist came to perform in our capital, contracted by the management of the theater of regional art, the Maravillas, which is also offering the group headed by Carmen Amaya. Montoya has been associated with the art of *cante jondo* for more than a quarter of a century, in which his dexterity as a guitarist has linked him with such figures of significance in flamenco expression as the Macarronas, La Niña de los Peines, and Antonio Chacón. Throughout the interview that the celebrated guitarist gave us in the Maravillas, all the big names that have made a cult of the popular song of the Andalusian people paraded through his memory, and he sprinkled the conversation with episodes, some picturesque, others sentimental, in which the actor Manolo Vico appeared frequently, for he has been tied to Montoya's artistic life by more than one performance on the Peninsula.
>
> The features of Montoya belie completely his native region. With his lively face, you would say that he is a man from the north of Spain, but when speaking, he resembles a perfect Andalusian. But, in the first questions, Ramón speaks freely and details all one would wish to know about him.
>
> —What region are you from?

---

[1]Montañés, p. 32.

"I am from Madrid, from the one and only barrio of Lavapiés, that foolish barrio that so well defines the capital of Spain. And you can be sure that on some occasions I have had to show my personal papers to demonstrate that I was *Madrileño* on all sides. [On another occasion, Ramón said that Andalucians often told him, 'Montoya, you are immense! With a guitar at your fingers, you are the best that God has put on this earth. You have only one defect, *chaval*...you are not Andalusian!']

"I was to go to Buenos Aires some seven years ago, when García Malla proposed that I perform in the Casino Theater, but the fear of going by boat—I am, besides being from Madrid, also gypsy—made me turn down that tempting offer. I always remember how Manolo Vico, who already knew this country, told me more than once, 'Don't be stupid, Ramón, go to America, where you will become conceited with all the money you will earn!' But I confess that just the idea, knowing that I would have to spend so many days in the middle of the ocean, removed all interest that could have been offered by those contracts"

The conversation turned to his recent performances and plans for the Maravillas.

"I have been performing in Paris for about eight months, extended from five. I had to come to Buenos Aires but they wouldn't let me go. I gave various recitals of flamenco music in the Salle Pleyel and two in the Opéra Comique accompanying Encarnación 'La Argentinita,' who had extraordinary success there. How your countrywoman can dance! For me, she is the most complete artist among the *bailaoras* that Spain has known. Even when singing in that little voice that she has, she does it beautifully. Hers is a pure art, first class, that the public in Paris, as previously in Spain, knew how to value in its true expression. Later, I performed in Brussels, London, and Switzerland, until I was able to go in the direction of Marseilles and board a ship to pass those days on the high sea—something I want to forget so that I will be brave enough for the return trip.

"In my performance in Buenos Aires, my repertoire will consist of interpretations on the guitar, on my *Leona*, of purely classical flamenco art, such as the *soleares, malagueñas, mineras, tarantas, rondeñas, bulerías, tangos* in major and minor, *guajiras, farrucas,* and *siguiriyas,* and I will execute each one of them in an arrangement according to the desires of the audience."[1]

---

[1] *"El arte popular andaluz: Ramón Montoya recuerda figuras del cante jondo." La Nación,* Buenos Aires. May 11, 1937.

García Matos implied that Montoya was with them for two years, but Rodrigo de Zayas insists that Ramón was back in France some five months later: "In September of 1937, Montoya returned from a tour of concerts in Argentina. I recall it perfectly, because he brought me a little guitar, my first instrument, which I still have."

Sabicas had been working with the popular *cupletista* Estrellita Castro when the civil war broke out. He recalled:

> She was a very good singer...very nice. People loved her... One day, we finished our act and the people were applauding. Suddenly she said to me, "Play!"
> I asked her, "What are you going to sing?"
> "I don't know, but play!"
> "But you don't even have an idea of what you want to sing."
> "Play..."
> And she sang something, and I followed her with the guitar. The people applauded for ten minutes. When we went upstairs, she lit a match and burned all of our music. I said, "Woman, why are you burning them? With whom are you going to sing now?"
> "With you."
> "But, do you think that I am your orchestra?"
> And that is the way it was. She would go out on stage, walk around, speak to the audience, and I would be waiting for her. You can only do this with the guitar. It was a revolution. She burned all the music. She was free. We earned a lot of money. We used to go on tours to Barcelona, to El Paralelo [Barrio Chino]—the theater district.
> When the war broke, we were in Barcelona. The following day I was to leave for France. Estrellita came and said, "Let's go to Valencia, for a benefit!"
> My mother said, "Estrellita, my child, Sabicas is sick." I was in bed, pretending to be sick, because I didn't want to go back.
> "Well, he has to come, otherwise I will get the police to come for him."
> I told her, "Go to Valencia and find someone else to play for you, I'm sick!"
> The woman left and the following day we took a ship for France. There, we met the rest of the company and we all left. It was a new French ship...very big. We left for Buenos Aires. The trip took a long time, about three weeks. When we arrived in

Buenos Aires, it was so big, so pretty, so clean—all of the streets.[1]

According to Diego Castellón, Sabicas and the rest of the company had been brought to Buenos Aires by an agent named Alcoriza, a big name in Spain. When the war broke out Sabicas had been working with Estrellita Castro and the *cantaor* Juan Mendoza, better known as El Niño de Utrera. Along with another popular *cantaor* named Pena, *hijo*, they were performing in a theater piece called *La Novia del Cante*. When they all broke with Estrellita and fled to France, they met with Alcoriza in Marseilles and formed the company that went to Argentina.

On another occasion, Sabicas explained: "I left Spain in '36. We arrived in Buenos Aires with a company that included the singers El Niño de Utrera and Pena, *hijo*, and a group of actors. We were doing a play called *'El Padre Castañuela.'* Carmen was already in Buenos Aires, creating an uproar. She went for four weeks and stayed nine months in a sold-out theater. They sold tickets one and a half to two months in advance. Later, we got together and stayed together for seven years."[2] "Everybody was talking about Carmen. Even the alphabet soup spelled Carmen—what a commotion!"[3]

Sabicas brought his family with him. His brother, Diego, spoke of that time:

> Carmen had been there for some months, and that was all they talked about. She was in the Teatro Maravillas and we were in the Teatro Mayor, on Avenida Mayor—an important street like Fifth Avenue in New York. You had to buy tickets a month in advance [for Carmen] because the best in Spain were there: Ramón Montoya, Conchita Martínez—the best singer in Spain— Asunción Pastor, Anita Sevilla—who sang and danced so well it was scary—and Los Chavalillos de España...
>
> *Señor* Maya was one of the two Spanish impresarios in the Teatro Maravillas. He was the one who brought Carmen from Lisbon. He brought all of the show and became a millionaire, taking advantage of people fleeing Spain and paying them very little.[4]

Diego added: "When we first got there, not many people came to see us, because there was Carmen Amaya. But later we presented *Padre Castañuela* and people began to come. That man made a lot of money and finally he could pay everybody." Apparently it was some time before Sabicas and Carmen Amaya got together. According to Diego, "She [Carmen] had been in the Teatro Maravillas for a little over a year, and then she went on a tour of different cities and countries...When they came back, they made a show

[1]Molarsky interview.
[2]Interview on Spanish television, in a program called "Madrid Flamenco." Onda Madrid, 1987.
[3]Molarsky interview.
[4]Goldberg interviews.

in the Teatro Mayor, with Carmen and Sabicas, and people came."[1]

While in Buenos Aires, Carmen appeared in some short films featuring the popular singer/dancer Miguel de Molina. According to Montañés, she received up to 70,000 *pesetas* for each, but concerned herself more with the quality of her appearance in films rather than the amount of money. She always demanded the right to preview her films and refuse their release if she was not satisfied. Many a day's work ended up in the fire before she was satisfied. Such was the public demand for these films, that often they had to be shown in the theaters up to five times daily.

Toward the end of 1938, the company that had seen so much success for two years began to break up. Montoya had already returned to France. Los Chavalillos went off on their own. One source says, "The brilliant Antonio had a very difficult personality and argued often with Carmen; he decided to create his own company..."[2] The dancer José Greco wrote: "...there was bad blood between Carmen Amaya and the dance team Rosario & Antonio. She'd been their boss and had taught them much of what they knew. When they left her, they 'borrowed' her choreographies and routines and became a big success, thereby earning her eternal enmity."[3]

Manuel García Matos and Anita Sevilla (romantically linked at this time) went to Mexico, while Carmen remained in Buenos Aires. The next year Carmen would embark on a whirlwind of tours through Uruguay, Brazil, Chile, Peru, Columbia, Ecuador, Venezuela, Santo Domingo, Cuba, and Mexico.

Sabicas recalled that they experienced their first earthquake in Chile. It was the famed 1939 *terremoto de Chillán*, in Valparaiso, where 15,000 lives were lost. "It caught me in the middle of a *farruca*. People began jumping from their seats and running out of the theater. For a while I thought they didn't like the way I was playing, but then I saw the big chandelier swinging from the ceiling. To tell you the truth, I had no idea what an earthquake was. If I had known, I would have dropped dead then and there. Luckily, nothing happened to us. The building housing the theater was new and stayed in one piece."[4] He added, "Poor Carmen was holding tight to me. We were already engaged at that time...Our involvement dated back to Spain. Her brother, Paquito, a good person also, married a gypsy woman named La Chata. I was at their wedding, when I was in Barcelona. We were there together. I used to tell them often, 'I was at your wedding.'"[5]

While in Cuba in the fall of 1939 to perform in Havana's Teatro Nacional, the Amayas made a short film entitled *El Embrujo del Fandango* (*The Spell*

---

[1] Goldberg interviews.
[2] Odette Lumbroso, quoted in Bois, p. 118.
[3] Greco, p. 56.
[4] Chileno, El Niño, p. 6.
[5] Molarsky interview.

of the Fandango). According to Goldberg, the film was El Chino's idea and he created the rather thin thread of story that linked the musical performances. The action opens in a cafe with El Chino, as the waiter, singing a bit of *fandango* to himself. El Pelao comes in, elegantly dressed and thin as a whip; his posture and movements are those of a dancer. Antonia Amaya makes her entrance and dances to orchestral accompaniment. It is immediately apparent that she was not an accomplished dancer. Her attempt to imitate her sister Carmen is almost embarrassing to watch. She teeters and stumbles off balance, attempts awkward leaps and turns, and doesn't know what to do with her short hair, tossing it around in an attempt at passion. The explanation was revealed many years later in Goldberg's interviews with Leonor and Antonia Amaya. The two sisters had not been professional dancers before coming to Argentina in mid-1937, almost a year after Carmen's arrival. They began their formal dance training in the corps de ballet of the Maravillas Theater, learning regional folk dances. Therefore, at the time of the filming in Cuba, they had been dancing for only about two years.[1]

At the close of Antonia's dance, Sabicas offers a toast to her. Paco walks in, playing the part of a bullfighter. Soon he is joined at his table by Carmen Amaya. He borrows a guitar and plays *por soleá* for Carmen at the table, showing himself to be a very strong, clean, and expressive player. The foundation of his technique is a strong thumb, but he also demonstrates a forceful *picado* and a good tremolo. The solo completed, a man comes from another table to offer a drink to Carmen. She declines, and the man says he would like to dedicate a *fandanguillo* to her if Paco would play for him. Paco replies, "I play only for her!" The waiter, El Chino, comes to the rescue, offering his services by saying, "What am I here for? I play as well as I sing and dance!" With that, he dashes off a quick step and a turn, and then takes up the guitar. He too shows that he is an accomplished guitarist, with a very crisp and rapid thumb.

Following the *fandango*, Carmen dances *"Embrujo del Fandango,"* an orchestral neoclassical piece composed by the pianist José María Palomo. Palomo had begun to play for Carmen after the departure of Manuel Matos. According to Diego Castellón, Palomo and Sabicas collaborated on a number of musical scores, based on flamenco but orchestrated by Palomo at Carmen's request. These included a *taranto* that Carmen would dance for years and the *"Embrujo del Fandango"* that would be Carmen's opening number throughout most of her life.

"Embrujo del Fandango" had the flavor of bullfight music, but was indeed a stylized *fandango*, with one complete *copla* and part of another. For this number, Carmen wore a costume that would be immortalized that same year, in Mexico, by the renowned painter of bullfight posters, Ruano Llopis.

[1]Goldberg, p. 198.

Llopis painted Carmen wearing a feminine version of a matador's suit of lights: A green wrap-around skirt, fitted tight at the hips, a white blouse, and a matching short jacket with the armpits cut out and polka-dot-like cutouts in the sleeves, all decorated with glittering metallic appliqués and dangling gold baubles. Carmen's dancing in this number can best be described as "tight." Everything is tight and compact: her variety of rapid turns and spins, her arms, her castanet playing, and the posture that would become her trademark—back straight, but leaning markedly forward from the hips over her deeply bent knees to form a partially opened "Z".

Without further pretext at story, the film moves to a raised circular stage, made to look like an enormous tambourine. Five guitarists are seated behind the drum, dressed colorfully in polka-dot blouses and traditional manchego cheese-shaped *calañés* hats (left to right: Agustín Castellón—Sabicas' father—El Chino, Sabicas, Paco, Pelao). Sabicas' brother, Diego, did not make this trip, remaining in Buenos Aires with his mother. It is possible that Leonor Amaya did not go on this tour either, as she does not appear in the film. Carmen dances an *alegrías* wearing pants and black shoes with attention-getting white heels. The dance contains all of the elements of a modern *alegrías*, but without its defined structure. Carmen appears to mix at random the rhythmic marking sections, melodic passages (*silencios*), footwork segments (*escovillas*), and the special rhythmic section called *castellana*, exploiting again and again the sudden change from strong and exciting rhythm to slow and dramatic expression.

Later that year, in Mexico City, Carmen worked in two places at the same time, the Fábregas Theater and the cabaret El Patio. Rosario said, "...she was performing in El Patio, an extremely famous place among flamencos. When she finished her contract, Antonio and I began there. We lived in the same apartment tower."[1]

While in Mexico, Carmen reunited with García Matos and Anita Sevilla. And, according to Carmen, she had her first contact with the legendary impresario Sol Hurok. Like most of Carmen's accounts, this one, told to a reporter in New York, is colorful if not one hundred percent believable or in agreement with the facts as seen by others.

Sol Hurok, the "P.T. Barnum of the Arts," had come to America in 1906 as a penniless teenager. He went on to become the leading manager of musical talent, importing acts from around the world. His discoveries included artists of the caliber of Marian Anderson, Isaac Stern, and Roberta Peters. Along with managing such talents as Anna Pavlova, Isadora Duncan, Martha Graham, it was he who brought Vicente Escudero and La Argentinita to the United States.

[It was in 1940] ...in Mexico City, that Sol Hurok first saw her

---

[1] Verdu, p. 25.

[Carmen]. It took only one glance to convince him that what this country and Sol Hurok needed was Amaya. A Spanish dancer is one if the hardest things to sell to an American audience, so what possessed him to think that she had dollars in her, nobody could imagine. They do say he gets these prophetic flashes from the Delphic Oracle, and nobody can guess to what dark gods he sacrifices for their blessing on his new ventures. He offered her a contract for herself and was surprised out of ten years of his life when Carmen nearly fell over backward refusing him—*him*, Hurok! She would go nowhere without her family, so she and they went back to Buenos Aires, and he went back to Radio City with a permanently surprised look on his face.[1]

The Spanish dance environment in New York City in 1940 was very much defined by the presence of Encarnación López "La Argentinita." Two years earlier Argentinita had returned to the United States for the first time since her difficult debut there in 1932. This time she brought a small company with her. *The New York Times* ad announced: "Sol Hurok presents ARGENTINITA and her Spanish Ensemble, in one performance only." That ensemble consisted of Argentinita's sister Pilar López, Antonio Triana, the pianist Rogelio Machado, and guitarist Carlos Montoya, who had been hired after Argentinita could not come to terms with Gabriel Ruiz.

Critic John Martin described Argentinita's premier in November 13, 1938:

> After an absence of eight years, Argentinita returned to New York in a recital of Spanish dances at the Majestic Theatre last night, accompanied this time by her sister, Pilar López, and a male dancer, Antonio Triana. To those who were fortunate enough to see her in her previous appearances here, the rather surprising news this morning is that she is an even finer dancer than she was then. The same superb carriage, the same simple and unaffected approach, the same richly native color, are all in evidence, but here is a new economy of method and a greater mastery of nuance...
>
> Certainly there is nothing lost of the old sense of comedy. The atmosphere is predominantly gay and bits of more pointed humor punctuate the program throughout... Argentinita is not one to set the dance apart in a strictly choreographic frame. On the contrary, she sings and mimes and makes use of all good theatrical means to achieve a spirited end. It is apparently part of her theory that good art can also be good fun...

[1] Dzhermolinska, Helen, "You Must See Amaya." *The American Dancer,* May 1941.

> As for the ensemble, there will undoubtedly by those who, like the present reviewer, prefer their Argentinita straight. Both Miss López and Mr. Triana are able dancers, however, and it must be admitted that their presence makes possible three of the program's high points. These are the *"Anda Jaleo,"* danced to García Lorca's song about the romantic smugglers, the "Castilian Dance," and the beautiful Peruvian festival dance which was added to the program by way of good measure... Carlos Montoya, who is by no means a stranger here, is the assistant guitarist and Rogelio Machado plays the piano accompaniments.[1]

The mention of Carlos Montoya not being a stranger here refers to his previous appearance on American soil, in 1932, with the company of Teresina, "the sensation of London and Paris."

The success of Argentinita's recital led Hurok to book "Spain's Number One Dancer" (according to *Time Magazine*) for seven more performances in the 51st Street Theater after completing a tour to the Pacific Coast. In San Francisco, renowned columnist Herb Caen had written:

> Argentinita, Spanish "Queen of the Dance," vowed yesterday, "If the Loyalists lose the war in Spain [which, of course, they did] I will never dance in my homeland again [she didn't]."
>
> Small, raven-haired, Argentinita fled Spain, where she was head of the first all-Spanish ballet, when civil war broke out.
>
> "I could no longer dance at home," she said, "so I went to the more peaceful countries of Europe, and now I am in San Francisco on my first tour of the United States, and I like it."[2]

Back in New York, John Martin singled out some of the highlights of Argentinita's concerts: the enchanting *"Anda Jaleo,"* the "delicious nineteenth century madrilene mazurka," the *"Huayno"* of Peru, "with its picturesque admixture of Spanish and Indian movement colored by a simple ceremonial dignity," a foolish little "Castilian Dance," a duel between two dancers in the comical "Café de Chinitas," and Argentinita's "Gaucho song and *'Malambo'* and Mr. Triana's virtuoso *'Jaleo Andaluz,'* both of which succeeded in stopping the show."[3]

Martin summed up Argentinita's unique qualities as a performer in an extensive analysis:

> Argentinita is as different from Argentina as day is from night, in spite of the fact that her medium is basically the same and her professional name confusingly similar. In her particular approach,

---
[1] Martin, John, "Argentinita Seen In Dance Recital." Copyright © *The New York Times*, December 14, 1938. Reprinted by permission.

[2] Caen, Herb, *San Francisco Chronicle*, December 9, 1938.

[3] Martin, John, "Argentinita Gives A Dance Program." *The New York Times*, December 28, 1938.

she, too, is unique, and because her unassuming art is so simple and so personal, it is, in the literal sense of the word, inimitable. So obviously so, in fact, that it is doubtful if many of the pseudo-Iberians will even attempt to imitate her...

Argentinita ignores virtually all of the clichés, for her whole approach is so thoroughly "castizo" that, just as the well-bred man does not have to think about his manners, she does not have to worry about being Spanish. There is a total absence of self-consciousness therefore in her style...

Argentinita's voice is a little one, clear and engaging in quality, and exactly in scale with all the other elements of her work. Hers is a lyric personality and a lyric art, in every way dainty, feminine, cameo-like. The eloquence of what she does lies not in its force but in its concentration, which is no less potent because it is easy and effortless...

The exaggerations frequently found in Spanish dancing not of the best are, of course, nowhere in evidence, but even beyond this there is surprisingly little movement in the body, especially in the torso. Oddly enough, there is no effect of rigidity or of staticness; on the contrary, one has rarely seen a more beautiful carriage. She is unusually light of foot, brilliant in taconeo, skillful with the castanets, and a thoroughly ingratiating dancer, with a style quite unlike that of any of her compatriots who have come this way...[1]

Martin said of Argentinita's male partner: "Antonio Triana presented two new solos, 'Polo,' to the music of Albéniz, and a 'Zapateado' of his own arrangement [very likely accompanied by guitar]. Both were brilliantly danced, but the former, with its opportunity for the kind of clowning which Mr. Triana so enjoys, is by all odds the best thing he has done."[2]

After a brief tour of the South, Argentinita gave one last recital, her ninth in New York, in Carnegie Hall on January 16 and then returned to Europe. Antonio Triana's daughter, Luisa Triana, gives some background on these tours. She says that Hurok had seen Argentinita and Antonio Triana in Paris and had contracted them for the American tour of 1938. "Afterward, they returned to Paris to prepare a new program for the following season, an extensive tour of North and South America.. My father realized that France was preparing for war and convinced my mother to let me go with him, with the promise that he would arrange for the rest of the family to join him as soon as he arrived in New York. In Buenos Aires, Argentinita became ill and the tour had to be postponed for six months. While she recuperated, Antonio and Pilar gave concerts alone. Meanwhile, the war escalated in Europe and

---

[1] Martin, John, "The Dance: In Praise Of Argentinita."Copyright © *The New York Times*, January 1, 1939. Reprinted by permission.

[2] Martin, John, "The Dance: Argentinita in New Program." *The New York Times*, December 30, 1938.

many Spanish refugees, including my mother and sisters, had to return to Spain."¹

By January of 1940, Argentinita was able to dance again and opened a series of performances in New York's Hollywood Theater. Among the new numbers was a *tanguillo de Cádiz* entitled *"Tacita de Plata,"* danced by Argentinita to the guitar of Carlos Montoya. The flamenco repertoire had been expanded to include *farruca, zapateado,* a couple of *tangos* (almost certainly *tanguillos),* an *alegrías*— considered to be one of Argentinita's finest numbers—and a closing *bulerías* danced by the whole ensemble and described in the program as "a gypsy jam session" (Carlos Montoya would later use this description in the jacket notes of his record albums). Another new number, *"L'Espagnolade,"* was described by John Martin as "...a broad burlesque of the approach of the non-Spanish dancer to the Spanish dance, and it employs not only some ludicrous travesties of movement, but also a veritable notion counter of stage properties—castanets, a cigarette, a pair of banderillas, a mantilla, a rose between the teeth, and practically every thing except a bull. It is not exactly subtle, but it is very funny."²

Between tours across country, the ensemble gave a full concert in Carnegie Hall on February 28, 1940. New numbers included *"Orgía"* by Turina, *"El Piropo,"* a comedy danced by Argentinita and Antonio Triana, and *"Goyescas,"* in which Pilar López showcased her maturing talents. In March the company returned to the Hollywood Theater to debut *"La Boda de Luis Alonso."* On April 4, Argentinita appeared as guest artist with Sol Hurok's Ballet Russe de Monte Carlo, in the Metropolitan Opera House, dancing *"Capriccio Espagnol"* with Leonide Massine. The two had collaborated on the choreography of this freely adapted suite of folk dances the previous summer and had danced it in Monte Carlo.

Eight months later, as Argentinita prepared for her first appearance in another new season, in a student dance recital at Washington Irving High School, the following small notice appeared in *The New York Times* (December 15, 1940): "Carmen Amaya, gypsy dancer-danseuse, arrived in New York last week from Mexico accompanied by what is officially described as 'a retinue of relatives, guitarists, and dancers.' She is to make her debut here in mid-January in a theater to be announced."

Luisa Triana says that her father had recommended Carmen to Hurok as a replacement for the ailing Argentinita and suggested that he go to see her in Mexico City. That would lend credence to the story of Hurok being turned down when he first saw Carmen in Mexico. Diego Castellón said that he had heard that story also, but didn't know if it was true. Perhaps the truth can be

[1] Triana, Luisa; personal correspondence, May 1998.
[2] Martin, John, "The Dance: New Argentinita Program." *The New York Times,* January 4, 1940

found in the account by Antonio Triana's biographer, Rita Vega de Triana, which asserts that it was Antonio, representing Hurok in Mexico City, who had been turned down because Carmen had to return to Buenos Aires to honor committments.

At one time, Carmen Amaya was earning $14,000 (more than $120,000 in 1997 dollars) a week in Buenos Aires, and a theater was built and named after her, a theater which she later purchased. Toscanini, the renowned conductor, on a good will tour with the NBC Symphony in April of 1940, saw her perform and wrote back, "Never in my life have I seen a dancer with such fire and rhythm and such a terrifying and wonderful personality."[1]

A few weeks later, Leopold Stokowski and his All American Youth Orchestra, on tour in South America, arrived in Carmen's theater too late to see the regular show. The conductor asked Carmen if she would go through her dances again. She was willing, but an Argentinian law prohibited theatrical performances after midnight. "So *Señor* Stokowski asked me to please go ahead," Miss Amaya recalled later. "He and his orchestra were the entire audience for me, and when I finished, he had to pay a large fine (several hundred dollars to government officials as a special tax). But he said he was happy." He also asked, "What sort of demon do you have inside you?"[2]

Diego Castellón told of the eventual meeting with Sol Hurok in Buenos Aires. The impresario's stepson, "a very cultured young man of about twenty who spoke perfect Spanish and acted as interpreter," came and told the Amayas that the "best impresario in the world was interested in taking them to the United States:"

> They [Hurok and his stepson] came to the show together and sat in a box close to the stage. And all of us were waiting for the decision of that man, who was big and fat...And that woman burned up the stage for that man, and the people ate her up, and that guy was stunned.
>
> After the show: "Look, I am Mr. Hurok's son and we have come from New York, with the Ballet Russe, and we are here in Buenos Aires...because the famous musician Stokowski told him, 'You have the best in the world—you have me, you have Segovia, and I don't know how many more. All you lack is one thing—a gypsy woman who is here in Buenos Aires: Carmen Amaya, the best in the world!'
>
> "Since we have stopped here in Buenos Aires, I want my father to talk with you to arrange for you to go to the United States"[3]

Dance critic Helen Dzhermolinska described the trip north:

[1] *Newsweek*, January 27, 1941.
[2] Sugrue, Francis, "The Greatest Gypsy Dancer." *New York Herald Tribune*, November 20, 1963.
[3] Goldberg interviews.

In December, 1940, they set sail for North America. But not before licking Uncle Sebastian into shape again. He swore they would all drown if they went; in fact, voices came to him in the night telling him so. Indeed, he would rather drown himself than see them all go down in a watery grave with his own eyes. They took him at his word. They drowned him in Argentinian wine, and two days later they carried him aboard, well-soaked and unprotesting.

They arrived in New York in January, and Sol Hurok, confronted by sixteen gypsies, stared at them and quivered in every muscle at his own daring in bringing them. They stared back and waited. Then it evolved that there was to be no tour. In fact, nobody knew quite what to do with them. They were offered to Monte Proser for $2,000 a week [c. $15,000 today]. The enormity of this sum in itself must have had an exhilarating effect on Monte, who, incidentally, is the Knight on a White Horse of the swank nightclub belt. It is almost a cliché that nobody fails under Monte's banner. He has an instinct for a "sure thing" in entertainment that is as unfailing as an otter hound going straight for an otter. Monte sweated a quart a minute over the prospect of sixteen gypsies sitting around on his Beachcomber stage and shaking their hairpins into the surrounding Zombies. However, he too heard voices in the night telling him what to do. He accepted, groaning loudly as he did so.[1]

According to Montañés, Carmen's original contract with Hurok had stipulated twenty-five days of performance for $15,000 (c. $100.000 today): "When the amount was translated into *pesetas* for Carmen, she said, 'In other words, a sackful...' One of her family replied, 'A sackful? More like five sacks!'"[2]

Antonio Triana recalled: "Now, I heard that Carmen was in Mexico City. I recommended her to Mr. Hurok who gave me full authority to sign her for her first American tour. She came to New York with her entourage of eighteen, which included her chauffeur (no car—but a chauffeur). She first performed at the old Beachcomber nightclub, and during the day I was busy giving her and her sisters, Leo and Antonia, instruction in the choreography necessary to fill the two-and-one-half-hours concert program. Their entire gypsy repertoire took only about forty minutes."[3]

According to José Greco, after La Argentinita had a falling out with Antonio Triana, Hurok dropped her, feeling that Triana was the more important of the two dancers. This would further support Antonio Triana's assertion that he was instrumental in bringing Carmen Amaya to New York, and

---

[1] Dzhermolinska, Helen, "You Must See Amaya." *The American Dancer,* May 1941.
[2] Montañés, p. 34.
[3] Pohren, p. 368.

it explains why Sol Hurok was so anxious to sign a new Spanish dancer. Luisa Triana says that Argentinita's sister, Pilar, never forgave Triana for bringing Carmen into the picture and avoided mentioning him in her autobiography.

While Sol Hurok tried to figure out what to do with Carmen Amaya, Argentinita headed west on her own. Christopher Stull wrote in the *San Francisco Chronicle*:

> That Spanish dancing is a form even more rigid and set than ballet one would never suspect in watching it performed by Argentinita, Pilar López, and Federico Rey. They bring it to a technical virtuosity and vividness of expression which represents the whole spirit of Spain, at least to those who are not Spanish.
> Rey this year takes the part in the ensemble previously held by Antonio Triana. He is a more spectacular dancer than Triana and also, I suspect, one with a broader foundation, for his work looks as if he may have had ballet experience.
> As for Argentinita and Miss López, each in her own way seems to have achieved the ultimate degree of excellence.[1]

While Carmen Amaya displayed her dynamic fire in the Beachcomber, Argentinita returned to New York for a single performance in the 51st Street Theater in January. Responding to popular demand, she presented a farewell recital in February. The biggest change in her programs was the absence of Antonio Triana. While Triana settled into teaching in New York, Argentinita had been training his replacement, the American dancer Federico Rey. New numbers that season included a *malagueña*, a *"zambrilla"* from Granada [*zambrilla* is not a dance form seen elsewhere; Carlos Montoya would include it as a highly syncopated *zambra* on his later albums, calling it a combination of *tanguillo* and *zambra*], *"Zorongo Gitano,"* which had been dedicated to Argentinita by García Lorca, *"Rapsodia Valenciana,"* and *"Segovianos"* by Gamboa.

John Martin wrote of the 51st Street Theater performance:

> The program was studded with playful twosomes and threesomes, of which none had so much vitality and good, solid earthiness as the closing *bulerías*. This year it has experienced a radical interpolation, for in its closing measures none other than the demon guitarist, Carlos Montoya himself, is separated from his instrument and forced to dance, which he does with great gusto. Earlier in the evening he played his customary solo (which one of these

---

[1]Stull, Christopher, "Superb Argentinita Work Makes Audience Want More." *San Francisco Chronicle*, December 9, 1940.

days is going to shock us all by being different)...[1]

García Matos related further details about the Amayas' arrival in New York:

> One thing for sure, there were difficulties related to entering New York. We had to go back to Havana because Carmen didn't know how to write and they wouldn't let her enter. So the members of the company spent twenty days teaching her how to sign her name. Once she had it half-learned, we were able to come to the city of the skyscrapers, in early January, 1941, and we made our debut in a cabaret on Broadway called the Beachcomber. And it was a clamorous success, so much so that in the first shows could be seen such enthusiastic spectators as Charlie Chaplin, Greta Garbo, Wallace Beery, Victor MacLaglen, Dolores del Rio, Ramón Navarro, etc.[2]

Carmen was not the only one to struggle with handwriting. Biographer Donn Pohren wrote of an incident involving her father and El Pelao: "El Pelao did not know how to write, and signed hotel registers with a fingerprint, planting an inked finger on the sheet and twisting in his print slowly and carefully, much to the astonishment of sophisticated hotel clerks. After one such operation he turned to El Chino and stated gravely: 'Look, Chino, each day I write better...'"[3]

The troupe moved into a luxurious suite in the Waldorf-Astoria Hotel, but were soon evicted due to what the gypsies called a *rareza* (peculiarity) of the management. It seems that what they called a *rareza* was the fact that the hotel would not permit them to fry fish in their rooms. Diego Castellón recalled that they also stayed in the Hotel Meridan, "...where they set fire to the drawers in order to fry their sardines. We all lived together, although the family had the penthouse, where they made their gypsy meals—usually fried sardines. The legend is that they took apart the dressers to fry the sardines."[4] Alfredo Mañas says that he once asked Carmen about the truth of the stories he had heard concerning her family making a fire on the floor of their suite in the Waldorf-Astoria in order to cook sardines. She only laughed and replied with gypsy evasiveness, *"Pero hijo,* how could we have eaten grilled sardines on the floor like savages? And if we had roasted them on a cushion?" Mañas never did find out if it was true or not.[5]

Carmen Amaya made her debut in the United States on January 17, 1941. Here is how *The New York Times* reported it:

---

[1]Martin, John, "Argentinita Seen In Dance Recital." Copyright © *The New York Times,* January 14, 1941. Reprinted by permission.

[2]García Matos in his memoires.

[3]Pohren, p. 235.

[4]Goldberg interviews.

[5]Mañas, p. 16.

> Another evidence that you never can tell what is going to happen where is the fact that the gypsy dancer, Carmen Amaya, hailed by Toscanini and Stokowski, did not make her debut in the United States at Carnegie Hall or the Metropolitan Opera House or even at the Guild Theatre on a Sunday night, but at the Beachcomber at midnight Friday, with virtually no advance notice. Miss Amaya, of whom rumors have been floating from Mexico and South America for some time, has brought at least a fraction of her family with her. Her father and brother Francisco both dance and play the guitar, and in the company are also an uncle, Sebastian Manzano (who is said to have two wives and eighteen children, not on the program apparently), a sister Antonia, another sister Leonor, and two guitar-playing cousins, Agustin and Diego Castellón Sabicas. Mama Amaya is present, too, but not professionally. Antonio Triana, who used to be with Argentinita, is also in the company.
>
> Whether Miss Amaya's future in this country is to be in nightclubs, concert halls, or revues is still uncertain, for she seems to be a bit difficult to classify.[1]

It is ironic and fitting that Carmen "the beachcomber" should make her United States debut in a cabaret called The Beachcomber. The Italian-born American Spanish dancer, José Greco, just starting his own career, had the following impressions of Carmen:

> She was to play at the Beachcomber, next to the Wintergarden Theater, at the present site of the Hawaii Kai Restaurant. Tickets to her opening were twenty dollars each. I didn't have that kind of money, but I desperately wanted to take Meda to see this famous Spanish dancer. I remember hocking something—a watch, perhaps—to come up with the price of admission.
>
> Meda and I sat there, drinking rum zombies (the cost included two drinks) and watching the famous Carmen Amaya. This incredible dancer was the same age as I was, but she'd already made a name for herself throughout Europe.
>
> Carmen Amaya was born a gypsy. She was a true child of the "bronze-skinned folk." She learned to sing and dance just as other children learned to walk and talk. Her father had been a famous flamenco guitarist.
>
> Now, with her two sisters and her guitarist brother and the now-famous Sabicas, she did her dances for us. Her repertoire was sadly lacking—she did only two dances. But these were the most astounding dances we'd ever seen, more intoxicating than the zombies we

---

[1] "Carmen Amaya at the Beachcombers." Copyright © *The New York Times*, January 19, 1941. Reprinted by permission.

were drinking. She was the Queen of the Gypsies and of the flamenco.

Carmen Amaya was not physically attractive. But while she was performing she was beautiful and passionate almost beyond belief. Also, she had an enormous technical capacity. Never have I seen anyone heel tap with such intensity, with so much speed. Later I used this sort of thing in my own shows, but I was never able to equal her skill.

So remarkable was her performance and her personality that she completely captivated her audience. But with her limited repertoire she was never able to find the proper showcase for her talents—she fit comfortably neither into nightclubs nor theaters nor concert halls. This, unfortunately, limited her popularity in the Unted States.

Eventually she learned something about showmanship and production, following my pattern, and finally achieved undisputed recognition, not only throughout the rest of the world, but also in the United States.

That night at the Beachcomber was magical.[1]

Greco goes on to state that in the audience were Frank Sinatra, Boris Karloff, and Dorothy Lamour. *Time* magazine reported that Carmen's contract actually called for $1,000 a week plus a percentage of the gross, which totalled about $2,000 a week. The magazine wrote: "It is Carmen Amaya who stops the show with the wrigglings of her round rump and wiry body, the tossing of her disheveled hair, the animal fury of her tough, splash-mouthed face... Amaya's incredibly swift foot-stamps, finger-snappings, and castanet-clacks are something to see and hear. 'When I dance,' says she, 'my heart comes out of my mouth.'"[2]

El Pelao told *Time* that he had two wives back in Spain and eighteen children. And the magazine also said that Carmen was investing her money in furs and diamonds and that she wore a dirty bathrobe around her house, topped off by a silver fox cape. Her English was said to consist of *'ello, goo'night, hokay,* and *t'ank you.*

Newsweek lauded Carmen in the Beachcomber only a week after she began there, calling her "a green-eyed, raven-haired Spanish gypsy..." And *Life* said that she took her dancing seriously, and if someone talked or laughed while she was dancing, she would glare at him until he adopted a more respectful attitude. The same magazine also reported that Carmen was already negotiating Hollywood contracts, which she would have to sign with an "X" because she had not learned to write.[3] All of the magazines reported

---

[1]Greco, José, *The Gypsy in My Soul.* Doubleday & Company, Inc, New York. 1977. p. 39.
[2]*Time,* February 17, 1941. p. 86.
[3]*Life,* March 10, 1941.

that Carmen was nineteen years old and complained that the family could not be certain about her birthdate. If she were nineteen, that would have placed her birth in 1921 and made her too young for her many accomplishments of the 1920s (five years old on tour with Manuel Vallejo and eight with Raquel Meller—far too young).

Diego Castellón described the Beachcomber as having a Philippine decor and said they called it *"el restaurán de las esteras"*—the restaurant of the woven mats. According to Diego, the club held a thousand people, yet lines began to form for the second show by eight-thirty.[1]

New York writer Edward Denby described Carmen and her clan:

> Carmen Amaya opened at the Beachcomber in January and they have had to change the battered rugs on the stairs to the club four times since her arrival. And the end is not yet even in sight. The New York press made a Roman holiday out of Carmen. A "natural" like her hasn't struck Broadway in years. She sneezes and it makes good copy. She grinds her teeth in a reporter's eye and immediately the front page is cleared of all foreign and domestic news. The boys have, in fact, gone so far in making copy out of her that they've met themselves coming back. They have formed a movement for putting her back in the caves of the Albaicín, because she would be so much more colorful if she couldn't read or write, they gleefully figure. The uncolored truth is that she is as literate as a college graduate, and knows more than most.
>
> The Amaya menage, if one can get the Open Sesame to it, is a chapter out of Spanish life that cheers the heart. It is of all places a modest apartment in the West Forties. On entering, your face turns a bright green with envy at the sight of something like eight fur coats handsomely thrown over the furniture, all Carmen's. The coats belonging to her sisters and cousins, added to hers, reach heights unheard of by America's best dressed women, who thank God for a mere mink or sable. A banquet is in progress at five o'clock in the afternoon. It probably began when they arose at two and will continue until four a.m. with only a recess at the club. The air resounds with the unearthly wailing of a *malagueña*. Their voices beat the air, and your long-suffering ears shatter to bits of bombardment of telephone, radio, phonograph, and hoarsely gutteral conversation. The room is full of guests, and now in and now out are three or four children whom Carmen embraces passionately at intervals. Of all the family, the children were the first to pick up English, which they talk with a solemn air of pronouncing deathless statements. The brightest and most *simpático* of these is

[1] Goldberg interviews.

Antonio, her ten-year-old brother. She tells you proudly there is soon to be another little one. You look at the mother. She is the most inarticulate one in the room, but the most compelling. No patina of Western civilization covers her as it does the others. She is unadorned gypsy. Her hair is sleeked down from the center and on her forehead sits a spit curl. She wears dead black and sits among her people like a queen on a throne. For her mother, whom she adores, Carmen has bought a great estate in Argentina, out of the proceeds of a South American tour. Of all the family, the mother never joins in the ritual of dances. She alone cooks for her beloved family. No one else touches their food. And such food deserves the name of manna. The table staggers under fish and chicken and unimaginably delectable rice. Everyone eats with unashamed gusto, which is the least you can do such food. Everyone eats, that is, except Carmen, who shows an amazing indisposition to eat at any time and who lives in constant dread of paternal chastisement if she is caught lowering her quota of food for the day. Where she derives the energy for those orgies of rage and ecstasy on the stage is a fine point for speculation; it is cetainly not from her food.

The table groans under the weight of the wine which was brought this day as a present by a rich Spanish marqués who is visiting there. He has seen Carmen in Spain and is her devoted aficionado. Sometimes the brothers and sisters spring to their feet and dance or sing as the mood seizes them. This is tribal life in a form probably not seen since the days of Abraham. Their love for one another is patent, unchanging. It would have to be love to permit of their continual living in one another's pockets. They are not a dull or backward race. Their acumen is painfully sharp, and of these the sharpest is the father of Amaya. Of course, no one in the family can ogle like Pelao, the "hairy one," which is Uncle Sebastián's nickname, but they are all *simpático* as well as suave. Their daily lives are a round of continual inner-family singing and dancing. They perform at home like they do at the club or the theater. A visitor there tells you of their recent trip to Washington last month, to dance at the White House Press Conference dinner. The publicity agent who escorted them left them at a hotel and cautioned them not to leave until he came to fetch them. When he returned, the room was empty, and, after tearing out handfuls of hair, he happened to look out the window, and down the street, about a block away, were the Amayas, on a Washington street corner, singing and dancing for all the world as though that was the very thing for which they had all been born.

Of all the faces in the family, hers alone bears the stamp of that tortured ugliness with a profound inner beauty that is more satisfying than the mere prettiness of any gypsy Venus. She reflects today that she would have liked to have been pretty like her sisters, but that it would make no essential difference. She cannot make pretty faces when she dances.

Carmen Amaya, the dancer, is transfigured, unspeakable emotion. She appears on the stage, set off by her accompanying guitarists, singers, and dancers, a figure of almost frightening magnificence, who dances unto herself, with a ferocity that unseats the placid spectator who has been dreaming over his long zombie. At first sight it is disturbing to see such savage contortion so close to the naked eye; it scares the uninitiated into embarrassed tittering. They cannot easily cover their fear of this raw emotion, so deep in every human soul, exposed so brutally and at such close range. They laugh nervously. They twist and gape. But they never forget. She has given birth with her untaught, unteachable art to a cult which grows. The rare flower of flamenco dancing has taken root here in a way nobody could have prophesied.

Probably six months from now, after she has been to Hollywood and back, it would not amaze us to find in this country, as in Spain, dolls made in her image, trains and cars named for her, new passionate shades of color called Amaya red or Amaya purple. She is the germ that brings to new life in every soul that understands, old and withered and long forgotten depths of emotion.[1]

The mention of furs piled high in Carmen's apartment recalls an often told story. In one of the great fur shops on Fifth Avenue there was a unique piece, a one of a kind jewel, a white mink jacket. One of the clerks inside saw a gypsy woman pass by the window again and again and alerted her boss. What intention could a gypsy have other than to rob the place? But how could she do it? The people in the store strained their eyes watching all the coming and going and thinking in front of the white mink in the window. Finally, a stifled cry as a clerk called out, "Come in, come in, come in!"

The gypsy went in and, planting herself directly in from of that display of employees, said confidently, "How much is it?"

"How much is what?"

"The jacket in the window."

"Look, that is a one of a kind piece, only within the reach of our special clients."

"How much is it?"

Finally, they told her the price, and the gypsy said, dryly and to the point,

---

[1]Denby, Edward, *Looking at the Dance*, March-April 1942, January-February 1943.

in the voice of a tribal queen, "Give me three of them!"[1]

Regarding the truth of this account, a close family friend, Alfredo Mañas, said, "Is it truth, or is it legend? It is all one and the same with Carmen!" Another version, which may be the original, was related by Montañés:

> "One morning Carmen goes into a furrier on Fifth Avenue. She asks the salesgirl to show her a silver fox stole that she has seen in the window. She tries it on, likes it, and the salesgirl thinks she is hearing things when Carmen says, 'Very beautiful! I'll wear this one, and will you wrap up seven more just like it for me to take also!'" That night, all the women of the company showed off their silver fox stoles. Carmen didn't forget the men. She presented them all with gold watches, saying, "Now let's see if you can be on time for the shows!" When a reporter asked Carmen about her extravagant spending, she answered, "You call buying gifts for my family an extravagance? Well, aren't you the tight one!"[2]

Sabicas gave a very different picture, one perhaps a little closer to the truth and reflecting the fact that Carmen did not always have access to the money; the father controlled the family purse strings:

> I remember one time in San Francisco [probably in 1941] she told me, "Keep this for me and don't tell anyone!" She gave me a stack of bills. "I am going to buy a little fur coat."
> It was a very beautiful coat, small like Carmen. It was perfect for her. I still remember the price: $2,540... But, why did she have to go home with it? The other women began to say, "A fur? What about us?" The following day, everybody had a fur coat. They bought coats for themselves—of course, not at the same price, but they each had a fur coat.[3]

Another account of Carmen's beginning in New York says:

> In the capital of the skyscrapers, the beginnings were hard. Somebody planted a seed of doubt in the ears of Hurok about the artistic quality of the *gitana*, so she was presented in a second-class cabaret. But Carmen was not discouraged. She danced as only she knew how and soon the cover charge, which had been eighty-five cents, rose to three and a half dollars. Famous personalities rushed to see her: Greta Garbo, Edward G. Robinson, Orson Welles, Dolores del Rio, Dick Powell, Wallace Beery...
> From the Beachcomber, she went to Theatre 51. She was called

---

[1] Mañas, p. 16.
[2] Montañés, p. 34.
[3] Molarsky interview.

to the White House to perform for President Roosevelt.[1]

President Roosevelt invited the Amayas to a party in the White House. Carmen turned down the honorarium offered her and agreed to perform on the condition that it be for free, saying, "I want to say thank you to the man who governs this country that has given me much more than I deserve." Sabicas was afraid to fly to Washington, so he, El Chino, and El Pelao took the train while the rest of the company went by air. He described the experience:

> A man came to tell us that there was an airplane that would take us there. I said, "Don't bother, *señor*, we will take the train!" I was so frightened by airplanes.
>
> The whole company wanted to go by air, except for Carmen's father—the poor man was also scared. Carmen, her sisters, everybody went by plane and had a fiesta in the air, while her father and I were too scared.
>
> I went to greet Mr. Roosevelt. He was very nice; he shook my hand and said, "Thank you very much!" But Carmen said to her father and me, "You two are sissies."
>
> "Why are you calling us names?"
>
> "Because, while you two take the train we are having fun in the air."
>
> So we went back by plane. The plane was so small, like a toilet room. I heard one engine, then the other. I wanted to get off and take the train.
>
> "Look, *señorita*, can you stop this? I want to get off!"
>
> And the *señorita*, would take me back to my seat. I had seen airplanes that would fly on their side and turn over. I had never been so nervous in my life. Carmen's father, poor thing, could not even speak. I looked down at the houses in Washington—they looked so very tiny. Forty minutes. I got off the airplane dizzy from fear.[2]

Montañés wrote: "Carmen Amaya 'La Capitana,' the gypsy from the Somorrostro in Barcelona, smaller and darker than ever in those huge white salons that are steeped in a history she could hardly understand, dances her red dance of passion and genius. The President of the United States presents her with a short jacket completely embroidered in gold. But the jacket disappears immediately afterward. According to Carmen, all of her relatives have as much right to it as she does. The best solution is to take it apart and share the gold with the whole company. Within a few weeks the little jacket of President Roosevelt has been converted into bracelets, rings, chains, and necklaces, to

---

[1] Góngora.
[2] Molarsky interview.

be shown off by the gypsies in the streets of New York."[1]

Other honors came Carmen's way: She was made an honorary captain by the New York police force, and General MacArthur assigned her the same rank in the U.S. Marines. That meant that Carmen was *La Capitana* three times over.

At the time Carmen Amaya was making her mark in New York, the city was crawling with Spanish dancers in exile. World War II had trapped some of them in the United States, while others could not return to Spain because of the political climate there. La Argentinita's sister, Pilar, said, "At that time, which was a very beautiful period for the dance, we were all there together, Rosario and Antonio, Carmen Amaya, and my sister and me. Rosario and Antonio were very young. They went to do their dances in a show and had a phenomenal success, and, of course, it was there that they made a name for themselves. My sister went crazy over those youngsters. They also worked in the Rainbow Room and made some films, with a lot of success. Carmen was also in a nightclub, with an outrageous success." In another article, Pilar elaborated further on Carmen: "To me, Carmen Amaya was and will always be unique. I saw her for the first time in New York, when I was with my sister Encarna, as everybody called her, although she was known artistically as La Argentinita. For both my sister and me, she made an extraordinary impression on us. Hers was an exemplary way of dancing and completely original."[2]

Los Chavalillos had been in the famed Copacabana in Rio de Janeiro in 1939. Toscanini saw them and sent rave reviews back to the USA, but Rosario and Antonio were too heavily booked to get to New York until 1940. The American agent Marcel Ventura, who specialized in Latin American talent and represented the well-known composer of the *"Malagueña,"* Ernesto Lecuona, found the duo in Mexico City and booked them into the Sert Room of the Waldorf-Astoria Hotel. A newspaper critic wrote:

> My "Cafe Society" was "out on the town" last night—and how!... For the majority it was a case of "breakfast in bed" this morning— and a delightful memory of Rosario and Antonio, the most fantastic Spanish dancers New York has seen in years.
>
> Last night in the Sert Room at The Waldorf, the "plush" ones clapped until hands were calloused, the feminine contingent threw flowers, and "bravos" echoed through the room as frenzied demands were made for encores by this youthful pair who landed on Park Avenue from Seville via South America.
>
> Here at last, in Rosario and Antonio, we have a pair of REAL Spanish dancers, utterly devoid of Broadway patina.

---

[1]Montañés, p. 36.
[2]Hidalgo Gómez, p. 117.

> Their costumes reek of a small Spanish town, their hair is as disheveled as if they were dancing in the village square for a goup of their fellow villagers—and their routine is so magnificently "different" it must be seen to be appreciated. Let's hope the management never will permit them to become "Broadwayized." They're "tops" as they are.
> Being young and enthusiastic, they dance with an abandon that is miraculous to behold—leaving the spectators spellbound and enchanted.
> I want to go back again and again to the Sert Room—to watch this inspired young pair of Spanish dancers go through their routine, which Allah be praised, does not include a rumba or a conga.[1]

Other reports said that the audience practically buried the two dancers in flowers. Both Antonio and Rosario had brought their families with them. One reporter said that they traveled with sixteen trunks containing, among other things, all of their money. After Antonio lost seven thousand dollars that way, the only change he made was to try to be more careful. Antonio lived in an apartment on West 55th Street with his mother and, later, with his sister, Pastora Ruiz, who would begin to dance with him in 1944. Rosario lived on West 54th with her mother and her husband and three-year-old son—who, the family boasted, could already sing "The Star-Spangled Banner."

Mr. Ventura wanted to insure the two dancer's legs. According to him, the Kids said yes, "but their mothers just stared at me and made the sign of the cross. I said that Fred Astaire had his legs insured for half a million dollars, but that didn't make any difference to them. 'Why do you put the evil eye on our children?' they asked me. 'Why do you want they should break their legs?' So the Kids had no insurance."

After the Waldorf, the Kids moved to a long engagement on Broadway, dancing in Olsen & Johnson's *Sons O' Fun*. They went on the road with this show and also performed in the Havana-Madrid cabaret and later Radio City Music Hall. In 1941, "The Kids from Seville," as they were billed in the credits, appeared in the film, *Ziegfield Girl*, starring James Stewart, Judy Garland, Lana Turner, and a number of other stars. Rosario and Antonio were among many vaudeville acts featured in the movie. Their dance to orchestral accompaniment was laughable by modern standards. The partners danced like carbon copies of each other, Antonio looking very much the woman with his effeminate movements and gestures. It seems clear that they attempted to mimic Carmen Amaya in posture and fury, but the exaggerated leaps and gymnastics make it very hard to watch today with a straight face. However, this did not seem to diminish their popularity at the time, and they were invited to appear in other films of the period.

---

[1] By Cholly Knickerbocker, quoted in an undated concert program, c. 1950.

Paco Amaya and El Chino in the Decca studio, June 1941.

Carmen Amaya, El Chino, Paco Amaya, Antonia Amaya and Leonor Amaya in 1941.

* * *

Carmen Amaya's growing celebrity status led to new opportunities. Decca Records contracted her for two albums, to be recorded the first week in June, 1941. Over a six day period, the company—minus Sabicas—recorded fifteen songs that would come out on 78-rpm disks. Carmen did most of the singing, in a very rough voice, frequently off-pitch, and definitely not with the caliber of her later recordings. The numbers were for the most part festive—*bulerías, fandangos, tangos*—and many of them had been composed by Manuel Matos and José Palomo in Buenos Aires. In the first session, Carmen sang the *zambra* "La Tana," supported by the company with castanets and *jaleo* (cries of encouragement). This fiesta in the Sacromonte closes with a build-up of footwork. Carmen sang *fandangos* to Paco's guitar and then two *bulerías*: the first, entitled *"Tondero,"* was adapted from a Peruvian song, the other, *"Fiesta jerezana,"* is a *bulerías* of Cádiz with the typical *aire* of the gypsies of Granada. To complete this session, Antonia recited *"Gitana y mare,"* a poem by Rafael de León, to the guitar of Paco Amaya, and Leonor sang *por fandangos* and *bulerías*.

Two days later, on June 4th, the Amayas returned to the New York studio to record three more *bulerías* and a *tientos*. One *bulerías*, "Adelfa," was credited to the songwriters Quiroga, Valverde, De Leon; another, *"Canasteros de Triana,"* was said to have come from the film *Ziegfield Girl*, but there is no song like it in the movie; the third *bulerías*, *"Vete con los tuyos"*, previously sung by Anita Sevilla, is so badly sung that it is really unlistenable—only in live performance could Carmen, with her energy and physical presence, get away with singing like this. In the *tientos*, El Chino again showed his playing to be crisp, strong, precise, and filled with flavorful touches. He usually sounded more youthful and modern in his playing than did his son, Paco.

In the last session, on June 6th, there were more *bulerías* and *fandangos*, another *tientos*, and a recitation with *fandangos* entitled *"Noches Huervanas Pesqueras"* ("Fishing Nights in Huelva"). Two albums with three records in each were released (Decca A-269, Decca A-288). One *tientos* and the two recitation numbers were not included (it is likely that Spanish recitation was not considered to be commercially viable in an English speaking market).[1]

These Decca albums are generally considered to be Carmen Amaya's first recordings. However, there is another series of records that may predate them. Two versions of the *zambra* "La Tana," some *fandangos*, and a *bulerías* were re-released as 45-rpm records in 1964 by the Gramófono-Odeón Company of Barcelona. They had been technically "reconstructed," presumably from the 78-rpm originals. When were these songs recorded?

---

[1] Dates for these recordings are taken from *Ethnic Music on Record, Vol 4*, by Richard K. Spottswood. University of Illinois Press, 1990.

Might it have been after 1950, when Carmen had returned to Spain? Several factors appear to rule out that possibility: Several songs are credited to José Amaya and bear his unmistakeable stamp, but he died before the return to Spain. Also, the songs were from an earlier era and not part of Carmen's active repertoire at that late date. And, finally, long-play records and 45s had come out by that time and it is unlikely that the records would have needed to be "reconstructed" a decade later.

Might these recordings have been made at the time of the Decca recordings, not used at that time, and then sold to the Spanish company at a later date? This seems unlikely. The treatments of "La Tana" are so different that it would seem that they could not have been made at the same time. There are three guitars on the Odeón recording, only two on the Decca. The Odeón version has no women present in the background, no castanets, and no fast build-up to close. In the Odeón recording there is a point where the guitars drop out and Carmen sings to percussion only, and, throughout, there is the presence of her powerful fingersnaps—not heard on the Decca version.

Several factors suggest that Carmen might have made these recordings in 1936, before leaving Spain. The *bulerías* that she sings in a very youthful and flexible voice is her version of *"María de la O."* That song did not figure prominently in her later repertoire and would most likely have been recorded shortly after the release of the film of that name. The same would hold true for the *zambra*, which she favored in the early part of her career and phased out once she reached the United States. The absence of women's voices in the background of the recording of "La Tana" might be explained by the fact that Carmen's sisters had not yet begun to work with her. One problem that arises with this scenario is the generally accepted fact that Manuel Matos created "La Tana" for Carmen. Matos did not join Carmen until later, after the two of them left Spain. Although this version of the famous *zambra* is credited to Carmen's father, not Matos, it is identical to those recordings that do give credit to the composer. One has to wonder what Matos' contribution to this number might have been, for it is very traditional in all aspects except perhaps the words. It is possible that Matos did not compose this *zambra*, but only lent his name to it for copyright purposes.

In 1941, Hurok commissioned the documentary film, *Original Gypsy Dances*, to promote the Amayas. Since *María de la O*, before the civil war, Carmen had appeared in a number of films. In some unexplained manner, she danced in two films made by Spanish companies during the war. *La Casa de la Troya* was produced by a company in Málaga, and *Martingala* featured Pepe Marchena and an upcoming gypsy singer-dancer, Lola Flores. Since Lola Flores did not leave Spain during the war, it is clear that Carmen's scenes were either filmed separately, in South America, or were scenes that had been filmed before the war. In South America, she had appeared in the film, *Don Viudo de Rodríguez* and a number of others.

Original Gypsy Dances features Carmen in two dances. She opens with a number to orchestral accompaniment, demonstrating superb control of her tiny, high-pitched castanets. It only takes three of her whip-like, wind-up turns to send two large flowers flying from her head and release her mat of thick black hair. During the finale she looks a bit awkard in a series of high-kicking *jota* steps, but recovers by reeling off five rapid turns in a row. Sabicas (Savicas in the credits) then takes the stage for a solo *malagueña* with the *cejilla* placed on the third fret. His playing is filled with touches of the showman: He opens by strumming back and forth from bridge to fingerboard, follows with a tight, efficient tremolo and crystalline *picado*, and finishes with a guitar version of the *cante* that closes with a long passage played by the left hand alone. In a grand gesture, he rises from his chair while still playing.

Carmen dances an *alegrías* that is similar to the one she danced in *Embrujo del Fandango*, with alternating slow and fast passages. She wears white pants with a black vest and jacket. The five guitarists wear the *traje corto* (traditional suit with the short jacket and high-waisted pants) and the *calañés* hat. Carmen's dancing is very masculine here. Her movements are sharp and angular. Her hands either grip the bottom of her vest or are held closed as she snaps her fingers like gunshots. In the few moments that she permits her hands to turn gracefully, she does so in the masculine manner, fingers together. Ironically, Carmen's dancing is as masculine as Antonio's was feminine during this period.

Sol Hurok could not ignore the impressive triumph of Carmen Amaya. He decided it was time to put her to the test. She would undergo the traditional initiation endured by so many great artists before her. The public and the critics would judge her and decide her future. She would make her debut in New York's hallowed Carnegie Hall.

A young New York girl, Lola Montes, suddenly found her life tied to the Amayas. She described events leading up to the Carnegie Hall concert:

> I had been doing Spanish dancing all my life, character dancing, but I had a ballet background and really wanted to be a ballet dancer. My family was artistic, poor as church mice, but artistic and cultured. My mother had been training for opera when she married and I was exposed to a lot of theater. The rest of my family are all professionals with college backgrounds, but when I was ten years old I knew I wanted to dance—I didn't know what I wanted to do with it, but I wanted to dance (my mother had started me in dance to help me lose weight). I studied in a very fine school in the Metropolitan Opera House, where we came in con-

tact with many great artists. A turning point came when the Met held an important audition and I had to miss it because I was still in school. My parents insisted that I at least finish high school. When I missed that audition, I felt that life was completely over. So, one day, I packed my suitcase, told my parents that I was just going to do a little audition, and went downtown to a club that was looking for a dancer—some cute kid to open the show. They hired me, and I was so thrilled that I stayed there all night watching the floor show. At two in the morning I realized I had forgotten to call my parents. When I got back home, my brothers were in tears and my parents had gone to the police station to fill out a missing persons report. The police told my parents that they hoped it had been a good lesson and that they wouldn't let their daughter out again. But somehow I convinced them and went on to work in several clubs, including El Chico, the most prestigious club of the time [opened in 1925].

I had studied with most of the Spanish dance teachers in town, including Angel Cansino, and I was thrilled when I heard that Antonio Triana was teaching. Triana was revered by students who had seen him with Argentinita. Now *there* was a concert! Argentinita, Triana, and Pilar López. Pilar has always been my idol. Some think she danced even better than her sister. Argentinita was the artist, so intelligent and cultured. She had been nurtured by people like Lorca, and it was she who had the imagination. Then, with Rogelio Machado, the pianist, and Carlos Montoya, you had five artists who mesmerized you. Their costumes were not very elaborate, with the exception of their authentic regional costumes, but after a couple of dances you were only aware of their art, their placement, their ability to mimic [act].

When Triana began to teach we all went to study with him. Before long most of the girls were flirting with him, but I just came for my lessons. Perhaps that is why he was attracted to me. We began to go out. It made me feel so important to go to clubs with him. He got me a job dancing in the Havana-Madrid while Carmen Amaya was in the Beachcomber. Times were not easy for Triana and he thought he could form a little company. We did a number of performances to get him some exposure, and Sol Hurok even presented one of his shows in the Guild Theatre.

When the Amayas arrived and began in the Beachcomber we would all save our money and go to see them as often as possible. We would stand outside on the corner as they pulled up and got out of their car swishing their full-length furs. Watching their show was like heaven! We had seen the great Spanish dancers and, inspired by Argentinita, I had made up my own *"Lagarteranas,"* a Mexican *jarabe*, a Cuban *rumba* and an Argentine *tango*. But this was different, with the women sitting and doing *palmas*, and all that fire. We tried to imitate them. And then, suddenly, I knew somebody who knew them! At that time Carmen had only a *cuadro* show, with her flamenco. Hurok needed a program suited to a concert format, so he engaged Triana to work with them. They needed one more girl to make trios, and I was chosen. Everyone knew that the Carnegie Hall appearance was very important, that it was needed to launch a successful tour. Triana set the concert repertoire: *"Orgía," "Goyescas,"* "Córdoba" for Carmen, *jota* for the sisters, and *farruca* and *"Capriccio Espagnol"* as duos for himself and Carmen. We rehearsed hard, and then Hurok sent us out on a sort of vaudeville tour. He had to pay salaries every week and needed to do something with Carmen in order to have some money coming in. So he would contract her wherever he could, and we would rehearse around her appearances. I recall very well a couple of weeks in Boston.

When they felt everything was ready, Mr. Hurok began to come around to make final decisions about the show. He cut or changed numbers and whittled the company down to Carmen and her sisters, Antonio Triana, Lola Montes, Sabicas, El Chino, Paco Amaya, and Manuel Matos at the piano. He felt that Carmen was too strong in the duos with Triana; he wanted someone more feminine. First they tried one sister in the *farruca*, and then the other, and it didn't work. I was the only one left, and they said, *"Niña, tú lo sabes?* [Do you know it?]" I meekly said, "Yes." So I was given the *farruca*, a gloriously magical experience for me, with Sabicas accompanying on the guitar. And I inherited the *"Capriccio Espagnol"* as well. I had memorized all of the numbers. When you are young, you don't have anything on your mind; I soaked up things like a sponge. Once, when they were working on "Córdoba" and couldn't remember how it went, I jumped out of my chair, saying, "I know, I know!" I did it for them. But the looks I got, My God!... I slunk back to my chair.[1]

The Carnegie Hall performance took place on Tuesday evening, January 13, 1942. *The New York Times* announcement read: "Sol Hurok presents CARMEN AMAYA with ANTONIO TRIANA (type size equal to Carmen's) and Sabicas (smaller type, but given importance) at Carnegie Hall." Argentinita's influence on the repertoire was quite evident. In the Carnegie

[1] All of Lola Montes' recollections are take from conversations with Paco Sevilla in February of 1998.

The Amayas with Lola Montes before the Carnegie Hall performance in 1942. Clockwise left to right: Paco Amaya, Leonor, Lola Montes, Antonia, El Chino, Antonio Triana, Carmen Amaya. *Photo courtesy of Lola Montes*

Hall concert, they would dance *"Goyescas"* by Granados, *"Jota"* as played on piano by Manuel Matos (who had dropped the "García" part of his name), and several dances from *El Amor Brujo*. Antonio and Lola Montes danced to piano in *"Capriccio Espagnol"* by Rimsky-Korsakoff. Even Carmen got into the classical act, dancing *"Córdoba"* by Albéniz and *"Sacro Monte"* by Turina.

Guitar solos introduced the flamenco in each half. José and Paco Amaya played a duet *por zambra* (the Moorish music from the Sacromonte) and, later, Sabicas performed his renditions of *granaínas* and *"Gallegos"* (aires from Galicia). The first flamenco dance comes as a surprise, for it was none other than *tarantos*, danced by Carmen to the guitar of Sabicas. Many have claimed to be the first to dance *taranto*, but here is Carmen Amaya performing it in 1942. The fact that she would feature it as the important opening flamenco number in her important debut suggests that she had been working on it for some time. It is impossible to know the nature of this number. Palomo and Sabicas had collaborated on a *taranto* in Buenos Aires that very likely bore little resemblance to the flamenco dance that would evolve later. The version danced in Carnegie Hall is credited only to Sabicas and may represent a step in the evolution of this dance. It also casts some doubt on Rosario's emphatic claim that she was the first to dance the *taranto*.

Some years later, Leonor Amaya would be the first to record the *cante por tarantos* in its modern form, with an incessant, *zambra*-like rhythm. Originally, the *taranto* had been sung in the same manner as the *tarantas*, in a loose 3/4 time typical of the *fandangos* family. Logically, it would be a family of specialists in the *zambra* and with close connections to the gypsies of Granada who would apply the droning 4/4 time of the *zambra* to the *taranto*.

In the second half, Antonio Triana and Lola Montes danced *farruca* to Sabicas' guitar, and Carmen performed her best known dance, the *alegrías*, wearing pants as she usually did for this number. It is almost certain that she had not yet incorporated into the *alegrías* what would later become her trademark—a footwork solo without musical accompaniment. If she had, it certainly would have shown up in the reviews. Diego Castellón said of this part of the program: "That would be the *cuadro*, with everybody: the guitar, *farruca*, *alegrías*, *verdiales*, *peteneras*—which Antonio Triana must have danced, because I don't believe Carmen would have danced it [she could have; this concert predated the *petenera* superstition]. *Las sevillanas, las bulerías...*"[1]

The concert was an overwhelming popular success, but reviews were mixed. Here is what John Martin had to say in *The New York Times*:

> Carmen Amaya, the Spanish gypsy who has danced previously

[1] Goldberg interviews.

only in nightclubs hereabouts, last night made her New York recital debut in a program in Carnegie Hall, assisted by Antonio Triana, the guitarist Sabicas, and half a dozen other assorted dancers, guitarists and pianists answering chiefly to the name of Amaya. After the tremendous reports that have been circulated about the dancer's fiery abandon, primitive passion and so forth, the evening was something of a let-down, as was virtually inevitable. Carnegie Hall is far too big and a full evening is much too long to make possible the same results that can be obtained in the intimate spaces of a nightclub with a handful of picked numbers.

Amaya needs a small and informal frame with as little division as possible between herself and her audience. In such surroundings, with a show carefully built about her highly personal talents, she would probably be as great a popular success as she has been on the dine-and-dance circuit and certainly a greater artistic one. For, make no mistake about it, she is a vivid personality, and a fine dancer within a range that is limited but quite sufficient. She has a wonderfully lithe and slender body, keyed to a high nervous pitch but aways under control. The "human tornado" myth has been somewhat overdone, for though she is speedy, intense, and brimming with physical excitement, she makes use of her dynamics entirely legitimately and with admirable artistry. All this, of course, when she is at her best, which is to say when she doing characteristic gypsy dances, improvising, mugging and generally playing with her audience.

The program was more than half over last night before this best made its appearance. For the most part she was smothered by a conventional and largely mediocre Spanish dance evening. She should never do such a number as her first solo to the "Cordoba" of Albeniz, dressed in classic costume with castanets and presenting, according to the program, a "fiery characterization of the gypsy spirit." There is nothing classic about her, and when she is stuffed into the routine things that every other Spanish dancer does, she is no better than any of the rest of them, lacking nuance, variety, and distinction. When, however, she trails her ruffled skirt across the floor and breaks into the wonderfully strident singing of *"Ay! Que tú,"* grimacing, crossing her eyes, making mock of her imaginary lover, things begin to happen. And they continue to happen through the *"Alegrías"* in which she dances superbly, every fiber of her body sentient of line, mass, and dynamics.

Otherwise, except for Triana's always excellent *"Polo,"* which came early on the bill, there was not much rewarding, unless one happened to be as passionate about incidental guitar numbers as

Spanish audiences always seem to be. Certainly this one was, and Sabicas was a definite success. So, for that matter, was everything else. The house was jammed to the doors, with scads of standees.[1]

Lola Montes added a few of her impressions:

> When I walked out on the Carnegie stage I was in heaven. I had been in the audience so many times to see great artists. The *farruca* went really well—we usually got an encore with it. They had given me a *desplante* [variation] for the *bulerías* at the end of the show. I had practiced it to the hilt and got a big hand. The audience went crazy that night, but some of the reviews were critical. Carmen had been so oversold, "an erupting volcano" and things like that...expectations had been raised too high. And I remember that even she didn't like the "Córdoba" number that she danced in a white lace dress that didn't suit her. I don't know why she agreed to do it, it just wasn't right for her.

Less than a week after the concert, the Amaya company gave three recitals in the Forty-Sixth Street Theatre and immediately thereafter set out across country. Hurok had booked them solid. The record is incomplete, but they worked their way across the northern cities—Detroit, Chicago...By February 20, they were in Seattle with a show that was pretty much the same as the Carnegie Hall performance, but without the controversial "Córdoba." The *Seattle Times* wrote: "Amaya's opening number was the fiery and tempestuous 'Soleares,' with superb castanet work adding further stimulant to the excitement of the dance...Amaya has injected so much of her own vibrant personality into her dances and those of her troupe that it is a truly individual style."

The following night in Tacoma, the *Tacoma News Tribune* reported: "Miss Amaya disproved in Tacoma, as she has been disproving all over the country, the claim once made in New York that she needs the intimacy of a nightclub floor to win complete appreciation from an audience. The crowd at the Temple theater appreciated her to the tune of applause that recalled her and her company time and time again...Carmen Amaya, a tiny bit of fine-tempered steel whose wildly urgent movements sometimes seemed too fast for the eye, whose dances, following the sedate beauty of the opening numbers, became faster and faster as she flashed along with stamping heels, snapping fingers, and clapping hands until they reached the furious pace of the 'alegrías.'"

The *San Francisco Chronicle* described the Amayas' arrival in the City by the Bay:

---

[1] Martin, John, "Premiere Recital by Carmen Amaya." Copyright © *The New York Times*, January 14, 1942. Reprinted by permission.

Small touring company that included Antonio Triana's students, prior to setting out on the first national tour in 1942. Back row, left to right: two dancers, Manuel Matos, dancer, Leonor Amaya, dancer, Carmen Amaya, Antonio Triana, Lola Montes, front row, left to right: Domingo Blanco, dancer, Jerónimo Villarino, Paco Amaya, El Chino, dancer, Sabicas. *Photo courtesy of Lola Montes*

A San Francisco hotel room turned into an encampment yesterday afternoon to accomodate the amazing Amaya family, gypsy dancers from Granada whose fame travels with them around the world.

Everyone talked at once—in Spanish, English, and possibly Romany—as photographers wished for sound equipment and reporters thought wistfully of international dictionaries. And the center of the group was Carmen Amaya, small, vivid, dark, intense, and voluble, and somehow managing to be everywhere at once. To cries of "Carmencita!" and *"Aí, aí!"* Miss Amaya demonstrated why critics have exhausted adjectives trying to describe dances that are almost too quick for the eye to follow...[1]

The concert took place several days later:

The sacred rafters of the Opera House rang yesterday afternoon with cries that emanated not from the stage, but from the audience, as Carmen Amaya danced for the first time in San Francisco. At first, a demonstrative gallery of her countrymen provided the audience participation... but so irresistible was the Amaya fire that eventually even the American section became unmindful of its sedate concert manners and joined the shouting, and then the Amayas—Carmen, Leonor, Antonia, Paco, and Father José—and the rest of their company really hit their stride...

...the Amayas and their associate, Antonio Triana, are flamenco dancers and that above all distinguishes them from other Spanish dance troupes, for flamenco is perfectly spontaneous. Put any ordinary company of dancers on the stage without previous rehearsals or a choreographic plan, and you would have absolute chaos. But the Amayas go on the stage under those circumstances and the ordinary observer might never know they are improvising except that even in an encore performance they never do a dance twice the same way...[2]

The reviewer went on to single out Lola Montes' excellent work in the classical and folk dances, the *jota* by Leonor and Antonia that was the fastest and most exhilirating he had ever seen, the virtuosity of the guitarists, and Carmen's flamenco numbers, the *tarantos* and *alegrías*, which were "so vivid that they literally left you breathless."

From San Francisco the company traveled south to Los Angeles, where they would remain for more than a month. In the Philharmonic Auditorium on March 10, every number had to be repeated. The *Los Angeles Times* called her

---

[1] "Amayas Give a 'Preview' of Flamenco." *San Francisco Chronicle,* February 28, 1942.

[2] Stull, Christopher, "The Amayas Bring Down The House." *San Francisco Chronicle,* March 2, 1942.

"a young tiger" and wrote: "There is something wild, intuitive, and fascinating about this child of nature. Her dancing is pure flamenco, with something added by herself that strikes fire. She is tempestuous, controlled, practiced, like well-tempered steel, and as dangerous." Like all reviews, the *Times* praised her interpretation of the song *"Ay! Que Tú,"* calling her "an actress," "an impressive and passionate artist," and "a delicious little peacock."

Lola Montes recalled the days of touring:

> We always traveled by train. I was paid seventy-five dollars a week and was responsible for my own food, lodging, costumes, and even taxis. I had to stay in the same hotel with the Amayas and they always stayed in the most expensive hotels. There was a manager who took care of the business end and arranged our travel, and a stage manager who knew our show and set everything up and did the lighting. We had a lot of wardrobe. Each one was allowed one personal suitcase and a trunk that had drawers for flowers and makeup. In the big towns costumes were ironed, but in the small towns...well, let's just say, I would press mine!
>
> Everyone pretty much stayed to themselves on the train. Sabicas would be practicing or studying music. Carmen was always working on her writing. Regarding her English, I recall that even in later years she was not fluent, and certainly not in the beginning. She could order food and that's about it. We always spoke Spanish, and she was always with her family. She never went anywhere. The men went out, but not the women.
>
> By that time, Antonio and I were married. We stayed pretty much to ourselves. I was in a state of shock through my whole experience with those people. I couldn't believe it was happening to me. It was like a dream, something really unbelievable. The Amayas seemed to like me, but I think they felt sorry for me. When we got to a theater, I was deposited in my dressing room and that's where I stayed. I never visited Carmen's dressing room, so I didn't see their private life. I wasn't in on the details of the company. There were very few times that we all sat down together to eat. I was like a chair; I sat in the corner and kept my mouth shut. I watched and learned. Also, Antonio always kept me at his side, under his supervision. Usually I stayed sequestered in my dressing room. But I was always in the wings to watch Carmen dance. I didn't really get to know her until many years later, when she toured without her family, and then we became very close.

Sabicas remembered:

> We were taking trains all the time. It was the Second World War. The trains did not run on time, they could not run on time. We

would ask, "What time does the train leave for Los Angeles?"
"It leaves at midnight."
We would arrive at in the station at eleven o'clock. Soon it was twelve, one, two, three, four, five o'clock. We were cold and hungry. The train that was to leave at midnight was not there at five in the morning. Then we were told that there would be a train at six. At 5:45 the train was there. We had to be ready with our luggage all the time.[1]

Carmen had a contract to appear in the Metro Golden Meyer film *Panama Hattie* while they were in Los Angeles. Sabicas spoke about the movie, which starred Red Skelton and Ann Sothern:

> We had a contract for five weeks of work. We looked for a house nearby... I will never forget that house; it was in front of the studio. What a house! It had a handball court, five or six bedrooms, a garden. How much rent do you think we paid? Twenty-five dollars a month! We used to laugh. It was a palace. There were seven or eight of us in the house.
> We waited the first week, and nothing. Second week, nothing. Third, nothing. Fourth, nothing. People were asking us, "Why have you come here?"
> "We came to make a movie."
> "But when? You have been here four weeks."
> They paid us $25,000 for five weeks of work, and we were there four weeks with nothing to do. Of course, we were ready to work at any time—that was why they paid us. Finally, after four weeks and five days, we were called to the studio. They said, "Tomorrow." We said, "Fine."
> I put on my white gypsy suit—I was very thin then. I took my guitar and arrived at seven in the morning. We were to start at eight. Of course, I did not speak English. I used to say hello backwards. So I said, in Spanish, "I am hungry." The people looked at each other, not understanding. I repeated, "I am hungry and would like to eat something." I decided not to bother anybody and I would go look for something to eat. I said, "I am leaving my guitar here; just watch that no one takes it!" They looked at me funny because they didn't understand. I left my guitar in its case and went to eat. I was hungry and ate eggs, ham, toast, juice. I bought cigarettes. I took a stroll. I even saw a movie scene being filmed. I went back to the studio.
> "Mr. Sabicos, it is nine-twenty Mr. Sabicos!" Poor Carmen looked desperate. She asked what I had been doing. I told her I

[1] Molarsky interview.

had had breakfast. "Okay Mr. Sabicos."

Finally, Carmen danced every day. And they focused on my hands. My hands looked so big on the screen. I have never seen bigger hands. They looked like squid. I played only a few things, and then they focused on Carmen's feet. And that was all. When I saw those two and a half minutes—it couldn't have been more than three minutes...that was all!

Then a friend told me to charge for my music. I told him, "They paid us $25,000 for two and a half minutes. I think that is all right." He said, "No, that has nothing to do with you. It is your music." I had written four *alegrías*, but I didn't play them—I played something else. But they didn't notice. The person who came with us told them that flamenco is very difficult...so for the *alegrías* I wrote, they gave me one thousand dollars.[1]

Diego Castellón added: "Sabicas smoked a lot... When there was a scene that needed a lot of smoke, the director told him to smoke inside so that they would have smoke for the film. There was a fire and they used Sabas' smoke."[2]

In spite of all the expense and time, Carmen Amaya did not appear in the finished version of *Panama Hattie*. According to Vega de Triana, she was unable to dub in the sound of her feet to match the on-screen performance and had to be cut.

After the month-long sojourn in Los Angeles and a performance in San Diego, the tour continued. By April 21, they had reached New Jersey for a concert in Princeton, and two days later they performed in the Academy of Music in Philadelphia, where Carmen had been promoted as the "human volcano" and a "bundle of TNT." The overly exaggerated hype resulted in disappointment on the part of the reviewer: "If her performance last night fell rather short of such extravagances, it may well have been due to circumstances she could not control. Miss Amaya is a gypsy. Her style is that of a gypsy rather than that of a formal Spanish dancer, and the gypsy style in dancing, as well as in music, is essentially improvisational...There was little stimulus in last night's formally and conventionally arranged program for a dancer of her type to get underway...she was too severely restricted by being confined to set pieces, and the full effect of her personality was dissipated in the Academy."[3]

Back in New York in May, Carmen danced in the *Greek Festival for Freedom*, a fund-raiser for the Greek war effort held at midnight in Radio City Music Hall. The company continued to rehearse new material for a second Carnegie Hall concert only four months after their debut there in

[1] Molarsky interview.
[2] Goldberg interview.
[3] Pleasants, Henry, "Amaya and Troupe Dance for Forum at Academy." *The Evening Bulletin*, April 24, 1942.

January. This time, Antonio Triana's name appeared considerably smaller than Carmen's in newspaper announcements. Two music critics told the story of the performance on May 17th. John Martin of *The New York Times* felt that Carmen had improved her program, but he still had reservations:

> Carmen Amaya returned to Carnegie Hall last night after a sojourn in Hollywood, bringing with her the rest of the populous Amaya tribe of dancers and guitarists, plus Antonio Triana, Lola Montes, and the pianist Raymond Sachse, who are non-Amayan, according to the record.
>
> The program on the whole was superior to that of the Amaya concert debut earlier in the season, largely because Carmen's material was less classic, less conventional, and more characteristic of her personal style. Instead of one song, she sang several; and if the rowdy *"Ay! Que Tu"* is still the best of the lot, it is good to hear her cut loose with her surprisingly large and husky voice, and use every medium in her possession.
>
> The truth of the matter is that Amaya is a very talented dancer, as well as a gifted clown, and that she is desperately in need of a fitting show built around her. Her family is no doubt dear to her, but they are not helpful on the whole, and Mr. Triana, who is credited with the supervision of the program, could scarcely have put together a more heterogeneous bill. He himself dances extraordinarily well, as always, and his *"Polo"* comes near to being the high spot of the evening from a dancing standpoint, but he would be well advised to use his editorial blue pencil on at least a half hour of the schedule and perhaps a half dozen of the people...
>
> A large audience deserted the balmy evening outside for the promised tempests within, and the applause and cheering seemed to indicate that they were well satisfied with their choice.[1]

The dance critic for the *New York Herald Tribune*, Walter Terry, was more enthusiastic:

> It was a rousing, dynamic, fiery performance that Carmen Amaya chose to give last evening at Carnegie Hall for her final appearance of the season. Of course, the diminutive Spanish gypsy is famed for her volcanic qualities, but last evening's program seemed more explosive than ever...New works and repeats from the earlier performance constituted the program, but novelties are not particularly important, for it is the way that Amaya dances that matters.
>
> Because of her success in a recent performance with the dance-song, *"Ay! Que Tu,"* others have been added. They are fine, but *"Ay!*

---

[1]Martin, John, "Program Offered by Carmen Amaya." Copyright © *The New York Times*, May 18, 1942. Reprinted by permission.

Que Tu" remains the best of the lot, for Amaya sings the title's words with all the innuendo of an Hispanic Mae West. Her voice is far from attractive, in the lyric sense, but it is lusty and the flamenco wailing, accompanied by hilarious gestures, adds up to knock-out entertainment. The new *"Leyenda"* [*"Asturias"* by Albéniz] finds Miss Amaya in fine gypsy fettle, churning her skirts until they brush her head, stamping out the fastest heel-beats in all Spanish dance, shaking loose bits of costuming with the violence of her movements. In *"Tango de la Abuela,"* she sings, dances, and exchanges banter with the guitarists, and in *"Enamorado,"* a typical romantic trio reminiscent of some of Argentinita's pieces, she and her sister, Antonia, play havoc with Señor Triana, who tries to flirt with them both.

"Valenciana," also a trio, but this time for three girls, again found Carmen Amaya in vocal form. The three sisters also appeared in *"Las Cuevas Gitanas"* and danced their pounding gypsy rhythms with wonderful skill and communicative excitement. Highlighting the program was the "Fire Dance" from *El Amor Brujo*, which Amaya and Triana danced to brilliant effect. It is in a dance such as this that one realizes that Amaya merely uses Spanish dances as a starting point, that her use of traditional technique is flawless but that her greatness lies in the personal dynamics, the personal fire, and the purely animal movements which she brings to all her dances...

The Amaya clan, including both dancers and musicians, contributed their individual skills to the program, and Sabicas, the guitarist, earned a goodly portion of the evening's applause...[1]

These reviews hint at the underlying influence of La Argentinita on Carmen Amaya's programming. It is impossible to stress too strongly the impact that La Argentinita had on all subsequent Spanish dance companies. Her ideas and choreographies accompanied dancers as they changed alliances and moved from one company to another and even crept into the repertoire of a gypsy like Carmen Amaya. Of course, Argentinita's predecessor, La Argentina, has to be given credit for being the first, but La Argentinita exerted a much broader and longer lasting impact on the Spanish dance world. Her contribution has been well summed up by La Meri, an ethnic dancer who specialized in Spanish dance in the early part of the century and wrote extensively on the subject:

> Spanish dances in the early twenties and thirties were of four primary groups: regional, neoclassic, flamenco, and *ballet español*. Of the regional dances, very few actually made it to the concert stage. The *jota aragonesa* was the most popular—nearly every Spanish dancer has a number built on this dance in his or her pro-

[1] Terry, Walter, "Carmen Amaya Closes Season at Carnegie Hall." *New York Herald Tribune,* May 18, 1942.

gram. It was not really until La Argentinita came along that they were incorporated into theater dance. Having studied in every region of Spain, she put these dances onto the stage in the form of *bosquejos* or dance sketches using traditional music, costumes, and steps, drawing from humorous or comic themes...

The best known of the regional dances was and is, of course, the *sevillanas* of Andalucía. This dance has been the inspiration for the neoclassic forms. Neoclassic refers to a form of dance created and made famous by La Argentinita—the dance interpretation of music of the Spanish composers (Albéniz, Falla, Turina, etc.). There was great controversy when it first came out, even among the Spanish, for it was generally believed that these composers were to be listened to, not danced to. In this dance form, La Argentinita created her own dances, making visual interpretations of the music, to use her words. With neoclassic choreography came compositions that respected air, floor, and music design in one, and were very much groomed for the theater. The mood that inspired this style was felt at the beginning of each piece, and the dance was then created in clear memory of that mood. The castanets were played in counterpoint like a second melody in the music.

Up until the early twenties, the flamenco style had a sharply defined technique for men and women. Simply defined, women used their arms, men their feet. The dance of the arms was considered highly feminine and passionate. La Cuenca and Carmen Amaya were the first women to wear masculine clothes and dance in the all-male style. The use of castanets began in the early thirties. Before that, they had been used only in the dances of folk origin, and men never used them at all. Into the thirties and early forties, flamenco was not routined, but rather, improvised on a theme or mood.

The *ballet español*, choreographed using Spanish rather than ballet technique, was seldom seen in this country prior to the forties. It was an outgrowth of the Spanish *zarzuelas* that were popular in the middle of the 19th century. These little operetas grew in popularity and can be compared to our own musical comedies of the '40s and '50s. The Madrid ballet [La Argentinita], collaborating with the poet, Federico García Lorca, choreographed many famous works, including *El Amor Brujo* and *Café de Chinitas*. Using music of many of the famous composers of the day, these dances were choreographed to tell a story, usually involving a plot of love and intrigue.[1]

[1] Mahan, Patricia, "An Interview with La Meri." *Jaleo, Vol. IV, No. 10*. August-September 1983.

It can be seen that La Argentinita was pivotal in developing three of the four types of Spanish theater dance, although it must be remembered that it was Antonia Mercé "La Argentina" who had pioneered these dance forms, especially the neoclassic. Argentinita's creative genius was least felt in the flamenco. Carmen Amaya, a master of the flamenco, could not resist being drawn into Argentinita's sphere of influence. Dance critic Edwin Denby brilliantly analyzed Carmen's struggle to resolve the conflict between the two styles in his reviews of her two Carnegie Hall performances. After the first, he wrote:

> On the Carmen Amaya question, it was her comic *"Ay! Que Tu"* number that convinced me she is an extraordinary dancer. A gypsy girl sings to her lover, "You can't make me jealous; you go on pretending to make love to others, but you always come back to me and say, 'There's only you, beautiful, there's only you!' Amaya was wearing the typical flamenco dress, with its many flounces and long train, but she looked like a girl of thirteen, angular as a boy, in her first evening gown. She fought her train into place like a wild animal trainer. Her voice was hoarse and small, her gesture abrupt and awkward. All this, with the defiance of the song, made the dance comic. But the figure of the tough slum girl Amaya suggested was as real to you as the stranger sitting next to you in the audience. You felt its private individual life, its life before and after the glimpse of it you were catching. And there was nothing pathetic, no appeal for help in it. So you grinned and laughed.
>
> Realness in comedy is very rare among dancers, and the cruelly comic is, of course, one of the special gifts of Spain. Now that I've seen Amaya do it, I have the greatest admiration for her. Before, I had been rather disappointed. Compared to the other Spanish stars in town, I had not found in her dancing the limpidity, the exquisite flow and nuance of Argentinita, nor the diamond glitter, the superb force of [Juan] Martínez, the greatest of the dancers here...And Rosario and Antonio—somewhat like Amaya in fiery temperament, in exuberant blurring of detail, in speed and theatricality—have the advantage of being a couple of kids happily matched, a relation which makes the dance look open and natural.
>
> True, even in disappointing numbers, Amaya has first-rate personal qualities. She has sometimes, for instance, a wonderful kind of rippling of her body in movement, more like a young cat's than a girl's. She has an extraordinary cutting quality in her gesture, too, as if she meant: here only, and never elsewhere. She has a thrilling speed and attack. But these impressions of real movements were confused by others when she seemed to be faking, forcing her "tem-

perament" or driving her dance into the floor, like a pianist who pounds too hard. Or she would lose control of the continuity of her dance, put all her fire into a half minute of it and not know what to do with the remaining two minutes, so they went flat. Sometimes she seemed determined to cow her audience, and I had the feeling I was watching not a dancer but an ambitious person. On the other hand, that in the course of her first recital she could adjust herself to the glum expanse of Carnegie Hall and finally take charge was proof of her personal stage power. But Amaya's unevenness does not bother me anymore. Instead, I now understand why all other flamenco dancers respect and admire her.[1]

A year later, he continued his evaluation:

Several straight flamenco numbers ended Carmen Amaya's Carnegie Hall program. They were each one much too short to have their full effect, but in them everybody can see that she is a great and very individual dancer. That, however, isn't the curious part of the story. Four-fifths of the evening was reserved for Spanish dancing, recital style, a form made illustrious by the great Argentina and of which Argentinita is now the star (at least here). Amaya as a flamenco dancer in the process of becoming a recitalist has naturally chosen the best model she could find, and she has worked hard— the improvement in detail over last year is obvious. But, actually, in the kind of number that Argentinita turns into a marvel of polish, Amaya, right after some real stroke of genius, next looks as if she had lost the thread of her story; she looks plain or out of place. Well, she carries off the number by the force of her presence on the stage, and it is wonderful how silly she invariably makes the Granados or Albéniz music sound by the force of her attack. But the whole thing is off balance.

Off balance, but highly interesting. Because Amaya is a completely honest character and what you watch is the struggle between two opposite dance natures—Argentinita's, which she wants to reproduce, and her own, which she can't destroy. Argentinita's nature is that of a sensible artist; she completely understands the logical line of a recital dance; she dances a piece through from A to Z without a false stress or gap. Similarly, she is a purist of movement and her transitions from one gesture to the next are a technical delight. She is also a witty and charming lady who takes the audience into her confidence in a vivacious and cultivated way. Some lovers of Spanish dancing even find Argentinita too polite to be thrilling. Amaya, on the other hand,

[1] Denby, Edwin, *Looking at the Dance*, March-April, 1942.

has none of these qualities. Form for her is not logical; it is a successive burst of inventions; the rhythmic shock is wherever you don't expect it; gesture is expression and attack, it's a gamble and there is no sense in saving and budgeting; and she has no patience with illuminating delightful anecdotes on Spanish life—she wants to say straight out what she knows is so.

Technically speaking, Amaya's dancing was more controlled and more varied than last year. She has also checked her former mannerisms; she doesn't repeat her lightening turns again and again, she doesn't shake down her hair every time, nor dance male parts too frequently. Her magnificent rapidity, her power, and her fine originality in handling the sex character of Spanish dancing, are all singular virtues. And again and again she can dance as if nothing else existed in the world but dancing and death.[1]

---

[1] Denby, Edwin, *Looking at the Dance*, January-February 1943.

CHAPTER EIGHT

ACROSS THE FRUITED PLAIN

A passion for Spanish music continued to sweep America in 1942. Theaters around the country featured films like *Blood and Sand*, with Tyrone Power, Anthony Quinn, and Rita Hayworth and a soundtrack by flamenco and classical guitarist Vicente Gómez, and *Carmen la de Triana*, a take-off on Bizet's *Carmen* with Imperio Argentina in the lead role. These movies would soon be joined by others featuring the dancing of Carmen Amaya or Rosario and Antonio. In May a short film (not named in the press) that the Amayas had made in Hollywood was shown in a New York film festival. Carmen also appeared on Broadway in *Laugh, Town, Laugh*, a revue produced by Ed Wynn.

According to Diego Castellón, when Carmen was not touring, Hurok put her in nightclubs like the Havana-Madrid, the Conga Room, and the Rainbow Room of the Plaza Hotel in New York, as well as others in Boston, Washington D.C., and Chicago. The shows were smaller and shorter, a half-hour in length without breaks. Antonio Triana only performed in the concerts and did not involve himself in club or cabaret shows.[1]

In the fall, the company set out on tour once more, duplicating many of the stops of the previous spring, but also including a swing through the Southwest. Notably absent was pianist Manuel Matos. He had been replaced in May, before the Carnegie Hall concert. Something must have been troubling the brilliant composer/pianist, for one of the last reviews of the spring tour revealed that, "The pianist, Manuel Matos, seemed to be reading the music and not very well. Perhaps the regular pianist was ill or something. This one had to be helped by the musical castanets and the heels of the dancers too often. The familiar music of De Falla, Turina, Granados, and Infantes was bungled inexcusably..."[2] Diego Castellón said, "García Matos was somewhat lazy in his execution at the piano."[3] Lola Montes suggested that Matos' departure may have been a management decision, since he was basically a composer and conductor, not a piano soloist. His

---
[1] Goldberg interviews.
[2] *Los Angeles Times*, March 11, 1942.
[3] Goldberg interviews.

replacement, Raymond Sachse, from Massachussetts, would receive universally high praise for his work with the Amayas.

The Amaya company overwhelmed its audience in a high school auditorium in Colorado Springs: "Carmen Amaya herself is one of those individuals who can carry all before her thru the sheer vitality, fury, and brilliance of an electric, indeed a high voltage, personality." Again, in Phoenix, Arizona, an audience not so jaded and critical as those of New York, was swept away by what they saw: "The curtains of red and gold swept back to reveal a stage empty and black-curtained except for the pianist and piano half-hidden in the left wing. Then there flashed into view three women dancers in as gorgeous costumes as this community has ever seen. Two of Carmen's sisters, Antonia and Leonor, with Lola Montes as the central figure, gave the audience its first pulse-accelerating taste of what was in store for the whole of the program…"

The Phoenix newspaper also had high praise for Sabicas: "A lonely chair in the front center of the stage was occupied then by a handsome Latin male with a guitar. Guitars are a dime a dozen. But not the guitar of Sabicas. It was not apparent at the very first, as he started into the first notes of *'Motivos Arabes,'* his own composition. Then suddenly it became apparent. Every finger was an orchestra. This was an artist. Sabicas made the guitar a new instrument, a bevy of instruments."

Sabicas was clearly becoming more and more consumed by the idea of playing solos. The press sometimes criticized him for playing too long—up to five pieces at a time (normally two). On this tour he played *zambra, panaderos,* or *farruca* in duet with Paco Amaya. His own solos included *alegrías, bulerías, granaínas, gallegadas, malagueñas,* and *"Motivos Arabes" (zambra).* Sabicas would become the only concert soloist to specialize in *zambra* and *danza mora* (*zambra* is the Moorish flavored *tango* of the Sacromonte, while *danza mora* is an attempt to imitate Arabic music, often employing an altered tuning of the guitar). Without a doubt his interest in this type of music stemmed from his relationship with the Amayas. In the 1936 film *María de la O,* El Chino's playing *por zambra* is identical in sound to that of Sabicas some ten or fifteen years later.

Exactly how the Amayas became so proficient in the *zambra* is not clear. It was not a music commonly found in the cafes. Although the Amayas' family ties with Granada were not very strong, there was significant contact with the gypsies of the Sacromonte during Carmen's visits there, as well as in the 1929 Exposition in Barcelona that had featured a *cuadro* from the Sacromonte, and during the filming of *María de la O* in Granada. In the early years, the Amayas often performed the *zambra.* Sabicas would compose numerous solo versions of *zambra,* in at least five different keys.

The fall tour continued into Los Angeles for two performances. The reviewer there expressed her frustration at not being able to understand

Carmen's songs and asides, but assured her readers that those who did were doubled over with laughter. She pointed out that Carmen dominated the whole troupe except when her father put down his guitar to dance, and indicated that "all but Carmen are slightly overweight by Hollywood standards." After an appearance in Fresno, Carmen opened in San Francisco on November 8th:

> Carmen Amaya has none of the refinement, scholarship, and intellectuality of her predecessors [Argentina and Argentinita]. She is a large-featured gypsy hell-cat who, in the course of one dance, generates and burns up enough energy to run a battle cruiser from here to the Solomon Islands and back without refueling.
>
> The stage of the Opera House has never resounded to so furious a battering of heels, nor so ear-splitting a bombardment of handclaps, nor so demoniacal a clattering of castanets. Why Amaya does not dance her costumes into shreds is a mystery; pieces of them did, to be sure, whirl the width of the stage, but the main seams, obviously sewed with steel thread, remained intact.
>
> All the usual metaphors for gypsy dancers apply, and to a transcendental degree. Amaya is a whip, a flame, a cyclone, a ton of dynamite, and then some. Doubtless there is much art, in the sense of something learned and rehearsed, in all she does, but what one carries away is a sense of improvisation, possessed rather than inspired, incendiary, nerve-scraping and violent, and occasionally carried out of this world to a point where the grotesque and the tragic, the vulgar and the noble, are fantastically mingled...
>
> Her singing is something else again. As a singer she employs all the old tricks that have been exploited by the prima donnas of burlesque since the days of Caligula—the annoyance with the unwieldy costume, the whiskey baratone, the spoken asides, the cross-eyed mugging, the frequent wheeling flip of the derriere...
>
> ...The guitar player, Sabicas, is an amazing virtuoso with very bad taste in his style of arranging...[1]

Two thousand turned out to see Carmen's first appearance in Portland, Oregon. Then, poor scheduling required the company to turn south again, to San Diego, for its second performance in Russ Auditorium, which "...took quite a scorching last night when Amaya turned on the old flamenco." The *San Diego Union* wrote of Carmen: "Her face pantomine is as fascinating as her footwork. She wears no set smile. Neither does she try to look pretty all the time. Sometimes she looks as vexed as though she has just seen a crocodile in the geraniums."[2] Sabicas was a hit with his solos—"*Variaciones*

---

[1] Frankenstein, Alfred, "Amaya Gave A Dynamic Recital." *San Francisco Chronicle*, November 9, 1942.

[2] "Carmen Amaya Gives Spirited Dance Program." *San Diego Union*, November 14, 1942.

por Bulerías" and *"Recuerdo a Málaga,"* (with its virtuoso effects and passages for the left hand alone).

After San Diego, the tour turned eastward, eventually reaching Allentown and Philadelphia, where the paper wrote: "The whirling miss has come a long way in style since her initial local appearance last April...Miss Amaya still dances like lightning, her arms, legs, torso, castanets, and vocalisms being one visual and oral blur at times. But there is more form to her numbers, and it is now more than ever suited to a theater stage instead of primarily for nightclubs, where Carmen scored her first great success. This, perhaps, may be credited to Antonio Triana, the group's superlative male dancer."[1]

When the group crossed the border into Canada for a performance in Winnepeg, Antonio Triana's papers were not in order and he had to remain behind. Of course, Lola Montes had to stay with him. According to the newspaper, Paco Amaya was also absent and the company had to work doubly hard to make up for the loss of duos and trios in their program. Carmen took it on her shoulders to give a good show, and the audience responded: "Carmen Amaya, gypsy spitfire, lived up to advance inflammatory press terms when she appeared in Winnepeg on Thursday night...Her elemental passions, violent gestures, incredibly quick movements of hands and feet, and dizzy whirls, electrified the large audience upon every solo occasion." In the "Ritual Fire Dance," Carmen was "the most startling human dynamo in action one has ever witnessed...and one was held breathless under the terrifying ritual." Papa José was singled out for his agile dancing.

Back in New York, the company made its third appearance in Carnegie Hall in less than a year. Revues were lukewarm, one critic implying that Carmen had an off night. John Martin gave a vivid picture of the gypsy dynamo:

> ...As usual, at the rise of the curtain the stage was set in high gear and remained there without fluctuation. If the energy seems by now a little like routine mechanics it is nevertheless still energetic, fast, and loud. For the tiny little wiry creature that she is, Amaya can make more noise with her "palmas secas," her pounding heels, and her amazing baritone voice than half a dozen riviting machines.
>
> She is apparently not happy until she can shake half a dozen flowers out of her coiffure, cause her hair to fall into her face, and virtually knock herself out by the end of a number. As a result she wastes no time; if her first dance is to such a poetic bit of music as the "Córdoba" of Albéniz, it is all one to her. And...it soon becomes all one to the spectator as well; before the evening has

---

[1] Singer, Samuel L., "Gypsy Dancer Gives Academy A Dusting." *The Philadelphia Inquirer,* December 11, 1942.

got to the halfway mark one number looks very much like another. The paying customers (and plenty of them) love it, however, so who are we to cavil? Mr. Triana provides the best dancing of the program, if dancing is what you are looking for, and his zapateado stopped the show cold last night. Miss Amaya is at her best, as far as this reviewer is concerned, not when she is tearing herself to well-rehearsed pieces, but when she gets tough and sings and mugs her way through such low-comedy numbers as *"Herencia gitana."*[1]

After that December 13th performance, the company continued to tour through the early winter, with shows in New York and neighboring states.

When La Argentinita was dropped by Sol Hurok, she fell on hard times. On top of the loss of the famed impresario, she had to face competition from Carmen Amaya and Los Chavalillos de España (upgraded from "Chavalillos *de Sevilla*"). But she continued to work, appearing in variety shows like *Topnotchers* and *Priorities*. In February of 1942, after a serious (unspecified) illness, she gave a concert in New York and presented Ravel's "Bolero."

One of the novelties of this performance was the inclusion of the Inca Trio, a group of Peruvian musicians who played solos and accompanied Argentinita's *"Huayano."* The international flavor of her program was further enhanced by the addition of a new Mexican dance. Pilar's dancing was singled out as getting "better and better."

Argentinita faced a new problem in early 1942: The United States had entered the war and Federico Rey was drafted. Argentinita had to find a new dance partner—not an easy task considering all of the training that was necessary to fit a new dancer into her choreographies. On at least one occasion she teamed up with Antonio (of Rosario and Antonio) to dance Ravel's "Bolero" in a concert to raise money for the war effort. Antonio was at that time appearing on Broadway in *Sons o' Fun* with Rosario. When, a former member of Argentinita's company, Teresita Osta, recommended a young man she had rehearsed with a few times, La Argentinita called Costanzo Greco and set up an audition.

Costanzo "Gus" Greco had been born December 23, 1918, in Italy. His family moved to New York in 1928. At age fifteen, following in his sister's footsteps, he began dance lessons with Madame Veola (with whom Lola Montes also studied). During the following eight years, Gus learned from a variety of teachers in New York and performed in the recitals and little

---

[1]Martin, John, "Amaya Group Seen At Carnegie Hall. "Copyright © *The New York Times*, December 14, 1942. Reprinted by permission.

restaurant shows that nourish young, aspiring dancers. In the late 1930s he took some classes with Antonio Triana and began to absorb the style and choreography of La Argentinita. But after only a week, he and Antonio disagreed over money and Gus could not afford further classes. He said that he also took some classes with Anita Sevilla. In Madame Veola's studio he met Vicente Escudero, "...an elegant figure with a great deal of personal magnetism, a man who radiated virility—though he was already in his fifties."[1]

Fortunately for Gus Greco, he had also rehearsed with a couple of former members of La Argentinita's company and had begun to absorb her style and routines. When La Argentinita called him to audition for her, he was ready and amazed her with his knowledge. Encarnación hired Gus for the company and baptized him with a new name—José Greco. According to José, it wasn't long before he and his boss began a long-running clandestine affair; he was twenty-four, she forty-four. With the addition of another male dancer, Manolo Vargas, to partner Pilar, the small company was complete and began to tour the region, working with local orchestras in each city. The enthusiasm generated by the group didn't escape the notice of Sol Hurok, who re-engaged La Argentinita and sent her out on a schedule that included hospitals and military bases. José related an experience with their guitarist, Carlos Montoya:

> In those days, Montoya was a young man, about my age, a little rough, a little wild, a friendly fellow but unpolished. Montoya was really the only fellow in the company with whom I could have a few laughs.
>
> He was a gypsy from Madrid, a strange combination of sophistication and primitivism. He sometimes warned me to be careful with Argentinita and Pilar because they were powerful women who could "really do the voodoo on you," if they wanted.
>
> Mostly, though, we talked of Spanish music and Spanish dance. "I want to dance better," I told him. "I want to dance as well as anyone has ever danced. I want to learn everything there is to learn about the Spanish dance."
>
> "Oh," he said, "if that's the case, I can teach you. I can teach you an *alegrías*."
>
> An *alegrías* was a typical flamenco dance—exactly the sort of thing I wanted to learn. "You know how to do an *alegrías*?" I asked. "Show me!"
>
> He did a few steps. And I said to myself, my God, this man really knows how to dance. But maybe that wasn't so surprising. All gypsies—whether they're singers or guitarists or even janitors—seem to know how to dance, at least a little. "Okay," I said, "teach

---

[1] Greco, p. 38

me."

"Fine. That will be fifteen dollars a class."

A member of my own company asking money to teach me a dance? I could hardly believe it. When I was teaching Manolo [Vargas], that idea had never occurred to me. But this, too, was typical of a gypsy. "That's too much money," I said. "I'll pay you fifty dollars if you teach me the whole routine."

We made a deal. For the next few weeks, Montoya taught me what he knew—a few small things, it turned out, but quite effective in their way.

Later, I told Argentinita about our transaction.

"What? He charged you money? I can't believe it!"

"It's true."

She laughed. "That gypsy! Well, at least he was honest and straightforward about it."

Over the years, Montoya changed. He became a man. More than that, he became a gentleman. Some of this, no doubt, was due to the very positive influence of his wife, Sally, who played a role in his life not unlike Meda—and Argentinita—played in mine.[1]

Carlos Montoya first met Sally McLean in 1934, when she was taking flamenco dancing lessons in Paris. She was descended, as she put it, "from a long line of New England Congregational ministers and Highland Scots" and "as American as apple pie." When they met again, in New York as World War II was getting underway, she asked the musician-dancer to teach her some flamenco steps. Six weeks later they were married. Using the name "Trianita," Sally performed with Carlos in small clubs around New York in the early years of their marriage. Carlos would become an American citizen in 1946 and proudly play for President Truman after the ceremony.[2]

José Greco made his debut with Argentinita in Carnegie Hall on March 21, 1943. Argentinita delighted the audience by playing the guitar in addition to dancing and singing. But, in the words of John Martin, the "...novelty of the occasion lay in the presence of two new male partners who proved to be distinct additions. José Greco is cool in style, light, controlled and objective in approach. At the other end of the scale is a lad named Manolo Vargas, fleet-footed and fiery, who quite won the hearts of last night's audience. He is definitely somebody to watch..."[3]

A month later the company filled in at the last minute for a cancelled Ballet Theatre production of *Romeo and Juliet* at the Metropolitan Opera House. They presented Ravel's "Bolero" to orchestral accompaniment.

---

[1] Greco, p. 55.

[2] The date of Montoya's citizenship has been given variously as 1940, 1941, and 1946. Obviously, if he played for Prsident Truman, it had to be after 1945.

[3] Martin, John, "Argentinita Here With New Dances." *The New York Times*, March 22, 1943.

Argentinita was praised for her ability to fill such a large auditorium to the farthest wall with the intensity of her dramatic understatement.

Argentinita was definitely expanding her conception of the Spanish dance, performing with orchestra and on larger stages. On May 17, 1943, *The New York Times* announcement read: "S. Hurok presents 'Spanish Festival' at the Metropolitan Opera House, with Argentinita • López • Dalí • Iturbi and the sixty member New York Philharmonic Orchestra in 'Dances from *Carmen*,' 'Bolero,' and Lorca's *'Café de Chinitas.'*" One of Argentinita's admirers, the Marquis de Cuevas, sponsored the Festival. Salvador Dalí did the sets, José Iturbi conducted the orchestra, and La Argentinita hired all the local dancers she could find to enlarge her company. The night was a tremendous success and put her back in favor in the eyes of the critics and the public. John Martin described the event:

> ...the always admirable Argentinita Saturday night gave what was undoubtedly her most sumptuous performance hereabouts, but not by the same token her most brilliantly successful one. With the presence of José Iturbi conducting an excellent orchestra...with a setting by Salvador Dalí and an augmented company of some ten or twelve dancers to supplement the excellent permanent group of four, the evening could scarcely have failed to be a gala occasion. When all is said and done, however, it is the art of Argentinita herself that is of first importance and it is to be feared that it was a bit smothered under all this affluence...
>
> *"El Café de Chinitas"* is now a *"cuadro flamenco"* as presented in a famous music hall of Málaga in the late Nineties. As such it has a wealth of atmosphere and a feeling of authenticity, but it does not always escape the fringes of dullness. The material is, perhaps, too authentic, too little dressed up theatrically, and crowded too far away at the back of the stage. Dalí has designed for it a beautiful back drop and a magnificent full-stage setting which, despite its psychological inappropriateness and its characteristically revolting qualities, is quite the finest work he has yet done for the stage.[1]

Martin went on to point out that the orchestra drowned out much of the footwork and castanets and that the lighting was poor and masked the dancer's movements. Clearly, Argentinita still had some work to do if she wanted to present Spanish dance on such a grand scale. Martin's description of Dalí's setting for *"Café de Chinitas"* gives some idea of the challenge the dancers faced in competing with its visual impact:

---

[1]Martin, John, "Spanish Festival Stars Argentinita." Copyright © *The New York Times*, May 17, 1943. Reprinted by permission.

Its two high and deep side walls covered with guitars lead to the huge center panel filling the back of the stage with a design that holds the eye remorselessly. It is an enormous guitar with a woman's disheveled but flower-trimmed head hanging limply forward from its neck and a woman's arms, with castanets in hand, stretching broadly from its shoulders as if crucified, with streams of blood forming a shawl across their length. It is utterly joyless, macabre, inversive, as a setting for Argentinita's straightforward, folkish, good-humored dance scene.[1]

Undaunted, Argentinita continued to experiment with Spanish dance in large venues. In July she and her ensemble danced in Lewisohn Stadium before a crowd of 10,000. In such a setting, and with Iturbi leading an enlarged orchestra, much of the subtlety and delicacy of the dances was lost. However, the enthusiastic audience appauded heartily and demanded repetitions of many numbers. José Greco stopped the show completely with his brilliant performance of the "Miller's Dance" from *The Three-Cornered Hat*.

Later in the year, Argentinita closed out the season with another concert in Carnegie Hall.

Not to be outdone, Carmen Amaya, too, took her dancing to the large stage. In August of 1943, "The World's Most Sensational Flamenco Dancer" would appear in Hollywood Bowl. But earlier, the company had spent the winter in the cabaret La Conga and apparently did some touring. An aficionado, Charles Teetor, described his meeting with the Amayas:

> I was a provincial boy from Indiana with absolutely no Spanish, gypsy, or even Mediterranean blood in my background. My only exposure to anything foreign had been one year of high school Spanish, a modest exposure at best.
>
> It all started one rainy night in January, 1943, when, with nothing to do, I found myself standing in front of the St. Louis Concert Hall [Missouri]. The posters proclaimed that Carmen Amaya and her company would perform in a few minutes. I bought a ticket. The next four hours changed my life.
>
> It is impossible to explain the euphoria that Carmen and her company produced in me that evening. Looking back, it may have been one of the best flamenco touring companies... Sol Hurok knew how to package a dance company: costumes, orchestra, scenery, and staging were of a scale not seen in later companies. When the curtain finally fell, I refused to let go of the spell the

---

[1] Martin, John, "The Dance: Spanish Theatre." Copyright © *The New York Times*, May 23, 1943. Reprinted by permission.

Amayas had woven. For the first time in my life I found the stage door and waited. I simply had to see those people again!

The first two artists to come out were Antonio Triana and Sabicas. It was Fate that made them ask me where to get a taxi to the train station. In my high school Spanish, I replied that it was only a two-block walk and that I would gladly guide them. By the time we arrived at the station we were sufficiently acquainted for them to ask me to come in for a coffee. Within a few minutes the entire company had gathered in the Fred Harvey Lunchroom to wait for the midnight train to Chicago. The war was on and transportation was difficult. To my everlasting joy the train was two hours late. During that two hours I discovered that true flamencos are exhilarated but constrained by stage performance and frequently can't wait to get off stage and start performing "free form." The tile floor of the lunchroom and the marble-topped tables were, perhaps, somewhat reminiscent of the cafes of Andalucía, and while waiting for that train to arrive I experienced my first *juerga*. Sabicas' guitar came out, the girls sang, and there was much knuckling of the tables. Antonio Triana was an electric spark that got everything and everybody going.

When the college semester ended, Charles boarded a train for New York:

By great good luck, the train paused in Newark and two Latin types got on. I asked them if they knew where I could find Carmen Amaya. They had not heard of her, but by a quirk of chance they knew of a cafe on 52nd Street where Spanish entertainers sometimes gathered. It was named El Flamenco. I went there directly and was not disappointed. Around 2:00 a.m. some members of the Amaya company drifted in. They were kind enough to pretend that they remembered me from St. Louis. In retrospect I think this was the ultimate kindness. While there was no *juerga* that evening, I did find that the company had a full winter's engagement in a Times Square nightclub called La Conga. I also found that there were a number of other clubs in New York that featured flamenco shows: Havana-Madrid, which catered to a cafe society crowd, Chateau Madrid, and El Chico in Greenwich Village.

I went to all of the clubs, but the obvious choice was La Conga with the Amayas. Between shows the action was in the dressing rooms. When it was too cold to go out for a walk, what did the flamencos do? They played, sang, smoked, and told jokes. Carmen's father, José, dominated the group. He was dictatorial not only in what and how they performed, but also when it came to who the girls talked to. Carmen seemed to treat him with great respect, but went her own way. The two younger sisters, Leonor and Antonia, were on a tight rein and after performances were generally escorted back to the brownstone house they rented in the West Forties. There were other younger children, but I was never clear as to their relationship [certainly Carmen's younger brother and sister, Antonio and María, would have been among them]. It seemed to be very much what we now call "an extended family."[1]

There had been ongoing friction between Antonio Triana and the Amayas. In spite of his pivotal role in the success of the Amayas, Triana really had little voice in the doings of the company. On the other hand, his contribution to the artistic merit of the Amaya concerts cannot be underestimated. Without him there might have been no Hurok tours. His intelligence and command of English was invaluable, and he was responsible for all of the dance numbers except Carmen's flamenco solos and some flamenco segments. He was very knowledgeable about theater and had a good feel for it, down to makeup and costume design. As we have seen, his background in all types of dance was extensive. And then there was his own dancing. Critics universally lauded his brilliant technique and winning stage presence.

Certainly Antonio was aware of his worth and it grated on him that he did not get appropriate recognition. In spite of a contractual agreement calling for his name to be equal in size to Carmen's in promotions and programs, his name often showed up in smaller print. The promotors tried to gloss over it, attributing it to "typographical error," but it was a constant source of irritation for the proud dancer. Lola Montes said, "It was holy war every time his name was too small."

For this and other reasons, Antonio left the company. He and Lola moved to Los Angeles where they had contacts and could teach. The absence of Lola also represented a considerable loss to the Amaya company. She had been unfailingly praised by critics, who had called her "lithe and graceful," and "lovely to look at, arresting in performance, and in no sense a letdown from the leading artist."

In the summer of 1943, Carmen was back in Hollywood to make a film, perhaps *Follow the Boys* or *Knickerbocker Holiday*, which would be released the following year. Sol Hurok saw it as an opportunity to bring Carmen and Antonio Triana back together. "He contacted Triana in his studio. They met in Hurok's Beverly Hills hotel suite, and after hours of haggling, followed by bracing rounds of vodka, plans were put in action for two Hollywood Bowl performances."[2] Hollywood Bowl, a natural outdoor amphitheater in the hills of Los Angeles, had been built in 1919 to house the

---

[1] Teetor, Charles, "The Flamenco Scene in New York in the Forties." *Jaleo, Vol. VI, No. 4*, January 1983.
[2] Vega de Triana, p. 52.

summer concert series, "Symphonies Under the Stars." Antonio and Lola began the arduous process of preparing their dance students for supporting roles in the production. The Amayas arrived shortly before the August concert dates and Triana, desperate to find another male dancer to play the ghost, assigned the role to guitarist Paco Amaya. To the relief of all, he turned out to be an excellent dancer. The newspapers gave Carmen and Antonio Triana equal billing, and said they would perform Falla's ballet *El Amor Brujo*, Ravel's "Bolero," and *"Café Flamenco."*

Problems began at the first rehearsal, when orchestra director Morris Stoloff could not agree with the dancers on how the music should go. Carmen was finding it difficult to dance within the confines of the orchestral scores and the director had no experience in trying to follow an unpredictable dancer. The sold-out show was threatened with cancellation.

Sabicas's brother recalled: "In the afternoon, Sabas and Matos were sitting and watching the orchestra rehearse. The director couldn't get the part where Carmen Amaya and Antonio Triana danced a *bulerías*. Matos told Sabas that, since they hadn't called him to direct, there would be no concert, because it wasn't going well... Antonio Triana told Hurok that his brother had to direct it, and he did!"[1]

Manuel Matos, who had come to Los Angeles to watch the performance, described the impasse:

...in order to direct Carmen Amaya it was necessary to follow her with the conducting, given that *El Amor Brujo* is very difficult, with its three types of *bulerías*—the most complicated thing in flamenco. Its difficulty lies in the fact that you have to accent very precisely, because it is a music of "accent." Carmen Amaya was accustomed to being choreographed and directed by my brother, Antonio Triana, who did it very well, making room for the *desplantes* [rhythmic variations] that the *bulerías* has in the middle. (The *tango de Cádiz* and the *alegrías* also have the *desplante*. The *desplante* consists of the *llamada* [a step that warns the guitarist of a change to follow], a break [dancer's improvisation], and then a return to the basic rhythm.)

So, to settle the matter, my brother, Antonio Triana, intervened. He went to the piano (that he played very well since childhood, although never as a professional) and began to finger Carmen Amaya's number, until the director finally caught on to the *compás*. My brother wanted to resolve the problem, so he explained to Stoloff everything I have mentioned here about *El Amor Brujo*: that the number required accent, that it had three different types of *bulerías*, one in the beginning, one in the middle, and one at the

[1] Goldberg interview with Diego Castellón.

The Amayas and friends after the Hollywood Bowl performance of 1943. Standing left to right: Argentine dancer César Tapia, Antonia Amaya, two local aficionados, Manuel Matos, niece of Anita Sevilla, El Chino, pianist Norman Secon, Sabicas, guitarist Jerónimo Villarino, Paco Amaya, Antonio el Chaqueta (Paco's son), Diego Castellon. Seated, left to right: local dancer, Lola Montes, Carmen's mother Micaela Amaya, Anita Sevilla, Carmen Amaya, Luisa Triana, Antonio Triana, Paco's wife La Chata. *Photo courtesy of Lola Montes.*

end, and it also had a *siguiriya* that followed a count of 3 [fast] and 2 [slow] beats and had to be marked very well if Carmen Amaya were to be able to dance it. (Carmen Amaya had a very rudimentary knowledge of music and all of her dance was very spontaneous.) He was explaining it all to Stoloff, but there was no way they could come to an agreement—the pride of the great director wouldn't let him give in to the advice of others.

Another problem with Stoloff's directing was the following: The Hollywood Bowl requires the use of the Los Angeles Symphony Orchestra, which is made up of one hundred professors who are paid ten dollars an hour each for rehearsal, which means a total of $1,000 an hour. On top of that, Morris Stoloff claimed to need three hours with the orchestra alone and an additional three hours with the orchestra and dancers. That meant a total of $6,000 just for rehearsal! The impresario, Sol Hurok, told Stoloff that what he wanted was very expensive. They debated a long time but couldn't come to an agreement, and finally began arguing, with Stoloff throwing his baton, etc.

Present at the rehearsal was the great guitarist Sabicas, who was very interested in seeing *El Amor Brujo* presented because it would free him to play separately, as a soloist.[1]

Sabicas had pointed out to Hurok that Antonio Triana was the one best suited to direct *El Amor Brujo* because he had done it before, not only for Carmen, but previously for Argentinita. Now he suggested to Triana that Matos lead the orchestra. And that is how it was: Triana directed and Manuel Matos conducted the orchestra (although the programs, printed beforehand, indicated Stoloff as director). Along with Falla's ballet, they did *"Goyescas"* by Granados and *"La Orgía"* by Turina. Matos wrote, "...these were not a problem for me because I had been doing them daily for years. We also included a composition of mine, *"Los Canasteros de Triana,"* a very popular piece that features gypsy women making baskets on the bank of the river. There was also the debut of another of my compositions, *"La Bulería de los Pastores."* In the second part of the evening, we did Ravel's "Bolero," which is not difficult if you follow the rhythm without getting lost, because what changes is the instrumentation—the rhythm is carried by the timpani drums from beginning to end."[2]

A rather naive reviewer for the *Los Angeles Times* backed up Manuel Matos' account: "Carmen Amaya and her partner in the dance, Antonio Triana, and a company of gypsies entertained a large audience in Hollywood Bowl last night. The music was furnished by the orchestra conducted by

---

[1] García Matos. Reproduced in Hidalgo, p. 120.
[2] García Matos. Reproduced in Hidalgo, p. 120.

Manuel Matos. The change in conductors was made in order to facilitate the Spanish style of improvisation which Amaya exemplifies." *El Amor Brujo* was "colorful and remarkable, if limited in style." The company "danced many a fandango to cheers from the audience." "The abrupt, angular, and percussive school, which is known all over the world as Spanish dancing, was used throughout the evening." *"Goyescas,"* danced by the trio of Leonor, Lola Montes, and Antonia, "was not vivid enough for the Bowl." Finally:

> The footwork of Señor Triana in *"Zapateado"* by Sarasate was appreciated by the comparatively few who sat near the stage. Even Escudero, the greatest of them all, was not able to hold a Bowl audience in this type of solo work.
> Carmen Amaya danced the *"Inspiración"* by Granados with guitars accompanying. This raised the temperature to a white heat and the brilliant turns and vivid footwork which she displayed were loudly applauded. The program closed at a late hour with flamenco dances to popular music and they proved to be of the same character throughout. This colorful program in which the footwork is loudly amplified and the orchestra seems largely superfluous will be repeated this evening.[1]

Hurok, elated by the huge popular success of the Hollywood Bowl performances, asked Triana to repeat the program in New York. But the dancer, exhausted by the pressure of late-night rehearsals, backstage directing, and playing out the parts in the wings for the dancers to follow, declined the offer. He preferred to remain in California where he had established himself as a teacher and he and Lola were forming their own professional company with Jerónimo Villarino as guitarist. Hurok showed Matos his gratitude for saving the show by paying him one hundred dollars—while Stoloff received three thousand dollars for doing nothing!

The Amayas remained in Hollywood for some time, working in clubs and making films. El Chino bought a house in Hollywood, at 4955 Los Feliz Boulevard, that had formerly belonged to Diana Durbin. One source says that they paid $45,000, but Carmen claimed in an interview that it had cost $150,000. Goldberg describes it as "a beautiful old stucco California home with two stories around a central patio, a garage, and a big living room in what at that time was a very exclusive, private and quiet area..."[2] Lola Montes says they had no furniture and danced and ate on the bare floors.

Diego Castellón spoke about the Amaya homes:

> We were in New York for two years and then they bought a house

---

[1] Jones, Isabel Morse, "Carmen Amaya and Troupe Entertain Large Audience." *Los Angeles Times,* August 28, 1943.

[2] Goldberg, p. 247. Goldberg says this house was destroyed by fire in 1980.

in Long Island. Then we went to Hollywood on various occasions—for Carmen to make films. On one of the last occasions, in 1943, the father bought a house in Beverly Hills, where all the artists had their residences. There was a politician, a Nazi, who wanted to sell his house so that he could flee the country. So, a gentleman from Madrid who had been one of the great artists of silent film, Antonio Moreno [Carmen's co-star in *María de la O*], who admired Carmen very much and was a friend of the family, recommended to Carmen's father that he buy the house—a beautiful chalet in Beverly Hills that I think cost $88,000. So she had that one, which was smaller, and the one in Hollywood where the family stayed during most seasons.[1]

On January 4, 1944, Carmen opened her second season in La Conga. In March she danced her *alegrías* in the long-running show "Three Cheers for the Boys." Carmen would return often to dance in this benefit revue that raised money to aid wounded soldiers. Diego Castellón: "During the war they would have benefits for the military or the Red Cross, and there were artistic benefits with all of the artists of Hollywood. And Carmen was so famous that they also brought her into those shows...And she got to know all those famous people of Hollywood films...That group admired her more than anyone because of her great artistic capacity. And I met all those people through her, because I went with her many times and had many opportunities to get to know those people, those famous Hollywood stars."[2]

Carmen's generosity with young Spanish dancers is legendary. Two young Puerto Rican students of Lola Bravo, dancing under the names Roberto and Alicia, replaced Rosario and Antonio in the revue *Sons o' Fun* in Chicago. Carmen asked them to come to her dressing room at La Conga and complemented them. She suggested they adopt the name *"Los Trianeros,"* which they did. On another occasion a Spanish dancer from New York, Giovanni Rozzino, came to see her. She gave him a photo and signed it: "To the famous *bailaor* Giovanni Rozzino, a good friend. Carmen Amaya." Her handwriting—in Spanish of course—was flawless. Giovanni would be a mainstay of New York flamenco for many years.

Rosario and Antonio had left the show in Chicago, where they had been for a over a year, to return to New York for their first appearance in Carnegie Hall, on April 18. For that performance, Antonio brought his sister, Pastora Ruiz, over from Spain. She would remain in America and work with various dancers, including La Argentinita the following year.

Carmen appeared in at least two films in 1944. Most of the films she made in America were war-related, and many were just thinly plotted excuses to present celebrities in a series of vaudeville acts. Carmen was just one more

[1] Goldberg interviews.
[2] Goldberg interviews.

dance act. Various biographers have credited her with appearing in too many of these films, however. Some of those in which she does not appear include *Stage Door Canteen*, *Hollywood Canteen*, and *Hoorah for Hollywood*. She did perform, with Sabicas, in the United Artist film, *Knickerbocker Holiday*, directed by Harry Joe Brown and starring Nelson Eddy, Charles Coburn, and Shelly Winters.

The Universal Pictures film *Follow the Boys* can still be seen today. It stars George Raft and Vera Zorina, but is essentially a series of musical acts. The long list of performers includes Orson Wells, Marlene Dietrich, W.C. Fields, Artur Rubenstein, and Dinah Shore. The credits list Carmen as an equal of these stars, while a number of lesser artists, like Donald O'Connor, appear in smaller print. Carmen and her company entertain the troops in front of what is supposed to be a large mansion or government building in London. She dances *alegrías* in a gray *traje corto* (the traditional Spanish suit with high-waisted pants and short jacket). All of the sections of the dance had to be shortened to conform to her alloted time limit of something under two minutes.

Of great interest is the first filmed example of Carmen's *solo de pie* (footwork solo without guitar accompaniment). The guitarist Felix de Utrera has related the popular version of how this solo first came about: "One day, in the United States, [Carmen was] dancing *por alegrías*, doing the *escovilla* with the guitar, when Sabicas broke two strings. In order not to lose the number, Sabicas began to mark rhythm with his knuckles on the side of the guitar. And from that time it became the established norm."[1] The fact that Sabicas does not use his knuckles to beat out the rhythm in this film casts some doubt on Felix' account. The sisters keep the rhythm with their handclapping, but there is no sign of the strong three-count pulse that Carmen would exploit to the maximum in the future. Although it is hard to judge in this abbreviated example, it appears that Carmen had not yet fully developed the concept of this footwork solo. However, her mastery of footwork is clearly evident, as she fires off rapid combinations of ball-heel, toe.

The guitar playing in *Follow the Boys* is quite revealing. There are four guitarists: El Chino, Jerónimo Villarino, Paco, and Sabicas. While three of the guitarists concentrate on their accompaniment with deadpan expressions, the suave and exhibitionistic Sabicas puts on his own display of virtuosity. Ever the consumate showman and dressed in an elegant white *traje corto*, he grins, nods his head in approval, and makes grandiose flourishes with his right hand like a concert pianist, or strums back and forth along the strings from the bridge to halfway up the fingerboard. While the others play in A-major chords, he places the *cejilla* two frets higher and plays in G. In spite of some synchronized melodies, it is evident that the guitarists have not worked out their accompaniments in detail. During the *ida*—the formal end-

[1] *"Qué opina del estado actual del arte flamenco?" La Caña,* No 8/9. 1994.

ing sequence—Paco and Villarino play six beats in one chord and then six in a different chord, while El Chino plays only three beats in the first chord, then three in the second chord, and then repeats this sequence for the next six beats. The result is discordant and surprising, considering how long El Chino and Paco had played together.

Montañés described how Carmen came to appear in this film: "Orson Wells sees her perform in a cabaret and he jumps on the stage to offer her a contract... For doing one dance in the film, Orson Wells pays Carmen Amaya three times what he pays Marlene Dietrich, the star [actually, Marlene has only one very brief cameo appearance, so the difference in pay was not out of line]. Vera Zorina, who has a part in the film [she was the star], is the only one who protests the amount that Carmen Amaya was charging. Orson Wells kicks her out of the studios without offering any explanation."[1]

Montañés also described the mutual admiration that Carmen Amaya and Charlie Chaplin felt for each other:

> Charles Chaplin presents himself in Carmen's dressing room after her performance, and the only thing "Charlot" can do is to offer her his hands. "Charlot," emotional beyond words, looks into Carmen Amaya's eyes and it is the Spanish gypsy who begins to cry and says, "It was worth coming to America to meet you!"
>
> "Charlot" departs from the dressing room and reserves a table for every night that Carmen Amaya is performing. When they ask "Charlot" why he likes Carmen Amaya's dancing so much, he answers, "Just go see her!"[2]

Diego Castellón confirmed that Carmen became friendly with many of the Hollywood stars: "Here, there were many great artists who admired her very much, like one named Lana Turner, a very old-time artist. They would sit down together and have coffee, and they talked. I thought they didn't understand each other, because I often sat with them. But it turned out that they understood each other very well, because she spoke very good English. I said to myself, 'How can this woman be so smart to be speaking English in seven months [more like two years]?' What an ear!"[3]

In 1944 Argentinita began to have unexplained fevers. Her planned Carnegie Hall appearance in March had to be cancelled because of illness. In October of that year she danced Ravel's "Bolero" as guest artist with the Ballet Theater of the Metropolitan Opera House, and in February of 1945 per-

---
[1]Montañés, p. 35.
[2]Montañés, p. 35.
[3]Goldberg interviews.

formed in Carnegie Hall with Pilar, José Greco, and Manolo Vargas. At that time, José Greco noticed that her eyes had changed color and lost their luster. Her fevers came more often.

More problems arose when jealousies within the small dance company exploded into a fight between José and Argentinita's assistant. The police became involved and Sol Hurok insisted that Greco leave the company. Argentinita and José appeared together on stage for the last time in April, at the Metropolitan Opera House. *Dance Magazine* wrote: "The name José Greco is a comparatively new one in the dance world—but it is a name to watch. The handsome young man to whom it belongs came out of nowhere, it seemed, only a few years ago, and is now flashing across the horizon of the dance like a brilliant and exciting meteor."[1]

While José Greco attempted to put together his own company around a nucleus of himself and a dancer named Lucille Peters—to be renamed Nila Amparo by José and later become his wife—Argentinita was in and out of the Columbia Presbyterian Medical Center in New York all summer for tests. She had refused to stop performing, which proved to be her undoing. If she had not delayed treatment so long she might have been cured. Her friend Anton Dolin wrote: "Before many of her last performances, there she was sick with pain and fever, almost unable to move, lying flat on the floor. But she would not give up or fail her public. She was billed to dance and she would do so. For this was the great tradition that was her background. Her whole life was being spent in the giving of her art."[2]

Toward the end of the summer she felt sick while at a party in the home of a friend and had to be taken to the hospital. They operated immediately and found a malignant tumor in her stomach. A second operation and seventeen blood transfusions led to complications that finally took her life. On September 24, 1945, she awoke briefly from a coma that had lasted seventeen hours and died shortly afterward. She was forty-seven.

John Martin wrote of her: "Argentinita was much more than a Spanish dancer, though she was both dancer and Spanish to the core; she had taken the inherent multiformity of the Spanish dance and expanded it into a full and rounded theater art." Argentinita had almost single-handedly created the concept of the Spanish Ballet and molded its repertoire. Her legacy would be passed on by Vicente Escudero, Pilar López, Antonio Triana, José Greco, Manolo Vargas, and all of their many students.

---

[1] *Dance Magazine*. April 1945. p. 6.
[2] Dolin, Anton, "La Argentinita: A Tribute." *Dance*, November, 1945.

CHAPTER NINE

RETURN TO SPAIN

When Argentinita died, Spanish dance in the United States appeared to die with her. The six-year frenzy was over and press coverage became almost nonexistent, not to revive until some ten years later. The death of the most famous and influential Spanish dancer the world had known coincided with the end of World War II and perhaps the public no longer had the same need for distraction. Dancers who had been living in forced exile were free to return to their homelands or tour internationally. Among the first to do so was Pilar López. But first she had to see to the completion of a statue she had commissioned from the sculptor Rosario Murabito. The likeness of Argentinita would be put on permanent display by the Metropolitan Opera Guild the following year.

In December, 1945, Pilar and José Greco accompanied Argentinita's body to Spain. There, in Madrid's Teatro Español, 25,000 people filed by the coffin. After ceremonies in which the dancer was postumously awarded the "Order of Alfonso the Wise" and the "Garland of Isabella the Catholic," a procession filed to the San Isidro Cemetery, where the body was placed in an elegant pantheon adorned by a copy of the Murabito statue.

The following June, "Pilar López and her Ballet Español," with José Greco, gave its first performance, in the Fontalba Theater in Madrid. Their guitarists were Ramón Montoya, Niño Pérez, and Luis Maravilla. Pastora Imperio came out of semi-retirement to dance in these performances with the veteran *bailaor* Rafael Ortega. For the next two years the company would tour Spain with resounding success.

Judged by press coverage, Spanish dance seemed to have disappeared in America. But as a matter of fact, it persisted, unheralded and on a smaller scale. In Los Angeles, Antonio Triana and Lola Montes continued to teach and perform—although they had divorced and now did so separately. Triana was partnered by his talented young daughter, Luisa. Roberto and Alicia, "Los Trianeros," continued to be active. Federico Rey performed with La Meri. Rozzino teamed up with Antonio's sister, Pastora Ruiz, for a time before forming "Los Rossilianos." Later he would tour with Rosario and Antonio—who alternated tours of the United States with travels to Mexico and South America.

Carlos Montoya, on his own after the death of Argentinita, performed around New York. He accompanied local dancers, including his wife, but usually managed to slip in a few solo numbers. His solos were called "richly vibrant" in appearances with María Teresa Acuna, a former dancer with Los Chavalillos. Only a couple of years later Carlos would take the first steps toward liberating himself from the role of accompanist:

> In early 1948, she [Sally Montoya] placed ads in the *New York Times* for Montoya's first solo recital in a friend's studio apartment. "He had never given solos before," Mrs. Montoya explained, "because it never occurred to him. No one would want to sit and listen to a concert of flamenco...But he could embroider the rhythms of the dancer and the melodies of the singer..." And, on a cold February evening, 100 people—mostly friends—packed the apartment to hear Carlos Montoya play alone. Then, 300 people came to another apartment for a second recital, 400 came to hear him at Carnegie Hall, 700 people came to Kaufmann Concert Hall. "Then," Mrs. Montoya said, "we met a man named Art D'Lugoff. That was the beginning of fame."[1]

Carmen Amaya made another film in 1945. *See My Lawyer*, from Universal Pictures, was little more than an excuse for a parade of variety acts and was the last film to feature the comedy team of Ole Olsen and Chic Johnson (originators of *Sons o'Fun*).

In April, after almost four years of non-stop dancing in the United States, Carmen, "tired of hearing so much English,"[2] took her company and family to Mexico. After a concert in Mexico City, the press wrote, "The spectacular performance of Carmen Amaya in Mexico constitutes a complete success." It was in Mexico that Carmen first performed the *"Malagueña"* of the Cuban composer Ernesto Lecuona.

Carmen appeared in a number of Mexican motion pictures. In 1945 it was *Pasión Gitana*, in which she danced and sang a song called *"La bien pagá."* Goldberg cites another, entitled *Los Amores de un Torero-La Luna Enamorada* and released by Columbia Pictures. Sometime earlier Carmen had appeared in at least two other Mexican films: *Seda, Sangre, y Sol* (also called *Sangre Torera*) was a bullfight melodrama, while *Maravillas del Torero* featured the matador Gaona.

In his many interviews through the years, Sabicas always maintained that he went to Mexico with Carmen in 1945 and then she returned to Spain. But Carmen would not return to Spain for two more years, after extensive tours of South America without Sabicas. It is clear that tensions between Sabicas and the Amaya family came to a head in Mexico. In spite of the reluctance on the part of Sabicas or anyone close to him to speak of this matter, the

---

[1] Soper, Susan, "Carlos Montoya: His Heart is in His Hands." *Newsday*, September 21, 1975.
[2] Goldberg, p. 249

guitarist did hint at the problem on a few occasions:

> During his first trip to North America he had his idyll with Carmen Amaya, perhaps one of his greatest loves, although the maestro won't be very specific about that: *"Bueno, mire usted,* it must have been one of those childish things, because nothing ever came of it. We were good friends...we were together for a few years and then I stayed in Mexico and she came back here to Europe."[1]
>
> "Despite what you may think, I was not in love with her. I love women in general. I love every woman. And I loved Carmen's genius. But I did not love Carmen. She wanted to marry me, but I wouldn't do that. And besides, I couldn't take that family any longer!"
>
> —Did Carmen love Sabicas?
>
> "Yes, I think so, yes...What a life!"
>
> —He became painfully quiet.[2]

Sabicas was quite candid in some of his remarks to Mona Molarsky: "[I was with her]...until 1945, for eight years. I didn't want to give her any problems. She, the poor thing, already had enough with her family...She was always at home. If she ever went out, it was with her father or brother...I didn't want to make a big deal out of it. I didn't want to get angry, because it would have been a bitter experience for all of us. Finally, I said, 'I can't take it any longer. It's all over!' While we were in Mexico it all ended."[3]

Sabicas must have been truly frustrated in his relationship with Carmen. He remained an outsider, with the family controlling his fiancée's every move. Sabicas' brother, Diego, hinted at the stormy relationship when he said, "We used to go to the garden of the museum on 49th Street during the war, for benefits for the soldiers. Lana Turner, Gary Cooper, Myrna Loy, Charles Boyer, were all there. I used to go with Carmen, because her older brother, Paco, who played very well, drank a lot. She was always fighting with her boyfriend, and she would say to me, 'You're the only one I can go with, because Sabicas makes me suffer so!'"[4]

The fights between Carmen and Sabicas were legendary. It is said that when they fought on stage in Mexico City, Carmen stormed off and cancelled the show. It may have been just such a scene that brought about the breakup. It also appears that Sabicas had tired of the constant touring. He told Mona Molarsky: "We worked for five years without stopping, from

---

[1] Caballero, Angel Alvarez, "Today, 80% of What is Being Played throughout the World is Mine." *El País,* July 7, 1984.

[2] Molarsky, p. 7.

[3] Molarsky interview.

[4] Goldberg interviews.

forty-nine to fifty-two weeks each year. The year we worked the least, we worked forty-nine weeks. I was exhausted. I was smoking three packs a day. I ate when I could, I slept when I could."[1] Sabicas felt a need to settle in one place. He would remain in Mexico for ten years, marry a Mexican woman, and have two children.

Luisa Triana shared some of her experiences with Sabicas while she and her father were in Mexico City in the late 1940s:

> Sabicas used to come into El Patio almost nightly—I was working there with my father. After the show, a rather elite group of writers and a mixed assortment of artists gathered in *tertulias* in the Cafeteria of the Prado Hotel, with much reminiscing about Spain and the Civil War, and much lamenting about how flamenco was changing and in danger of disappearing.
>
> Sabicas had a sense of humor. He enjoyed telling jokes, and people marveled at how he never ran out of material. My father was a good story teller, but could not keep up with Sabicas' one-liners. He also amazed us by playing music on a three or four-inch match box with a rubber band. You could actually identify the melody of the *"Capriccio espagnol!"* [Luisa was not the only one to witness this feat—it was one of Sabicas' favorite tricks.]
>
> We performed at a benefit together, and I will never forget the presence and sound of his guitar. He was so perceptive to the dancer's timing.[2]

While Sabicas set out to make a life for himself in Mexico, Carmen left for Argentina. The Amayas returned to the city that had launched their American odyssey. By early September they were performing in the Avenida Theater in Buenos Aires. Then Carmen sprained her ankle and had to stay off her foot for several days. She explained to the newspaper:

> —How is that foot?
>
> "Very good. It's amazing what science can do. It is hard to believe that shortwave, which up until now I thought was only good for radios, is good for fixing dancer's feet...Happily, the doctor has told me that, in spite of my stature, *estoy de alta* [a play on words, meaning 'I'm tall' and 'I'm much improved'], and we will see if I can please the public once again. *Mire usted*, it is idiotic that we dancers have to suffer in our *pinreles* [gypsy word for 'feet']. *Bueno*, it is always the same: singers suffer in their throats and those who dance, the other end. More than anything, what makes me angry is the way this happened, what the doctors call a sprain or something like that.

---

[1] Molarsky interview.
[2] Personal correspondence, 1998.

"As you know, on that black Saturday, as I was coming out to dance the last part of *'Romance de bandidos en Sierra Morena,'* I had to come down by way of a platform located behind the branch of a fallen tree. It was prophetic—the fallen tree was me. When I reached the stage floor, I twisted my foot, producing such pain that I could only limp toward the wing, without attempting to continue dancing. There, one of my comrades just grabbed my foot and, with a strong blow that crunched all my bones, put my ankle back where it belonged. I thought that it had not been completely fixed, and while I complained of the pain, the dancer Miguel Herrero, under orders of the management, had gone forward to the footlights to explain to the audience that I could not continue dancing due to the accident that I had just suffered.

"The audience seemed resigned, but not me...Have you ever seen a goring in a bullfight? Well, that's what happened to me...I just came from Mexico, where Garza, *El Soldado*, Pepe Luis Vázquez, Rafaelillo, Rafael Ortega, Silverio Pérez, and others dedicated magnificent demonstrations of skill to my eyes on many afternoons. What happened to me on that infamous Saturday was that I had a bad bullfight, and even though I am not a bullfighter, like a very good countrywoman of mine who is there in Mexico, I am a gypsy. And, with the genius that the pharoah has given me, I couldn't quit...When a proud matador is wounded by the bull, if he hasn't lost too much blood, he returns to the ring and takes charge of the bull he had been assigned.

"The same thing happened to me. When I saw that what had happened to my foot was of little consequence, I escaped with dignity from the infirmary, just like the bullfighters, and returned to the ring. And, while Herrero was resigning the audience to the situation, I was repeating the phrase used by Curro Cúchares on many afternoons: 'Everybody out of the way!' and I signaled the maestro for the orchestra to return to the attack. The rest of the story you know or can guess: when the moment was past I found out the good part...Dear mother! What pain! Above all, the next day when I tried to get out of bed."

—We began to smoke and I offered her the pack, which she rejected:

"I'll dance all you want, but smoke—that's for the men..."

—Have you had a similar mishap before?

"When I was very young. When I was ten years old. Now I'm twenty-four [subtracting twelve years from her age]. It was in Barcelona, in the Romea Theater. I danced last and I was also working in Villa Rosa. Since I didn't have much time, I was always in a rush. When I reached the door of the theater, I jumped to avoid a puddle and twisted my foot. This shortwave wasn't known then...I was in bed for two months—I was hit with chicken pox at the same time..."

—On saying goodbye, the dancer said to us: "I hope to show the public my gratitude by dancing with all my enthusiasm and, in that way, repay the affection that Buenos Aires professes for me; especially when some witty fellow, who must have been a gypsy, came to the box office of the Avenida to ask for a seat near the stage, and they told him that for some days to come there were only tickets available from the fifteenth row back. This *gracia* came out of him: 'Can you sell me an orchestra seat in the fourth row to see Carmen Amaya sometime in the next three months?'..."[1]

Pepe Marchena arrived in Buenos Aires and was photographed with Carmen Amaya and Conchita Piquer on October 1, 1945. Marchena began in the *colmao* El Tronío and appeared on the radio every Thursday and Sunday, singing and explaining the *cante*. On November 20, he joined Carmen and Conchita in the Avenida Theater, in a musical comedy called *Feria de Sevilla*, written by Pascual Guillén and Gerardo Ribas. Later, they would do others like *Colores Andaluces* and *Sacromonte de Granada*.

Marchena had not changed his ways. As pompous as ever, he told the newspaper *Atena*: "I, who live dreaming of giving the *cante jondo* its most pure and severe expression, that which brings me closest to it in flesh and spirit, I who suffer it like a tear in my soul, have understood the pain of the *tango* [Argentine]... And I have approached it with the emotion of a beginner. Perhaps that is why it has taken such a hold on my soul. Perhaps that is why I am so comfortable in this city that sometimes seems like a piece of my Spain dressed in cosmopolitanism, such is its enthusiasm for things from there."[2]

For Carmen's thirty-second birthday Marchena sent her a mahogany furniture piece, two of its drawers filled with chocolates and a third with lottery tickets. Carmen would say of Pepe, "Marchena, pharoah of the *cante*, deserves to be a gypsy!"

In January of 1946, Marchena took his show, with the well-known singer Jesús Perosanz, Chato de Valencia, and Faíco, to Montevideo, Uruguay. The Amayas couldn't go because they had to perform in Rio de Janeiro, but they would go to Montevideo later, in March. Marchena returned to Spain in April to record a number of South American songs. It is likely that Carmen, influenced by Marchena and her surroundings, began to include Latin flavored songs in her repertoire at that time. She began to sing the *colombianas*

[1] *La Nación*, September 19, 1945. Reproduced in Bois, p. 109.
[2] Cobo, p. 98.

of Marchena and *"Cuando pa Chile me voy,"* which she sang and danced *por bulerías*. Carmen Amaya was now an international star and her name filled theaters. She couldn't possibly fullfill all of the contracts offered her. The company toured throughout South America, Cuba, and Mexico in 1946. They were in Peru in September, where twelve-year-old Toño Portuguez found himself warmly welcomed into Carmen's dressing room. He would never forget her kindness or her religious shrine, made up of statues, pictures, and candles. When he saw her again sixteen years later, she still had that shrine in her dressing room and he found that she had not changed. On that second occasion, she embraced him and said, "You are one of us, you have *nervio* [nerve, strength, toughness]." Toño described the special quality she had of listening and making you feel like she cared, even with a casual acquaintance.[1]

A photo of Carmen in her dressing room taken a few years later showed her shrine to be an elaborate display of religious icons, photos, candles, and flowers. She felt a special devotion to the Virgen de la Angustias, the venerated Virgin Mary of Granada, whose picture figured prominently in her shrine. In an interview, Carmen said, "I always have her with me. She is my guide and my hope, my salvation." The director of the Champs Elysées Theater would say about Carmen: "She was very religious and prayed every night. Before her performances she spent long hours alone and quiet in her dressing room, taking refuge in her religious objects. Carmen was purity itself."[2] Carmen would need her religious strength in 1946, for that year was not to be without grief: José Amaya "El Chino," the patriarch of the clan, died of throat cancer in Argentina.

Although her brother would continue to play a leadership role, especially when it came to business negotiations, the family would lean on Carmen more than ever for strength and guidance. One of her first moves was to incorporate more non-family members into the company. In Mexico she found nineteen-year-old Luis Pérez Dávila, a classically trained dancer who had been inspired to learn Spanish dance by seeing Carmen Amaya some eight years earlier. Luis, known ever-after as Luisillo, brought along his seventeen-year-old dance partner, New York born Teresita Viera Romero. Luisillo and Teresa had a number, *"El Relicario,"* originally popularized by Raquel Meller, that never failed to bring the house down. According to biographer Mario Bois, one night after this number had gone over unusually well, Carmen announced that she would like to dance it. Luisillo and Teresa didn't dance it again.[3]

While the Amayas crisscrossed the Americas, rumors of Carmen Amaya

---
[1] Personal conversation.
[2] Gabriel Dussurget, in Bois, p. 125.
[3] Bois, p. 57.

had begun to circulate in Europe. The newspapers wrote at length of her exploits in America. When El Pelao returned to Spain in 1946 to enjoy a fleeting moment of fame, he brought with him fifty suits for his children and spoke of the millions that Carmen had earned in the United States, the impressive Packard that she drove, the $70,000 home she had in New York, and the home in Hollywood that she had purchased from Diana Durbin for $150,000. People's imaginations took it from there. As one biographer put it, "from that time on, her biography and her legend became one and the same."[1]

In France, people saw her pictures in the magazines:

> One impresario remembers: "This is the gypsy woman who performed some years ago with Raquel [Meller]."
>
> Paris needed, during that postwar period, strong shows, with "vedettes" to attract people to the theaters...
>
> The French impresarios spend hundreds of *francs* on long-distance telephone calls and telegrams in an attempt to locate Carmen in the Americas. Nobody can account for her.[2]

The sister of Fernand Lumbroso, one of the most important agents in Paris, gave the details:

> In 1945, in Paris, Fernand thought about Carmen Amaya. "If I could get her to come to Paris? I'm sure it would be a success." It would be a risk, but he had to try. Where could she be? For some nine years she had been somewhere in America. Fernand sent a mountain of telegrams saying "I'm an agent and I want to present her in Paris" to Hurok, to New York, to Hollywood, to Mexico, to Buenos Aires.
>
> For the next two years there was no answer, nothing, until one day, at the beginning of 1948, a little gypsy dressed in black appeared unannounced in Fernand's office with four telegrams in his hand. It was Carmen's brother, Paco, the guitarist and "businessman." He could hardly write. They went to dinner together and the evening stretched until four in the morning, ending in a preliminary agreement signed on the tablecloth. The group would get a percentage and Fernand was charged with renting the Théâtre des Champs Elysées.[3]

Paco returned to Madrid, where the family was living in the flat they had purchased before the war. They had returned to Spain in early 1947. Certainly the loss of Sabicas and her father must have played a part in Carmen's decision to return home. She had been away for more than ten years. It is also possible that she had heard of the great success that Pilar

[1]Hidalgo, p. 129.
[2]Montañés, p. 38.
[3]Bois, p. 118.

López was enjoying in the aftermath of her opening in the Teatro Fontalba in June of 1946. Carmen must have felt the urge to make her mark in Spain. The Amayas lost no time. They appeared in the Teatro Madrid in a production called *Embrujo Español*. The *cantaor* Antonio Mairena went to see her. He recalled:

> I went to greet Carmen and was talking with her in her dressing room. She was happy to see me and asked me where I had been, since she had tried unsuccessfully to find me so that I could work in her company. She missed me a great deal and had sent a mutual acquaintance to Sevilla to try to find me. But instead of calling me as Carmen wished, and in spite of the fact that I was in Sevilla, this intermediary sent a different *cantaor* who, of course, was not suitable and had to be dismissed by Carmen. I was infuriated by what she told me, but at the same time it gave me satisfaction to know that she still remembered me.
>
> Carmen asked me if I would like to work with her during the two months she was going to perform in the Teatro Fuencarral. I accepted and was with her for that time. The dance of Carmen Amaya was a lot of dance for the public that rushed to fill the theater, a public unprepared to fully grasp the genius of that extraordinary *bailaora*—and she realized it. Nevertheless, the success was great every day, especially for the blacksmith number that had the poem from the *Romancero Gitano* by García Lorca, "*Romance de la Luna*," set to *cante* and *baile*. I appeared on stage in a blacksmith's shop while the reciter, Juan José, began to say the verses:
>
> | | |
> |---|---|
> | *La luna vino a la fragua* | The moon came to the forge |
> | *con su polisón de nardos.* | with her petticoat and stays. |
> | *El niño la mira, mira;* | The child looks at her, looks; |
> | *el niño la está mirando...* | the child is looking at her... |
>
> The *romance* continues until it reaches the part that says:
>
> | | |
> |---|---|
> | *Huye luna, luna, luna!* | Flee moon, moon, moon! |
> | *Si vinieran los gitanos,* | If the gypsies come, |
> | *harían con tu corazón* | they will make your heart into |
> | *collares y anillos blancos.* | white necklaces and rings. |
>
> And in that moment, symbolizing the moon, Carmen Amaya appeared in her white train dress and I sang *soleá* for her as she danced. I continued with more verses and *cantes*, while she danced around me—saying at times, "*Qué lástima de cante de baile! Qué lástima de cante y baile!* [roughly: What unbelievable song and dance!]"
>
> This forge number was a big hit. While I sang, she turned on her

left foot, slowly wrapping her very long train about her until it was completely wound around her—all with that unequaled art that she had. Then she made a sudden movement, sending the end of the train flying. Finally, I closed the *cante* as she was speeding up the dance, doing *desplantes* and moving that long train:

Yo te quería,	I used to love you,
ya no te quiero.	but now I don't want you.
Tengo en mi casa	I have new merchandise
géneros nuevos.	in my house.

Before the two months had passed at the Fuencarral, we had agreed that I would accompany her to Paris. I was thinking about the great future I could have with that extraordinary artist, when my dreams went up in smoke due to circumstances that I prefer not to explain. Powerful family reasons made it so that Carmen found herself practically obligated to take with her the *cantaor* Chiquito de Triana in place of me. So I had to stay in Spain. Destiny decided that the *baile* of Carmen Amaya and the *cante* of Antonio Mairena were not to be united this time either. And it was a shame, because Carmen was a brilliant *bailaora* who was delighted and danced fabulously when I sang for her.[1]

Luis Algaba "Chiquito de Triana," a twenty-seven year-old singer from Sevilla, had become engaged to Antonia Amaya. They would soon marry and Luis would be the singer for the Amaya company for a number of years. There seemed to be a subtle stirring as Spanish dance looked to its roots for inspiration. Both Pilar López and Carmen Amaya had begun to give flamenco a little more prominence in their programs, and for the first time in more than a decade they were using flamenco singers to accompany their dances.

In October, the Amaya company went south to Sevilla. The press wrote:

When the figure of Carmen Amaya appeared on stage she had to stop the first steps of her dance while the audience paid tribute to her with a great ovation...Carmen, after so many years, unperturbed by the exotic influences of her expatriation, returns a pure gypsy, with absolutely no signs of contamination or adulteration. Last night she danced in her dizzying style, with its sudden flamenco stops, revealing the rich sentimental venom of her gypsy race, the exuberance of her strong temperament, and the rhythmic testament of the inner fire that consumes her. Her tiny figure of bronze, with the magic breath of inspiration from the pharoahs vibrating in her heelwork, in the silhouette of her arms, and in the

---
[1]Mairena, p. 123.

snapping of her fingers, gave us a warm exhibition of her mastery and the untiring ease of her execution... Along with the group, a magnificent couple stood out, the Mexicans, Teresita Viera and Luisillo Dávila.[1]

Carmen was interviewed after the performance:

"*Ay, Sevilla, Sevilla de mi alma!* As soon as I finish my contracts in America I'm going to sell everything I own there and come here immediately, buy a *cortijo* [country home; ranch house] near here, and never leave Sevilla for anything."

—You have to go again?

"*Sí, hijo*, I have no choice. I may have escaped, but I continually receive telegrams telling me to go back. I have to fulfill some contracts that I signed in Hollywood."

—When do you go?

"When I finish this lightning tour that I am doing through Spain—within eight months."

—Tell me something: How much money did you earn in America?

"*Ay, mi vía*, I don't know! A lot, so much that I don't have it in my head. I have three homes there: One in New York, that cost me sixty thousand dollars; another in Hollywood, that I bought from Diana Durbin for one hundred and fifty thousand dollars, and a third in Buenos Aires that is valued at more than two hundred thousand Argentine *pesos*."

—What was the hardest thing to achieve in America?

"Learning English. *Ay*, in the beginning! For two months we had nothing to eat but ham and eggs. It was the only thing we knew how to ask for. My poor brothers and sisters—they turned yellow..."

—There are six of you, if I am not mistaken.

"Exactly, four women and two men."

—Since you don't want to tell me what you earned in America, tell me how much you have earned since you returned to Spain?

"In Madrid, where I just came from, I have made a million *pesetas*."

—That's not bad.

"*Sí, hijo*, but it cost more than a million just to put on the show."

—But...how about what you will save now?

"Let's not exaggerate!"

—What do think of Sevilla?

"It is more beautiful and more lovely than ever! It seems like a

[1] *ABC of Sevilla*, October 24, 1947. Reproduced in Bois, p. 177.

dream to find myself here. I will live in Sevilla the rest of my life."
—Were you fearful tonight?
"No! Fearful, no. Respectful, yes. A lot of respect for the public, which is not the same thing. This is the birthplace of my art. This is where I had to triumph, and where I wanted to triumph."
—Are you happy?
"Happy is not the word for it. I wouldn't trade this night for all the successes that I have had in my life. Say that...be sure to say that!"[1]

The time for the proposed April concerts in Paris was approaching. The sister of Fernand Lumbroso related the events leading up to it:

A month before the debut, Paco lets Fernand know, from Spain, that "there are difficulties" with their crossing the border. Fernand sends them a collective passport. Ten days later Paco cancels the contract. Carmen is in the hospital for an emergency operation. Fernand has already rented the theater. He goes to Barcelona and takes a room in the Hotel Oriente, where the [Amaya] group is staying. They take him to the clinic. Carmen pulls back the sheet and shows her abdomen and wound. What to do? Carmen has the solution. She will go to Paris and dance even if it has to be with a fresh scar.

And that is how it was. A few days later the company took the train, but as soon as they crossed the border they demanded to be allowed to remain in Port Bou to rehearse. They hadn't rehearsed the show. They were forty people in all: twenty-four family members and sixteen more, among whom were the young soloists Teresa and Luisillo. The Amayas included Carmen's brothers and sisters—among whom Antonio, a fantastic dancer, stood out—the aunt, La Faraona, the imposing personality of Micaela, the mother (who kept all their money in her apron), and the grandfather, the eighty-year-old father of El Chino. Carmen took care of all of them with infinite tenderness.

The morning of their arrival we went to wait for them at the Austerlitz Station. Who was in charge? Nobody. And the debut was that very night! Carmen spent the whole day in the theater attending to everything—lights, scenery, costumes. That night... all of Paris, those of interest to the press, were there...Carmen came out on stage and was like a storm; it was the triumph of one of those who define an era. The following days, the ticket lines reached all the way to the Place de l'Alma. Fernand had rented the theater for a week, but he had to extend the contract for a month

[1] Hidalgo, p. 138.

more, and then another. Later, they did a tour of all of France, London, and Switzerland.[1]

The press was exuberant in its praise. The Paris *Opéra* wrote: "Carmen Amaya has an almost diabolical power over the spectators in the Théâtre des Champs Elysées. She appears on stage with her company and, instantly, the stage floor begins to spit forth flames; the audience, which is normally apathetic, becomes inflamed and involved in the show...Throughout the performance, lovers of the dance never stop applauding and stamp their feet in time to the music on stage; the room inspires the dancers, and the dancers reciprocate by dancing better each time."[2]

Apparently the *"Olés"* began at the first number and didn't stop, and hats were thrown on stage like at a bullfight. Another account described "...the powerful sensuality of La Faraona [probably between fifty-five and sixty years old], the guitar of Paco, the youthful bravado of Antonia, Leonor, Antonio, and all of the Amayas. Above all, her, Carmen. Her power of attraction is not so much physical as it is the result of the ardor that seems to devour her. She is like a flame, she sings with a voice that embraces and woos you, sometimes ironic, other times caressing, or violent."[3]

In *Revue de la Dance*, No. 5 (April, 1948), Jean Silvant gave a description of some of Carmen's program:

...To the broken and reinvented chords of "Dance No. 5" by Granados, [Carmen] made her surprising entrance, her teeth clenched in rapture—the rapture of the dance, the sacred fever that she spread to all of the spectators, who were possessed by her rapture...

Shortly after, Teresa and Luisillo come on stage to dance a *malagueña*. The two dress in white and remind us of a volcano in the snow, a cyclone of complete purity, and then the sorceress returns to the stage to interpret the "Bolero" of Ravel. Her presence erases from memory all previous choreographies and gives a new vision of the work of Ravel. In this dance, which little by little becomes frenetic, Carmen Amaya bewitches the audience, as well as the dancers that accompany her...

Luisillo appears again to dance the *"Danza del molinero"* by Falla. He is such an extraordinary dancer that when he finishes the piece, the whole audience, delirious with emotion, rises to its feet to applaud him and the applause appears to break his neck when he bows his head in appreciation. But the star of the show is Carmen Amaya, provocative at times, as when she improvises a

[1] Bois, p. 118.
[2] Fabre-Le Bret, Robert, *Opéra*, Paris, April 28, 1948.
[3] Warnod, André, *Le Figaro*, April 29, 1948.

colombianas and sings in a rough voice. With the strength of a man, like a bullfighter faced with death, she interprets the *fandango* that closes that unforgettable show, one of the most intense nights Paris has known...

In this and subsequent stays in Paris, the Amayas led an extravagant and colorful life. The forty members of the company and family ate in the most exclusive restaurants, where Carmen paid for everyone, including friends and reporters. They stayed in the best hotels—the Plaza Athénée, the Ritz, the George V. One reporter gave the following account: "The neighbors in the adjacent hotel rooms are frightened. The doors that lead to the hallways are always open; the children never stop yelling; the men strum their guitars; the women sing while they sew and suckle their children. The floors are strewn with rags, the beds are unmade, and the floor is invaded by the strong odor of fried sardines, pepper omelletes, and stew. Because, the tribe always carries with it a grill, frying pans, and copper pots to make their daily meals in their rooms or in the dressing rooms of the theater."[1]

The daughter of Carmen's agent in France during later tours described the family: "In the beginning they stayed in the best hotels, but more and more often they were asked to leave, and it was Carmen herself who had to seek out third-class hotels for her people. What can I tell you? There was no way they could get used to the steak and potatoes of Paris. Carmen's mother made the *olla gitana*, a type of stew. She cooked, improvising a fire in the bathtub, lighting some small sticks and going at it."[2]

Another reporter wrote: "Carmen was always surrounded by her family; a world in itself that traveled and lived like a tribe; they could be seen wandering through the neighborhood of Montaigne, some dressed in luxurious furs, others in multicolored clothing..."

Gabriel Dussurget, who had helped Fernand Lumbroso bring Carmen to Paris, told Mario Bois:

> When we presented her in Paris, we had to pay her a lot: a million *francs* a night for the company. It was a great deal at that time. One day we accompanied her to the station. The tribe was agitated because some jewels that Carmen was keeping in a handkerchief had disappeared. Carmen was unconcerned and said to me, "Maybe I will have to go back to making baskets, like when I was a child!"
>
> ...On one occasion I saw her stop to contemplate with admiration a splendid white car, a Hotchkiss. At that moment she began to cry, "I want that car!" We found the owner, Carmen paid cash, and a few weeks later, when she left Paris to perform elsewhere, she just left the car parked in the street. Another time, when she

---

[1] Sirvin, René, *L'Aurore*, November 1973. Reproduced in Bois, p. 211.
[2] Souplet, Maruja, in conversation with Mario Bois. Bois, p. 115.

was staying in the Hotel George V, I saw her seated on a sidewalk bench, dressed in a mink coat and eating her breakfast, a herring sandwich. When she saw me, she directed her gaze to the hotel and said, "You know something? These things are not made for me!" Carmen used the mink coat as a bathrobe.

According to Montañés, Carmen paid a price for her high lifestyle:

> For those six months, Carmen had been the highest paid artist in Paris. When the contract ended, the company pooled its money. They had 3,700 *pesetas* [c. $60] between them! Twenty-some people eating in the most expensive restaurants in Paris, the Club des Champs Elysées, partially explained the sorry state of the company's funds. London offered a contract. Carmen answered with a telegram saying: "We're coming. Send money or tickets."
>
> Many years later, Carmen would say on Spanish radio, "You see, although it seems impossible, it is the English, as phlegmatic as they are, who give the most applause to a Spanish artist. England is where they best understand flamenco.[1]

In June, the Amayas performed in London's Prince's Theatre. One reviewer lamented the absence of authentic flamenco and felt that the inclusion of music by Ravel and Rimsky-Korsakoff was unjustified. He also was disconcerted by the sight of women wearing pants, feeling that this should have been an affront to their gypsy race. The British dance critics could be quite analytical and demanding. When Carmen returned to the Prince's Theatre exactly one year later, Arnold Haskell wrote:

> The critic might easily tear holes in this production. He might say that it belonged in the music-hall, that the music of Ravel and others was murdered, and so on. He would be right in all his strictures and at the same time he would be completely blind and more cold-blooded than any critic has a right to be. Here is dancing of tremendous technical skill and vitality, here is something that is completely honest and unpretentious.
>
> Carmen Amaya herself is a tremendous personality whether she is dancing, clowning, or merely taking a call with that wide smile of sheer pleasure that is so warming. She is not, I feel, the best dancer in the troupe, though the dance with the train [*"La Fragua"*—the *soleares* she had done with Mairena] is a jewel. Among the gypsies, the older and plumper La Faraona showed the most consummate artistry of all. When she danced, the rather tawdry scenery became Granada, the limes its burning sunshine. Every movement was per-

---

[1]Montañés, p. 39.

fection. The sensational dancers, and they could rouse any audience outside of a mortuary to a frenzy of excitement, were the Mexicans, Teresa and Luisillo. His combination of fire, rhythm, and absolutely classical precision are altogether incredible. This is something quite distinct from gypsy dancing, something more at home on the stage and not requiring the intimate collaboration of an audience. Yes, this belongs in the music-hall or cabaret. It has moments of incredible banality, but so long as I can be certain of seeing it again, I will not grumble.[1]

While Carmen toured Europe, Pilar López and José Greco were having problems back in Spain. The two dancers had fought over the name of the company from the beginning. José felt it should be "Pilar López and José Greco and their Spanish Ballet." Pilar insisted that it was *her* company. Their relationship deteriorated and, in the spring of 1948, José decided to go it alone. To form the nucleus of his new company he brought Carola Goya from America, along with his wife's brother, who danced under the name Luis Olivares. During most of the summer and fall, members of the company collaborated in the making of the film *Manolete* (a year after the death of the great matador). José danced in the movie to the playing of Pilar's guitarist, Luis Maravilla. When filming finished, Greco added some of the artists from the film to his company, including the gypsy *cantaor* Rafael Romero. His guitarist was Mario Escudero. Pilar López hired Manolo Manzanilla—another singer from the film—and replaced José with a Mexican dancer named Roberto Ximénez.

A two-week contract for Barcelona in January of 1949 was to serve as a warm-up for a debut by the Greco company in Paris and a later tour of Scandanavia. Unfortunately, things didn't go well in Barcelona. Audiences were sparce and reviews critical of José's audacity to perform in Spain after abandoning Pilar López. The press printed a series of negative exchanges between José and Vicente Escudero—then living in Barcelona and dedicating himself to painting. To top off these difficulties, Greco began to run out of money. In Paris, his problems multiplied. A number of his artists, grumbling about their pay, deserted him and joined Carmen Amaya, who was in Paris for her second season. Among these were the guitarist Mario Escudero, and two male dancers, Tomás Marco and Agustín de Triana.

Greco hastily assembled and trained a new company. Then disaster. Only days before the opening the new company leader was informed that he could not perform one of his most important numbers, Ravel's "Bolero." According to Greco, Pilar López owned the rights to perform it in France. Cleverly, José had his musical director change the melody without altering

[1] Haskell, Arnold L., *The Ballet Annual, 1949.* Adam and Charles Black, London. p. 29.

the underlying rhythmic structure, and they were able to dance the number. From those first concerts in Paris, the Greco Company would enjoy increasing success and a prominence that would endure for more than twenty years.

Both Carmen's company and the Amaya family added new members. Antonia had married the company singer, Chiquito de Triana, and they already had their first baby—Carmen "Chuny" Algaba Amaya. Antonio, perhaps in his early twenties, would marry the actress/*cupletista* Pepita Llaser, who was traveling with the company at the time and had to be at least twenty years his senior. And Mario Escudero began to court the youngest Amaya sister, María, who had begun to perform with the company. If María were "twenty-something" years younger than Carmen, as has been suggested by Goldberg, it is likely that she was about sixteen at the time. Luisa Triana said that she used to play with María when they were children and that the gypsy seemed a little older than she. Luisa was born in 1932, so María could have been seventeen or even eighteen.

The company would be further expanded toward the end of the year when they were joined by twenty-seven-year-old Rosa Durán, a dancer descended from a long line of flamencos from Jerez. She had been adopted by the great *cantaora* Isabelita de Jerez and another singer, José Durán, whom Rosa later married. Rosita began her dance studies in Madrid with Maestro Angel Pericet and made her debut with his company in the 1935 fundraiser for Fernando de Triana's book. Her most important teacher would be El Estampío. The Amayas called her *La Blanca* (the White One).

Both José Greco and Carmen Amaya were adding more flamenco to their programming, while maintaining the strong presence of Argentinita's choreographies. Back in Spain, Pilar López did the same. Pilar described her creation of the dance *por caracoles*:

> ...*Los caracoles* had never been danced. I recall that I said to the guitarist Luis Maravilla when we were in Sevilla, "Why don't we do something with the *caracoles*?" And so we made the *caracoles*...I recall that El Niño de las Marianas [the father of Luis Maravilla] used to come to teach it to the *cantaores* that I had at that time, one of whom was Ramón de Loja...and he taught him the *caracoles* and *la caña*. The *caracoles* [a *cuplé* in the rhythm of *alegrías*, its chorus based on the cries of the snail vender] were charming, because, since the verses are very beautiful, we gave them appropriate scenery and gave them a touch of the vignette...[1]

In January of 1949, Rosario and Antonio had returned to Spain. They discarded the "Chavalillos" label and henceforth would be known only as

[1] Espín y Molina.

"Rosario and Antonio." Their successful debut in the Fontalba Theater on the 27th marked the beginning of years of defining the essence of a Spanish ballet company. Antonio's skill as a choreographer allowed him to put large numbers of dancers on stage performing precision movements. He incorporated many elements from the classical ballet, but also advanced the flamenco repertoire—the *martinete* he would create a few years later being a notable example. The Spanish ballet that had been refined and enlarged in America had returned home. The companies of Carmen, José, Pilar, and Antonio and Rosario would spawn numerous imitators.

In this time of the Spanish ballet, the *ópera flamenca* held its own. Top artists like Pepe Marchena and Manuel Vallejo continued to enjoy extended engagements with revues or musicals in the major theaters. Manolo Caracol, the winner of the 1922 Contest of Cante in Granada teamed up with a gypsy *cupletista* named Lola Flores to become a dominant couple in films and on stage. Caracol, with the most profound of gypsy *cantes* surging through his veins, rose to fame with his *zambras*—orchestrated *cuplés* that had little to do with flamenco and bore no resemblance to the *zambras* of the Sacromonte. La Niña de los Peines came out of retirement briefly to sing in her husband's touring company, but then retired again, to be seen frequently seated in Pepe's bar on the Plaza Campana in Sevilla. Manolo de Huelva, more reserved than ever, restricted himself to private parties in Sevilla. Niño Ricardo, after a throat operation in 1945, had joined the company of *cantaor* Juanito Valderrama, a singer in the *ópera* style with whom he would stay until 1955.

Ramón Montoya, approaching seventy in 1949, continued to work as an accompanist, often teamed with Pepe Marchena. After his concerts during the Civil War, he had done little to further his solo career. His grandniece, the *bailaora* Rosa Montoya, described him:

> I was raised by Ramón Montoya's daughter, who is like a mother to me. My father was sick, half-paralyzed, and couldn't work much, so when I was very young my brother and I had to go live with my aunt—Ramón's daughter. All of my family is gypsy, but Ramón's wife, Mariana, was a *paya* [non-gypsy] and, besides that, the daughter of a Guardia Civil. In those times the gypsies and the Guardia Civil did not like each other. So the gypsies did not like her at first, but she was such a good woman and did so much for the gypsies that later everyone came to her and praised her. So the aunt I lived with was half gypsy. She married a *payo*, a lawyer. We lived also with Ramón, whom I called grandfather, and his wife.
>
> I remember that I always used to dance and Ramón didn't like it, because he didn't want any of the women in the family to be dancers. In those days the *bailaoras* did not have a good reputation. But all of the men were guitarists: Carlos [Montoya], the

other brother, Ramón, and one of Ramón's sons, also named Ramón. My mother said that when I was three years old I was always dancing, and I used to put on shows in our patio with the other little girls. I always danced to *"La Tani."* My uncle, Ramón Montoya, was very strict. In the house, like with most gypsies, there had to be a lot of respect. He was very serious. So there were not many fiestas. What I remember is that there were many musicians and flamencos who came to the house. There was Príncipe Gitano, El Gallina [Rafael Romero], Pepe Culata, Pericón de Cádiz, and musicians like Quiroga who would come and write down Ramón's music. We had a piano, and musicians would copy Ramón's music on the piano and then write it down. So there was music, but not gypsy fiestas; my uncle was very serious. Other flamenco people say he was not like that, that he was very funny and *muy juergista* [lover of *juergas*]. But at home he was not that way. He was *un señor*. He would come home at eight or nine o'clock in the morning and everyone had to be quiet while he slept.[1]

The guitarist Carlos Ramos recalled joining Pepe Marchena's company in 1948 to play second guitar to Montoya:

I liked him very much from the very first time I saw him play the guitar. I always thought he was the very best and he influenced all of us. Well, it is true that other, newer things have been done after him, but he was the source for all guitarists of today...He was a difficult man in many ways. For me, though, he was a very good friend, but in those times it was very hard to make a living. All artists were suspicious of each other and he had that suspicion. I remember the first time I rehearsed with him and the company. He watched me constantly, but not in a good way at first, as if saying, "Who is this guy? What does he want?" I noticed him looking at me like that, and I, who worshipped his art, nearly went crazy. But eventually he came to accept me and we became very good friends. We worked together for a year, but eventually Don Ramón became ill and left me in his place in the company. After we had finished the tour and I left the company, I went to see him in his home, when he was very ill. Sick as he was, he would grab his guitar and say to me, *"Mira lo que he sacao yo!* [Look what I have done on the guitar!]" The man was dying and yet still composing! He never recovered and finally died in 1949...[2]

On July 21, 1949, Don Ramón Montoya died of an internal hemorrhage. He was sixty-nine. Rosa Montoya tells us, "I recall very well when Ramón

[1] Sevilla, Paco, "Rosa Montoya: An Interview." *Jaleo*, Vol VI, No. 3, December 1982.
[2] Chileno, El, *"Conversaciones con Carlos Ramos." Jaleo*, Vol. V, No. 6, February 1982.

died, because it was so incredible at our house. There were long lines in the street, on Calle de Las Cabezas, which is between the plazas Tirso de Molina and Antón Martín—enormous lines of people who had come to see the body of Ramón Montoya. I was young, eight years old, but I remember all of the famous artists, artists from all around the world, who came to see him."

A reporter visited the Montoya home a week after the guitarist's passing:

The death of the great *tocaor* made me ask the question, "What will happen to his guitar?" And sentimental curiosity impelled me to know the answer. Nobody could supply it better than the artist's family. And it was thus that I found myself in one of the modest districts of Madrid, in a house where everything speaks of recent sorrow, with Maruja Montoya, the guitarist's daughter, and his faithful friend, Niño de Almadén [the *cantaor* Jacinto Almadén].

"Almadén and I," said Maruja, "held father in our arms up to his last moment."

—What will happen to his guitar? Has he left it to somebody?

"This," continued his daughter, "is a precious memory to us. There they lie, the three of them, in his working room, in their cases on the sofa."

—Did he call them by special names?

"By the names of their makers. The oldest of all is the one by Torres—it is eighty-two years old. Then came the Santos and the Ramírez."

—Were they made expressly for your father?

"No, the three of them belonged to a member of the Spanish nobility, whose name I dare not mention. You may rest assured that he belonged to the oldest nobility and was a great lover of the guitar. My father used to give him lessons. He held these guitars in great esteem. Shortly before he died—and indeed he died suddenly, just like my father—he said to him, 'Montoya, these guitars should not belong to anyone but you, and I am going to give them to you.' My father has had them ever since."

I turned to Niño de Almadén.

—What are your last memories of the *maestro*?

"There are so many. These last years I have always been at his side. We performed together. To my mind, Don Ramón died of deep moral suffering. He realized that his art did not receive the merit it deserved. He suffered very much when they did not understand his playing. Sometimes, when they asked him to take part in some big fiesta and he saw that people hardly knew how to listen to him, he would complain to me, 'If I had money to live on, I would not play for such people, Almadén. I am a bitter man...They do not appreciate my merit. They regard me exactly as a common player who does not know what to do with his hands..."'

—But you must have witnessed many triumphs of the *maestro*.

"*Sí señor!* I could mention many. Recently in Granada, in Jerez, and also in Málaga. We were performing in this latter city and were invited to a fiesta given in honor of a general. The audience rose to their feet and applauded Don Ramón again and again. He was deeply moved. Everything that had to do with his art went very deep inside him."

I had a vague suspicion that there was another famous guitar, well-known to the public, that had not been mentioned in the conversation.

—Has the *maestro* left only the three guitars you mentioned?

The artist's daughter did not reply at once, but finally she complied. "No. You wish to inquire about the guitar that they called '*La Leona*?'"

—Yes. That's it.

"It was a very old guitar—so old that you couldn't even have it varnished for fear of making it lose its sound. The Spanish public knew that guitar. Sometimes my father would take out a brand new guitar and the audience would protest, 'Not that guitar, we want *La Leona!*' And father had to take out his old guitar to please them. All I know about that guitar is that he used it for the first time the day I was born!

"Many wanted that guitar, which father had for twenty-five years. Finally he gave it as a present to a Mexican pupil of his, Don Mario Zayas, to repay his admiration and kindness. This gentleman has a chateau in Grenoble where he used to invite my father frequently. There, he has a collection of Spanish objects. Their friendship was so close that my father could not find a better way of showing his appreciation than by presenting him with the famous *La Leona* that the public knew so well and so frantically insisted upon in their desire to hear its notes."

I took my leave, having learned where rest the guitars of this great exponent of the flamenco art, Ramón Montoya, those guitars that no human hand will touch again: three in the house on Calle de la Cabeza, and one, the most famous of all, in a chateau in Grenoble. But the four are silent, indeed forever, because no other hands will know how to make them speak as he did.[1]

---

[1] "The guitars of Ramón Montoya." *Foto*, Madrid, July 30, 1949.

Odette Lumbroso traveled often with the Amayas during the early 1950s. She shared her observations with Mario Bois:

> [After the second triumphant appearance in Paris]...they began to disperse: some got married and didn't work anymore; others got tired of it and disappeared overnight; they argued, they stole from each other; Luisillo and Teresa abandoned the company. All of that influenced their work. Over the course of the following years, they went against the advice of Fernand who insisted that they prepare for their seasons in Paris, but they paid no attention. Paco, "the businessman," would decide: "The company has two weeks free!" So they rented the Théâtre de l'Étoile and began to perform with no publicity. They continued to do that sort of thing in different parts of the world, accepting contracts in places that continually were more and more mediocre—from a cabaret in Mexico to a casino in Belgium. The company had no leader, nobody responsible for the money, nobody in charge...
>
> When [Carmen] walked down the street, she dressed in such a way that she could pass unnoticed: no makeup and not very well dressed; nobody could recognize her. Men didn't turn and stare—in contrast to her sister Leonor, who always attracted stares (although the family would never have forgiven the slightest false step). Carmen, always exhausted by overwork, would fall asleep anywhere. I have seen her asleep in the hallways of the Théâtre des Champs Elysées, lying on a basket. She smoked excessively and drank coffee at all hours, but she never drank alcohol. She ate little and didn't place much value on money...After the death of her father, it was her older brother who took charge of the finances. He used to drink too much...
>
> All of the Amaya tribe were big gamblers, as was the orchestra director. When they traveled by train, the poker games lasted until dawn. Carmen didn't play and she would say to the others, "You have no money!" But she liked to watch them play. Since she was so short, she would climb up on one of the seats to see better. One night, going from Oran to Casablanca, we had reserved twenty sleeping compartments. Everyone spent the night gambling in one of the compartments and they never set foot in the other nineteen.
>
> We never arrived on time. We were always late, and I lived in dread that some day the curtain would open and we would not be ready. As much as I begged them to hurry, there was no way they would pay attention to me. Once, when we were an hour late, the car broke down on a bridge. We all got out, and to my surprise, they began to yell at me, "It's your fault, you have given us the evil

eye!"[1]

In early 1950, after almost four years of apprenticeship in Carmen's company, Teresa and Luisillo struck out on their own, creating a company that included Tere Maya—a gypsy from Granada—and the *cantaor* Jacinto Almadén. It is not clear whether Luisillo just wanted a chance to put his choreographic creativity to work, or if there were personal differences with others in the company. It is significant that Luisillo never mentioned his tenure with the Amayas in future interviews or biographical sketches. He always made it seem like he had appeared as a bright star out of nowhere.

The *Paris-Match* described a happier moment with the Amayas: "On the occasion of the baptism of Luisillo's son, Carmen and her gypsies entered Nôtre-Dame for the first time. For eight days they had searched for a priest who could speak Spanish. None of the gypsies knew the recitations of the baptism. When the priest, speaking in Spanish, came to the following words of the sacrament, '...of the dead and the living...,' the gypsies thought it was the very popular Andalusian song, *'La vida y la muerte'* ['Life and Death'], and they began to sing it. The priest almost fainted..."[2]

In April, Teresa and Luisillo premiered their new company to rave reviews in the Sarah Bernhardt Theater in Paris and then went on to a long and distinguished career. Meanwhile, a new guitarist would enter the Amaya company and bring about profound changes. There is a lack of agreement concerning the date that Juan Antonio Agüero joined the Amayas. Goldberg claims that Mario Escudero brought Juan into the company in 1948. She quotes Mario:

> And my intimate friend, Juan Antonio, was there and he said to me, "Mario, get me into the company!" And I said, "But, Juan..." Because he didn't know anything. And he said to me, "For free— I won't ask for any money." And I spoke to Paco, and I said to him, "Look, this non-gypsy is a good guy." And so he said to Juan, "Come in." And he started.[3]

Since Mario Escudero didn't join the Amayas until February of 1949, it would have to be sometime later that he introduced Juan Antonio to them. Escudero's view of the newcomer as an amateur guitarist is supported by Sabicas' brother. Diego recalled: "He [Agüero] played the guitar, but only for pleasure. He was from a very distinguished family from Santander...A very good person, a very educated guy, cultured..."[4]

But there is another side to the picture. Carmen's agent in France, Odette Lumbroso, stated that she introduced Juan Antonio to the Amayas in 1952.

[1]Bois, p. 119, 122.
[2]Salgues, Yves, *Paris-Match*, November 18, 1950.
[3]Goldberg, p. 260.
[4]Goldberg interviews.

Her date is impossible, for reasons soon to be made clear, but it could have happened in 1950 or '51. Odette said that Juan Antonio Agüero was playing for Rosario and Antonio when they returned from Egypt, thereby implying that he played well enough to be professional. It makes sense that Juan Antonio would already have known how to play the guitar—if not, why would the Amayas hire him, especially considering that he would be an outsider, a *payo*? He must have played well enough to inspire Carmen Amaya in her dancing, for Montañés wrote: "Carmen Amaya dances a little better, if that is possible, when the *payo*, with his head always soaking wet, draws forth gypsy notes from the strings of his guitar. That guitar guides, conducts, and applies the brakes to that passionate, red-hot dance of the gypsy. The new guitarist is respectful towards the 'star' of the show. The company is amazed the day they hear Juan Antonio use the formal *'usted'* to address the one that some call Carmen, others, Carmela or Carmelilla."[1]

Later, Carmen would tell a reporter: "With him, I don't have to force myself. With the others I have to pick them up; with him, no, because he comes out like a bullet. I dance first for him, and since he loves the dance more than anybody, it comes out of me without effort. Do you understand? He wheedles it out of me, and whether I want to or not, he makes me dance."[2]

The noted flamencologist José Blas Vega confirms that Agüero worked with Rosario and Antonio before joining the Amayas, and adds that, earlier, he used to hang out in Madrid's Villa Rosa, where he learned from Pepe Motos, Ramón Montoya, and Mario Escudero. Rosario and Antonio had returned to Spain in early 1949 and some time must have passed before they toured Egypt. Considering that there is no mention of Juan Antonio in the press before 1950, it seems safe to assume that he and Carmen met sometime in 1950—perhaps in May, as indicated below—during a whirlwind tour of France. Odette Lumbroso gave her account to Mario Bois:

> Rosario and Antonio's company was returning from performing in Egypt. They had a good *payo* guitarist named Juan Antonio Agüero, who belonged to a respected family from Santander. He told me he wanted to leave the group because Antonio was unbearable. I introduced him to Carmen in a *brasserie* in the North Train Station (it was May, if I am not mistaken). He didn't appeal to Carmen. He drank too much and was much younger than she—she was forty [probably thirty-seven; he was twenty-three]. I insisted, because the young man needed work. Carmen, always inclined to help everyone, hired him. And the company continued its tour throughout France, in casinos and in the beach towns during the summer season.

[1] Montañés. p. 47.
[2] Reproduced in Hidalgo, p. 232.

Carmen didn't like to go out alone at night. She had to be with her family, to dine with her family. Her mother and La Faraona used to take care of her. It was her mother who brought her packages of Chesterfields in the mornings, because Carmen never carried money, and many times I paid for our coffees.[1]

Montañés picked up the tale:

> Closing night. The Amaya company is busy gathering and packing all of their bags. It is around three in the morning and the next day they have to open in another city, with almost three hundred kilometers of travel before them.
>
> The *payo* guitarist and the gypsy *bailaora* run into each other in a hallway. With no preamble, Juan Antonio blurts out, *"A que no casaría usted conmigo?* [Why don't you marry me?]"
>
> The dancer, astonished, looks into the eyes of her guitarist. It is not a time for jokes. But the guitarist is there in front of her, respectful, but determined. He looks directly at the "star" and there is something in his eyes that tells Carmen that those unexpected words are not a joke, that this is something very serious. Carmen Amaya, a gypsy true to the ways of her race, feels that this *payo* is the man for her. Her response is brief, perhaps with a touch of gypsy *guasa* [humor, teasing] in her tone, *"A que sí!"* [a play on his manner of asking: *"A que no..."*]
>
> A half-hour later the bus with large letters on the side reading *"Gran Compañía de Ballet Español de Carmen Amaya"* abandons the city and heads down the highway. Inside, Carmen, wrapped in a huge blanket, tries to sleep. But there are some words, those words by Juan Antonio, that don't allow her to fall asleep, that keep her eyes wide open in the gloom of the night: *"A que no casaría usted conmigo!"*
>
> At the other end of the coach, Juan Antonio, the guitarist, stares at the highway, shrouded in darkness as it slips rapidly beneath the wheels. In his head, three words dance *por alegrías*: *"A que sí!"*[2]

Odette Lumbroso:

> On several occasions she told me she was tired of it all, of the family, and they looked badly on her romance with Juan Antonio. [She said] "Once in awhile, once a week, we manage to escape alone to have a few drinks—once to Juan les Pins, another time to Biarritz." She would confide to me, "Juan Antonio is charming, marvelous, and you know something, a few days ago he asked to

[1] Bois, p. 120.
[2] Montañés, p. 48.

marry me. You know what I answered? I told him yes! Now I have to meet his brother, prepare the wedding, arrange the papers...I will need your help."[1]

Odette said that it took quite awhile for the family to accept the *payo* guitarist. It is very likely that the family feared losing Carmen, upon whom they all depended. It didn't help that she wanted to marry a *payo*, although two of her sisters had married *payos*[2] and her brother, Antonio, had married a much older non-gypsy woman. Plans for the wedding had to be put aside until the completion of several months of intense touring in the south of France. Finally, with one more contract to fulfill, the Amayas crossed the border into Spain and arrived in Barcelona:

> After finishing the performance one night, one of so many, Carmen gathers all of the company on stage. When they are all there, she announces, "Tomorrow, everybody to Mass! At seven o'clock, in the Santa Monica Church...I'm getting married!"

The New York Times announced the marriage of Carmen Amaya to her guitarist on October 19, 1951. The plans for the wedding had been kept secret to avoid the press. But one reporter found out. Biographer Hidalgo described the scene as Josep Postius recalled it in his memoires:

> It was a mysterious voice that alerted him with a telephone call at two in the morning. When he was able to answer, still half asleep because the ringing had roused him from a deep sleep, a voice which at that moment he could not identify, in spite of its undeniable personality, said to him, "Postius, pay attention, because this morning, around six, Carmen Amaya is getting married!" And without further details, the unknown man hung up the phone. He reacted immediately and while he was dressing quickly he was trying to think of the churches where the ceremony might take place. But, since he could reach no conclusion, he left the house to begin a pilgrimage that might lead him to his objective. First he went to the Teatro Barcelona where Carmen was performing in those days [October 5-21], but the guard, the only one around at that hour, knew nothing. So he went into La Luna, a bar next door frequented by actors and reporters...But they didn't know anything either, although they gave him a clue that in the end proved useful. They directed him to the Hotel Oriente, where Carmen and most of her guests were staying. There, the night porter, whom he knew, told him very discreetly, and only after making him promise he would never reveal the source of his information, that the wed-

---

[1] Bois, p. 120.
[2] The cantaor Chiquito de Triana, Antonia's husband, may or may not have been a gypsy, but from his appearance and name, I suspect not.

ding would be at six in the morning in the Church of Santa Monica, just a few meters from the Oriente.

A little before six, Carmen's relatives, all gypsies, began to arrive. A little later, the groom made his appearance: Juan Antonio Agüero, who said he was the son of an important lawyer in that city, although other sources say his father was a bank employee.

A minute later Carmen's car arrived. She made an angry face when she saw the reporter, and even before the car had stopped, she yelled, "What are you doing here? Who told you that I was getting married?"

There were no further words and Carmen quickly entered the church and headed for the altar where the ceremony would take place. [A newspaper account said that Barcelona was wrapped in snow that early morning and that Carmen dressed in street clothes, with just a touch of white in her hair. A photo reveals that she wore a beige skirt and matching belted jacket with a fur collar, very high-heeled shoes, her hair in a bun and a large white flower over her ear.] After the ceremony, in the sacristy, everything was euphoria, hugs and kisses.

Later, in the Sícoris [bar], still open at that hour, the *aguardiente* ran freely, because everybody wanted to toast the happiness of the couple.The one who had alerted Postius about the wedding was the popular radio announcer Gerardo Esteban.[1]

Montañés:

...At nine that morning, in a tavern on Calle de Escudillers, thirty gypsies rushed to surround the newlywed Agüeros. To the cry of "Long live the newlyweds!" they toasted with chocolate and rotgut *aguardiente*. At two in the afternoon, anyone who entered the bar could hear the best gypsy *cantes* and attend a show of the best, purest, and most heartfelt dances by Carmen Amaya.

The wedding fiesta ended when La Capitana gave the order, "Now, everybody home, we have to work this evening!" That evening, and later that night, and the next evening and night, Carmen's company continued performing.[2]

Years later, the new husband would say, "The day of our wedding, Carmen and I performed in the theater as we always did. They say we had no honeymoon, but that is not true: our honeymoon lasted from the moment we were married until Carmen died eleven years later."[3]

And perform they did. Carmen Amaya, a true nomadic *canastera* gypsy,

---
[1]Corberó, Salvador, *Els racons de la memoria.* Described by Hidalgo, p.173.
[2]Montañés, p. 50.
[3]Hidalgo, p. 174.

traveled as no other gypsy before her had traveled—non-stop, year after year, with an exhausting schedule that depleted all those around her. The makeup of the company began to change regularly as new members came and went, unable to keep up with the woman of steel. From 1949 through 1951 the company traveled throughout Europe, back to Argentina, and into Africa—Morocco and the Belgian Congo, where a dance academy bore her name. The majority of Carmen's biographers have erroneously claimed that she returned to the United States during this period. But Mario Escudero explained: "I went with Carmen Amaya after the Greco tour and we worked in France and in South America, in Buenos Aires, Chile, Uruguay. Then I spent almost a year with Rosario and Antonio...In 1954, I came to the United States for the first time, with Vicente Escudero...I never was here with Carmen Amaya."[1]

Carmen may not have returned to the United States at that time, but she was not completely forgotten there. In 1950, just a little over a year after the first long-play records appeared on the market, Decca Records released a single, "long-play, microgroove, unbreakable record," containing music that had been recorded by the Amayas in 1941. *Flamencan Songs and Dances: Volumes 1 and 2* (DL 8027) included all of the numbers that had originally appeared as two albums of 78s.

In early 1951, before her marriage, Carmen had felt a pang of homesickness. She rejected numerous contracts and returned to the flat in Madrid, where she lived in luxury with her two enormous American automobiles, five fur coats, jewels, and a tremendous twenty-three carat diamond. All of that, and a six-figure bank account that she had saved from her earnings.[2] After a few weeks in Madrid, she flew to Barcelona, to see her birthplace for the first time in more than fifteen years. Television cameras were there to record the event:

> The arrival at the airport in the Ciudad Condal, surrounded by a few of her people, makes her so emotional that she begins to cry. No sooner does she descend from the airplane than she falls to her knees on the runway and kisses the ground, her long fingers, slender and hard, convulsing over the hard cement in a passionate gesture of violent possession.
>
> Photographers and reporters capture the moment. They ask her, "Will you perform soon in Barcelona?
>
> Carmen doesn't answer...She doesn't know. For the moment she only wants to saturate herself with her Spain, her Barcelona...[3]

At the prodding of a reporter, Carmen went to look for her childhood

---
[1] Chileno, El, "Mario Escudero." p. 21.
[2] Montañés, p. 42.
[3] Montañés, p. 42.

home. There had been so many changes that she could hardly recognize the Somorrostro. At one point she asked to stop the car so that she could get out and search for a familiar house. As she descended further into the Somorrostro, doors opened and gypsies poured out to greet the legend, yelling, "Carmen Amaya," "La Capitana," "The daughter of El Chino and La Micaela," "The granddaughter of Cagarrutas has returned!" By the time she reached the dirty gray sand of the beach, she was surrounded by hundreds of half-naked and dirty gypsy urchins. Josep Postius recalled:

> In the company of her husband [soon to be husband], her agent, Falgueras, the secretary, María Luisa, and Sempronio and me as witnesses, we went to the house where Carmen had been born in that densely populated barrio on the fringe of Barcelona, facing the sea and in the midst of a tremendous sea of mud—the product of recent rains. The memory I have is dominated by a genuine cloud of gypsies of all kinds and ages, pressing in upon her almost to the point of suffocating her. And all of them asking for something, from a souvenir to a coin to alleviate some current ailment, or perhaps to pay for one more drink of wine or *aguardiente* in the local tavern. The smallest of them, not any less demanding when it came to getting money, besieged Carmen completely naked...[1]

> Montañés: There on the sand of the Somorrostro, Carmen Amaya, the best paid dancer on five continents, takes off her shoes and, once again, as if there had been no passage of years, in a mysterious rite, with no music other than the clapping of hundreds of hands, dances for herself and her people...Only when the sea, the sky, and the sand merge into a single shadow, then and only then, does the fiesta come to an end.[2]

> Postius: When we finally managed to leave the Somorrostro, more drained by our fight against the gypsy populace than by the long walk on the muddy paths of that shantytown, Carmen Amaya invited everybody to Can Costa [*can: casa* in *Catalán;* a tavern] in that densely populated Barceloneta. And there, to show us the Catalonian within her that she had never denied, and in spite of being a gypsy and having her own language, she gave us an authentic demonstration of how to drink wine from a *porrón* [glass or ceramic pitcher with a long spout from which wine is poured at a distance, as with a wineskin], something that has to be practiced from a very young age to attain true mastery.[3]

---

[1] Hidalgo, p. 176.
[2] Montañés, p. 44.
[3] Postius; in Hidalgo, p. 176.

For a month and a half Carmen performed to sold-out houses in the Tivoli, one of the best theaters in Barcelona. She then returned to Madrid for a two-week contract that was extended again and again. This may have been when she appeared in the Fontalba Theater with a company that had been enlarged considerably. Luisillo had been replaced by Goyo Reyes, a dancer from Madrid.

Goyo had begun in the company of Vicente Escudero at age sixteen. He recalled Vicente's comments after his initial audition: "You are a daring boy; you do not know a thing about dancing...however...I like you; you have *madera* (the makings) and I hope to make a real dancer of you." Goyo says, "I rehearsed with almost religious fervor, without missing a word or indication from him. He taught me how to dance properly and with a virile style; he also put in my mind the usually neglected idea about theatrical discipline and I also learned a great deal about choreography. I will be ever grateful to that man!"[1] Before joining Carmen Amaya, Goyo had formed his own company and worked with Manolo Caracol and Lola Flores. He and Pepita Ortega (later to become his wife) performed mostly classical and folk dances with Carmen's company.

Other new members of the Amaya company in 1951, prior to Carmen's marriage, included Paco Laberinto, a dancer from Jerez known for his *bulerías*, and Nati Mistral, a singer of *cuplés* like Antonio Amaya's wife, Pepita Lláser. The three guitarists were Paco Amaya, Mario Escudero, and Juan Antonio Agüero.

In April the company performed in the Gran Teatro in Huelva, where the press reported:

> The audience welcomed her with an ovation when she appeared on stage to begin the *fandango* that opened the show, to give us all that genius and presence that she puts into the purest gypsy attack, and later the applause had to be even louder to give a stamp of approval to the *soleares*. And above all, among many things, the *siguiriya* that she elaborated in a prodigious manner in a true demonstration of all that was involved...And while everyone shared in the success—four Amayas in the group, with Antonio standing out—we mention an extraordinary dancer: we refer to Goyo Reyes, magnificent in the whole range of Spanish dances, in the *farruca*, as well as the *jota*, and the *bolero* that was definitely one of his most brilliant images."[2]

After another Paris season and a tour through France, the company had returned to Barcelona in October for two weeks in the Teatro Barcelona. There, Carmen was married on October 19th.

---
[1] From a Vicente Escudero program booklet, c. 1955.
[2] From an unspecified newspaper; in Hidalgo, p. 161.

The stirrings of the old flamenco that had been suppressed for more than two decades became more evident in 1952. The *ópera flamenca* didn't realize it yet, but its days were numbered. Where there had once been only a single touring Spanish dance company—that of Argentinita, with its sporadic appearances in Spain and emphasis on the classic and folk styles—there were now many. Competing with Carmen Amaya were the companies of Pilar López, José Greco, Antonio, Teresa and Luisillo, Mariemma, and Rosario. And they were using real flamenco artists—*cantaores*, guitarists, and gypsy dancers.

During the previous year, José Greco had been approached by Sol Hurok about the possibility of touring in the United States. Hurok wanted only a small group, along the lines of those of Argentinita, feeling that a large company would not work in America. But Greco insisted that he wanted to bring his whole company. Hurok even tried to apply pressure by bringing up the disagreeable incident that had led him to insist upon Greco's dismissal from Argentinita's company some years earlier, but the two could not come to an agreement. Another agent, Lee Shubert, saw José in the film *Manolete* when it showed in Cannes and signed him based on that film.

On October 1, 1951, José Greco and his Spanish Ballet opened in the Schubert Theater in New York. It was the largest company ever seen in America. Among its thirteen members were Lola de Ronda, La Quica (who danced *soleá* and *tangos*), two gypsy dancers from the Sacromonte—Tere Maya and her brother Juanele—singer Chico de Madrid, guitarist Rogelio Reguera, and pianist and musical director Roger Machado. Although Greco incorporated many of Argentinita's choreographies, he also showed that he was a capable choreographer himself. A dramatic *peteneras* was one of many numbers for which he received high critical praise. Held over after four weeks, the company had to move to the Century Theater for four more weeks. It was the beginning of America's love affair with José Greco. He would tour the country year after year, exposing the American public to the finest of Spain's flamenco artists. In 1952 he danced in the film *Sombrero* and in 1955, his appearance in Mike Todd's *Around the World in Eighty Days* would make his name synonymous with Spanish dance.

However, in spite of the critical and popular acclaim, the early days were not easy for José. His battles with musicians' unions would be never-ending. He had to pay membership fees and annual dues for all of his artists. In later years he would be required to hire local musicians (often not even flamencos) equal in number to those in his company. Rather than pay them for nothing, he sometimes had the locals play in the lobby before his performances. On top of that, he found that he had to withhold federal income taxes for all of his company—which came out of his pocket. A dispute with Schubert led to a split with the agency and Greco found himself on the verge of bankruptcy.

José resorted to dancing in Olsen and Johnson's vaudeville review,

Hellzapoppin', in the Palace Theatre. He says the mix of comedy and Spanish dance was a disaster, but the income sustained him until he found a new booking agent. Charles Green (who would later represent a number of other Spanish dance companies) soon had him on his feet financially. But one problem that always stayed with him was the difficulty of dealing with temperamental artistic personalities. The experience of celebrated photographer, Peter Basch, with one of Greco's gypsies gives an idea of what José had to deal with. Basch wanted to photograph the extraordinarily handsome and primal dancer, Juanele Maya. "His manager, however, made clear that this was virtually impossible, first because Juanele had never been known to keep an appointment and second, if by any chance he should turn up at the studio at any time, he would certainly be unmanageable... I had hoped to have his gypsy partner in a photograph with him, but was informed by the same manager that there was 'bad blood' between the two and that they were absolutely not allowed in the same room except for performances."[1] Basch did eventually make some impressive photos of Juanele.

José Greco and the other touring Spanish dance companies stimulated an interest in the excitement of flamenco. Tourists began to travel to Spain seeking the real thing. Demand for authentic flamenco led to the opening of the first new *café cantante* in Spain since the early part of the century. The *tablao* (new name for the *café cantante*) El Guajiro opened in 1952, on the outskirts of Sevilla, in a gypsy area known as Los Remedios. A rustic affair, El Guajiro consisted of four walls enclosing a large space, with a dirt floor and a canvas canopy for a roof. Dancers sometimes capped off their *bulerías* with a monkey-like swing around one of the tent poles adjacent to the stage. Just as in the *cafés cantantes* of seventy years earlier, a *cuadro* of six to ten dancers, a couple of *cantaores* and a pair of guitarists performed several times a night on a raised stage. After the *cuadro*, singers and other special attractions came out to perform alone. El Guajiro would be a training ground for a number of future flamenco stars, including singers Terremoto, El Chocolate, Romerito, and El Sordera, and dancers El Farruco, Matilde Coral, and Manuela Vargas.

Another landmark event of 1952 was the release of Edgar Neville's film *Duende y Misterio del Arte Flamenco* (*Flamenco* in foreign releases), a prize winner in the 1953 Cannes Film Festival. There was no plot, only a series of fourteen sequences, each devoted to a different *cante* or *baile*. Antonio premiered his groundbreaking dance *por martinete*. Pilar López and Alejandro Vega danced *la caña*. Roberto Ximénez did *zapateado* on two tabletops. A shriveled old woman and a young girl performed *alegrías* on a rooftop in Sevilla. Other well-known flamencos featured in the film include Jacinto Almadén, Antonio Mairena, Aurelio de Cádiz, Bernarda and Fernanda de Utrera, Pepe de Badajoz, and Luis Maravilla. The film broke new ground in

[1] *Dance Magazine*, July 1953, p. 22.

being the first motion picture dealing with flamenco to be widely praised by critics and intellectuals. It opened in the 55th Street Playhouse in New York on May 2, 1953.

In what appeared to be the beginning of a renaissance of flamenco, Carmen Amaya faced a certain amount of criticism for her programming. The major part of her concerts consisted of neoclassical and regional dances based on Argentinita's model. Carmen had choregraphed *"La Boda de Luis Alonso"* for the company, and one of the staples of the repertoire for a number of years would be the Argentinita classic, "Three Dances from the 18th Century" (*"Goyescas"* and two dances by Albéniz). One critic in London felt that Carmen's music often sounded anything but Spanish, and thought her costumes lacked authenticity and had the stamp of Hollywood films.

But, more and more, Carmen began to leave the dancing of these numbers to others in the company. She specialized in what she did best—flamenco. Where she had once done two flamenco numbers in a performance, perhaps a *soleá* or *farruca* and her *alegrías*, she now did at least three and as many as five on a single night. She might do her opening *fandango*, then *soleares*, *siguiriyas*, *bulerías*, and the *alegrías*.

Carmen never lacked for critics. In February of 1952, the company returned from performing in Portugal and a reporter asked:

—They say, Carmen, that your tour through Portugal was a disaster. True or false?

"A lie, and a big one! You just have to look at the reviews in the newpapers of Lisbon.

—That's true, they call you a genius, extraordinary. Nevertheless, it was said that your return to Spain...

"*Sí señores*. But I will explain: Somebody paid a certain reporter to spread that sort of thing."

—Who was that "somebody?"

"An artist. Don't ask me his name.

—Then, in truth, why did you return?

"Because of an accident. I broke two little bones in my back... You have seen the reviews. As far as the economics were concerned, I was paid 30,000 *pesetas* a day. Is that a disaster?[1]

Even Vicente Escudero got into the act, criticising Carmen's approach to the dance. Carmen responded to the press:

"Vicente has been a great artist..." Carmen affirms.

—Speak to us of the present.

"*Pues*...Today he is nobody, he is finished. That's why, because the newspapers are no longer interested in him, he dedicates his time to speaking badly of this one and that one. About me he has

[1] Source not specified. In Hidalgo, p. 175.

said that, before he would dance like I do, he would prefer to die of starvation. And he has said really nasty things about Antonio."[1]

During Carmen's London season of April 1952, the critics were still not sure about how to categorize her dancing. The *London Sunday Times* wrote:

> Carmen Amaya and her company of Spanish dancers are back in London, at the Cambridge Theatre. Since she last appeared here, we have seen dancers of the calibre of Nila Amaparo, Pilar López, Mariemma, and Rosario, to mention a few only. In comparison with their versatility, Carmen Amaya's range appears limited.
>
> A real *gitana*, broadfaced, slim-bodied, with sleek black hair and sculptural lips of a vivid red, she has a dynamic personality, explosive temperament, and a seemingly inexhaustible store of vitality. Her features have a certain dignity in repose, but she prefers to contort them into a demoniac mask. She plays the castanets well. She is skilled in the *zapateado*. She can dazzle with her swift turns in place, during which she jerks her head, shakes her shoulders, and whirls her arms with the vicious speed of a boxer's punch, and all with a savagery that borders on frenzy—but her dancing is not outstanding for elegance or style.
>
> Of the male dancers, I prefer Marcos Manuel, Antonio Marcos, who has good beats, and Goyo Reyes, who has speed and lightness.[2]

The dance critic Elsa Brunelleschi wrote:

> Barely had the boards of the Cambridge Theatre recovered from the rhythmic onslaught of Rosario, Antonio, and Pilar López when another Spanish dancer descends upon them. This time the spell is cast by Carmen Amaya, Spain's greatest gypsy dancer, a *gitana* on all four sides.
>
> Amaya seldom adheres to the canons of "flamenco." Within a few seconds of appearing she casts her feigned formality to the winds and her gypsy instinct manifests itself with the power of a tornado. Her split-second spins explode; her arms lash the air; her beautiful features are convulsed and her eyes glint with malefic fire. Other dancers before her have worn men's costume but none have carried it off with so individual a charm. Dressed in skin-tight trousers, Carmen Amaya makes one appreciate subtleties that frill might obscure.
>
> Paco Amaya and J. A. Agüero [Mario Escudero had left the company] handle their guitars like tommy-guns, firing volleys at Carmen's amazing footwork. In the *alegrías* an imperious gesture

---

[1] Reproduced in Hidalgo, p. 170. Original source not cited.
[2] Beaumont, Cyril, "A Real Gitana." *London Sunday Times*, April 20, 1952.

orders *son* [handclapping rhythm] and guitars to stop. Carmen stands alone, battling with her own rhythm. She reminds one of the matador ordering everyone to leave the bullring to face his enemy single-handed. Headed by Chiquito de Triana and the statuesque Faraona, the young company gives the star excellent support. The *"Cachucha"* was, however, played far too quickly. There is in Spain a recent craze for academic dances of the old bolero school. Carmen Amaya should remain exclusively in the field of gypsy dance. There she reigns supreme.[1]

Brunelleschi also described the Amaya tribe at that time:

The performing Amayas we have seen at the Cambridge Theatre are as follows: Carmen is the star of the show. Paco Amaya, her brother, the guitarist. Being the director and manager of the company as well as the arranger of flamenco tunes for the gypsy scenes, we sometimes find Paco in the programme as Francisco Amaya. His wife is Micaela la Chata and she takes part in a few ensembles. Their sons are Curro and Diego. The latter, a youngster about sixteen years old, was prevented by a knee injury from dancing in the early days of the season. Antonio and Antonia Amaya are brother and sister of Carmen; Chiquito de Triana, the flamenco singer, is married to Antonia, and they have one little three-year-old girl. Antonio's wife is Pepita Llaser, the *tonadillera* or singer of popular music hall songs. Lastly, there is Juana "La Faraona," the aunt of Carmen, and Juan Antonio Agüero, who recently married Carmen and may himself become an adopted gypsy by contact with this extraordinary family. On the whole, the chief merit of the Amayas is to be related to Carmen. Independently I do not think that any member of her family would go very far; she, on the other hand, would be handicapped without them. As with all gypsies her art is limited. The other Amayas render her service by undeniable personal sympathy that forces one to like them. In the finale, with her family and the other artists of the troupe around her shouting encouragement and beating a fantastic percussion of handclaps, Carmen Amaya, in tight-fitting trousers, tearing herself apart as if she were possessed by a thousand demons, is a unique savage sight...Most flamenco shows end with a grand *fin de fete* in which everyone participates. Carmen reverses the usual procedure. Quite alone, she closes the show with her magnificent solo *alegrías* proving that, after all, she and no one else *is* the show.[2]

---

[1]Brunelleschi, Elsa, "Ballet." *The London Observer,* April 20, 1952
[2]Brunelleschi, Elsa, "The Amaya Tribe" *Ballet,* June 1952

For reasons that haven't been disclosed, Mario Escudero left the Amaya company in early 1952, taking his wife—Carmen's sister María—with him. They joined the company of Rosario and Antonio, which would break up later that year. Rosario and Antonio each gave different reasons for the formation of separate companies. Antonio said, "We disagreed over the interpretation of a three-minute *jota*." Rosario put it more diplomatically: "It was only that Antonio needed to make a big company and I prefer small." Rosario took with her as a partner a young man who had been with the company for several years before leaving to form his own group. Roberto Iglesias, originally from Mexico, had learned classical ballet in California, with the San Francisco Ballet. After five years with Rosario, he would again enjoy success with his own companies.

The Amayas continued touring intensively through 1952. In 1953, Carmen performed a great deal in Spain. Dance writer Bill Butler saw her three times that year—in Sevilla, Málaga, and Madrid. He wrote: "...though I had heard extraordinary accounts of her, nothing prepared me for the reality. The figure that stalked into the light was flesh on steel, radiating the qualities of both. Her castanets whispered, chattered, or drummed thunderously at her command. Her heels stabbed the floor in a crisp staccato that drove stitches into one's skin. The impact was staggering and resistance to her was impossible... I blistered my hands and exhausted my arms in applauding, but my considerable demonstration was completely lost in the ovation she received from her countrymen..."

Butler saw Carmen again in an "ugly baroque theatre in Málaga" and "in the barbaric splendor of a great *caseta* in Sevilla." He said, "Neither repetition nor sober reflection has diminished my exuberance. She began each performance with a solo *fandango*, forewarning her entrance with the buzz of castanets that chilled the heart like the sound of an angry rattlesnake. Once on stage, she assaulted the audience, cowed them, whipped them to a frenzy, and divested them of any dispassion."

At that spring fair in Sevilla, Butler had occasion to see Carmen away from the stage:

> ...I witnessed the dazzling effect she produced in a tiny *caseta* when, to the astonishment of the host, the customers, and the gypsy children performing feverishly for rewards of wine or a nibble of fried fish, she entered and sat quietly at a corner table. Were Michelangelo to drop into a Florentine atelier or Shakespeare to stroll into a rehearsal at the present day Stratford, neither would create a comparable stir. These men were merely mortal. Carmen Amaya is legend, inspiration, a goddess, and a miracle to the gypsies of Andalucía, whose blood and heritage she shares...
>
> The important fact is the undisputable power of the woman her-

self. I saw the fever that swept the *caseta* in Sevilla when the dancers knew they were performing for Carmen Amaya...She watched the dancers intently and sympathetically. She spoke only once, and that time violently, when a well-meaning patron rewarded a child of five with a glass of wine. Sweating from her dancing, the little girl gulped the wine greedily.

"Take it away from her, you fool," Carmen Amaya suddenly yelled at him. "It will make her vomit. I know."[1]

---

[1]Butler, Bill, "The Legend of Carmen Amaya." *Dance Magazine*, April, 1954. p. 24-25.

CHAPTER TEN

THE NEW GOLDEN AGE

While Carmen Amaya embarked on a long tour of South America in 1954, the *cante gitano* and the old flamenco continued to emerge from a thirty-year hibernation. Pericón de Cádiz described the opening of a new *tablao* in Madrid:

> Perico el del Lunar [guitarist and former accompanist of Antonio Chacón] used to frequent the Villa Rosa, too, and one day he began to talk to me about a *tablao* that was about to open, that they would contract me for a fixed salary, and they would do this and that, and it wouldn't be something foolish, that it would be good for me...In short, he convinced me and I went to see the owner. I spoke with the owner and he says to me, *"Bueno,* I'll sign a contract for you for two weeks."
> *"Hombre,"* I say to him, "two weeks? If you will, make it for a month!"
> So he signed it for a month, and then I spent thirteen years there without missing a single day!
> The Zambra was the first modern *tablao* to open in Madrid, and there used to be a good number of artists there, but not in the same format as the fiestas of the Villa Rosa, because here there was a small stage and that is where we performed. First the big *cuadro* came out, made up of eighteen or twenty artists between the dancers, singers, and guitarists. At eleven at night they went out and did their thing on stage until almost one o'clock in the morning, and that is when we came out with Rosita Durán. And there we were—Perico el del Lunar, Juanito Varea, Rafael Romero, Manolo Vargas...and me too, of course.
> And in this *cuadro* everything was based on the *cantes güenos* [the good *cantes*]: we used to sing *por soleá,* we sang *por siguiriyas,* we sang *por la caña;* in short, we sang all the good stuff. And then the dances of Rosita, which were always something *grande* [great, important]. She used to dance the *peteneras,* which Rafael sometimes sang for her, or other times Jarrito, or me; she

used to dance the *caracoles*, which I sang for her. We would be on stage for about an hour, and then the big *cuadro* would come out again to close.

So, of course, there, for two or three hundred *pesetas* [c. $5.00] you could see all of those many artists, and the people began to like it more and more and became less interested in the fiestas. Because, in a fiesta just a "Good evening!" would cost you a lot more. But, in spite of that, some continued with the custom of the fiestas, and from the Zambra we got some good ones. The aficionados who used to come to listen to us arrived, they listened, they drank their whiskey, another whiskey, they got warmed up, and when we finished, they waited for us at the bar to invite us for a drink, and, of course, what happened, since they wanted more *cante*:

"Let's go to this such and such a *venta*, or that one!"

We would go and be with the *señores* until the morning. I got many fiestas like that, and many very good tips. Because many foreigners used to come and I would give them the commercial smile and they would begin taking out the dollars.[1]

La Zambra opened with the noble goal of continuing the work begun in 1922 by Manuel de Falla and García Lorca, that of seeking out and preserving the old, pure *cantes* that had all but disappeared and making them accessible to all. In the interest of authenticity, the owner, Fernán A. Casares, hired *cantaores* who had not participated in the *ópera flamenca*. The youngest of them was the gypsy Rafael Romero at forty-four, and the oldest, Pericón de Cádiz at fifty-three. A few others, younger, would be added in the ensuing years—Pepe el Culata, José Menese, and Enrique Morente. And, keeping them all in line, sixty-year-old Perico el del Lunar (named for a large mole between his eyebrows that had long since been removed). Until its closing, upon the death of its director in 1975, La Zambra enjoyed a reputation as the citadel of authentic flamenco and remained faithful to its founding ideals.

That same year, another important event evolved out of the Zambra. Pericón explained:

While we were in Zambra, some Frenchmen came to record the first "anthology" to be made of *cante flamenco*. They spoke with Perico el del Lunar, and he was put in charge of assembling the *cantaores* who would each sing their specialties. So he went and looked for Pepe el de la Matrona, Niño Almadén, Rafael Romero, Jarrito, Bernardo de los Lobitos, and me, and he told us the *cantes* that we had to do. El de los Lobitos would come out singing the *cantes de trilla* [threshing songs]; El de la Matrona would do the true *serrana*;

[1] Ortiz Nuevo, *Pericón de Cádiz*, p. 64.

Almadén, the *cantes* of Chacón; in short, each did his specialty, and I did the *malagueña* of El Mellizo, *alegrías*, and *tientos*. I recall that a blind man came with the French team, a recording technician, and he was unbelievable. He would get into his booth, we would begin to rehearse, and the instant somebody hit a wrong note, there was the blind man notifying him to correct it. The ear of that blind man was really something!

Afterward, they made other anthologies: Mairena made his, Caracol, El de la Matrona. But the first was the one we made with Perico el del Lunar and the French, that had a terrific success, above all outside of Spain, because in France they gave it the *Grand Prix du Disque* and it sold throughout the world.

On one occasion, a Japanese man came into the Zambra. He was here in Spain to buy rice, and he told us that seventy thousand anthologies had just been shipped to Japan. Another day I ran into a reporter friend of mine and when he saw me he gave me the biggest hug in the world: "Pericón, I am going to give you the biggest hug in the world because you have given me a tremendous moment of joy."

"What happened to you, *hombre*?"

"Look here: I had to go to the Congo to take care of some things, and while I was in the Congo who could have told me I was going to listen to some *alegrías* of Cádiz? And when I heard you sing them it gave me a happiness that I will never forget."[1]

Pepe el de la Matrona left his recollections of the anthology:

Perico el del Lunar came looking for me to record the Anthology. He told me that some Frenchmen had come to record the old *cantes*, and he called me to sing some *cantes por soleá* that were no longer sung.

This was around 1955. We went to record in the home of a friend of mine, *Don* Ezequiel Selgas, who said when he saw me come in, "*Hombre!* What is this, dead and revived?"

"What are you saying *Don* Ezequiel?"

"*Hombre*, they told me that you had died."

"Well, let it be known that I have come back to life."

"*Hombre*, I'm glad to hear it. I wanted to know about you, but up until now..., because the people who organized this didn't tell me a word about which artists would be coming."

And in that man's house we recorded the *Anthology*. It took several days; some days they recorded some things, other days other things, and so on until it was done. Various artists came: some

---

[1] Ortiz Nuevo, *Pericón de Cádiz*, p. 68.

sang *malagueñas*, others a *fandango*, a *saeta*; in short, each one did something. And I, well, I was not permitted to go beyond what they had originally proposed to me. I recorded the *serranas*, and some *cantes por soleá*—the old *cantes* of Paquirri. And that was the first time that a recording was given the title, "Flamenco Anthology."[1]

This first anthology (collection of *cantes* organized by type or region) represented a true landmark in the rebirth, re-evaluation, and dissemination of flamenco throughout the world. It signaled the birth of the new science of flamencology, intitiated in a literary sense by the Argentinian, Anselmo González Climent, who coined the term and popularized it as the title of a flamenco essay published in 1955. The three-record Hispavox anthology, and the many others that would follow, served as a repositories of the old *cante* styles that had fallen into disuse and as textbooks for a young generation of *cantaores* who had grown up in the era of the *ópera flamenca* and had not heard those songs. Even the *cantaores* who participated in the Hispavox anthology had to be taught some of the ancient songs by Perico el del Lunar.

Vicente Escudero had been relatively inactive in the dance since 1946. He lived in Madrid with his longtime companion, Carmita García, and focused on painting, writing, and lecturing. In 1947, he published *Mi Baile*, a book about his life and dance. The following year saw an exhibit of his drawings and then, in 1949, he intensified his lecturing. He spoke in Madrid, where he and Carmita illustrated his points to the guitar of Vargas Araceli. In a later interview, Vicente gave a summary of these lectures:

> Repeatedly I have pointed out on the radio, in the press, and in lecture-demonstrations in Madrid, Barcelona, Granada, Sevilla, Cádiz, and Jerez (the last four being cradles of flamenco art) the unfortunate corruptions that are presented today as flamenco dance. I have invited newspaper men, writers, professional dancers and the public in general to debate, but no one has written to deny the veracity of my words, which would seem to indicate that they were in agreement with me. But then, I ask, why do they write in high praise when they see a dancer do wild jumps, run on his knees like a clown in a circus, contort himself, do convoluted turns or an endless series of spectacular movements which are, indeed, often effeminate? Only very few Spanish critics have dared to make such observations in print, and in France and England the same timidity exists.[2]

---

[1] Ortiz Nuevo, *Pepe el de la Matrona*, p. 159.
[2] Escudero, Vicente, "What is Flamenco Dance?" *Dance Magazine*, October 1955.

Two more books followed: *Pintura que Baila* [Paintings that Dance] and *The Enigma of Berruguete* by Dr. Luis de Castro, to which Vicente contributed illustrations and an explanation of the principles of flamenco dance. Escudero, although outspoken and highly opinionated, was proving himself to be one of the first flamencologists—a student of flamenco history and a defender of its traditions. The man who had once placed no restrictions on his experimentation, now led the call for a return to the purity of the past. In 1951, he published a pamphlet entitled, *Decalogue of Vicente Escudero on the Pure Flamenco Dance*. He explained: "All who wish to dance with purity must, without question, adhere to the ten points of my decalogue. At present, I know of no one who uses them in every sense." The ten points were as follows:

> 1) Dance as a man: "The personality of the Spanish man is grave, austere, with strong passions that achieve their dance expression in reserved, composed movements; a vertical unbroken line of the body from the hips upward...The character of the Spanish man in the dance is without effeminate thrusts of the arms, without spreading or crooking fingers, and without angular or waving movements of the hips. Those are the woman's movements."
>
> 2) Sobriety.
>
> 3) Turn the wrists from the inside outward, fingers together.
>
> 4) Hips quiet: "They should remain within the vertical line of the body and support it."
>
> 5) Dance *asentao* [firmly planted] and serenely: Avoid nervous, frantic movement.
>
> 6) Harmony of feet, arms, and head.
>
> 7) Esthetic and plastic purity: Avoid incorporating styles foreign to flamenco.
>
> 8) Style and accent: Authenticity of body line and interpretation.
>
> 9) Dance in traditional garb: "Arbitrary additions like wide sleeves, open-necked shirts, sashes...are in poor taste and produce a vulgar and false effect."
>
> 10) Achieve a variety of sounds through the inner emotional interpretation of the dramatic character of the dance, without metal taps on the shoes, inlaid wood on the stage, or other externals.

Escudero did not endear himself to other dancers when he publically applied these principles to them. We have seen how Carmen Amaya bristled at his remarks. And Antonio could not have been pleased to read that Escudero had invited him, especially, to take note of the decalogue.

In February of 1954, Vicente's hometown of Valladolid paid homage to him in a farewell performance. He was assisted by the his countrywoman, Mariemma, who had built her career as a dancer on the now somewhat antiquated style of La Argentina (she had even inherited the costumes of that legendary dancer):

> As he stood, quietly acknowledging the tumultuous applause, an ecstatic voice called out from the balcony, "Vicente, *esto es*" (Vicente, that's it!) And indeed it was. For, despite more than a decade of comparative inactivity, Vicente Escudero, the great master of the flamenco dance, had lost little of his touch. True, the years had slowed him down a bit, but his arrow-straight body and richly shaded *zapateado*, his stern gypsy face and ominous clicking fingernails, combined to epitomize flamenco dance in its age-old dignity and power.[1]

That benefit performance raised money for Escudero's trip to Paris, where he had been invited to head a Spanish dance academy in the Salle Pleyel. Once in Paris, Vicente focused on performing, but he may also have done some teaching. Dancer Doris Niles wrote:

> When I knew him Escudero was a strict teacher. Nothing was allowed to pass that did not measure up to his stern standards of perfection. For hours we danced back and forth before the small mirror in his unpretentious apartment in the Rue Victor-Masse in Paris, close by the Bal Tabarin.
>
> A simple *zapateado* was the beginning step. Then it was doubled, and contratemps injected; then tripled, and more unexpected contratemps, until truly it became a dance without end, mounting and mounting in variation and excitement. This was undertaken in various rhythms of *alegrías*, *fandanguillo*, *zambra*, *soleares*, *farruca*, and his beloved *siguiriyas*. Sometimes he taunted me by making steps so difficult and fast that I could not follow his lightning feet. We would end up sweating and laughing at my bewilderment.
>
> Then he would take up his guitar and say, "Dance!" (He would also say, "Don't tell anyone that I play the guitar!")[2]

A reporter who met with Vicente in Paris at that time described the veteran dancer:

> "We found him spare, wiry, animated and energetic. Time had affected his appearance very little. Erect, looking taller that his actual height, he walked bending only his knees. He moved and

---

[1] Krinkin, Alexandra, "Vicente, Esto Es!" *Dance Magazine*, February, 1955.
[2] Niles, Doris, *"El Duende," Dance Perspectives 27*, Autumn, 1966.

spoke with neat, rapid gestures to emphasize his ideas. In conversation he was animated, with reserved intensity, describing and 'sketching' his thoughts with occasional movements of his arms or whole body and flashes of dry, ironic humor. His personality suggested elasticity and a fluid, but self-contained vitality—the poise and fleetness of a heron."[1]

One source says that Escudero performed with his new company in the Champs Elysées Theater. But in an interview he made it clear that he had no interest in shouldering the responsibility of forming a company. He would perform, but others had to put the ensemble together. In Valladolid it had been Mariemma. Then, in Paris, the guitarist Perico el del Lunar assembled many of the artists who would form the *cuadro* of La Zambra that same year—Juanito Varea, Rafael Romero, Pepe el de la Matrona, and Rosa Durán, along with Carmita García, and Andrés Heredia on guitar. *The New York Times* reported that the Paris season was extremely successful and was extended again and again—in spite of the emphasis on traditional flamenco and the absence of theatrical numbers.

When the invitation came to visit the United States, after an absence of twenty years, Escudero agreed on the condition that he would not be responsible for the company that would surround him. A small flamenco group was located in San Sebastián, headed by the dancer Rosario Escudero and her cousin, the guitarist Mario Escudero. Other dancers in the Escudero company included Mario's wife (María Amaya) and José Barrera. To this nucleus were added dancers Pepita Valle, Antoñita Millán, and José Melero, the *cantaor* Chiquito de Levante, and the guitarist Manolo Vázquez "Sarasate" (a nickname given him as a child when he made the rounds of the bars with his violin). And finally, nineteen-year-old María Marquez, who had been located dancing in a hotel in Mallorca and would become Vicente Escudero's partner many years later, after the death of Carmita.

The success of José Greco in the United States had spawned a rebirth of interest in Spanish dance. Spanish ballet companies once again descended upon New York and fanned out across the country. Lola Montes had signed a long-term contract with Columbia Artists Management and was to tour seventy-two western cities and then follow with a tour of the East. Teresa and Luisillo appeared in the Mark Hellinger Theatre in New York. In February of 1955, Antonio and his Spanish Ballet—fifty members plus an orchestra—opened in the Palace Theatre. After a month, he moved to the Saville Theatre with a new program. Six months later, when Antonio returned to New York, John Martin would write:

> When he was last seen hereabouts, Antonio was a precocious youth of indisputable talent, but with far more interest in offering

[1] Krinkin, Alexandra, "Vicente, Esto Es!" *Dance Magazine*, February, 1955.

his good looks and his virtuosity for applause than in creating anything substantial artistically. He was also annoyingly mannered, with ballet arms and hands and what looked like an overwhelming ambition to end up dancing 'Swan Lake.' There is not a trace of any of this now; the young man has grown up. He has discovered the innate dignity of the Spanish dance, has acquired a certain humility before it, and has become an artist."[1]

While Antonio continued to experiment in New York with a theatrical approach to Spanish dance, complete with scenery and complex ensemble choreography, José Greco toured up and down the East coast with his company. In Spain, Roberto Ximénez and Manolo Vargas had left Pilar López to form their own company. In July they opened to tremendous acclaim in Buenos Aires and would soon add to the number of companies traversing the United States.

Into this glut of Spanish dancers came Vicente Escudero in February of 1955. John Martin came away from his New York concerts very impressed:

> Well along in his sixties [approaching seventy], he has less of the incendiary quality than he used to have, but he is still a great dancer. His feet are as exciting as they ever were; his *zapateado* is as subtle, as sensitive and as truly virtuoso. If there are only whispers left of that curious animal quality so characteristic of him, they are effective whispers, and they are accompanied now by a kind of mellow comment that gives them added carrying power.
>
> It is strangely moving to see a man of his years dancing, and doing it with full conviction and as naturally as he breathes. Sometimes he has great dignity, as in the *"Siguiriya Gitana;"* but much of the time he is fairly bubbling with a kind of fun that goes all the way to the edge of clowning...[2]

Martin continued his assessment a few days later:

> In his famous unaccompanied "Primitive Flamenco Rhythms," now danced with a spotlight on his feet, he still presents the subtlest, most brilliant and rhythmic *zapateado* of our time. In his newly developed *"Romeras"* he achieves the fullness of his medium with the simplest and most pertinent sketches of movement, performed with an inner strength that fills them in and gives them dimensions. [Escudero once explained: "The *romeras* are not different from the *alegrías* except for the song, and I have adapted it to the style of the *alegrías* because I regard it as the more ancient

---

[1]Martin, John. "Dance: Antonio and His Spanish Group." Copyright © *The New York Times*, October 3, 1955. Reprinted by permission.

[2]Martin, John, "Dance: Escudero Troupe."Copyright © *The New York Times*, February 8, 1955. Reprinted by permission.

and sober. But the dance has the same technique, style, and rhythm as the *alegrías*."] In the "Sevilla" of Albéniz, which he dances with Carmita García, his long-time partner, he turns his rhythmic comedy skill to the business of flirtation, and the fact of his age adds a hilarious and waggish fillip.

...Everything he does is charged with comment, much of it playful, some of it touched with sadness, all of it mellow and genuine.[1]

The printed program for the Playhouse performances reveals that the members of the *"Bailete"*—as the group headed by Mario and Rosario Escudero was labeled—played a relatively minor role. Rosario, María Amaya, and Pepita Valle danced only in group numbers, including *zorongo*, *villancicos*, *sevillanas*, *jota*, and a long hodge-podge of fragments of *siguiriyas-caña-alegrías-martinetes-caña-soleá-bulerías-alegrías-bulerías* composed by Mario Escudero and entitled *"Suite Flamenca."* A recording by the *Bailete*[2] reveals that Mario had already developed the technically advanced and syrupy "classical" guitar style that would become his trademark. Aside from Vicente, the star of the flamenco dance had to be María Marquez, who stopped the show with her *soleá* and *tientos*.

Vicente Escudero's two-week season in New York's Playhouse Theatre was extended time and again. A twelve-week tour of twelve cities followed and then a return to New York for an April farewell performance in the Brooklyn Academy of Music. Escudero said he was anxious to get back to Madrid to spend a quiet summer. His guitarist, Manolo Vázquez "Sarasate," remained behind and became a mainstay on the American flamenco scene until his sudden death while visiting Spain in 1978.

Escudero returned to New York in the fall. On October 31, he gave a concert in Carnegie Hall and began another "farewell" tour, this time with a hastily assembled group of American artists to support him. Along with Carmita and José Barrera, the company consisted of Teresita Osta, Rosa del Oro, Fernando Ramos, and a group of student dancers that included Clarisa Talve, who would later dance with Carmen Amaya. Carlos Montoya did the guitar accompaniment and played *granaínas* and *jota* as solos, while the singer was listed only as "Juanillo". The press was not kind to the group. Only Escudero, Carmita, and Montoya were considered "convincing." At least one number demonstrated that Escudero still had a knack for the unusual—a *tientos* danced to the rhythm of a windmill! John Martin wrote of Carlos Montoya: "He is not only a virtuoso guitarist, but also a musician, and however much one may resent musical interruptions in a dance program, Mr. Montoya's interludes constitute a notable exception."[3]

[1] Martin, John, "The Dance: Escudero." Copyright © *The New York Times*, February 13, 1955. Reprinted by permission

[2] *Fiesta Flamenca* (MGM Records E3214).

[3] Martin, John, "Dance: Artistic Farewell." *The New York Times*, October 31, 1955.

Only a few months later, on Easter Sunday, 1956, Carlos Montoya's manager, D'Lugoff, presented the guitarist as a soloist in the 1,200-seat Brooklyn Academy of Music. To everyone's surprise it sold out. Carlos was launched on what would become a highly popular and lucrative career as a concert artist. He would eventually tour each year to Europe, Australia, Japan, and all points of America, giving two-hundred fifty recitals a year and filling the largest concert halls available. He became "Mr. Flamenco" to a generation of concertgoers. His more than forty recordings would dominate ethnic record sales.

A record album[1] released in the mid-1950s (although recorded much earlier, perhaps while he was still with Argentinita) illustrates Montoya's approach to solo playing. Most obvious is the complete lack of any connection with the styles of solo guitar that had been developing in Spain during the preceeding fifty years—the schools of Ramón Montoya and Niño Ricardo. In Carlos' playing there is an almost complete absence of arpeggios, and his tremolo, although smooth, is used in a very simplistic manner, without complex melody or creative bass line. He does not use the *alzapúa*. That leaves a lot of lively thumb and *picado*, almost always interspersed with *ligados* (unplucked notes, played with the left hand). Throughout his career he would make little use of the harmony and counterpoint that had been creeping into flamenco music, and he placed little emphasis on composition, his pieces generally consisting of melody, rhythm, melody, rhythm, etc. Montoya had spent a great deal of his life outside of Spain and it appears that he stayed with the basic accompaniment style of playing that he had mastered in his youth. He said on one occasion, "I have deliberately kept to the old flamenco, but have enlarged upon it in my manner of playing."

On this early recording, Montoya played the lightest of *toques* [guitar forms]—the *tanguillos, sevillanas, alegrías,* and *bulerías*. Most of these are based on his renditions of popular songs. The two *bulerías* are almost identical potpourris of songs he had learned with Argentinita—*"Anda jaleo"* and *"Los cuatro muleros"* from Lorca, and a variety of folk songs from the north of Spain. The same is true of two *tanguillos* and the *sevillanas*. An *alegrías* is almost indistinguishable from the ancestral *jota*. His version of *zambra* bears no resemblance to the Moorish pieces being recorded by others. In the *tarantas*, he showed that he had already developed the ability to play long passages with the left hand alone. And finally, in *saeta* (the religious song of Holy Week) he showed off a gimmick that would unfailingly earn him a standing ovation throughout his career—a snare drum effect created by plucking two bass strings held crossed one over the other on the fingerboard.

What enthralled Carlos Montoya's audiences and brought them to their feet was the emotion he conveyed in his playing. There can be no denying

---

[1] *Carlos Montoya* (Stinson Records, New York). The jacket notes indicate that the material had been recorded earlier and released on 78s.

that, whatever else his playing was or was not, it always had heart and energy. The guitarist himself explained: "Playing has been advanced *technically* very much over the years, However, I don't think it has advanced *musically* to any great extent. I don't believe that anyone has the feeling of the old artists."

Carlos was the first to give flamenco guitar concerts on a wide scale. Mario Escudero summed up his contribution: "One pioneer to whom we are much indebted is Carlos Montoya. Each person has his own taste in guitar playing—there is no accounting for taste—but we owe him a great deal, for he was a trailblazer who opened the way for the rest of us."

In late September, 1955, Carmen Amaya returned to New York. She was brought by Maurice Attias, who had also brought Escudero. Her company had spent the previous year giving concerts in South America and Mexico. During that time, the strain of constant touring and living in close quarters began to tell. Carmen's husband, Juan Antonio, had been challenging the control of Paco Amaya, attempting to put financial affairs in order, and stripping the company of dead wood—those family members who did not contribute their fair share to the performances.

Ironically, Juan Antonio was capable of extravagance himself. On one occasion, Carmen and her people had dined with a baron in one of the most expensive restaurants in Paris. When the long evening finally came to an end, Juan Antonio went to pay for the dinner and found that the baron had beat him to it. Angrily, the guitarist insisted that he be permitted to pay in the name of Carmen Amaya. His masculine pride and Latin possessiveness had led him to vow that nobody would ever pay for his wife. He demanded to see the maitre d' and then the manager, but to no avail. After raising a big fuss, he did manage to learn the amount of the bill: 200,000 *pesetas* (about $2,500). The following morning, Juan Antonio bought 200,000 *pesetas*' worth of flowers and had them sent to the home of the baron. "Carmen and all of her gypsies sat on a terrace in front of the mansion and, amid jokes, handclapping, fingersnapping, and songs, watched three truckloads of flowers, reaching to the roof, unload at the baron's home."[1]

The friction between Carmen's husband and her family led to changes in the company. Her sister María and Mario Escudero had already gone. According to Goldberg, Antonia did not get along with Juan Antonio; she and her husband, Chiquito de Triana, left the company in Guatemala. They would later be joined by Leonor and her husband, Roberto Rico, in Mexico City, where they would settle and teach dance.[2] Goldberg also states that Carmen had performed for the first two months of 1955 in El Patio, the same nightclub in which she had danced fifteen years earlier.

[1] Mañas, p. 13.
[2] Goldberg, p. 272.

While in Mexico City, Carmen reunited with Sabicas. The guitarist had married a Mexican woman and had a son. Apparently he was still on relatively good terms with his wife, for that year they conceived a baby daughter who would be born in 1956. The wife and children would join Sabicas in New York in 1957 and it must be assumed that they divorced shortly after that. Perhaps Sabicas' reunion with Carmen Amaya and the stresses of the touring life had put a strain on the marriage. Sabicas phrased it succinctly: "I was married once and it was a mess. I thought I could handle it, and I was handled!"[1]

Carmen needed to fill the gaps in the company created by the departure of family members. While in Buenos Aires, she found Olga Fernández, a young dancer of Spanish heritage, and immediately hired her. Olga would pair with Paco's son Curro, who had become a full-fledged performing member of the company. They would later marry. Then, in Mexico City, Carmen hired two new dancers: fourteen-year-old Begona Palacios and sixteen-year-old Lucerito Tena. Lucero would later head her own companies, become the headliner for years in Madrid's prestigious *tablao* Corral de la Morería, and achieve world-renown for her castanet playing. Unlike Luisillo, Lucero never failed to give credit to her mentor:

—What is flamenco, Lucero, and what does it mean to you?

Lucero laughs. "I could answer both questions in two words: Carmen Amaya!"

Carmen Amaya, called the greatest *bailaora* of all time, was Lucero's *"maestra incomparable."* It was she who transformed the Mexican-born and Spanish-naturalized young artist into what the critics have called "the dancer for whom the Spanish dance holds no secrets." She lived with Carmen Amaya and her sister for several years.

"I was with her constantly. She trained me, formed me, taught me everything I know about flamenco... Carmen revolutionized flamenco," insists Lucero, almond eyes sparkling. "Before her, it was danced from the waist up, but she danced it from head to foot, with all of herself. 'It should be danced and imagined,' she used to say, 'like a serpent rising and coiling from the earth.' She was wonderful, wonderful! There are no words to contain her art. She was a genius, and even that does not say enough. She was of a race whose moving spirit is mystery, and to dance flamenco you must *know* mystery; *duende* the gypsies call it; they have it in their blood. It is that which makes them a people who just hear the guitar and they already know how to dance."[2]

With the addition of these dancers, Carmen Amaya's company lacked only

---
[1] Molarsky interview.
[2] Grimble, June A. *Guidepost*, July 7, 1967.

one important element: a *cantaor*. According to Goldberg, Carmen contacted Antonio Mairena in Spain, asking him to find a singer for her. Mairena had toured with Teresa and Luisillo for several years and then had joined Antonio's Spanish ballet when he was offered more money. He spoke of the difficulties flamenco artists had faced in Franco's post-war Spain and how the touring ballets had been his salvation:

> When the Civil War was over, Sevilla went downhill and everyone went to Madrid, where there was life for this art. And it was necessary to go. Everyone who wasn't in the *ópera flamenca* went there—the guitarists, singers, and dancers. There, they had the *colmaos*, the *ventas*, and sometimes you would find a fiesta with some drunks for a few *pesetas*. When I would go to a fiesta full of drunks, I had a couple of *cuplés* I had practiced so that I could get by and earn something. That's how I earned a living.
>
> I almost died from the kind of life I led. The years went by and I never saw the sun. And drinking...I drank everything there was to drink. And I fell sick in bed, in a *pensión* in Madrid. And when I didn't have any more money to pay the *pensión*, I said to myself, 'Where am I going? I'll have to get out of here to earn a living!'
>
> Then they looked me up to go abroad with a ballet, with Teresa and Luisillo. They paid me whatever they felt like. And I went for the 3,500 French *francs* they gave me. I went as part of the group. But that got me out of the life of drinking and staying up all night, from that life that could have killed me. Many things happened. I wasn't treated with importance—I was just an adornment for the dance. Then Antonio realized that he needed me for his ballet flamenco. I was good for him. And it was lucky for me. The *cante* still didn't have a market, but in the ballet I started to become known. They renewed my contract and doubled the salary... because the press was starting to say that Antonio had a great *cantaor*.[1]

Mairena and the guitarist Manuel Morao would be with Antonio for almost ten years. The *cantaor* said that he got along well with the difficult Antonio, that they never had a disagreement, and that the dancer never criticised him. He claimed that they never had the need to rehearse together.

If Mairena was in Spain to help Carmen Amaya find a singer, it must have been in the summer of 1955, during a break in his American tours with Antonio's ballet. He recommended a young singer from Jerez named Domingo Alvarado. Carmen had wanted a gypsy singer, but she acceded to Mairena's recommendation and Domingo was soon on a boat headed for New York.[2]

---
[1]Delgado, José, and A. Ramos Espejo, "I was Strong as a Horse." *El Ideal*, November 1981.
[2]Goldberg, 275.

Friday night, September 30, Carmen returned to Carnegie Hall for the first of four concerts. The other performing members of the company were her brother Antonio, Paco and his sons, Diego and Curro (La Chata appeared only in a supporting role), Goyo Reyes (who shared credit for choreography) and Pepita Ortega, Olga Fernández, Lucerito Tena, Begona Palacios, the singer Domingo Alvarado, and five guitarists: Sabicas, Agüero, Paco, Diego Castellón, and an American guitarist, Juan Perrín. Goldberg states that Perrín would be instrumental in funding many of their American concerts. Diego Castellón told her: "The agent was Juanito Perrín, a young American who played the guitar. Attias represented us, but Juan Perrín, a very good person, financed it."[1] Other sources explain that Perrin would exhaust most of a family inheritance assisting the Amayas over the next several years. Carmen's pianist for some time had been Alfredo Speranza. Born in Uruguay and trained in Europe, Speranza composed a piece for her entitled *"Danza a Carmen Amaya"* ("Dance for Carmen Amaya") that she had been using as her opening number, alternating it with *"Embrujo del Fandango."*

The Carnegie Hall concerts followed the pattern established by Argentinita, although, in keeping with the times, placed considerably more emphasis on flamenco. With the exception of her opening number, Carmen left the non-flamenco numbers, those performed to piano and orchestral accompaniment, to others. Goyo Reyes danced the *bolero* and partnered Pepita in a classical *"siguiriyas"* entitled *"Dolor y Gozo"* (by Freyre). He was also highly praised for his *farruca* in the flamenco *cuadro*. In fact, Goyo was the only dancer aside from Carmen to be singled out for his excellent work. One reviewer wrote: "In his first number he takes your eye and you spend the rest of the evening watching for him." Other numbers included the opening "Sevilla," by Albéniz and a *jota* danced by couples.

Carmen opened the flamenco with her *soleá*. It was no longer the elaborate and theatrical *fragua* number she had done in Europe, but it *was* more than five minutes of impassioned flamenco dancing to the *cante* of Domingo Alvarado that left the audience breathless. According to Alvarado, the ovation had her bowing for minutes.[2]

If the audience reacted that way to the *soleá*, it is hard to imagine what they did for her *siguiriya*. When she entered, wearing a white ruffled dress with an immense train, her castanets growling and purring to the masterful guitar of Sabicas, the effect must have been awe-inspiring. Sabicas claimed that he and Carmen never rehearsed. The creative process could be seen on stage. When Sabicas played an elaborate melody, Carmen would accompany with her castanets, at first tentatively, feeling her way, and then when she had it figured out she would enter confidently, embellishing and crowning the *falseta* with her rhythm. Carmen's handling of train dresses was leg-

---
[1] Goldberg interviews.
[2] Goldberg, p. 276.

endary. The ability to move about the stage, turning and spinning while entangled in yards of starched cotton and then kicking the heavy train into the air far from the body is a skill not mastered by many. In truth, the length of Carmen's trains has often been grossly exaggerated, with estimates of ten to fifteen feet. A measurement of the trains in her photos shows them to be no more than five or six feet in length. Due to her tiny stature, they appeared much longer. The more than seven minutes of seemingly endless climactic build-ups, thundering footwork, and sudden stops in the *siguiriya* must have left the audience drained.

And finally, the *alegrías*. This trademark number had evolved into more than nine minutes (long by any standard) of what John Martin called "an incredible manifestation of Amayan dynamics," and it could be followed by no other number. It closed the program. The footwork solo alone, a prodigious display of subtle shading, fiery strength and speed, and intense passion, occupied more than four minutes. Carmen had created a model to be copied by all dancers after her.

The public and the press were overwhelmed by the new Amaya. John Martin wrote:

> ...she left us [ten years previous] a whirlwind gypsy without much form or discipline, she returns to us an artist.
>
> Her performance now looks as if she had spent the years making a study of herself until she has perfected a sharply etched, fiercely concentrated stage portrait of Carmen Amaya. All her old qualities are still present, but she has cut away the superfluities and stripped the characterization to its essence. She is the merest wisp of a woman, moving constantly in a state of hardly constrained violence. The quieter she is the more intense is the latent power behind her movement. Nothing is wasted; when she raises an arm, however slowly, it stays raised.
>
> When she cuts loose and unleashes her force for a phrase or two, the atmosphere fairly vibrates. There is not a square inch of her taut little body that is not alive with animal vigor, and there is as much passion in the sharp, hard pounding of the nervous feet.[1]

After returning to see Amaya again, Martin came away even more impressed:

> The new Amaya is overwhelming... She has awakened, quite without arrogance, to the fact that she is a great lady, and within the frame of this realization she shows us...the real beauty and essence of her art.
>
> ...she makes only five appearances, but in all of them she cuts

---

[1] Martin, John, "Dance: Carmen Amaya." Copyright © *The New York Times,* October 1, 1955. Reprinted by permission.

"...the new, the more austere, the more fiercely elegant Amaya"—John Martin

across the scene with such power and intensity that any more would be difficult to take. She is a tiny creature, lean and taut and electric. Every movement is animated by a feeling of latent violence, held in check only by an equal power of control. When she lifts an arm it is as if it were forcing itself through a weight of water...

...If it may seem regrettable that she no longer sings...that may really no longer be part of the new, the more austere, the more fiercely elegant Amaya.

In our time we have had a handful of great Spanish dancers—La Argentina, La Argentinita, Escudero, all striking personalities and artists of individual genius; now, in all fairness, we can do no less than add the name of La Amaya to the list.[1]

After the Carnegie Hall concerts, the company toured through the East for several weeks and then returned for an unannounced two-and-a-half-week engagement in the Holiday Theater, beginning on November 20. In the interim, New York had been visited by both Vicente Escudero and Antonio (described earlier), and Teresa and Luisillo had returned for a second American tour. But, in spite of the surfeit of Spanish dance in the city and the late notice, Carmen's opening night was attended by a large and enthusiastic audience. The company had shrunk again: This time it was Antonio Amaya and Pepita Lláser who had jumped ship. Several new numbers were of interest. Carmen demonstrated that she continued to believe in the importance of classical numbers by programming a suite of pieces by Albéniz—"Sevilla," "Asturias," and "Triana." *"Repiqueteo Flamenco,"* a duet danced by Lucero Tena and Diego Amaya, was credited to Mario Escudero and may have been a variation of the *zapateado* that Mario would record later as a solo.

Finally, Carmen introduced the American public to her *"Ritmos Carmen Amaya,"* a *bulerías* that she had been evolving for some time, in which she sang and danced. In later versions she would often sit and rap out a surprisingly complex display of rhythm with her knuckles on a table top. In the Holiday Theatre performances, Carmen would enter this number with blazing footwork, matched by the equally fiery *falsetas* of Sabicas, and then sing several verses interspersed with dance. The critic from *The New York Times* wrote: "Miss Amaya never ceases to dance; even in the midst of her song, the shrug of a shoulder or the sharp turn of her head was exciting movement." The rest of the program was the same as that of the Carnegie Hall concerts. As was so often the case, the critic did not think highly of other dancers in Carmen's company, writing: "Throughout the program, Miss Amaya danced with a completely unforced intensity that was, unfortunately, lacking in the other members of her group."[2]

[1] Martin, John, "The Dance: Spanish."Copyright © *The New York Times*, October 9, 1955. Reprinted by permission.
[2] *The New York Times*, November 21, 1955.

Immediately after the engagement in the Holiday Theatre, Carmen and her company traveled to Hollywood to work for almost two weeks in the Huntington Hartford Theater, finishing on New Year's Eve. Lola Montes reestablished her contact with Carmen and they began to evolve a deep friendship over the next five years. Lola says that Carmen would send notes announcing her arrival in Los Angeles and ask her to get ready to cook up some fried fish and roasted peppers. Lola describes the company in the Huntington Hartford as the best that Carmen would bring to Los Angeles, with Lucero Tena and Sabicas.

According to Goldberg, Juan Antonio had a disagreement with Maurice Attias and broke with his management company. The Amaya company would go it alone until they signed to tour with Charles Green (former manager with Attias) later in the year.[1] Back in New York, the company worked in the Chateau Madrid for six weeks and spent five weeks in the Lincoln Theatre. According to Diego Castellón, the company lost a great deal of money during this period and often depended on Juan Perrín to keep them afloat. Perrín had become close friends with Juan Antonio and often acted as agent for the company.

While in New York, Carmen recorded a long-play record that would become a classic and a monument to her art. Decca Records approached Juan Agüero with an offer. Sabicas described the contract:

> Her [Carmen's] husband came to tell me, "They are paying $1,200 for the record: four-hundred for the *palmeros*, the ones who do the handclapping, four-hundred for Carmen, and four-hundred for you."
>
> Imagine, a record for four-hundred dollars! How was I going to make a record for four-hundred dollars? Not unless I were a mariachi! He even came to my house: "Please Mr. Sabicas!"
>
> "No!"
>
> "Can't you see that it is publicity for us?"
>
> Well, they convinced me. There were twenty-five *tíos* against me, and I had to do it. We recorded it, and it was marvelous. A record gives a lot of fame.[2]

Apparently the recording did not go smoothly at first. Sabicas spoke of difficulty in getting started:

> Records are like everything else, very difficult. I cannot emphasize enough how difficult it is to do a record the way you want to. It is almost impossible. I hear a record and I know I can do it better. That is why I don't like any of them. You know that you can always do it better. One can always improve. But to do it at the

---

[1] Goldberg, p. 284.
[2] Molarsky interview.

moment that you are taping, that is very difficult. Sometimes it happens. Carmen and I taped a record when we came here.

Poor Carmen—she was smoking all the time. She would go into a room and smoke a whole pack by herself. I told her to stop smoking, but she never paid attention. I said it from the heart, because a woman who dances should not smoke. Finally, I stopped mentioning it.

She would say, "Sabas, do something with the guitar to cheer me up!"

"And who is going to cheer me up so that I can do these things for you?"

We began to tape, and I said, "I cannot play, Carmen, I do not feel well."

"Let's go," she said.

"What happened, Mr. Sabicas?" [the record executive asked]

"I do not feel well."

"But, what happened?"

I had everything—coffee...everything. The man came to hug me. "Mr. Sabicas, please!"

I didn't feel well. We went to the hotel, we had dinner, and we went to bed. I picked up the guitar again, I studied, and in two or three days we recorded it. It was wonderful—that's how Carmen was. I leave the record as proof for the centuries.[1]

Queen of the Gypsies: The Rhythms of Carmen Amaya (Decca DL 9816) is a stunning tour de force. Except for the background handclapping, the record is all Carmen Amaya, Sabicas, and the *cantaor* Domingo Alvarado. As a dancer, Carmen was particularly well-suited for audio recording because of the powerful rhythms she produced with her hands, fingers, and feet. As Sabicas put it, "She was immersed in the *compás*. She did it in such a way that you had the urge to say *'Olé!'* even when you were just listening to a record and could not see her."[2]

The album features the flamenco numbers that Carmen was performing in concert at that time. The opening *bulerías*, *"Ritmo de Carmen Amaya,"* explodes with rhythm. Unseen feet spit fire and sparks fly from steely fingers as Carmen sings to the crisp guitar of Sabicas. Carmen's full-length concert solos are all here: *soleares*, *siguiriyas*, and *alegrías*. In two other numbers, Carmen both sings and dances: The *tangos* had been in her repertoire for years and, according to Diego Castellón, she had often sung them for her sisters. The other number, entitled *"Rondeña,"* was a true innovation.

Rondeñas are *fandangos* from Ronda and thought to be the oldest form of

[1] Molarsky interview.
[2] Molarsky interview.

the *fandango*. The *rondeña* had already been made into a dramatic guitar solo (with little resemblance to the original dance form) by Miguel Borrull and Ramón Montoya. Following the model of the *taranto*, Carmen and Sabicas converted the simple and festive *rondeña* into a profound *cante*. They changed the rhythm from a lively 3/4 time to a heavy, droning 4/4 typical of the *zambra*, and played it in the tones of the *minera* (based on the somber G# chord) that had been developed as a solo by Ramón Montoya. Carmen's singing is anything but festive as she gives the *rondeña* the mournful *aire* of the *tarantos*. For the finale of this piece, Carmen dances to a rhythm that returns to the ancestral 3/4 of the *fandangos*, but maintains the dirge-like drone of the *zambra*.

Sabicas completes the album with four solos. The *taranta, soleares, siguiriya*, and *soleá por bulerías* are gems of composition and inspiration. They are short, two to three minutes each, but packed with innovation. Sabicas excelled in the ability to create beautiful melodies in *toques* that tend to be rather monotonous (especially the *siguiriyas*), and he did it without losing any of the essential flamenco flavor. For the solos on this record, he placed the *cejilla* on the fourth fret, effectively cutting the fingerboard in half, but brightening the guitar considerably. The virtuosity, creativity, and passion displayed here are truly unique in flamenco's history.

For the next year, Carmen criss-crossed America, from New York to California, from Florida to Canada, with forays into Mexico, Central America, and Cuba. The make-up of her company changed often. Goyo Reyes and Pepita Ortega returned briefly to Spain to get married. They were replaced by María Guzmán and Miguel Marín. Paco and La Chata left. Jesús Sevilla joined the company.

Performances ranged from small flamenco shows in cabarets and restaurants to full concert recitals in civic theaters. When the company returned to the the Holiday Theatre in November of 1956, the press reported that the costuming was not what it had once been and there was little in the way of stage decoration or special choreography. The focus was on Carmen Amaya and her flamenco. On January 4th and 5th, she gave recitals in the Brooklyn Academy of Music. A critic wrote:

> The opening program of Carmen Amaya and her company was almost amusingly chaotic. Spotlights wavered; straps snapped on costumes; seams split; shoe laces opened, hats flew off. And there was an irresponsible substitution of numbers without previous announcement. A Gypsy mood was rampant.
>
> And yet it didn't make too much difference. For, at best, Miss Amaya's company is a time filler between her solos... Her *solear-*

es with singer, guitarist, and two male dancers was almost balletic in its four-part structure. First her disdainful flirtation with the musicians; then the entrance of the men and her briefly savage response to them, followed by her departure. And her return to be mesmerized again by the singer. The dance created a complete emotional image, yet its surface retained the rough grain of welling anger...

While Amaya has grown and mellowed through the years, she has not improved in her ability to handle a company. She assembled a fairly presentable group of dancers, headed by the serious and sensitive Goyo Reyes. But their numbers were perfunctorily paced and choreographed in monotonous unison fashion...[1]

Yet, the following year, Carmen gave full concerts with a greatly expanded repertoire. An elaborate program booklet accompanied these performances. The 1939 painting by Ruano Llopis of Carmen in the dress she used for *"Embrujo del Fandango"* graced the cover. Photos and a fanciful biographical sketch by Domingo José Samperio completed the booklet. Samperio, an aficionado from Málaga living in exile in Mexico was instrumental in the recording of flamenco's second important anthology. The *Antología del Cante Flamenco*, produced in 1957 by the Orfeón Company of Mexico, was again organized by Perico el del Lunar and featured many of the same singers as the original Hispavox anthology. Among the almost fifty examples of *cante*, was a delightful *tarantos* by Leonor Amaya. The two *coplas* of *tarantos*, sung superbly by Leo in her soft, throaty voice, were recorded in Mexico with the guitar of Manolo Medina, and are very likely the first recording of this *cante* in its modern, danceable form.

Carmen's nomadic existence must have played a role in the constant need to revamp her company. Even her own family could not keep up with her—always on the move, day after day, month after month, year after year. With her family gone, she had to keep an eye out for new talent. For a period in 1957 she was joined by a cousin on her mother's side—Micaela Flores Amaya, better known in artistic circles as *"La Chunga"* ("The Ugly"—a name passed down in the family).

Nineteen-year-old La Chunga had been discovered as a young girl by the painter Francisco Rebés, dancing barefoot *rumbas* in the bars of Barcelona. Rebés used her as a model and found work for her dancing in the cabaret El Emporium, where she became a favorite of Catalonian intellectuals. In 1956, Pastora Imperio took the young gypsy under her wing as her protégé and put her in a *tablao* in Palamós. When La Chunga was ready, she made her Madrid debut in the new *tablao*, La Corral de la Morería. A movie producer saw her there and, captivated by her beauty and natural manner of

[1]*Dance Magazine*. March 1957.

dancing, brought her to Hollywood to appear in two films. After a brief stint with Carmen Amaya, La Chunga performed in Las Vegas and on the Ed Sullivan Show with a young guitarist named Juan Serrano—who had just arrived from Spain. A photograph of La Chunga in the clutches of a grinning Ed Sullivan showed her to be an exquisite beauty. With Carmen's help she was contracted to dance in El Patio in Mexico City and then she returned to Spain where her dancing career blossomed. But, just three years later she would marry and retire from dancing (to return some years later).

A young dancer in New York auditioned for Carmen. Clarissa Talve, who had studied with José Cansino in Hollywood and Vicente Escudero in New York, described her experience:

> Carmen Amaya and Company had arrived in New York. It was the summer of 1957, with the usual New York heat wave. She was looking for a dancer and all the young aspiring dancers were excited. The suspense and expectation was too much for all of us. Who would she pick? We all tried to remain calm, but really wished, hoped, and wondered.
>
> Weeks went by and finally the news came...I was chosen! My first meeting with Carmen was awesome. My idol. The great Carmen! To be in her presence...I could hardly believe it! At first glance she seemed fierce and I was very frightened. Seeing her so close, I soon realized that she only came up to my shoulders in height. Her body was like that of a young boy. Sinuey, muscular, and perfect. She was very dark-skinned, with her hair pulled back in a knot. I could feel her electric presence. After a few minutes of talking, I was amazed to find that she was so kind, lovely, and humble. I thought, "She is truly a great artist." She had quickly remarked that I looked like a gypsy (I was also dark-skinned, intense-looking, with a strong body). She was amused and quite fascinated with my Sephardic background. "Of course, how else could you dance like that," she observed, *"una americana!"* She was very pleased that I looked like one of the "tribe."
>
> The gypsies accepted me as one of their own and I loved to be with them. I was quickly rushed into rehearsals with the rest of the company—Sabicas, Diego Castellón, Domingo Alvarado... We used the old Alexandro studios on 57th Street for approximately two weeks. I recall that I had a lot of choreography to learn in a short time, but my excitement was so overwhelming that nothing but being with Carmen Amaya mattered to me.[1]

Goyo Reyes and wife, Pepita, had returned for the fall season. They were featured prominently in a greatly expanded repertoire, with emphasis on

---

[1] Talve, Clarissa, "Memories of Carmen." *Jaleo, Vol X, No 1.* 1987.

music by Albéniz—*"Puerta Tierra,"* (*bolero*), *"Rumores de la Caleta"* (based on melodies of the *fandangos* of Málaga), and "Castilla" (*seguidillas*) and "Cádiz" from *"Suite Iberia."* Carmen added a powerful *caña* and an intricate *zapateado* danced to the melodies of Sabicas' guitar. She also resurrected her *farruca* to further broaden an already ample flamenco repertoire.

The Los Angeles agent Mary Bran brought the Amaya Company to California for concerts in November. An aficionado recalls her disappointment when a Los Angeles performance had to be cancelled due to Carmen's ill health. It is not clear what particular ailment sidelined Carmen on that particular occasion, but she had been experiencing periodic severe back pains for some time. In New York, her husband had attempted to convince her to see a doctor, but she put him off, saying she would do it later.

On the 29th, Carmen danced in San Diego's Russ Auditorium. In spite of suffering a severe headache and other flu symptoms, she only cancelled one number. The *San Diego Union* reported that she danced with such fury that nobody in the audience could have suspected she was ill. Solos by Sabicas were among the most applauded numbers of the evening, and the dance critic added "A kind word, too, for Juan Antonio Agüero, a spare guitarist."[1]

Sabicas and Carmen parted ways once more toward the end of 1957. But before they did, they recorded again with Decca Records. *Flamenco! Carmen Amaya* (Decca DL 9925) is distinctly different from the previous album. Carmen had already recorded her dance solos, so the only dancing on the second album occurs incidently to her singing. Sabicas said of Carmen's singing, "She sang better than she danced. She had a lot of charm when she sang. I used to encourage her when I played the guitar. I was always on the lookout with her, because she always came out with something strange. She would come out and drive you crazy. I was always looking at her feet—that's why it always turned out well."[2]

It appears that Carmen and Sabicas were at a loss for material to record. Half of the numbers are solos by Sabicas. His *tientos-tanguillo*, *alegrías* (in A-major), *danza mora*, and *rondeñas* are superbly played concert solos, but lack the intensity of the work he did on *Queen of the Gypsies*. Carmen sings a lackluster *bulerías* entitled *"Cuando pa Chile me voy,"* the group does an insignificant set of *sevillanas* with the *cante* of Domingo Alvarado, and Sabicas plays a brief *malagueña-verdiales* with his brother, Diego. These appear to be fillers, thrown in to complete the album.

But the core of this record is three songs by Carmen: The *garrotín* is recorded for the first time in the modern era and very likely inspired its subsequent popularity. A nine-minute *colombiana* would be instrumental in the revival of this song and its elevation to a major branch of *cante*. The most

---

[1] Herreshoff, Constance, "Amaya's Dancing Vivid Despite Flu." *San Diego Union*, December 1, 1957.
[2] Molarsky interview.

unexpected number is the *"Jaleo Canastero."* Jaleos are a form of *bulerías* cultivated by the gypsies of Extremadura (well outside the flamenco zone of Andalucía); they did not enter the mainstream of flamenco until well into the 1970s. During a television interview, Sabicas spoke about recording this song: "I recall that we were rehearsing the *"Jaleos Canasteros"* in a studio and Carmen was singing it. When we began to record it, I went to put the *cejilla* at the right place for her voice, but Carmen wouldn't let me, because she said that if we stopped we would lose the heat of the moment. That's why, at certain moments, you can hear that the pitch is too low for her."[1]

One has to question this story, for while it is true that Carmen struggles with the low tones, it is equally true that Sabicas already had the *cejilla* at the eighth fret, where is is very difficult to play. At most, he could have moved the *cejilla* one fret higher—a relatively insignificant half tone. Sabicas could also have played at a lower fret by playing in different chords, but he would have lost the sound he was after.

Goldberg traces Carmen's travels in early 1958 to California, through the Southwest and its border towns, and on to Puerto Rico for six weeks in the summer. She had a new guitarist: René Heredia, a seventeen-year-old gypsy whose family had emigrated from Granada to the United States in the early 1940s. He told of his early days with Carmen:

> Carmen Amaya's father, José Amaya "El Chino," and my father, José Heredia "El Clavijo," were both *gitanos puros de los cuatro costaos* [pure gypsy on all sides] and very close friends. They were both gypsy guitarists.
>
> It was not until 1957 that Carmen heard me play the guitar for the first time. She was looking for a first guitarist to replace Sabicas, who had left the company to launch his solo and recording career in the United States. I was Carmen's guitarist for four consecutive years, from 1957 to 1960. At that time I learned more from her than from any other one person...Through Carmen I met all of the top artists in the flamenco world—singers, dancers, guitarists, and *juerguistas*.
>
> Playing the guitar for Carmen Amaya was a great responsibility that I respected. When you played for her it was like floating on a cloud... When she danced, she would carry the whole company. Everyone, audience and performers, would give her their undivided attention. It was like everyone was in a trance. In fact, when Carmen really wanted to dance, she would go into a trance. I'm positive she was in a world of her own. But yet she knew what everyone else was doing on and off stage. She knew where the guitarists were in their *compás* [rhythm], what the singer was doing with his *tercios*

---

[1] Television program *Madrid Flamenco*, on Onda Madrid, 1987.

[phrases], and what the dancers were doing with their *palmas* [handclapping]. She was a walking computer of *compás*. Her technique was not only original, but also impeccable.

Not only did Carmen transform the dance world, but she would improvise on the spot like no other dancer. In fact, she had such strength in her footwork that, at times, she would ruin the dance floors in the theaters where we performed. I remember in 1958, when we were in Cuba at the Riviera Hotel, she was doing her famous *alegrías*. She was off to one side of the stage. The guitars had stopped playing and she was dancing to the accompaniment of the *palmas*. There was complete silence except for her thunderous *zapateo* and the *palmas* of the other dancers. I was watching her feet and I could not believe my eyes. The floor of the stage started to splinter and crack! Carmen just moved over a little to one side of the stage and continued her dance. [According to Lola Montes, Carmen could go through a pair of shoes in one number.] Carmen's *palmas* were so loud that you could hear them over the other dancers—sometimes as many as twenty people. Then she would start with her fingersnaps, the strongest I've ever heard![1]

Carmen returned to Spain at the end of 1958. Hidalgo places her in Paris in October, for performances in the Étoile Theater, but the press called her concerts the following January the first in many seasons. And it would have been difficult for her to perform immediately, for she had returned essentially alone, with only her husband, her nephew Diego, and the guitarist René Heredia. Paco and la Chata stayed behind, as did Curro and Olga, who would eventually make their home in Puerto Rico. The Amaya family was settling down. But Carmen couldn't stop. Something compelled her to continue, even if it meant going on alone. In her childhood she had danced through the nights to support her family. As a teenager she often worked two jobs each night, rushing from one cabaret or theater to another in such haste that she had sprained her ankle on one occasion. Then she had traveled the world under the heavy burden of maintaining an ever-increasing number of family members. The family knew that without Carmen they had little to offer and jealously cloistered her and discouraged any relationship that might take her away from them. Now the family had abandoned her, but she still wouldn't or couldn't stop.

The impression of many has been that Carmen was only really happy when she danced. Off stage she was just Carmen. On stage she was Carmen Amaya! Diego Castellón said, "Carmen was always demure, very quiet; she was never robust socially. Yet when she would go on stage, she was an animal; you thought you had run into a demon...!"[2] Odette Lumbroso put it this

---
[1] Heredia, René, "A Carmen Amaya." *Jaleo, Vol IV, No 4*. December, 1980.
[2] Goldberg interviews.

Carmen with guitarist René Heredia c. 1959. Standing left to right: El Chino Amaya, Diego Amaya, Alejandro Manzano. *Photo courtesy of Marilyn Perrin*

way: "On stage she was proud and arrogant; on the contrary, in her private life she was reserved, spoke little, and was not particularly happy, like an unfortunate child who takes refuge in his dreams (until the day she met Juan Antonio and from then on she appeared more expressive)... Her life was not easy, you know. For her nothing existed except the dance. She was an introverted person accustomed to living with the painful feeling of sacrifice..."[1]

On the same subject, British critic Elsa Brunelleschi wrote: "To her, flamenco dancing has been, since her earlier days, a positive physical necessity; one has the feeling of something smouldering inside which would cause an explosion if she were not able to dance."[2] When Carmen was once asked how long she would continue to dance, she replied, "As long as my body can take it." And did she really love it? *"Mucho!* If I go a week without dancing, I become like a caged lion!"[3]

A few years earlier Carmen had expressed the first hint of a desire to get away from the grind of endless travel. During an interview in Sevilla she spoke of retiring to that city after the next tour and never leaving. Now she would talk more and more of finding a quiet place of her own. But first she had to do one more series of tours. There were commitments to fulfill in Paris, London, Spain...

Carmen had left her former company behind in America—Sabicas and his brother, Diego, Domingo Alvarado, Goyo Reyes, and most of her dancers. Once back in Madrid, she had to assemble an entire company and teach them the repertoire. She ended up creating her largest company. It is not clear how many of the twenty-two artists went with her on the road outside of Spain (the French press called her company "much reduced in size"), but they all worked with her during the Spanish tour in the fall.

To replace Sabicas as soloist, Carmen engaged José "Pepe" Motos, a dynamic and innovative guitarist with a forceful, flambouyant style. Pepe, a licensed lawyer, had an abandoned, almost savage attack on the strings and literally devoured guitars. Highly original in all styles, he was far ahead of his time in the *bulerías* and *fandangos de Huelva*. If he wasn't a gypsy, he certainly played like one. He would receive applause second only to Carmen Amaya during their tours.

The lead dancers would be "the lively and supple" Carmen Mota and her partner (and husband), Joaquín Robles. Mota had been with a number of ballet companies, including those of Mariemma, Pilar López, and Antonio, and she probably had her own repertoire well established. The same would be true of the great *jota* dancer and choreographer, Pedro Azorín, who also joined the company. Among the male soloists were Carmen's nephew Diego and another nephew, José Santiago Amaya, the younger brother of La Chata,

---

[1] Bois, p. 122.
[2] Brunelleschi, Elsa, "The Lone Gypsy." *Dancing Times*, May 1959.
[3] Hidalgo, p. 233.

who had been baptized and nicknamed "El Chino" by Carmen's father. A twenty-five-year-old gypsy dancer named Isidro López "El Mono" (The Monkey) would stay with Carmen for the next four years. Other dancers making up the company included Rosa España, Pilar Caballero, Angelina Chocano, Pilar Juárez, Zoilo Gómez, and José Ardiz.

Carmen took three singers with her: Rafael Ortega, a twenty-nine-year-old gypsy from a long line of distinguished *cantaores* from Cádiz;[1] Antonio Núñez Montoya "El Chocolate," a gypsy from Sevilla; and Cecilio Bueno, a specialist in *jotas*. The guitarists were Juan Antonio, René Heredia, and a guitarist from Cádiz named Juan Doblones.

René Heredia described rehearsals (date not specified):

> When we were in Madrid, rehearsing at Amor de Dios studios for over a month to prepare for one of our year-long tours, all the top dancers would come by to see and learn from Carmen as she rehearsed the company. Other dancers would often say, *"Carmen es un fenómeno, pero de un baile no más, las alegrías!"* ["Carmen is a phenomenon, but has only one dance, the *alegrías*!"] People who say such things are just showing their ignorance about her. Carmen could dance anything she wanted. Since she dominated *compás* and technique, it was no problem for her to do this...
>
> There was one dancer in the company by the name of Isidro López "El Mono." He was practicing a *farruca* and asked me if I would help him with it. So I got my guitar and we started to do the *farruca*. Every time we would get to the *llamada* [a signal to close a section of dance], he would do it wrong. I told him, "That is wrong, it's out of *compás!*" As most flamencos do, we got into an argument. Luckily for both of us, Carmen had overheard what was going on. She came out of her dressing room and said, "No, Isidro, you are doing it wrong! The *farruca* is danced like this." Then she proceeded to show him how to dance the *farruca* of El Gato. Of course she danced *fenómeno*. After that, Isidro knew how to dance the *farruca*.[2]

Carmen opened in the Théâtre des Champs Elysées in early January. Although the public received her with its usual enthusiasm, the critics were a bit cool. In *Le Monde*, Olivier Merlin wrote: "What did we see last night? An unrecognizeable Carmen Amaya, vulgar, with nothing of the gypsy and even less of an authentic *bailaora*." (January 7, 1959). On January 10, François Guillot de Rode wrote in *Figaro Littéraire*: "Carmen returns with a smaller and less turbulent company than on past occasions, and a little paler; no number really stands out... I believe that you either like Carmen

---
[1] The father of modern-day singer Manzanita.
[2] Heredia, René, *Jaleo*, December 1980.

Amaya or you don't, and I have to confess, without shame, that I belong to the second group." Finally, Antoine Golea wrote in the *Carrefour* on the 14th: "The billboards of the Théâtre des Champs Elysées announce the performance of Carmen Amaya and her company. It would be better if they announced only Carmen Amaya, given that the show begins and ends with her. While she is on stage, Carmen is a prodigy of natural force, a cosmic phenomenon…but the rest…they are a sad lot! Is it Carmen Amaya's fault? Does she destroy everything in her path?"

From Paris, the company continued on tour in France. In Montpellier, Carmen's travels were interrupted by an important notice from the city government of Barcelona. Some time earlier, while she was dancing in New York, a Spanish newspaper correspondent based in Washington D.C. had shown Carmen an article in the *Diario de Barcelona* describing a new roadway that was to be built on the site of her childhood home. The dancer had become quiet, and then asked with sadness in her voice, "What will happen to my fountain?" She referred, of course, to that miserable little brick fountain with the lead spout where she had gone so often for water in her childhood. The news correspondent wrote to the author of the article, describing Carmen's concern and suggesting that perhaps the fountain could be preserved and named after her.

In 1956 the Urban Commission of Barcelona had proposed the construction of a stretch of thoroughfare along the waterfront. The Paseo Marítimo would be 1,500 feet of roadway and wide sidewalks lined with plants and trees that would pass through the area of the recently demolished Somorrostro slum. In the future, the Paseo would be extended many times, until it connected a number of coastal communities. The Commission agreed to dedicate the fountain to Carmen Amaya, but not the old one; they would build a new one.

> In Montpellier, Carmen Amaya receives a letter on official stationery of the government of Barcelona. It says that in less than a week, on February 14, 1959, at the same time that the first section of the Paseo Marítimo will be inaugurated, to be named for General Acedo, there will also be the dedication, at the same location as the humble fountain of her infancy, of a new fountain which will bear the name, *"Fuente Carmen Amaya."*
>
> The day the *bailaora* received that official notification she cried as she had seldom cried before. Her decision was immediate: "Everyone to Barcelona!" The impressario in Montpellier roared in fury and threatened Carmen with a lawsuit for breach of contract, for failure to work, and even for inciting public disorder…
>
> The night of February 13th, no sooner had they finished their performance than the company of Carmen Amaya was heading

full-speed toward Barcelona. It was a race against the clock. The car ate up kilometers and kilometers at dizzying speeds. Finally, at eight o'clock in the morning, Carmen was in Barcelona with just enough time to clean up a little.[1]

On the Friday before the inauguration, the *Vanguardia* of Barcelona published the following:

> After seven years without performing in this city, Carmen Amaya returns to offer us her incomparable art in a *gran recital* with all of her company and the Symphony Orchestra directed by Maestro Angel Curras.
>
> To reciprocate the kindness of the city that is dedicating to her the fountain that has been placed on the Paseo Marítimo, and which will be dedicated to her with great solemnity this Sunday, Carmen has cancelled various contracts in France and, at the head of her company, is coming to Barcelona expressly to attend that ceremony Sunday morning in the same barrio where she was born—although it is completely transformed—and to offer us a single recital in the evening at the Palacio de la Música, the proceeds of which are being donated to the contruction of the San Rafael Asylum Hospital that is being built in the Valle de Hebrón.[2]

The newspaper went on to describe Carmen's company as being the same one that had performed in Paris. If accurate, then the company certainly was not "reduced in size," as the press had called it, nor was it smaller than those of earlier years. In fact, it included many of the artists who would make up her very large company later in the year. There is no mention of her family, of Diego or El Chino, but new artists with her here included Rafael Ortega's wife—a dancer from Málaga named Trini Heredia—and dancers Lolo de Cádiz and Antonio Amaya "El Pillín," from the Sacromonte. Sharing singing duties with Ortega was José Díaz Sarria, known as Chato de Osuna [The Snub-nose from Osuna—in the province of Sevilla]. El Chato had begun his career in Barcelona and it is possible that he joined Carmen just for this one recital in Spain. Later, he would go with her to America.

> On a sunny [Sunday] morning, a spring morning in the middle of winter, among government officials, authorities, and reporters, Carmen Amaya, the dancer who had been born in the Somorrostro, was attending the official ceremony to cut the tape leading to the Paseo Marítimo, the pride of the city... But Carmen's eyes were escaping toward a short stairway of red brick that she knew, that she felt, must lead to her fountain...

[1]Montañés, p. 55.
[2]Reproduced in Hidalgo, p. 192.

While the official retinue advances slowly, with the sluggishness of protocol, a cloud of little gypsies crosses the Paseo yelling, *"Viva Carmen Amaya!"*

And, thus, amid a mixture of authorities and the people and a deafening uproar, the dancer finds herself in front of her fountain. The location is the same, but the fountain that had, in reality, been nothing more than a lead pipe embedded in a wall is a now a vaulted niche decorated by a relief sculture in which three childen, like three gypsy angels, raise their arms to the sky in an eternally flamenco gesture, while two other children strum guitars, and above, to the right, some tiles that announce, *"Fuente de Carmen Amaya."*[1]

The civil governor, Acevedo Colunga, pronounced the following words:

"Carmen Amaya: The Urban Commission, believing it speaks for the city and the city government, has sought to perpetuate the fountain that flowed in your childhood, that fountain surrounded by shacks that has been converted into an artistic fountain, a sign of civilization. In that way, we have sought to pay homage to your merits, to all that your personal style signifies, to your *garbo* [style, class, graciousness], to that mystery of our race that is translated into art, into something that cannot be performed by other races and other peoples, something that is carried in the blood, is manifested in our faith, and signifies style, spirit, and soul. This thing that you have had since birth, that felt the light of the Mediterranean Sea, and which you have since transported throughout the world, making you an ambassador of our art and our race.

We have sought to perpetuate the memory of this woman from Barcelona who was born on this beach of Somorrostro..."[2]

Carmen, with tears in her eyes, spoke in response:

I don't know if I really deserve it or not. I only know that what little value I have I owe to you, to everyone. I would like to say many things and it is impossible. I will be eternally grateful. As long as I live...this will remain in my soul until I die, because my artistic career, with the many years of work that I have had, it has been, it had to be, my native land, Barcelona, that has remembered me. What more can I ask?

To all of you, with all of my soul, I give thanks with all of my heart. Believe me, because I owe it to you, I owe you for this. At

---

[1]Montañés. p. 55.
[2]Reproduced in Hidalgo, p. 196.

least, as his excellency the governor said before, something will remain, something in Barcelona to recall this poor little gypsy who travels the world doing what she can. But one thing for sure, the little that I do, I do with much pride, spreading the name of Spain and, above all, Barcelona. Thank you very much![1]

Carmen approached the fountain, wrapped in plush mink stole:

When the dancer reaches the fountain, there is a tremendous silence. For a few brief seconds nobody makes a sound, nobody says a thing. Carmen Amaya contemplates her fountain. Through her moist eyes she can see herself dancing *por bulerías*, there in that same spot...she contemplates herself dreaming of being the best artist in the world...

Ceremoniously, which she too knows how to do when the need arises, she leans over the fountain, reaches one hand into the crystalline stream of water, fills the dark-skinned hollow of her palm, and lifts it to her lips to drink the first sip of water to flow from the brand-new *"Fuente Carmen Amaya."*

Only then do the applause, ovations, and cheers burst forth again. Three little gypsies, in mended clothing and with shiny hair, offer Carmen a bouquet of flowers [Hidalgo says the gypsies gave bouquets to all of the women present, and those who presented the flowers to Carmen included her little cousin, Nuria Flores Amaya—the youngest sister of La Chunga.] Immediately after, much too soon for Carmen, who looks at her fountain as if she had an eternity to contemplate it, the photographers arrive, more speeches... Protocol imposes itself again.

In the Barceloneta [the barrio bordering the Paseo], the police and other security officials find themselves helpless to control the multitude of people who want to see Carmen Amaya, their Carmen, close up more more time.

That night, in the Palacio de la Música of Barcelona, Carmen Amaya offers a function to benefit the San Rafael Hospital. The Palacio de la Música records the most packed house in its history. In the boxes, all of the authorities of Barcelona; in the orchestra pit, all of the gypsies of Barcelona in a herterogeneous intermingling with the best of Barcelona's society. In the aisles, people of all classes who have bribed the doormen of the theater or have slipped in by every trick imaginable...

The opening prelude is listened to with respect, there is soft applause for three dances of the 18th century, and suddenly, from behind the curtain, the strumming of a guitar can be heard. The

[1] Hidalgo, p. 197.

strumming increases as the curtains opens, and then, like an exhalation, like a ray of light, Carmen Amaya bursts onto the stage. A unanimous outburst irrupts and the Palacio de la Música becomes an immense *tablao flamenco*, in the center of which Carmen Amaya, the genius from Barcelona, prances to the *"Hechizo del Fandango."* [the press got the name wrong].
From that moment on, yells, applause, *"Olés"*... Carmen Amaya dances while seated in a chair, at a table that creaks and wobbles; the audience applaudes, cheers her on...
When the show finishes, the audience is on its feet asking for more, and Carmen Amaya gives more, she gives all that could be desired... After two in the morning, on a stage completely filled with baskets of flowers, Carmen Amaya, smaller, more gypsy, and belonging more to Barcelona than ever, says thank you to the audience and, in a voice broken by emotion, "to that man that you have here, your governor, who has made possible this great work for my Barcelona..."
Moments later, in the dressing room, beautiful mink coats rub shoulders with bright polka-dot blouses and genuine diamonds shine beside arrogant costume jewelry. [1]

Carmen did not alter her program for the occasion. She might have been tempted to emphasize the flamenco, but instead presented an evening weighted in favor of the classic numbers: *bolero, seguidillas, malagueñas, "Goyescas," "La Boda de Luis Alonso,"* and more—many of them arranged for her by the director of the orchestra, Angel Curras. The newpapers pointed out the enthusiastic applause for the facil solos of José Motos. At the end of the first half, the writer César González-Ruano presented Carmen with the *Medalla del Oro* [Gold Medal] *del Círculo de Bellas Artes de Madrid.*

Carmen spoke to a reporter in Barcelona about her dancing:

—Carmen, in these last ten years there has been a lot of folk dancing here, but very little flamenco. What is that about?

"Flamenco is something incomprehensible. It is centuries old, the very best."

—Have you evolved?

"Ever since I began here—I'm from the Barceloneta—at four years of age, and in the Teatro Español with the Catalonian company Santpere, up until now, I have danced the same. What has happened is that now I dance with common sense, knowing what I am doing."

—What is the foundation, or where lies the truth of flamenco?

"In three things: placement, footwork, and arms. And in all of

[1] Montañés, p. 56.

this, that the audience is obliged to say *Olé*."

—If you see a *bailaora*, how do you judge her?

"If she positions herself as God has ordained, does footwork, raises her arms, and does turns as they should be done, I say, 'first-rate, she is a phenomenon.' But to move the hands with neither rhyme nor reason, to beat the dress as if to shake off the dust and expose what one can expose, along with movement from her—indicating her hips—that is not flamenco."

—In flamenco there is no movement?

"There is a certain cadence…I don't know how to explain it…something that comes out because it has to, that is, to do something reasonable within the art. And to give your all."

—Does dancing require effort?

"Don't you see the face I make when I dance? I clench my jaws and am completely unaware of the audience. If there were a *gachó* in the front row with a pistol, I wouldn't know it."[1]

In another interview about that time, Carmen said, "I, personally, don't need to rehearse. When I dance, I forget everything and the dance surges out of me spontaneously. My little niece says that she doesn't know me when I dance, as if I had been transformed into something else… Because the dance has to come from far inside, freely."

The newspaper printed an article expressing appreciation to Carmen for having left her tour in France, for having driven all night to get to Barcelona, and for her patriotism. They said it was a symbol of her big heart that she had donated all of the flowers she had received to the church where she had been married. And they underlined their gratitude to her for having donated the proceeds of her concert to the San Rafael Hospital for handicapped girls. The article finished with: "Barcelona, with its ovations, puts its seal of approval on a biography begun on the beaches of Somorrostro, when a little gypsy girl used to come to a sad little fountain and saw in the waves, in the wind, and in her blood, a rhythm that would be triumphantly translated into dance."[2] Two weeks later, Carmen performed in the Teatro Barcelona. The following day she participated in a benefit performance in the Municipal Sports Palace.

Between the money she had to pay the impressario in France, the cost of travel, and lost earnings, the dedication of the fountain had cost Carmen at least 300,000 *pesetas* [c. $5,000 in 1959 dollars; probably close to $30,000 today]. But she said to the press: "To have seen this in my life is something marvelous! Even if it had cost me twenty million, I would have come!"

In an interview, Carmen spoke of her fountain:

---

[1] Reproduced in Hidalgo, p. 232.
[2] Hidalgo, p. 198.

—You have again drunk the water [of that fountain]. Is it the same?

"It tasted the same to me."

—What is your impression of the new fountain and the honor of having named for you?

"I swear by my mother that it was the strongest emotion that I have received in my life. I couldn't see the fountain because of the tears!"

—Which flowers moved you the most?

"Besides those of the governor, the ones of the children of the orphanage, for whom I danced in the Palacio de la Música, and also those of the little gypsies."

—How many relatives do you have in the slum district?

"At least two hundred."

—When you saw yourself standing before the fountain, what was your first thought?

"I saw my reflection in the water, and I believe I didn't see myself as I am now, but as I was when I was seven years old, barefoot and running on the beach."

—How long were you in the Somorrostro?

"Until I was ten, when I went to Madrid. But I always carry Barcelona inside me. So much so that I want to buy some land near the fountain, to build a house, and ask God to let me die."[1]

Carmen had long wanted to build a home in Barcelona, but with her busy schedule she kept putting it off. Then, while in Barcelona in 1959, she saw a picture of a rustic manor near the small town of Bagur (Begur in *Catalán*). Bagur is located some one hundred kilometers (sixty miles) north of Barcelona on the rugged Costa Brava and lies three kilometers inland from the coves and precipitous cliffs of the coast. It is a typical small Spanish town, huddled around the base of a hill crowned by a medieval castle, and had a population of less than two thousand. The building Carmen saw in the photograph occupied a rocky promontory outside of Bagur with a magnificent view of the town, the castle, and the Mediterranean. Perhaps Carmen was attracted to its 14th century tower, or maybe it was the harshness of the barren terrain and the stark simplicity of the stone structure that she identified with. She fell in love with *El Mas Pic* (untranslatable), as it was known by locals, or *La Masía* (The Country House), as it was dubbed by the press, or simply *El Manso* (The Mansion), as it was to be called by the Amayas. She purchased the property and had some work done on it, but had no time to enjoy it at that time. Another grueling tour of Europe awaited.

[1] Hidalgo, p. 200.

CHAPTER ELEVEN

COMING HOME

Throughout 1959 the movement to revive the old flamenco continued to gather steam. New *tablaos* appeared with regularity. Pastora Imperio opened El Duende. Corral de la Morería had opened its doors in 1956, and the next couple of years would see Torres Bermejas, Las Brujas, and Arco de Cuchilleros added to the flamenco nightlife in Madrid. On the academic front, the *Cátedra de Flamencología y Estudios Folklóricos Andaluces* had been founded in 1958 for the study, preservation, and dissemination of flamenco. This scholarly organization in Jerez de la Frontera would encourage investigation into all aspects of flamenco, award annual prizes, and sponsor contests. Flamenco *peñas* (clubs) proliferated by the dozens throughout Spain. Their members would debate the origins and merits of *cante* styles by the hour.

Contests had come into vogue again. As early as 1952, an attempt had been made to hold a yearly national contest of *alegrías* in Cádiz. The effort failed after its second year, but in 1956, Córdoba held it first national contest. That contest launched the career of a young *cantaor* from nearby Puente de Genil: Antonio Fernández Díaz—better known as *"Fosforito"* ("Little Matchstick"—no relation to the legendary Fosforito of fifty years earlier) walked off with first place honors in all the major categories of *cante*. Three years later, the second edition of the *Concurso Nacional de Arte Flamenco de Córdoba* brought to light a number of *cantaores* who had never succumbed to the *ópera flamenca*, preferring to remain secluded in their small towns rather than submit to the demands of commercial success. Juan Talegas, a 68-year-old gypsy, won in the *siguiriyas* and *soleares*. Two gypsy sisters, Fernanda and Bernarda de Utrera, won for their *bulerías* and *tientos*. And finally, the now legendary gypsy *cantaora*, La Perla de Cádiz, won with her *alegrías* and *bulerías*. Gypsy *cante* was finding its way back into the limelight and gypsy artists were again awarded celebrity status. Columbia Records featured the winners of the Córdoba contest on the superb record, *Sevilla: Cuna del Cante Flamenco*.

Carmen Amaya fit into this renaissance of gypsy flamenco by dancing primarily the purest of gypsy dances. Her only concessions, on a personal level, to the neoclassic movement of the previous quarter century were the *"Embrujo del fandango"* (usually described as a *fandango*, but fitting that mold only by the greatest stretch of the imagination), the *"Danza"* by Speranza, and *"La Boda de Luis Alonso"* by Jerónimo Jiménez, a dance favored by Carmen for its interminable crescendos and seemingly endless false finales that gave free reign to her passion for furious footwork. But she surrounded herself with a company that largely followed the "Argentinita model" in its programming.

Lacking a strong choreographer in the company of 1959, a Goyo Reyes or Antonio Triana, Carmen was left to her own devices and it is not clear how much original choreography she did for the company. She had the routines that she had learned from others, of course, and it is likely that dancers like Carmen Mota and Joaquín Robles brought choreographies with them from other companies. But, judging by the mixed praise from the critics, the onstage result lacked cohesion and often failed to convince. Carmen's dances were "spontaneous and fiery," but were "not well choreographed;" her concert programs were "filled with exciting surprises," but "poorly arranged;" she "danced with energy and creativity never seen before," but lacked femininity and danced like a man."

After her March appearances in London's Westminster Theatre, one critic wrote: "Perhaps a legendary fame and her own unique quality make Carmen Amaya the lonely personality that we see, surrounded by people of her race, yet not joining in their dancing, nor they with her. Amaya dances solo throughout the performance and in many ways it is no wonder, for dancing as she does, like nobody else, nobody would dare to measure up to the furious pace of her footwork, the quickest I have ever heard or seen anywhere."[1]

Another critic, Peter Williams, praised Carmen, but could not refrain from letting his preconceived notions of flamenco dance creep in:

> Where I feel that Carmen Amaya fails to touch the heights of flamenco is that, though she is all-woman, she never brings to her art the femininity of the greatest gypsy artists, such as must have been the case with a "La Macarrona," "La Malena," or a Pastora Imperio. Carmen approaches her art like a man and she dances with all the fire of a man and with a great deal more speed than is the case with many male Spanish dancers. She has developed something that is entirely personal to herself and made her dancing extremely theatrical. Anything stately or undulating would be entirely contrary to her naturally dynamic and ebullient personality...
>
> Her spare and compact body is the most perfectly attuned instrument and you get the impression that there is not one particle of it that is not under immediate and absolute control. Her

---

[1] Brunelleschi, Elsa, "The Lone Gypsy." *Dancing Times,* May 1959.

speed in *zapateado* is geater than almost any man alive; her hands are so dry in *palmas* and *pitos* [fingersnaps] that they sound like a volley of bullets fired at some hard, unresisting object. She never looks better than when she appears in trousers, and must be the only woman in the world who can dance as she does in these all-revealing garments without causing a second of embarrassment...

In her first programme at the Westminster Theatre, she gives five numbers which collectively contain the very essence of Carmen Amaya's very personal development of, and approach to, the art of flamenco. From the moment she enters, with the proud strut of a matador, it is obvious just why she was called "La Capitana." The fact that her red dress is not very becoming is immediately forgotten as she swirls and stamps her variations of the *fandango*...Brilliant as Carmen is in this, and it is a formidable display of technique, I feel that she lacks a sensuous quality and somehow the dress never becomes part of the dance.

In a way, this same criticism could be applied to her next solo, *soleares*. That long flounced train, whose serpentine coils should be an extension of the body, is an integral part of this dance, generally considered to be the original source of *cante flamenco*. Yet Carmen has replaced sensuousness with something that is in a way far grander. With her arms raised, her whole presence suggests the remoteness of the plains and the mountains of her country. One gets the impression that, come flood and earthquake and the collapse of the Triana bridge over the Guadalquivir (a symbol in Andalucía as important as the Eiffel Tower or the Statue of Liberty in other countries), she will remain as symbolic of the earth's endurance. In the space of a few moments she can convey the contrasting sorrow and joy which is such an essential part of the Spanish character and of the gypsies in particular. To be able to achieve this in dance is obviously to have reached the pinnacle of art.

The humor and joy of the gypsies is conveyed no more clearly than in the *bulerías* which she sings later in the program. Here the rhythms and counterpoint are very complex and it is wonderful to watch and hear how Carmen, with her eyes and shoulders and hands, points every line. Though possibly not one member of the audience understands one word of Spanish, the humor is infectious and in a few moments she can have them in stitches.[1]

René Heredia recalled:

> One time that I remember in London, Pilar López and company were in town. They all came over to see our show—we were per-

---

[1] Williams, Peter, "The Art of Carmen Amaya." *Dance and Dancers*, June 1959.

forming in the Westminster Theatre near Buckingham Palace. At that time, Antonio Gades was her first dancer, along with Nana Lorca. Ricardo Modrego was her guitarist and El Güito the guest artist. El Güito was seventeen or eighteen years-old and was the hottest dancer to come out of Spain in a long time. Just before Carmen was to do her *alegrías*, one of the younger dancers in our company came running up to Carmen and said, "Carmen, Carmen, there is El Güito!"

Carmen looked up with a very stern gypsy face and said, "And who is El Güito?" And with that, she went out and danced an *alegrías* that lasted about half an hour. It blew everyone away—including El Güito. She received thirteen curtain calls that night. That is not easy to do in London, where the English are so reserved. But they have always loved Carmen Amaya.[1]

René related another incident that occurred during the subsequent tour of Great Britain:

Carmen also knew a lot about guitar. She knew how the *falsetas* [melodies] should sound, since her father and brother were both guitarists and spent many years with Sabicas. She knew whose *falsetas* were whose—if they were from Ramón Montoya, Niño Ricardo, Sabicas, or Manolo de Huelva. In 1959, when we were in Scotland, at the King's Theatre in Edinburgh, I was in my dressing room warming up before the performance, working on a new *falseta* that was not working out for me. Carmen was four doors down the hallway in her dressing room. From there she could hear what I was playing. After hearing me do this *falseta* several times, she came in and told me what I had to do to play it correctly. Then she told me whose *falseta* it was and where it had originated. To play, sing, or dance for Carmen Amaya was not as easy as it appeared, since most of the time she knew more than the guitarists who were accompanying her![2]

In the fall of 1959, Carmen toured Spain. She held nothing back for these concerts in her homeland, nor did she alter the programming to feature more flamenco. If anything, she included more folk and classical dances for her company. Her reception by the Spanish press and public was overwhelmingly enthusiastic. On September 23rd, the *Diario de la Tarde* wrote:

The International Festival opened its arms last night to the return of the whirlwind of light and *gracia*. After an absence of seven years, the bronze empress danced again in Sevilla. An absolute,

---

[1] Heredia, René, "*A Carmen Amaya.*" *Jaleo, Vol IV, No 4.* December 1980.
[2] Heredia, René, "*A Carmen Amaya.*" *Jaleo, Vol IV, No 4.* December 1980.

complete, and unforgettable success! Just the announcement of her name left the large theater without a free space. Her unique style, delivery, and presence excited the crowd and brought forth the most enthusiastic acclamations. Carmen Amaya triumphed completely, as did her very gypsy and well put together company of flamenco stars...

Carmen, dancing *por lo derecho* [correctly], without cheap corruptions to win over an unfamiliar crowd, opened fire with all she had and surpassed by far the general artistic level of this edition of the *Festivales* in Sevilla. She was temperamental in *"Embrujo del Fandango,"* perfect in her admirable *zapateado* of *"Las Bodas de Luis Alonso,"* and captivating in the *bulerías*—where she reached her highest point of artistic genius, accompanying the *cante* of Tomás Pavón[1] and the *duende* of Antonio Núñez Montoya "Chocolate." A truly admirable *bulerías*. Carmen, with a white train dress more than fifteen feet long, exactly measured the *tercios* [sung phrases] in order to irreproachably elaborate this most *airoso* of the *bailes gitanos*...[2]

Another newspaper pointed out that Carmen's company was completely different in concept and technique from others seen in that city, and that the " ballet of Carmen Amaya is Spanish—very Spanish! The genius of the artist—and Carmen Amaya has a very distinct personality—shone at all times, whether she was on stage or not; when not performing, her artistic soul makes itself felt and animates everything... Individually and as a group all of the artists are very good...among these we would like especially to mention René Heredia and José Motos, who played a magnificent solo."[3]

Three days later, the same show was presented in Madrid—according to Goldberg, in the Teatro de la Zarzuela. The Madrid periodical, *Ya*, wrote: "With the theater totally filled, Carmen Amaya presented her company last night... *Bravos* and *Olés* burst out at her turns and *desplantes*. The ovation was as great when she first appeared on stage as when she finished the program..."[4] The critic singled out for praise all of Carmen's numbers, as well as the *jota* by the "magnificent dancer, Pedro Azorín," *"Las Hojas Verdes"* (a dance from Castilla), and the three dances of the 18th century—although the *"Goyescas"* had "suffered a vulgarization through the use of continuous castanets."

And finally, in her hometown:

Performances by our countrywoman, Carmen Amaya, whirlwind

---

[1]Not the brother of La Niña de los Peines, who had died in 1952.

[2]*Diario de la Tarde,* Sevilla, September 23, 1959.

[3]*El Correo de Andalucía,* September 23, 1959.

[4]Franco, José María, Ya, September 26, 1959.

of the dance, epitome of *gitanería*, and breaker of rules, disciplines, and academics, are not very frequent in Barcelona. Carmen is discussed by captivated audiences in Europe and America with the same frenzy that she puts into her dances. The night before last, in Barcelona, before a packed house, Carmen Amaya reappeared with her company to offer us a program of Spanish dance in which the great artist had ample opportunity to demonstrate all facets of her undeniable personality...

"*El Embrujo del Fandango,*" by Maestro Palomo, gave the Barcelona gypsy her entrance in an expectant atmosphere that, more than warm, was ardent. Carmen Amaya sparkled as always, her movements sudden and electric...

In the second part, Carmen danced *por bulerías, soleares,* and *alegrías,* and her creations were often harsh, with a vigorousness bordering on ferocity. Her hands, her eyes, and her feet all danced. The footwork of our gypsy is clean, artfully in *compás*, rhythmic, well-rounded, mathematical, and without needless *barroquismos* [elaborate ornamentations] or cute bastardisms. Just as in the good times in Somorrostro, during her escapades in the streets, *colmaos,* and flamenco taverns, Carmen created enthusiasm with her genius, her *desplantes,* her deep wisdom, and her witchcraft...

And, finally, an *alegrías* by Carmen and the company that brought the house down. Carmen's attempt at thanking the crowd was drowned out by ovations of that Barcelona public that understands her, esteems her, and loves her.[1]

It is hard to reconcile this passionate response by a Spanish public that embraced Carmen with that of the French critics only a month later, when she returned to Paris:

...Lacking a greater creativity in movement, they often barely manage the simple expression of a school dance. There is also a notable influence of the music hall that adds nothing to the quality of the performance. These dancers, for whom the choreographic tradition of their country prohibits scanty clothing, don't hesitate to show too much leg above the knee, and the back as well. Where Carmen Amaya is concerned, she is the only one of the company who has the stage wisdom to temper her fire. Nevertheless, the excess of passion compromises the plasticity of her movements. I would reproach her for the abuse of male costuming.[2]

---

[1] Junyent, José María. Barcelona newspaper, 1959.
[2] Acheres, Victoria. *Les Letres Françaises,* Paris, November 9, 1959.

Perhaps the French compared Carmen's company with the polished ballets of Pilar López or Antonio and found it lacking in structure or discipline, while the Spanish took Carmen at face value and compared her only with the more spontaneous flamenco dancers of her homeland. The following spring, when Carmen returned to the Étoile theater with a smaller company, the French critics finally warmed to her. Critical praise did not extend to her company, however:

> The applause that Carmen hears when she no more than sets foot on stage helps her to maintain the fire of her peformance. Just her presence is sufficient to galvanize the eight members of her ballet, who seem to be flamenco in name only. Her face is surprisingly expressive. Her frenzy and rhythm make one forget the inadequacy of her group, and the *alegrías* that closes the show is the high point of the night.[1]

Another critic underlined Carmen's need for a male dancer of her stature to partner her, and yet another, three weeks later, found her "in better form than ever."

The exhausting tours of Europe continued through 1960, on a smaller scale than in the past and often on a shoestring. One night, while in Madrid preparing for an upcoming tour of America, Carmen dined with the Spanish playwrite, Alfredo Mañas. Mañas had just premiered a new theater work entitled *La Historia de Los Tarantos*—a gypsy *Romeo and Juliet*. He recalled that evening with Carmen Amaya:

> The night that Carmen called me to talk I had the feeling that my life might be about to profoundly change, that the wheel of destiny would turn, and that, just by being with her, the dawn of something new and unknown might be about to begin.
>
> We dined with her that night in Casa Garrido on Calle Jacometrezo. Along with her husband, there was Aurora Bautista, Paco Rebes, Esteban Agüero—her brother-in-law—and his wife. We had no more than said hello and begun to eat when Carmen turned to me: "Would you like to write a show for me?" she said with that almost masculine voice she had, that voice of the responsibility she had shouldered since age eighteen, the responsibility of taking a whole clan of gypsies dancing through the world, that voice of a Queen of the Tribe.
>
> "If time permits, Carmen..." I answered with boastful calmness. Ever since that moment, I have asked myself, could there have been a more stupid response? I should have rolled about on

[1] Santerre, François de. *Le Figaro*, Paris, February 3, 1960.

the floor in joy and sung psalms of praise...! There were hundreds of writers dreaming of creating a work for Carmen. Nobody had written anything for her. She danced accompanied by her people and traveled the world that way to the scent of glory and throngs of admirers... She was offering me the chance to travel the world as an author!

She said, "Tomorrow I begin a one-year tour of America. The following year I will return to Spain and we can begin to rehearse!"

I had just premiered *Los Tarantos* in the theater, and most producers wanted to buy it from me to make it into a movie. Just between us, my inflated vanity led me to continue gambling with my fate. "I will do a show for your if you will appear in my film *Los Tarantos*."

Carmen remained motionless looking at me, then turned to Juan Antonio and asked, "What should I do, Juan, *hijo*?"

"You're the boss, Carmen. Whatever you say!"

So Carmen extended her hand, as if we were a *payo* livestock dealer and a gypsy closing a deal on a pair of horses in the fair, and said to me, "I'll be in America. Whenever you do the film, call me, and wherever I am I will return by airplane and be here with all of my people. Then we can begin to rehearse the show. How does that sound to you Juan, *hijo*?"

"Whatever you want will be done, Carmen," said Juan Antonio, who when he married had sworn to do two things and had carried them out without fail: to work wherever Carmen wanted and doing whatever she wished, and never to permit, after the wedding, anyone to invite Carmen to eat or drink. Never! Wherever they went nobody would pay except Carmen Amaya...

We were together all night, until the morning, when they said to us, "We are going to Barajas [Madrid airport], we have to catch a plane." Going out at night with Carmen in Madrid is a little like wandering about Sevilla drunk with La Macarena [the Virgin Mary] on your arm. In the midst of that confusion of people who saw us and waved, and the emotion, Juan Antonio Agüero caught me by the arm with herculean strength and pulled me aside: "Carmen is dying. Hurry and write. She has a year to live. And I want her to die dancing. Today Doctor Gisbert gave me the results: If she doesn't dance she will die from blood poisoning. Each time she dances she loses three *kilos*. She has only one kidney, enlarged and hypertrophied, and she eliminates toxins by dancing. If she stops dancing she will die from a heart attack. Hurry, she's dying. And I want her to die dancing!"[1]

[1] Mañas, p. 12.

When Carmen came to America at the beginning of 1961, it seemed that she was seeking to return to her ancestral roots, for she brought with her a small company of gypsies, the majority from the caves of the Sacromonte. Along with the *cantaor* Chato de Osuna and her nephew, José Amaya "El Chino," the group included Luis Flores, Antonio Amaya "El Pillín" (whose paternal grandfather, Juan Amaya, had headed the first performing *zambra* in the Sacromonte), and a *gitana* who would later marry El Pillín, Rosario Salguero "La Morita." The guitarists were Antonio Pérez, usually listed as Antonio de Linares (after his birthplace), but also known as "Pucherete," and Juan Santiago Maya, better known as "El Marote."

At age twenty-four, Juan Maya "Marote" had begun to establish a reputation for his hard-driving guitar style. Carmen found him in the *tablao*, Torres Bermejas, where he had begun to popularize a new way of strumming for dance accompaniment. Guitarists had previously created rhythm with individual fingers, finger-rolls, or simple up-and-down actions of the hand and thumb. Marote introduced a stacatto machine-gun triplet, created by whipping the thumb and fingers with a rapid wrist action, a powerful technique that arose out of the need to be heard over the din of the gypsy *zambras*. Marote's brother, Manuel, who would become the charismatic and innovative dancer "Manolete," described the early life of his family and his impressions of Carmen Amaya:

> I started dancing in the caves of the Sacromonte in Granada, for the tourists, because we needed money for food... I liked the atmosphere of my family, where there was no theater of any kind. We would have a wedding, a baptism, a party among ourselves. I've always liked that, then and now. Maybe I appreciate it more now... I think it was a way for us to move beyond the limits of our lives, of expanding ourselves, because we really didn't have much to eat, much to drink, or much sleep. We didn't have houses. I think it was a way of escaping boredom... My maternal grandfather was a guitarist. His name was also Juan Maya. He was well-known in Granada... My father was a fruit seller. My mother has always danced, in the *zambra*, in the Camino del Monte where lots of people went for vacation. The typical things to see there were the Alhambra and the Camino del Monte, which is where the gypsies lived. They didn't go to see the dance—they went to see where the gypsies lived, how they lived, whether they were dirty, whether they wore mustaches or were badly dressed...I remember that it was more or less a people living very poorly that they went to see.
>
> It has probably been a hundred years since they started dancing in public in the caves of the Sacromonte...It started in a cave

where people began to enter. Not tourists, but Spaniards who would come into a cave and have a drink. Since we had to eat, we had to say, "Come in sir, and have a drink!" And they stayed and enjoyed themselves, and they gave us money to eat. And that is how the *zambra* got started. Then they began to promote it, they made records in the Sacromonte and started to work with the hotels: "You must see the *zambra* of the Sacromonte, it's very cheap!" In the end, people came to see it, but in the beginning they came to see a people living very poorly.

The caves also had another history. The caves of the Sacromonte used to be the stables of the Arabs. Hundreds of years ago the caves were where the Arabs kept their horses and where we lived... I don't know how, but I think the Arabs must have taken something with them, maybe not from the gypsies, but from Spain, from Granada or the other Spanish cities. And we must have picked up some Arabic things, in our dance...

But we used to work for the tourists without knowing how to dance...we didn't know how to dance! ...Juan Maya Marote, who is now a guitarist, used to dance. I started to dance because of him. I had help from my brother, but he learned on his own, from all of the people who used to dance in the caves. There has always been a fountain to learn from. There was a man named Miguel Heredia who used to dance... He used to teach all the kids, like Mario Maya, Juan Maya, Juan Habichuela—a guitarist who also used to dance. There is always someone older than you to learn from...

My brother went to Madrid. He brought me to Madrid when I was twelve, because he thought I could do something with my dancing. I started to study, to work, and developed myself little by little... I didn't like to study much, hardly with anyone. I studied by myself, because my brother made me go into a studio and work alone... I got bored a lot. I was by myself, and you know what it is to be young. I loved to dance, but still I got bored. I worked a little, because I was afraid of my brother Juan, who used to reprimand me a lot. I had to go in, but I didn't want to... But I got better, little by little, with practice, and with the dancers who were famous then, like El Güito, Farruco, Mario Maya, and Antonio Gades, within the school of Pilar López. She developed almost all of the male dancers who are famous today and was the fountain for all of us who are a little younger than those dancers...

Carmen Amaya invented something that had never been done before. She danced with the rhythm of percussion, with *palmas* and no other accompaniment. Before her, people only danced with the guitar. She used the handclapping as percussion, just as if it had been played on wood or other drum surface. It was very valid, because, aside from good sound, it had such strength that even today all dancers repeat things of hers. I think that a hundred years could go by and we'll still be using her steps... My brother, Juan, worked for eight years with her [probably closer to three or four years], and he would bring me all of her steps, and of course I still do many of her things.

[Asked to comment on the masculinity of Carmen's dance, Manolete replied:] She was just as masculine doing footwork as she was feminine wearing a long train-dress. [Is the difference between male and female dance very important in flamenco?] It used to be. There exists much less difference now, because a person has to be complete in all aspects of the dance. You can't have no arms and no body sensitivity and footwork like a machine. Neither a man nor a woman. You must have footwork and feeling; you must have arms and body; you can't dance like a stick! The idea that a man has to dance one way and a woman another is dying. The audience wants that change—we are the ones who don't want to change. We talk about one quality as opposed to the other, but the audience doesn't even notice the difference. Twenty percent might notice if a woman has more feet than arms, or a man more arms than feet. We are the ones who say that a woman should have more arms than feet. I don't know why. A person who gets to be somebody, a dancer, has to be complete. If they weren't, they wouldn't be anything![1]

The Amaya company began an eight-week engagement in New York, in the Chateau Madrid. While in New York, Carmen again recorded with Decca. *Furia! Amaya* (DL 9094) is a surprise with respect to Carmen's choice of songs and dances. Carmen sings only two numbers, leaving most of the singing to her *cantaor*, Chato de Osuna. Her first song is a driving gypsy *rumba catalana*, and then she does a credible job with the very un-gypsy *fandangos del Albaicín*—for all practical purposes, a *verdiales*. She does not sing in her *"Ritmos Amaya."* Her voice had deepened considerably since the last recording several years earlier, perhaps due to age and incessant smoking. But she still retained the flexibility of voice needed to sing the difficult *fandangos*, and, in fact, sang with more control than on some of her earlier records.

Carmen dances three numbers on the record. The *fandangos de Huelva* amounts to little more than a solo for her *cantaor*, since her presence is practically undetectable. It is perhaps significant that she dances to one of very

---

[1]Paisley, Helena, Lisa Rosal, and Meira Weinzweig, "Interview with Manolete." *Jaleo, Vol IX, No 2.* Summer 1986.

few styles of *fandangos de Huelva* that carry a clear *bulerías compás*—those of Santa Eulalia. Her family had always seemed to prefer their *fandangos* with a gypsy rhythm (*soleá* or *bulerías*) rather than the 3/4 time of the typical *fandango*.

In *romeras*, a relative of the *alegrías*, Carmen dances to the *cante*, with very little display of virtuosity or choreography. That leaves *la caña* as the sole concert dance number on the album. And here Carmen leaves no doubt that, in spite of age and failing health, she could still dance. She develops this *caña*—an ancient relative of the *soleares* that had all but died out in the previous century—to its fullest, in its modern dance form. Her powerful footwork displays her unique concept of rhythmic phrasing, in which she often seems to float over the rhythm of the guitar with unexpected and fluctuating patterns, rather than marking a clear and predictable rhythm.

The remaining numbers on the record are a *bulerías* by the company and two solos by Juan Maya, a *soleá* and a *granaína*, played in a remarkably reposed manner and with great technical virtuosity.

Carmen did not care for the photograph selected for the album cover, perhaps because it made her look even older than her forty-seven years. When she traveled to California after completing eight weeks in the Chateau Madrid, she gave the photo that she had preferred to Lola Montes to hold for her. She would never see it again.

The company arrived in Los Angeles at the end of April, 1961, for a series of recitals in the Friday Morning Club Playhouse on Figueroa Street. The printed program illustrates that even while working on a reduced scale with her small group of gypsies, Carmen sought to recapture the grandeur of her earlier concerts. The performances opened with the musical director, Manuel Torrens, playing *"Orgía"* as a piano solo. Two classically trained dancers, Vargas and Peralta, did the "Córdoba" of Albéniz, and Carmen followed with "El Albaicín" by the same composer. Juan Maya's solo and Carmen's *soleá*, with the guitars of her husband and Antonio de Linares (Pucherete), completed the first half.

Another piano solo and a *bolero* by Vargas-Peralta opened the second part. Then *bulerías*, with Carmen, Antonio Amaya, and the guitar of Juan Maya. Another dance by Vargas-Peralta, a solo by Juan Maya, and Carmen's *alegrías* finished the evening. Only seven dance numbers. Audiences were enthusiastic, but did not fill the hall.

Lola Montes recalls that one of the dancers—probably Rosario Salguero "La Morita," who specialized in the *rumba*—wrapped a large shawl around her body during the performance in an attempt to hide the fact that she was very pregnant. When the company moved on to perform in San Diego, word came back to Los Angeles that La Morita had given birth there—that's how far along she had been, and still dancing!

The tour continued into Mexico and South America, through the summer and fall of 1961. According to Goldberg, Carmen returned to New York in November for a six-week engagement in the Chateau Madrid. Domingo Alvarado joined them for those performances and said that he could see a difference in Carmen, that she didn't dance the same and was not well—although she tried to hide it. Before Christmas she flew back to Mexico.[1]

The return of traditional flamenco and the *cante gitano* continued in 1962. The third edition of the National Contest of Flamenco Art in Córdoba proved to be merely an excuse to honor the *cantaor* Antonio Mairena. Word had spread that Mairena would be awarded the third *Llave de Oro del Cante*, that strange Gold Key that had been spontaneously presented to Tomás el Nitri in the 1860s and to Manuel Vallejo in 1926. The Gold Key would be the only prize in Córdoba thirty-six years after its previous presentation, so most *cantaores* stayed away from the contest. The only other "contestants" were Fosforito, Juanito Varea, El Chocolate, and Platerito de Alcalá. Mairena would hold the Gold Key until his death. Two years later Mairena would collaborate with flamencologist Ricardo Molina in the publication of *Mundo y Formas del Cante Flamenco*, an extensive examination and documentation of the *cante*.

Another book, published in 1962, proved to have far-reaching influence outside of Spain. American Donn Pohren had gone to Spain as a guitarist, married a Spanish dancer, and opened a flamenco club in Madrid. His book, *The Art of Flamenco*, gave foreign aficionados their first glimpse into the inner world of non-commercial flamenco and inspired them to flock to Spain in search of the "real thing." To aid these seekers, Pohren maintained a flamenco ranch near Morón de la Frontera through most of the 1960s, where aficionados could go study all aspects of traditional flamenco.

The First International Contest of Flamenco Art, held in Jerez in 1962, showcased a number of traditional gypsy artists, but it was fourteen-year-old Paco de Algeciras who astounded the flamenco world with his technique and knowledge. Only seven years later, this young guitarist, his name changed to Paco de Lucía, would lead flamenco down a new path, away from tradition and the strictures of the past and into a fertile and feverishly creative period that might eventually prove to be every bit as decadent as the era of the *ópera flamenca*.

The call came from Spain in early 1962. Filming had begun on *Los Tarantos*. As promised, Carmen interrupted her tour in Mexico to fly back to Spain for what were to be a few brief scenes. She left her husband behind to explain and

[1]Goldberg, p. 303.

smooth over her absence with agents. She had continued to be sick with back pain and had taken to bed after each performance on the tour. During filming she would have to take days off to rest.

The director of the film, Francisco Rovira Beleta, had wanted Carmen Amaya because they needed an authentic gypsy dancer to play Rafael Taranto's mother, a dancer free from classical or folk dance influences. Rovira also felt that Carmen would be a box office draw and help to guarantee success for the film. But when shooting began, Carmen surprised everyone with her presence, talent, and naturalness, and they began to add scenes and dialogue for her. Before long she had become the dominant figure in the story and was to be the only one listed as a star in the credits.

Rovira and the author, Alfredo Mañas, had fought over the concept of the film. Rovira wanted to do *Romeo and Juliet*, as had just been done by United Artists with the Jerome Robbin's musical, *West Side Story*. Mañas felt that, although his work contained elements of *Romeo and Juliet*, his story was unique. He told Rovira, "If you want to do *Romeo and Juliet*, adapt it directly from that!" Whatever agreement they came to, the film *was Romeo and Juliet*, complete with a balcony scene where Juana ("Juliet," played by Sara Lezana) plans her escape with Rafael ("Romeo," played by Daniel Martín) from high on an embankment. The dancer Antonio Gades has a minor role with a number of spoken lines that parallel those of his counterpart, "Mercutio," in *Romeo and Juliet*. When he says, for example, "Damn both your tribes," he paraphrases Mercutio's "A plague on both your houses!"

The story revolves around two feuding clans of gypsies, the Zorongos and the Tarantos, plus a subgroup of bad guys—Los Picaos—who side with their Zorongo cousins. The inevitable love affair takes place between a girl and boy from opposing clans. The setting is the Somorrostro slum in Barcelona where Carmen Amaya grew up. Since the Somorrostro had been demolished several years before, they had to build a new one in the Montjuic area, where they successfully captured the bleakness of the squalid slum. The beach scenes were filmed fifteen miles down the coast in Castelldefels. Snowy Christmas scenes were the result of fortuitous circumstance. That year Barcelona experienced a freak snowstorm, the snowstorm of the century, with sixteen inches of snow. So they wrote it into the script.

Speaking about *Los Tarantos* some years later, Rovira said, "This is not a flamenco film, although flamenco certainly plays a large role. But no, it is a film that portrays the gypsies, their customs, and the way of life in the Somorrostro." In fact, there is very little of authentic gypsy custom portrayed in the movie. Unlike *María de la O*, filmed more than twenty-five years earlier, *Los Tarantos* contains only a few tired clichés. There are a couple of fleeting scenes of a gypsy wedding, but little is revealed in the way of gypsy custom. The gypsies didn't want to sing the wedding song, the *alboreá*, because they believed it would bring bad luck to sing it outside of gypsy circles. The director finally convinced them, but the resulting song is brief and barely audible.

The gypsies were portrayed with knife in hand at the slightest provocation, and they punctured each other left and right. They seemed to enjoy being stabbed, offering little resistance. Rovira said, "I argued a lot with the gypsies, one of whom came after me with a knife—because he said that I was painting a picture of the gypsies not as they are, but always with a knife. To prove me wrong, he came after me with a knife...But there was no blood let."[1]

Rovira might have benefited from listening to the gypsies, for he was guilty of another cliché: In almost every view of the slum, the gypsies are dancing. The result is quite comical at times. But in spite of this emphasis on dance, most of the dance scenes are quite brief and not permitted to develop. Among the dancers given prominence in the film was Antonio Gades. Gades had begun to attract attention in 1957 when he and Eduardo Serrano "El Güito" were serving their apprenticeships with Pilar López. During the making of *Los Tarantos*, Gades was working as principle dancer, choreographer, and ballet master for La Scala in Milan and had to shuttle back and forth between Spain and Italy for filming. He said that he saw little of Carmen Amaya because they shared no scenes and did not dance together. But he did describe his impressions of Carmen at that time:

> When I first began dancing, I knew Carmen Amaya only by name, her fame as a "giant," a phenomenon, and the famous poster by Ruano Llopis. I had never seen her dance, not even in movies. I saw her for the first time in Paris, when I was dancing in the ballet company of my teacher, Pilar López. I don't remember where we were working, whether it was in Bobino or the Champs Elysées. But, on the other hand, I recall very well that Carmen was dancing in the Théâtre de l'Étoile.
>
> Carmen Amaya destroyed all my prior conceptions of the dance. Up until then, when I used to see the great dancers, I would think, "Someday I will dance as well, or better." But suddenly, for the first time in my life, I realized that Carmen Amaya was impossible to imitate. I had encountered something that broke all the rules and principles of dance, of everything that one had studied. It was hard to grasp, and it was something else: a force, a feeling. I realized that that fire, that halo, that energy, was impossible to learn. Impossible even to be injected.
>
> That first time I saw Carmen Amaya I couldn't even applaud— I was paralyzed. When the performance was over, I went with

---

[1] This and other quotes by Rovira Beleta were taken from a lecture he gave during the Bienal de Sevilla on September 17, 1988. It was reproduced in *"Opiniones sobre Carmen Amaya,"* in *La Caña, No 1*, December, 1991.

Pilar López to say hello to her. I entered her dressing room crying and I left crying. I embraced her and she embraced me.

I remember her humanity, her simplicity. She never talked about dancing. She spoke about the simple things of life—always with a pack of light tobacco and a lighter in her left hand, and a coffee... There are things that cannot be put into words. That woman was an example of class, of dignity, of humanity. And a natural force. How can a stamina like that have such strength? And she always had a natural comment for everyone. She was straightforward. She was natural.[1]

In *Los Tarantos*, Gades is featured dancing a *farruca* in the middle of the night, on the tables and pavement of the major thoroughfare known as Las Ramblas. The dance shows a little of his classical style, although it is quite brief, and the incongruous orchestral accompaniment that appears from nowhere is a bit distracting. It is said that drunks staggering home along Las Ramblas late at night were astonished to come upon this scene as it was being filmed.

One delightful revelation in the film was fourteen-year-old Antonia "La Singla," who played Rafael Taranto's sister. Antonia does not appear in the credits, although her father, Antonio "El Singla," does. The father dances briefly with his daughter and then later, before the funeral, dances alone on a hillside. Antonia had several opportunities to show her natural barefoot *gracia*— *por bulerías, rumba,* and *garrotín*.

Sara Lezana, "Juliet," showed herself to be an accomplished dancer in a bit of *tientos-tangos*, and a more extensive segment of *bulerías*. Carmen Amaya responded to her future daughter-in-law's *bulerías* with one of her own—usually cited as the highlight of the film. It is the *bulerías* she had been doing for some years entitled *"Ritmos Amaya,"* variations of which can be heard on both *Queen of the Gypsies* and *Furia! Amaya*. One critic quoted in a Carmen Amaya biography called it "a *bulerías* for eternity, the quintessential *bulerías*." But is it? Carmen begins with a bit of footwork on some planks thrown down on the sand. Much of the effect is lost in the confusion of poorly dubbed sound. She then sits at a table to sing a verse to the guitars of Andrés Batista and Pucherete. It is a simple old-style *letra*, giving the viewer a taste of the deep, throaty voice that had captivated audiences for more than thirty years. Again, the words don't match her lip movements. The director tells us that, in order to match the dubbed rendition that Carmen did later in Madrid with her on-screen performance, they had to speed it up a little, resulting in a higher pitch to her voice in the finished film. Carmen's face, which has been described as "an ageless face that appears to have been hewn out of the scorched rock of Andalucía," nevertheless shows every one

---

[1] Hidalgo, p. 210.

of her forty-eight years and more, putting to rest her claim that she was only forty shortly before her death.

The brief song finished, Carmen uses her knuckles and fingers to rap out an impressive display of rhythm on the table top. She then rises to dance. But instead of vintage Carmen Amaya, there is about a minute of furious and frenetic thrashing about, arms spinning like a windmill—"Much ado about nothing!" Sometimes older dancers, no longer able to carry out the dizzying spins of their youth, attempt to give an impression of turns by doing only the armwork that would normally accompany them. Carmen appeared to be doing just that. Age and ill health seem to have taken their toll. She did better in other dance fragments. El Chocolate sings a letra of *soleá por bulerías* for her and then, just when it looks like she is about to settle into some excellent dance *por soleá*, the camera pans away. Perhaps the best piece of dancing is a *tarantos* that gives a hint of what she was like at one time. Sadly, the director of the film later reported, "In editing, we threw away many meters of film of her dancing. I don't know where they ended up—surely, they have been lost."

The soundtrack of *Los Tarantos* presented some difficulties. All sound, including dialogue and dance, was added after filming was completed. With the spontaneous nature of flamenco, it is almost impossible for artists to match their on-screen performances exactly. And in *Los Tarantos* they almost never did. Voices seldom match lip movements. Footwork and handclapping sounds don't match what is seen on the screen. Guitarists do *picado* to the sound of strumming and strum during melodic passages. When Peret, who had almost single-handedly put the *rumba flamenca* on the map, appears briefly in a crowd playing the guitar and singing, his lips are terribly out of synch, sometimes not moving at all during his song.. Most of the musical action takes place outdoors, but the studio sound, complete with echo, often sounds unrealistic, like a record played in the distance. In fact, some of the background music appears to have been taken directly from records: a *soleá de Alcalá* by Juan Talegas, a *fandango* by Manolo Caracol... The classical music by guitarist Emilio Pújol is really the only appropriate mood-setting music on the soundtrack.

After its release the following year, *Los Tarantos* would enjoy great critical acclaim. It was shown in Cannes and at the International Film Festival in Montreal, and would be nominated for an Academy Award in 1963. In spite of its many defects, the film would remain as a monument to Carmen Amaya, to be preserved for future generations.

Filming finished, Carmen returned to the road. And the terrible back pains persisted. Montañés described her torment:

> This tour, Mexico, Chile, Peru, is absolute torture for Carmen and a hell for Juan Antonio. Now it is the tireless dancer who, as soon

Carmen's smile warms a fiesta in the home of Paul Heffernan, May 1962. Antonio Pucherete plays guitar.
Photo courtesy of Ana Maria Lievano-Ruiz de Galarreta.

as she finishes her performance, goes directly to the hotel and prostrates herself on the bed until it is time to return to the theater the next day.

Juan Antonio insists: "You have to go to a doctor…you have to rest…"

But Carmen's answer is always the same: "Okay, very well! After we finish Chile…" But after Chile, there was Peru, and after that, Israel…

Finally, Juan Antonio convinced her. A doctor saw her and diagnosed: "This dancing thing is finished. Now you must rest and take care of yourself…"

But Carmen also had a diagnosis: "If I have to stop dancing, it is better that I should die!"

So Carmen continued living, because she continued dancing, against all medical advice.[1]

In May of 1962, Carmen returned to New York for an extended engagement in the Village Gate. After the Sunday, May 27, performance, the company attended a party held in the home of college student Paul Heffernan's parents, in Harrington Park, New Jersey. Carmen had been invited by Spanish *bailaora*, Amor Sirvent. A local newspaper reported: "A motorcade of New York taxis and a few private cars slid into this quiet sleeping town at 4:20 A.M. Monday morning and deposited the greatest living group of Spanish gypsy flamenco dancers and guitarists at 31 Parkway, home of Mr. and Mrs. Paul Heffernan. Straight from the Village Gate, a Greenwich Village club where she finished her midnight show, came Carmen Amaya, world-famous flamenco dancer, and her troupe, consisting of about seven guitarists and twenty dancers, to 'start' their evening of performing and feasting…And so, at 6 A.M. Monday morning, when this borough was waking up to start another week, the Spanish gypsies were tuning their guitars and clicking their heels—about to start the festivities of their day."

The party was attended by dignitaries from Washington D.C. where Paul went to school, and a photographer from *Life*. The large "company" reported by the press was, in fact, made up of family, friends, and hangers-on. Paul says that guitarist Gabriel Ruiz was there to get drunk with Paco Amaya and Fernando Sirvent.

From the Village Gate, Carmen moved to the Players' Theatre. Dance critic Doris Hering described Carmen's performance on June 17, 1962:

> Our first reaction was, "Is *this* what she has come to?" For Carmen Amaya and her company were appearing in one of those musty Greenwich Village theatres that are little more than a handful of seats, a curtain, and a stage. But the dancers embraced the squalor

[1]Montañés, p. 60.

and transformed it into an exhilarating intimacy—a joyous mélange of spectators in shirtsleeves, aficionados squatting in the center aisle, even a stray dog.

We've never been to a *cueva* in Spain, but this felt like it...

In her first solo, with its gleaming white *traje de cola* and crimson rose in her hair, she [Carmen] seemed particularly changed. True, the mischief was there, as she snapped the tail of her dress (as only she can do). The power was there...But there was a new majesty, as she completed a phrase by driving her arm straight down, or as she enticed the singer and then willfully ignored him. This was not what one might call feminine dancing. It was more fundamental. It was female.[1]

Accompanying Carmen in the Players' Theatre were Diego Amaya, El Chino Amaya, Isidro López "El Mono," Angela Hernández Comuñas (El Mono's wife, according to Goldberg), and Rosario Ortiz, "an almond-eyed *gitana*" with a "deliciously impersonal vulgarity." The singer was El Chato de Osuna and the guitarists, although not named, were probably Juan Antonio Agüero, "Pucherete," and Andrés Batista (it appears that Juan Maya did not return to America with Carmen after the filming of *Los Tarantos*). The review of this performance closed with: "...as for Amaya, she is to be cherished."

"She is to be cherished!" Lola Montes reiterated that sentiment when she reflected: "Carmen should be treasured. I have always thought of her as a little hot-house flower—although she really was not fragile—something so unique, so beautiful, and so precious that she should be treasured and taken care of, not just worn out. She worked all of her life and what did she have to show for it? She wasn't appreciated enough, especially in Spain, where I heard her called a *bailarina de exportación* [a dancer suited only to dancing for foreigners]!"

Carmen Amaya's small band of gypsies headed west and descended upon the stage of the Los Angeles nightclub, Casa Madrid.[2] The well-known dancer, Teo Morca, recalled that time:

> She stayed in Los Angeles for quite a few months and performed at the old Casa Madrid where, nightly, she danced miracles. I can say that those months gave me some of my most important lessons in flamenco—just watching that energy, that emotion in motion,

---

[1] Hering, Doris, "Reviews: Carmen Amaya and Company, Players' Theatre, June 17, 1962." *Dance Magazine*, August, 1962.

[2] I have been unable to establish the year of this Casa Madrid appearance with certainty. The press had ceased to cover Carmen's activities and the dancer's acquaintances give dates ranging from 1960 to 1962. Most insist it was before making Los Tarantos, i.e. 1961. But Juan Maya was with her at that time and I am assured that he was not in the Casa Madrid. It is possible that Maya left Carmen in late 1961 and she appeared in Los Angeles at that time rather than early 1962.

not the steps, but Carmen becoming or being the essence of flamenco. She was an individual, an innovation. She danced, acted, and sang with her total body and soul movements, rhythms, and interpretations that are still copied and recopied by today's flamenco artists.

Carmen was so generous off stage and on and would give benefit performances for needy causes, such as dancing in the old Plaza Church in downtown Los Angeles and receiving only a bouquet of flowers. She let me watch her rehearsals, and I found her knowledge of all forms of Spanish dance to be incredible. She loved the classics and seemed to be a perpetual student of all forms of Spanish art.

The last time I saw Carmen in person was when she came to see me dance. I did not know she was there, as she came in with a big party of people and sat next to the stage, right in the center... It was opening night for me and our group, "Los Flamencos," at the Casa Madrid. Typical first-night nerves were there, but with great artists like Pepe Segundo singing and guitarists Benito Palacios and Rogelio Reguera, I was looking forward to a month of fun and exciting flamenco... Also adding to the nerves was the fact that we were following the long engagement of Carmen Amaya...

We opened with *sevillanas* and when we had finished I heard some ringside *jaleo* coming from a familiar voice. It was Carmen Amaya! My knees almost buckled. Carmen had never seen me dance, and for me to dance my *alegrías* for this person who had revolutionized that *compás* was a bit much. She gave me a big smile and I knew she was there to enjoy. Pepe started to sing and I began to dance. I don't remember a thing, but I guess it went well for that time in my life.

After the performance, I joined her table and she passed me her glass of champagne. I will never forget that evening. She was a great lady and I feel so fulfilled to have been able to see such a great artist and to know her as a great and giving person.[1]

According to Lola Montes, Carmen and her husband stayed with an attorney named Anthony Newman and his Spanish wife while she was in Los Angeles. The Newmans had arranged her contract with the Casa Madrid. Lola noticed that Carmen was dancing for the first time with her hair in a bun. Previously, she had always put her hair up loosely with one or two very large hairpins. Then at a certain point in the *alegrías* her hair would come loose and fall down—a dramatic effect. When Lola asked her why she had

---

[1] Condensed from two articles by Teo Morca: "Inspiration of Carmen Amaya," *Jaleo, Vol II, No 11* (June 1979), and "Carmen Amaya, Creator, Innovator, and Inspirational Force," *Jaleo, Vol III, No 3* (November 1980).

changed, Carmen replied, "Everyone is copying me now and wearing their hair down. So, to be different, I have to put my hair up!"

Lola recalls that she used to take Carmen to the club each night and after the show they would go out to eat in a coffee shop on Sunset Boulevard. Carmen always ate the same thing—she loved their potato salad. She also spoke often of her dream of returning to the little house in Bagur.

Guitarist Benito Palacios said that the musician's union in Los Angeles refused to permit Carmen's guitarists to play for her, saying that she had to use union musicians. Benito went to the union and told them that he would be doing the playing. Of course he didn't play. He also took members of the company out to the beach, where they were astonished to find abundant mussels and barnacles for the taking. They collected buckets full and took them back to their rooms to cook.

At the end of her contract, as Carmen turned over the Casa Madrid to Teo Morca, a surprise visitor showed up in Los Angeles. Mario Escudero had come to America again, with José Greco, and settled in New York. By 1957, he and Sabicas had already cut an album of duets.[1] That same year, Mario also recorded with Antonio Triana's daughter, Luisa, and a *cantaor* who had also come with José Greco—Chinin de Triana (no relation to Luisa). And, in yet another recording endeavor in 1957, Mario appeared as accompanist to Vicente Escudero on the aged dancer's album *Flamenco! Vicente Escudero*.[2] Vicente's face adorns the record jacket, wrinkled as a mummy, with a harsh slash of painted lips and a toupee plastered onto his head leaving very little forehead. On the record he dances several classical numbers to the piano of Pablo Miguel and then shows off his newly developed talent as a flamenco singer.

Vicente Escudero had kept busy in Spain with his lecture-demonstrations and had planned to open a dance school for foreign students in the town of Escorial. He and the dancer Antonio had continued their verbal sparring in the press. Mario Escudero said that the last time he worked with Vicente was in Cuba in 1957 or '58. The recording must have been done at that time. The two would renew their friendship a few years later, when Vicente came to live in New York. Mario said of Vicente, "He took everything he did very seriously. He was a lover of the arts, a true artist. He had known Picasso well. Vicente's arms were unique, very masculine; there are many artists today who follow his style, especially his arm movements."[3]

Mario spoke about the move to California, with his new wife, dancer Anita Ramos (Mario separated from María Amaya after the tour with Vicente Escudero): "My headquarters had always been New York City. I moved my family to California for a few years, but New York was always

---

[1] Sabicas and Escudero: Montilla FM-105.
[2] Columbia CL-882.
[3] Chileno, El, "Mario Escudero."

the center of my activities. I went to California when Carmen Amaya finished at the Casa Madrid in Los Angeles and I went there to play solos for thirty minutes or so between the performances of the *cuadro flamenco*. I was just a soloist and went under contract with an agent."

Mario continued to elaborate on how he eventually began his concert career: "I was living in San Gabriel, near Los Angeles, and played in a place owned by a Mexican, called El Poche. It was a big place, with many rooms and a dance hall. There was a round area near the restrooms where he used to store junk. I said to him, 'Why don't you put a flamenco corner here?' He said, 'And what is that?' I replied that he could decorate it and have a flamenco guitarist. The room was round, narrow but tall, and it had a domed roof; the guitar sounded glorious. We put in a small stage, a few tables, and some dim lights, and decided to try it out for a few months. I ended up staying three years and grew tired of it—I thought they might end up burying me there. During that period I began to give concerts, at first in universities. My first concert in New York was at Town Hall in 1963 and I received very good reviews."[1]

When the contract at the Casa Madrid ended, the Amaya company was more or less stranded in Los Angeles. But they had a commitment to honor in Mexico City, where they were to perform in El Patio. Juan Antonio bought an old car and they headed south. After a breakdown and with Carmen not feeling well, they reached their destination and would spend the rest of the year touring Central and South America. The trail of Carmen's travels during the next year is not well-documented. Aficionado Toño Portuguez saw her in Peru and reported that she complained of not feeling well and had a special diet that emphasized eggs. Goldberg places her back in New York in the fall of 1962, and in Mexico City for an extended stay in early 1963. Montañés described the end of her wandering:

> ...one day, in mid-tour, she collapsed while performing.
>
> Now it was impossible, completely impossible to continue dancing. Juan Antonio, with tear-filled eyes, said to her: "Let's go back to Spain! There you will recover from everything..."
>
> This time, and only this time, Carmen obeyed without protest. With infinite sadness she nodded in agreement. Sadly, the *Gran Compañía de Ballet Español de Carmen Amaya* returned to Spain.
>
> In Spain, the doctors came up with the same diagnosis: "Absolute rest!"
>
> Carmen consulted with every possible doctor, looking for one who would give her life, who would say: "This does not stop you from dancing..." But she couldn't find one.[2]

Carmen retired to her house in Bagur to rest. From her hilltop home she

---

[1] Chileno, El, "Mario Escudero, Part II."
[2] Montañés, p. 60.

could contemplate her beloved Mediterranean and the tranquil coastal village below. But she remained restless, and when she found out that the government of Bagur planned a series of festivities to raise funds for the lighting of Bagur's castle—the castle that she could see from her window—Carmen could not resist offering her services.

> She overcame the opposition of Juan Antonio and, on a typical Mediterranean night, before an expectant crowd that had come from as far away as Barcelona and Gerona, Carmen Amaya, accompanied on the guitar by Juan Antonio Agüero, danced once again. The castle of Bagur would have its lighting. In just that one evening, more than enough money was collected to make it possible.
>
> When Carmen Amaya finishes her performance, she collapses. She has to accept the applause of the frightened public while seated in a chair; the audience rises to its feet and pays tribute with the greatest and most emotional ovation ever given to a dancer. At the back of the stage, in a corner, Juan Antonio, embracing his guitar, cries with a great suffering. He is sure that this has been the last dance of Carmen Amaya.
>
> Here, at the edge of the Mediterranean, La Capitana also knows that she has danced for the last time.[1]

Carmen returned to Madrid for more in-depth tests. The doctors continued to order complete rest. Rumors flew in the press. One day the newspapers would report that Carmen would undergo surgery, only to recant the story the next day. Nobody wanted to speak of the truth they feared. Juan Antonio assured Carmen that she only needed to rest a few months. They decided she could receive the same treatment closer to home and returned to Barcelona.

Carmen entered the clinic of Doctor Antonio Puigvert, Spain's top kidney specialist. He confirmed a diagnosis of sclerosis of the kidneys. At that time, she had only one enlarged kidney still functioning. Popular legend has it that she had been told by a doctor at one time, "Dance child…if you don't you will die!" It was believed that kidney failure prevented her from eliminating body toxins, but dancing as she did, she sweated enough for four people and thereby staved off her death. However, medical fact appears to contradict this scenario. Sweating cannot eliminate toxins through the skin, and strenuous exercise puts a greater burden on the kidneys. A likely cause of Carmen's sclerotic kidney disease would have been recurrent or chronic kidney infection—which would have explained the frequent illness and severe back pain she had suffered for years. Carmen's reluctance to see doctors and receive antibiotics could have led to her eventual kidney failure.[2]

Relatives tried to comfort the dancer, assuring her that it was only tempo-

---

[1] Montañés, p. 62.

[2] I thank Dr. Robert Mallon for this insight.

rary. Carmen, in turn, tried to put up a good front, eating heartily of bread and stewed tomatoes in order to demonstrate that she was doing well. According to one reporter, Carmen stayed confined to bed in a luxury hotel in Barcelona. She didn't feel particularly comfortable in that setting and said, "For me, who has had everything—diamonds, furs, money—it would be all the same to return to living in a shack, sleeping on a sack, and, for food, a potato and a slice of tomato." News cameras came to film her and days later her hollow, darkened eyes looked out from movie screens across Spain. Audiences became emotional at the sight of the shrunken, emaciated dancer who had once been a symbol of strength and vitality. Ironically, as Carmen lay in bed, *Los Tarantos* played in local movie houses. She would never see the finished film.

At the beginning of November, 1963, when it had become clear that nothing further could be done, Carmen asked to be moved to her home in Bagur "to wait for spring." She tried to cheer her family by saying, "Now you will see how I get over all of this!" Ten days later, on November 12, *The New York Times* reported: "The noted Spanish gypsy dancer Carmen Amaya was given, at her own request, the last rites of the Roman Catholic Church today, a member of the family said."[1]

Now the local doctor in Bagur became like a member of the family. Word spread and gypsies began to arrive from around Spain. Many of her family joined the around-the-clock vigil.

> Micaela Amaya, the mother of Carmen, old and heavyset now, seated by the fireplace, her eyes fixed on the flames, moves her lips, perhaps in prayer, perhaps in an exorcism...
>
> Carmen's nights, restless, filled with terror of the darkness, worry everyone. Doctor García—now called Paco by everybody—remarks, "It's amazing. This woman is made of iron." Doctor Puigvert comes and goes from Barcelona to Bagur. Juan Antonio's father arrives. Some cars with registrations from the other side of the Pyrenees begin to arrive. Their occupants, photographers and reporters, find rooms in the hotels of Bagur and settle in to await what will be news for all of the world. The central telegraph office of Bagur never rests. Telegrams arrive from around the world inquiring about Carmen's condition.
>
> Gypsies roam around El Manso like shadows of an ancient ballad. Mattresses and blankets are found in every corner of the house, layed out in improvised campsites. From time to time a gypsy goes into Carmen's room. When he comes out, the others, silent and expectant, look at him and it is always the same phrase, the same answer to their unspoken question: "She is tranquil!"

---

[1] "Miss Amaya Gets Last Rites." *The New York Times*, November 13, 1963.

And indeed, in her bed, Carmen is tranquil...tranquil at the cost of injections and tranquilizers...[1]

On November 13, the Spanish Government awarded Carmen its highest civil award, the *Lazo de Dama de la Orden de Isabel la Católica*. The governor of Barcelona traveled to Bagur to make the official presentation to the bedridden dancer. Carmen responded to the honor with a sad and lifeless smile, saying, "Now? What good is it to me now?" And turning to Dr. Puigvert, "Take it Doctor, keep it!"[2] Two days later, the city government of Barcelona presented Carmen with the Medal of the City, for artistic merit.

A newspaper reporter described Carmen sitting in her window to catch the warmth of the sun:

> You [Carmen] were cold. You covered yourself with a gray blanket and rubbed your small, boney hands, weak as those of a child, over a blue hot water bottle. Night was falling and you were too. You were saying, "The sun has left me." Night was coming, the night that had always brought you good things and now brought nothing but bad: insomnia, agonizing sweats, the long and desolate hours of nights that never seems to end. The night, that takes the sun from you and brings the fear that you will never see it again.[3]

For several days Carmen could not eat, vomiting up even the little milk she managed to swallow. One night, a week after receiving the last rites, Carmen grew unusually restless. Even the pills could not make her sleep.

> A whisper: "Hold my hand..."
> Juan Antonio's father takes the hand of the dancer. Hours pass. The sick one opens her eyes. She looks at those around her bed for a long time...Then: "Give me a kiss, Papa..."
> Juan Antonio's father tenderly kisses Carmen's sweaty forehead; the dancer asks the same of the others...Diego, her mother...She continues to try to rest, without success. The dawn makes its timid appearance. Another night has passed. The sun is high in the sky when the clock of the church of Bagur chimes nine times. A few minutes later, Carmen squeezes Juan Antonio's hand tightly and whispering something that only he can understand, kisses him. And nothing more.[4]

Carmen Amaya Amaya died on November 19, 1963. She had just turned fifty. She once said, "If I have to stop dancing, it is better that I should die."

---

[1] Montañés, p. 66.
[2] Hidalgo, p. 213.
[3] Serrano, María Dolores, *"Carmela, mi niña, mi Carmela..." La Vanguardia*. Reproduced in Hidalgo, p. 219.
[4] Montañés, p. 67.

She had waited until she was sure. When it was absolutely certain that she would never dance again, she died. The official account read:

> At five minutes after nine in the morning, in her ranch, La Masia, in Begur, the brilliant Spanish dancer Carmen Amaya has died.
>
> Throughout the night her family took turns watching over her... At eight this morning, the invalid fell into a cold sweat and those at her bedside suspected that the end was appoaching...
>
> At the moment of death, those at bedside included Dr. Del Río, assistant to the emminent urologist from Barcelona, Dr. Antonio Puigvert, and the doctor of Begur, Don Francisco García. Also, attending to spiritual matters, the priest from the local parrish, Reverend José María Mir.
>
> Carmen Amaya was lucid up to the last moment. No complaint escaped from her lips. Only prayers and, at the end, a nervous kiss for her husband, whose hand she held tightly.[1]

Amid the grief of her family and her people, reporters and photographers descended on El Manso. Pictures of her before and after her death would appear in major magazines. The telegraph office of Bagur would work non-stop to spread the news worldwide. Within days, more than 2,500 telegrams and letters would arrive from as far away as South America, the United States, and Japan. Most of population of Bagur filed up the steep paths from the town and passed through El Manso to pay homage to their adopted daughter. Carmen lay in state in a mahogany coffin, dressed in white, a white *mantilla* over her face and her hands holding a rosary. She appeared serene, resting at last.

The city of Bagur officially mourned Carmen Amaya by flying flags at half-mast, draping balconies and windows in black, and leaving the lights on in the castle day and night. The city donated a parcel of land in the municipal cemetery and artisans worked through the night to prepare a tomb for the burial the following day. Fellow artists came for the funeral. Pilar López and Rosario hired a taxi to bring them from Madrid. Antonio Gades made the rounds of the flamenco establishments in Barcelona to be sure that they all closed down and then drove to Bagur with friends. Flowers of all types, in bouquets or immense arrangements and wreaths, filled El Manso. It is said that flower supplies were completely depleted in Bagur and neighboring towns.

On November 20th, business shut down in Bagur and the populace turned out en masse to accompany Carmen on her final journey. Shortly after ten o'clock in the morning the funeral procession began its trek down the dusty road from El Manso, headed by a contingent of cross-bearing clergy from local churches and barefoot friars from the Palafrugell Convent. The casket

---

[1]Reproduced in Hidalgo, p. 214.

was carried in shifts, first on the shoulders of the husband, brother-in-law, and other family members. A group of older gypsies took the second turn, followed by younger gypsies, and finally, neighbors and friends from Bagur. Family, including the mother and aunt, La Faraona, and intimate friends accompanied the casket, and were joined by a large group of officials, mayors, governors, and representatives of artists unions and agencies.

The procession reached the local church as the bells sounded twenty to eleven. The crowd, estimated at more than two thousand, was far too large to be accommodated by the small chapel and the majority had to remain outside in the street during the funeral. Montañés described the trip to the cemetery:

> At noon the procession gets under way. On the shoulders of the gypsies, Carmen Amaya, the body of Carmen Amaya, descends the dusty road from her house. An immense crowd gathers with an almost mystical fervor to watch Carmen pass by. From mouth to mouth spreads the terrible name of the illness that has carried her off: sclerosis of the kidneys.
>
> It takes the cortege two interminal hours to reach the cemetery of Bagur, two hours under a sun that also wanted to say goodbye to Carmen. The masons have worked until the last moment to complete the simple mausoleum. Yesterday the spot had been occupied only by the wildflowers that grow in the countryside. Now there is a grave, a small one—it wasn't necessary to make it very big—destined to shelter the body of Carmen Amaya.
>
> A simple and fragile wooden fence is inadequate to hold back that multitude that wants to be close to the dancer at that moment, a multitude that, just like when she danced, wants to see her from up close...
>
> In absolute silence the coffin descends to the bottom of the grave, and a hand drops a simple bouquet of red carnations in after it. Juan Antonio throws the first fistful of earth. Then, handful by handful, shovelful by shovelful, the soft earth, moist and dark, hides forever the most brilliant *bailaora* that has ever set foot on a stage.
>
> Slowly the crowd abandons the cemetery. The last to do so is Juan Antonio. The gypsies return to El Manso. Each and every one wants to take away some keepsake, some memory of Carmen. Her costumes are for Micaela; Carmen has left them to her. The car is waiting and it is getting late. Frantically, large bundles are gathered up. From here a *bata de cola*, from there a polka-dot blouse; shoes worn-out on the stages of the world are going to come to rest in a straw basket. Multicolored polka-dot blouses, Spanish

combs, lace *mantillas*, fans, castanets, all in dazzling disarray, are packed and carried to the open area in front of the house.

Little by little the house is emptied.

Carmen Amaya's people begin the trip home, some to Barcelona, others to Gerona, to Palafrugell…home.[1]

A Spanish newspaper described the aftermath of Carmen's death:

> Even as her bed still held the shape of the body of Carmen Amaya, the last gypsies, the last of her people, were leaving in tears, loaded with packages of "remembrances" of their *capitana*. It was a brazen robbery, but at the same time an act of devotion that few will understand…they all fled crying and loaded to the maximum with packages. Nobody stopped them, and nobody would have tried…
>
> Nobody knows anything. Everything disappeared, as things tend to disappear. Nobody knows when, nor how, nor why. The stables of El Manso were always full of glossy horses that were happy to carry the small body of the *bailaora* on rides along the coast. They were rich stables. Where are the horses now? One day they disappeared. Where are the automobiles? At times there were two or three automobiles at the doors of El Manso…they are all gone! And the furs. Where are the rich furs of Carmen Amaya?
>
> Her sickness was long, very long. The expenses were great, but I don't know if they could have been that much. Carmen Amaya gave everything, because everything she had she gave. It was for "her people." "Her people" needed it. She would never deny her race. She was, above all, a gypsy, and she wished to die like a gypsy. She died the most gypsy of them all. She died with nothing, almost as she had been born, believing that she still owned her home, when nothing was left to her, and believing that "her people" respected her.
>
> Now there are no more thefts from El Manso. I know that for certain. After passing several deathly hours in the desolate rooms of what was Carmen Amaya's house, I have come to this conclusion: There have been five burglaries in El Manso, five that are known…there could have been more. But nobody will ever rob El Manso again, because there is nothing left to steal. It has been left denuded, with nothing.
>
> For Carmen, nothing is left, unless it is the memory of her great art. Only her tomb, where her remains are at rest. But it is a blank tomb, indistinguishable from the rest. It is a tomb without inscription—neither name nor dates. That is what she ordered before she

[1] Montañés, p. 70.

died. "I want a white tomb with nothing on it, as the tomb of a gypsy should be."

And so it was.[1]

---

[1] Valverde, José Antonio; in an unidentified Spanish newspaper.

EPILOGUE

According to Francisco Hidalgo, Carmen Amaya's remains were eventually moved to Santander, to be placed in the pantheon of her husband's family. Juan Antonio retired from playing the guitar, although an American living in Spain in the mid-1960s reported the rumor going around that, "Juan Antonio Agüero, who has acquired a number of Santos guitars, has hidden himself in a little town in the Lérida Pyrenees. 'Nobody can get him out of there,' his friends say. 'Not his family, not even his friends—nobody. Night and day he plays his Santos and laments the death of Carmen Amaya.'"[1] The fact is that, three years after Carmen's death, Juan Antonio remarried and had two children.

Carmen had streets named after her in Buenos Aires, Barcelona, Bagur, and l'Hospitalet de Llobregat. A plaza in Cornellà de Llobregat bears her name. And the fountain in Barcelona continues her memory.

Twenty-eight years after Carmen's passing, biographer Mario Bois undertook a pilgrimage to see what remained of her monuments. On the site of the Somorrostro stood the Olympic Village constructed for the 1992 Games. After a great deal of searching, he came across Carmen's fountain, squeezed between two modern buildings, in ruins and covered with painted graffiti. In the Plaza del Dante, he located a magnificent ten-foot bronze sculpture of Carmen in a train dress. In Montjuic, in the Pueblo Español built for the 1929 Exposition, he found the Tablao de Carmen, a functioning *tablao* decorated with remembrances of Carmen Amaya—including the celebrated poster of her painted in Mexico in 1939.

Two years after Carmen's death, José Antonio Valverde wrote: "Carmen's home in Bagur was nicknamed 'El Manso.' It was owned by an American named Wilson, who was a great admirer of Carmen. The trail of ownership disappears, but after Carmen's death El Manso seems to have belonged to a Señor Picamau, who then sells it to the city of Bagur. Now, two years later, from a distance the tower rises majestically; it seems to be a regal mansion in the middle of a small jungle. But only from a distance…Now El Manso is dead. The doors were permanently closed the day the queen of the gypsies died—November 19, 1963."

Years later Mario Bois found that the city had built the *Centro Cultural Carmen Amaya* below El Manso. A dirt path leads up to Carmen's home, which has been preserved and restored. Apparently the only evidence of Carmen Amaya is a set of eight large photos in one room. The guard told

---

[1] George, David, *The Flamenco Guitar*. Society of Spanish Studies, Madrid. 1969. p. 103.

Bois that during the intervening years he had played hide-and-seek as a child in the abandoned building.

After leaving Carmen Amaya in 1957, **Sabicas** spent the rest of his life working out of New York. He never achieved the level of public acclaim enjoyed by Carlos Montoya and often looked back on his years with Carmen as the height of his fame, when, "even the stones knew my name."[1] But he was revered by flamenco aficionados everywhere, and when the more than thirty-seven long-play records he made in the United States began to filter into Spain in the 1960s, he became a dominant influence on a new generation of guitarists. In 1967, almost thirty years after he left, Sabicas returned to Spain to receive an award. He said that his failure to return before that had not been a political statement, merely a matter of commitments and other priorities. About that return, he said:

> What a great thrill! After almost thirty years! What emotion, to see the places where you grew up. There wasn't enough time to see everything, as I was there for only four weeks—two in Málaga and two in Madrid. I would have liked to stay for six months or a year, but I had other commitments... I was not going there to work, but the television found out and talked me into it. I told them I wasn't prepared, that I had not studied anything, but I just couldn't get out of it. Ever since, every time I have been back, I have had to do a television appearance. I recorded a few albums there. In 1971 I went with *Festivales de España*, which is one of the best groups of its kind. We did a tour of Spain, and in 1974, I went back for the last time. I have not been back since, because there are no ships from New York. And if there are no ships, I won't go.[2]

Sabicas continued to be active giving concerts through the 1980s. But gradually he cut back, claiming that he did not feel well and did not enjoy the pressure of performing. He gave his last concert in Carnegie Hall in June of 1989. After suffering a stroke in his home the following year, he passed away on April 14, 1990. He was seventy-eight. As of summer, 1998, his brother, Diego, was still living in New York.

Vicente Escudero lived in New York for a period in the early 1960s. He attempted one more national tour, but according to José Greco, his company walked out on him in the middle of a performance because they weren't being paid. That was the end of Vicente's touring career in the United States. By 1964, he was back in Spain, performing with María Marquez and the guitarist Andrés Batista. The following year, eighty years old, he danced in the Madrid *tablao*, Cuevas de Nerja, and toured Europe. His home town of

---
[1] Molarski interview.
[2] Chileno, El Niño, *"Conversaciones con Sabicas."*

Valladolid honored him for a third time in 1966, and he continued giving lecture/recitals during the next several years. He was honored on a national level in a 1974 homage that included performances by Antonio Gades, Luisillo, Pilar López, Rosario, and others. Vicente Escudero died in poverty in 1980, at age ninety-five, but was buried in a pantheon alongside other notables of Valladolid.

Mario Escudero continued to lead an active flamenco life in America, cutting more than thirty record albums and influencing young guitarists with his (for that period) avant-garde style. He moved to Spain in 1983, where he enjoyed a period of celebrity, served on contest juries, and opened a flamenco school in Sevilla. By 1989, he was experiencing diminished mental faculties, a condition that would continue to worsen over the next decade.

Juan Sánchez "Estampío" continued to teach in Madrid in the 1950s, when he was well into his seventies. Diego Castellón had said of him: "The best dancer I have seen in my life was Juan Sánchez 'Estampío,' and he didn't even have money for cigarettes. He used to go into Los Gabrieles [early 1930s] in Madrid and they would say to him, 'Take one...two...Take the pack!' I used to go into Los Gabrieles and I saw that man practicing in a dark room, old and without work. I have never seen anyone dance better—and he was sixty years old! They said he was better even than Antonio de Bilbao."[1]

José Greco said: "I never saw El Estampío perform. I only appreciated him as a teacher, and he taught extraordinary technique. He was one of the greatest flamenco dancers, and he specialized in footwork. He had great expertise in his *desplantes*—the breaks between variations. Then he would go into the *escovillas*; in these he excelled. He was quite a personality, even in his late years."[2]

A young American dancer, Lydia Torea, studied with Estampío in the early 1950s:

> El Estampío lived in an old section of Madrid. We went up three flights of rickety steps to his apartment. The master teacher couldn't have been more than five feet tall. He was wearing a shabby little robe and slippers. He looked at me in surprise and jabbered, "Onononono, much too young! You'll be here only four weeks? You can't learn anything in that time. I take only professionals."
>
> Mama pleaded and begged until he finally weakened, but he had a warning: He had four schools of *zapateado* (footwork) and he thought I would only learn the first school...
>
> Apparently I was a quick study with Estampío, because we stayed six weeks rather than four, and I learned all four schools. He cried the day we left for America. He wanted me to stay and

---
[1] Goldberg interviews.
[2] Iran, The Shah of, "Interview with José Greco." *Jaleo, Vol VIII, No 1*.

study with him, but Mama wasn't about to leave me there. I promised I'd be back as soon as I'd finished grade and high schools. We kept in touch, but he died just three months before I returned to Spain.[1]

El Estampío died in 1957.

Manolo de Huelva could usually be found playing for private fiestas during the 1950s and 60s, often in the Venta Manzanilla outside of Madrid. Encumbered by his eccentricities, he generally restricted his playing to *juergas* or practicing in his apartment above the Villa Rosa. However, in 1964, at age seventy-two, he filled in at La Zambra for six months while the regular *cuadro* was performing at the World's Fair in New York, and he accompanied the *cante* of Enrique Morente at a lecture by flamencologist José Blas Vega. By 1969, he had returned to Sevilla, where he continued to play in bars for private fiestas. Manolo passed away in 1976. He was eighty-three years old.

José Greco continued to tour until well into his seventies. His successful career included appearances in six movies and the release of at least eight long-play records. As his abilities began to wane with age, José founded dance academies in Spain and the USA, and three of his children rose to prominence in the Spanish dance. After consolidating their reputations in Spain's *tablaos*, the Spanish National Ballet, and their father's company, José Greco II, Carmela, and Lola eventually formed their own dance companies to carry on the family name.

Pastora Imperio continued to operate the *tablao*, El Duende, through the 1960s and opened a second club in Marbella. After a long retirement, she died of a heart attack on September 14, 1979, at age ninety.

Antonio Mairena compiled an encyclopedic archive of *cante* with his many recordings. Some question the authenticity of many of the ancient songs he recreated, but the fact remains that his versions are the only ones known today. As holder of the Gold Key of *Cante*, Mairena had reached the pinnacle of his profession and remains as a symbol of an era that sought to preserve tradition in flamenco. His biography, *Las Confesiones de Antonio Mairena*, is a valuable source of historical and anecdotal information. When he died of a heart attack in 1983, shortly after recording for the last time, he left behind a vacuum in the panorama of the *cante*—a vacuum that has yet to be filled.

Pepe Marchena sang until the end. In 1969 he married the woman he had lived with for twenty-five years. When he was diagnosed with stomach cancer in 1976 and given only a few months to live, he told his friends calmly, "It's not worth getting all worked up about. These are things that have to happen." As his condition worsened, he said, with no hint of sadness, "This is coming to an end. From the moment we are born we begin the road to

---

[1] Olmsted, Maxine, "Lydia Torea." *Jaleo, Vol VI, No 10*, August 1979.

death, and the hour has come for me." Less than a week before his death on December 4, 1976, Marchena, with his usual flair for showmanship, sent a statement to be read in a festival held in his honor. In it, he apologized to all those he might have offended during his lifetime, and ended by stating: "Thank you to everybody, and goodbye forever!"[1]

Lola Montes remains active with her company in the Los Angeles area.

Carlos Montoya maintained his position as the people's flamenco guitarist right up to the time of his death on March 3, 1993. He had brought a great deal of pleasure to hundreds of thousands of fans through his constant concertizing and his more than forty record albums. After his passing, at age eighty-nine, his friend, Ivor Mairants, said, "He certainly was a happy man who enjoyed life."

La Niña de los Peines made a brief appearance at a 1961 performance organized in her honor by Antonio Mairena. She amazed the press and the huge audience by singing and dancing *por bulerías* as well as ever (a tape recording attests to this fact). For the next eight years she would rarely be seen except when she sat, dressed in black and wearing dark glasses, outside her husband's tavern, the Bar Pinto, on the Plaza Campana in Sevilla. Her health and mental condition gradually deteriorated due to arteriosclerosis, so that, when her husband died on October 6, 1969, she wasn't even aware that he was gone. Less than two months later, on November 26, she united once again with her beloved Pepe. The year before, aficionados in Sevilla had erected a bronze bust of her on what had once been the glorious Alameda de Hercules, but had become a shabby avenue of garages and homeless derelicts.

Niño Ricardo spent most of the last two decades of his life accompanying the maximum exponents of the *ópera flamenca*: Juanito Valderrama, Antonio Molina, and Pepe Marchena. This association put him somewhat out of the mainstream in a period in which the *ópera flamenca* style was falling into disfavor. However, his recordings were the primary source of inspiration for a new generation of guitar revolutionaries, headed by Paco de Lucía, Victor Monje "Serranito," and Paco Peña. Ricardo recorded with his protégé, Paco de Lucía, in 1969. He died in 1974.

Antonio Triana remained in Los Angeles for many years, teaching and participating in more than twenty films. When he remarried and retired to El Paso, Texas, he left his daughter Luisa behind to carry on his school of dance. His wife wrote that he continued to teach until age seventy-eight and passed away in 1989.

---

[1] All quotes taken from Cobos, p. 176-78.

Glossary of Spanish Terms

afición: love or liking (for something).
aficionado: fan or supporter; nonprofessional performer.
aire: air; flavor or attitude in behavior or performance.
alegrías: song and dance form that originated in Cádiz; from *alegría* (joy, happiness).
alzapúa: from *alzar* (to raise or lift) + *púa* (plectrum; pick); a thumb technique that creates chordal rhythm and melody at the same time; involves back-picking/strumming, i.e. "raising the pick."
ambiente: environment; mood of a situation.
Andalucía: the region that occupies the south of Spain; made up of eight provinces. Flamenco is primarily an Andalucían phenomenon.
apoyando: in guitar playing, the use of the rest stroke, i.e. plucking with fingers or thumb coming to rest on an adjacent string.
arte: art.
bailaor (a): flamenco dancer.
baile: dance.
bamberas: a song based on verses sung to accompany the swinging of girls in the spring; usually done to the rhythm of *soleá por bulerías*.
banderillero: in the bullfight, the man who places the *banderillas* (colorful barbed sticks) into the bull's neck.
bulerías: lively and festive gypsy song, dance, and guitar form; most difficult and improvisational of the flamenco styles.
café cantante: a cafe where flamenco performances are presented; *tablao* in modern terminology.
canastero (a): basket maker; often used as a generic term for nomadic gypsies.
canción: non-flamenco song.
cantaor (a): flamenco singer.
cante: flamenco song.

cantiñas: the family of songs to which the *alegrías* belong; also includes *romeras, mirabrás, caracoles,* and modern inventions *"por alegrías."*
caracoles: a song in the *cantiñas* family; traditionally played in C-major chord patterns.
cartageneras: a free rhythm *cante* from the mining districts; named after the city of Cartagena on Spain's east coast.
cejilla: a small device, usually made of wood, that clamps across the guitar strings on the fingerboard to alter pitch.
colmao: in flamenco circles, a restaurant where artists hang out looking for work.
colombianas: Latin flavored *cante*; named for Colombia, but actually invented in Spain.
compás: rhythm; includes accentuation and length of rhythmic cycle.
copla: verse.
corto: short: a style of singing or playing without elaboration; short in repertoire, a specialist in only a few styles.
cuadro: a flamenco performing group consisting of singers, dancers, and guitarists.
cuplé: a non-flamenco song done to a flamenco rhythm.
cupletista: one who specializes in *cuplés*, usually a woman who also danced and played castanets.
debla: an ancient and little sung gypsy *cante*; one of the *tonás* family of songs that are sung without musical accompaniment.
desplante: short sequences of steps in certain dances, especially the *bulerías*, that give free reign to the dancer's imagination and spontaneity.
duende: soul; an undefinable spirit that inspires a performer to rise above his usual level of performance.

escovilla: sections of dance that emphasize footwork.
estribillo: chorus or repeated part of a song.
falseta: a melodic variation on the guitar, as contrasted with strumming.
fandangos: a class of flamenco songs that appear in different forms throughout Andalucía; dating back to the Moorish occupation, they were originally spritely dance songs, but have evolved in some areas into profound *cantes*, such as the *granaínas*, *malagueñas*, and *tarantas*.
fandangos de Huelva: a variety of styles of lively dance *fandangos* from the province of Huelva.
fandangos de Lucena: a style of *fandangos* from the town of Lucena (Córdoba).
fandangos de Triana: a free-rhythm profound style of *fandangos*, derived from those of Huelva; also called *fandangos grandes* or *naturales*.
fandanguillos: common name for *fandangos de Huelva* in the early 1900s.
farruca: a song from Asturias in the north of Spain, seldom sung today; a masculine dance emphasizing footwork and strong poses.
flamenco: a form of music, including song, dance, and guitar, that arose in Andalucía through the fusion of gypsy elements with Andalucían folklore.
flamenco (a): one who performs and lives flamenco; having a personality typical of flamencos.
flamencólogo: flamencologist; one who studies flamenco in an intellectual manner.
garrotín: a gypsy song and dance in 4/4 time with a gay major tonality.
gitano (a): gypsy.
gracia: humor, cleverness, and personality in performance or way of being.
granaínas: profound style of *fandangos* developed in Granada; the guitar music has a haunting Moorish quality.
guajiras: a song style developed from Cuban music; a dance based on the song.
hombre!: "man!"; an exclamation widely used for emphasis.
ida y vuelta: round trip: refers to *cantes* derived from Latin American songs.
jaberas: a seldom sung fandango from the Málaga area.
jaleo: clapping and shouting used to inspire a performer.
jaleos: a style of *bulerías* that originated with the gypsies of Extremadura.
jondo: the Andalucían pronunciation of *"hondo,"* i.e. "deep" or "profound."
jondura: profundity.
juerga: a flamenco gathering or fiesta.
ligados: notes played on the guitar with the left hand alone, i.e., unplucked by the right hand.
malagueñas: a class of profound *fandangos* from the Málaga area.
marianas: a *tango*-like *cante* based on the songs of the itinerant circus performers.
martinetes: songs of the gypsy blacksmiths; member of the *tonás* family of *cantes* that are sung without musical accompaniment.
milonga: a flowery *cante* in 4/4 time with roots in Argentina.
mineras: profound style of *fandango* from the mining region of eastern Andalucía.
monstruo: monster; a "giant" in one's field.
ópera flamenca: the generally decadent theatrical flamenco typical of the period 1920-1955; emphasis was on the *fandangos* and the Latin American influenced *cantes*, often sung in a falsetto voice and with great liberties taken in the structure in order to display virtuosity.
palmas: handclapping.
pasodoble: music played during the

bullfight; popular dance to this music.
payo: non-gypsy.
peseta: Spanish monetary unit approximately equal to a USA penny; value has varied through the years, from 60 to the dollar to over 130; changing values and inflation over the years make it difficult to give equivalents in dollars.
peteneras: a dramatic *cante* of uncertain origin.
picado: the playing of scale passages and melodies, often at great speed, using (usually) alternating index and middle fingers.
por derecho: correctly; in the traditional manner.
rajo: the rough, raspy quality of voice that is desirable in flamenco and most often found in gypsy singers.
rasgueado: strumming techniques on the guitar.
rondeña: a *fandango* from the area around Ronda; a guitar solo created by Ramón Montoya which requires an alteration in the tunings of two strings.
rumba: festive song, dance, and guitar style that originated in Cuba and was incorporated into flamenco by the *Catalán* gypsies of northern Spain and southern France.
seguidillas: a pre-flamenco, 3/8 rhythm dance song that gave rise to the *sevillanas* and related forms.
señor: Sir, gentleman.
señorito: a gentleman with money; a term applied, sometimes derogatorily, to those with money who hire flamencos for their private entertainment.
sevillanas: a folk song and dance from Sevilla that is a fringe element in flamenco.
simpático: friendly, likeable, charming.
siguiriyas: the most profound gypsy *cante*, with themes of death and misery; the guitar music is intense, but less profound than the *cante*, and employs an unusual rhythm of three fast and two slow beats.
soleares, soleá: from the word *soledad* (loneliness); the most popular of the serious *cantes*, based on a twelve-beat rhythm cycle, and having many styles; the guitar music is also one of the more popular for solo playing; equally popular as a dance form.
soleá por bulerías: verses of *bulerías* sung to an uptempo *soleares* rhythm; a rhythm in between those of *bulerías* and *soleares*.
tablao: a nightclub featuring flamenco entertainment.
tangos: a lively song, dance, and music in 2/4 time; many styles.
tanguillos: lively and humorous songs typical of Carnaval in Cádiz.
tarantas (os): deep *fandangos* songs from the mining regions of Andalucía; possibly the most profound of the guitar styles.
temple: singer's warm-up, consisting of sounds of *"ay," "lele,"* or *"titititrán."*
tercio: a phrase of *cante;* may or may not coincide with a line of verse.
tientos: a slow form of *tangos*, done in a highly syncopated 6/8 time.
tío: uncle; guy.
tirando: plucking of the guitar strings with free strokes, i.e. into the air without coming to rest on an adjacent string.
tocaor: flamenco guitarist.
tonás: from *tonadas*; originally popular songs, but now referring to a series of gypsy *cantes* that are sung chant-like, without musical accompaniment.
toque: flamenco guitar playing; a guitar style or musical form.
tremolo: sustained melody played by the fingers while the thumb accompanies in the bass.
verdiales: danceable *fandangos* from the countryside around

Málaga.
vidalita: a practically extinct *cante* based on Argentinian peasant songs.
zambra: a style of *tangos* from the gypsy caves of Granada, having Moorish overtones; a fiesta in the caves of the Sacromonte; a performing group from the Sacromonte.
zarzuela: Spanish light opera.

References

Alvarez Caballero, Angel, *Historia del Cante Flamenco.* Alianza Editorial, Madrid. 1981.

Blas Vega, José, "*Manolo de Huelva (1892-1976): El Guitarista que inspiró a Falla.*" La Caña, No 4, Winter 1993. Asociación Cultural "España Abierta," Madrid.

_____ , "*Ramón Montoya: La Guitarra Flamenca.*" in: *Guitarra en la Historia, Vol V.* Colección Bordón, Córdoba. 1994.

_____ , *Vida y Cante de Don Antonio Chacón.* Excmo. Ayuntamiento de Córdoba-Area de Cultura, Córdoba. 1986.

Blas Vega, José, y Manuel Ríos Ruiz, *Diccionario Enciclopédico Ilustrado de Flamenco.* Creaciones Internacionales y Coedicciones S.A.-Cinterco, Madrid. 1988.

Bois, Mario, *Carmen Amaya o la Danza del Fuego.* Espasa Calpe, Madrid. 1994.

Butler, Augusto, *Javier Molina, Jerezano y Tocao: memorias autógrafas de su vida artística.* Jerez. 1938.

Chileno, El, "*Conversaciones con Mario Escudero.*" Jaleo, Vol VI, No 11, October/November 1983; Part II: Vol VI, No 12, December 1983.

Chileno, El Niño, "*Conversaciones con Sabicas.*" Jaleo, Vol IV, No 8, April 1981.

Claus, Madeline, "Baile Flamenco." in: *Flamenco,* edited by Claus Schreiner. Amadeus Press, Portland, Oregon. 1990.

Climent, Anselmo Gónzales, in *Candil: Revista Flamenca de la Peña de Jaén,* September-October, 1989. Jaén, Spain.

Cobo, Eugenio, *Vida y Cante de Niño de Marchena.* Virgilio Márquez, Córdoba. 1990.

Dos Passos, John, *Rosinante to the Road Again.* George H. Doran Company, New York. 1922.

Espín, Miguel, and Romualdo Molina, *La Argentina y Pilar López.* V Bienal de Arte Flamenco, Sevilla. 1992.

Gasch, Sebastián, *El Molino.* Dopesa, Barcelona. 1972.

Goldberg, K. Meira, *Border Trespasses: The Gypsy Mask and Carmen Amaya's Flamenco Dance.* Temple University. 1995.

Goldberg, K. Meira, Interviews with Diego Castellón in New York between November 1985 and April 1989.

Góngora, Rafael de, "*Una Vida Fulgurante.*" Blanco y Negro, November 23, 1963.

Hidalgo Gómez, Francisco, *Carmen Amaya: Cuando duermo, sueño que estoy bailando.* Libros PM, Barcelona. 1995.

Magnussen, Paul, "Sabicas." *Guitar,* August 1982.

Mairena, Antonio, *Las Confesiones de Antonio Mairena.* Universidad de

Sevilla. 1976.
Mañas, Alfredo, "Carmen Amaya." *La Caña*, No 1, December 1991. Madrid.
Maravilla, Luis, in *Sevilla Flamenca*, No 68, November 1990.
Matos, Manuel García, *Mi Vida, Mi Obra, y Mis Recuerdos*. Servicio Municipal de Publicaciones, Alcalá de Guadaira. 1985.
Molarsky, Mona, "Salt and Enchantment: An Encounter with Sabicas." *Guitar Review*, No 82, Summer 1990.
Molarsky, Mona, Interview with Sabicas in New York, April 1989.
Montañés, Salvador, *Carmen Amaya: la bailaora genial*. G.P., Barcelona. 1964.
Ortiz Nuevo, José Luis, *Las Mil y Una Historias de Pericón de Cádiz*. Ediciones Demófilo, Madrid. 1975.
───────────── , *Pepe de la Matrona: Recuerdos de un Cantaor Sevillano*. Ediciones Demófilo, Madrid. 1975.
Pohren, Donn E., *Lives and Legends of Flamenco*. Society of Spanish Studies, Madrid. 1988.
Puig Claramunt, Alfonso, *Ballet y Baile Español*. Montaner y Simón, Barcelona. 1951.
Puig Claramunt, Alfonso, y Flora Albaicín, *El Arte del Baile Flamenco*. Polígrafa, Barcelona. 1977.
Rodríguez Cosano, Ricardo, "*Marcheneros de Pro*." *Sevilla Flamenca*, No 69, December 1990.
Samperio, José, *Carmen Amaya*. Luo Dunetz and Paul Lovette, New York. c. 1955.
Sugrue, Francis, "The Greatest Gypsy Dancer." *New York Herald Tribune*, November 20, 1963.
Triana, Fernando de, *Arte y Artistas Flamencos*. Ediciones Demófilo, Córdoba. 1979.
Vega de Triana, Rita, *Antonio de Triana and the Spanish Dance: A Personal Recollection.* Harwood Academic Publishers, Luxembourg. 1993.
Verdu, Juan, and José Manuel Gamboa, "*Entrevista a Rosario*." *La Caña*, No 1, December 1991. Madrid.

Index

Agüero, Juan Antonio: 305-309, 331, 364, 387
Alvarado, Domingo: 333, 369
Amaya, Antonia: 12, 14, 223, 243, 253, 295, 299, 331
Amaya, Antonio: 236, 295
Amaya, Carmen: birth and early life, 11-27; Bar de Manquet, 25; Madrid, 29, 38; Vallejo, 39-42; El Español, 38; Villa Rosa, 44; Sacromonte, 45-49; dances for the king; 50; with Raquel Meller, 80; dance style, 97; Barcelona World's Fair (1929), 103; *colombianas,* 114; Barcelona (1933), 129; meeting Sabicas, 162; Madrid, 163; meets Antonio Triana, 167; Barcelona (1935), 177; with Luisita Esteso, 177; *La Hija de Juan Simón,* 177; Sevilla (1936), 178; *María de la O,* 179; on tour in Spain, 182; Lisbon, 187; Buenos Aires (1936), 209-215; *Embrujo del fandango,* 222; New York (1941), 229; Beachcomber, 232-235; fur coats, 237-238; President Roosevelt, 239; recording for Decca (1941), 243; *Original Gypsy Dances,* 244; Carnegie Hall, 247; on tour, 251-256; *Panama Hattie,* 255; Carnegie Hall II, 256; Carmen compared with Argentinita, 258; on tour (1942) 263; Carnegie Hall III, 266; La Conga and touring (1943), 271; break with Antonio Triana, 273; Hollywood Bowl (1943), 273; Carmen's homes, 277; *Follow the Boys,* 279; Hollywood celebrities, 278, 280; *See My Lawyer,* 284; Mexico (1945), 284; romance with Sabicas, 285; Buenos Aires (1945), 286; Spain (1947), 290; Teatro Fuencarral, 291; Sevilla, 292; Paris, 294; gypsy lifestyle, 296; London, 297; Paris (1949), 304; marriage, 307; *Flamencan Songs and Dances,* 310; Barcelona (1951), 310; tours (1952-53), 315; New York (1955), 331-334; *Queen of the Gypsies,* 338; American tours (1955-57), 340; *Flamenco! Carmen Amaya,* 343; Spain (1958), 345; Paris, 348; Carmen's fountain, 349; Home in Bagur, 355; European tour (1959), 358-363; *Los Tarantos,* 363, 369; New York (1961), 365; *Furia! Amaya,* 367; Los Angeles, 368; New York (1962), 375; Casa Madrid, 376; Bagur, 380; illness, 379; last performance, 380; death, 382; epilogue, 387.
Amaya, José Santiago, "El Chino": 347
Amaya, José "El Chino": 12, 13, 15, 223, 243, 249, 266, 289
Amaya, Leonor: 12, 14, 223, 243, 248, 253, 295, 304, 341
Amaya, María: 299, 331
Amaya, Micaela: 11-12, 236, 381
Amaya, Paco: 14, 189, 223, 249
Amor Brujo, El: 23, 56, 65, 67, 110, 169, 186, 274
Anthology of Flamenco (Hispavox): 322; (Orfeón): 341
Antonio: 197, 216, 224, 240, 278, 299, 306, 318, 327
Antúnez, Fernanda and Juana: 116, 168
Argentina, La: early life, 63; castanets, 65; New York, 67; Paris,

80, 81; USA (1929), 83; photo, 90; USA (1931), 171; (1934), 174; Fernando de Triana, 176; death, 186; also, 226, 258, 260

Argentinita, La: early life, 72; recording, 74; New York debut, 84; Sánchez Mejías, 84; photo, 90; Lorca, 93; *Las Calles de Cádiz,* 167; Paris (1936); New York (1938-42), 225-231; contribution to Spanish dance, 258, 260; on her own, 267; illness and death, 280; burial, 283; also, 193, 205

Baeza, Angel: 36, 77, 145
Ballesteros, Salvador: 63, 75
bamberas: 149
Bar de Manquet: 26, 104, 129, 162
Barbero, Paco el: 159
Barcelona: 14, 19, 24
Breva, Juan: 150, 183
Bilbao, Antonio de: 55, 57, 78
Borrull, Miguel, *hijo:* 38, 75, 103
Borrull, Miguel, *padre:* 35, 38, 42
bulerías: 20, 139, 147
café cantante: 18
Calles de Cádiz, Las: 167, 207
caña, la: 197, 299, 314, 368
campanilleros: 118, 133
caracoles: 31, 54, 205, 299
Cepero, José: 33, 53, 185
Chacón, Antonio: 31-34, 40, 53, 54, 79, 112, 115, 119, 120, 147, 156, 184
Chavalillos de España: 216, 224, 240 (see also: Rosario and Antonio)
Chiquito de Triana: 292, 299
Chunga, La: 341
Civil War, Spanish: 186, 205
Colección de canciones populares españolas: 93
colombianas: 113, 288

contests: Granada, 40, 153; Córdoba, 357, 369
Copa Pavón: 40, 41
Cuenca, Amalio: 40, 59, 205
Cuenca, La: 44
cupletistas: 63
debla: 155
duende: 124, 201
Durán, Rosa: 299
Duende y Misterio del Arte Flamenco: 197, 314
Escudero, Mario: early life, 198-202, 298, 299, 305, 310, 316, 318, 327, 329, 331, 378, 389
Escudero, Vicente: early life, 54; Paris, 57, 59; debut in Spain, 60; New York (1932-35), 105; with Argentinita, 186; Paris (1936), 193; dances *siguiriyas,* 195-198; Madrid (1946), 324; *Decalogue,* 325; USA (1955), 327; end of life, 388; also, 104, 195, 201, 312
Escuela bolera: 64
Estampío, El: 44, 56, 61, 62, 78, 389
Faico: 26
fandangos: 111
Faraona, La: 45, 80, 81, 189, 295, 297, 317
farruca: 26
Flamenco! Carmen Amaya: 343
Flamencan Songs and Dances: 243, 310
fountain, Carmen's: 26, 349
Frasquillo: 82, 216
Furia! Amaya: 367
Gabrieles, Los: 32
Gades, Antonio: 360, 370, 371
garrotín: 26, 148, 162, 343, 383
Gato, El: 25, 44, 104
Generation of '98: 23
Granada, 1922 Contest of *Cante:* 40, 153

Greco, José: 233; early life, 267-269, 271, 283, 298, 313, 390
guajiras: 112
Güito, El: 360
Habichuela, Juan Gandulla: 38, 143
Heredia, René: 344, 346, 359
Huelva, Manolo de: early life, 135-138; recording, 139-142; technique, 139; also, 152, 170, 205, 300, 390
Hurok, Sol: 105, 224, 228, 230, 241, 271, 273, 281, 313
ida y vuelta, cantes de: 30, 112
Imperio, Pastora: 21-23, 63, 145, 180, 186, 283, 390
jaleos canasteros: 344
Jeroma, Currito de la: 120, 153
Joselito, La: 43, 59, 81, 95, 205
Llave del Oro del Cante: 41, 369
López, Pilar: 74, 170, 190, 225, 228, 283, 298, 299, 314, 363
Lorca, Federico García: 40, 74, 84, 86, 148, 169, 170, 171, 187
Lucena, Paco de: 34, 139, 160
Lucía, Paco de: 369
Luisillo y Teresa: 289, 293, 295, 298, 304, 305, 327
Lunar, Perico de: 37, 321, 327
Macandé, Gabriel: 78
Macarrona, Juana la: 37, 63, 78, 99, 100, 168, 169, 170, 178, 207, 216
Mairena, Antonio: 54, 125, 144, 168, 178, 291, 333, 369, 390
Malena, La: 168, 169, 170, 178, 207
Maravilla, Luis: 33, 185, 283, 298, 314
Marchena, Pepe: 24-31, 37, 40, 54, 79, 110, 114, 127, 158, 288, 300, 390
María de la O: 179
marianas: 148
Mariemma: 59, 205, 326

Marín, Rafael: 35
Marote, El: (see: Maya, Juan)
martinete (danced the first time): 197, 314
Matos, Manuel García: 169, 187, 212, 222, 224, 232, 263, 274
Matrona, Pepe el de la: 36, 43, 61, 323
Maya, Juan: 365, 368
Maya, Manuel "Manolete": 365
Medina el Viejo: 143, 150
Medina, *hijo:* 143, 151
Mejías, Ignacio Sánchez: 74, 84, 86, 116, 124, 126, 167, 171
Meller, Raquel: 63, 76, 80, 94
Meri, La: 94, 258
milonga: 112
Miracielos, El: 56
Molina, Amalia: 63, 73, 83, 92
Molina, Javier: 122, 139, 151, 156, 160, 169
Molina, Luis: 36, 57, 77, 103, 115, 151, 152
Mono, El: 348
Montes, Lola: 245, 251, 254, 273, 274, 368, 376, 383, 391
Montoya, Carlos: 38; early life, 76, 80, 92, 191, 193, 225-226, 231, 268, 283, 330, 391
Montoya, Ramón: 26, 34-38, 55, 60, 77, 114, 135, 139, 148, 151, 161, 200, 202, 204, 218, 220, 283, 300
Morca, Teo: 376
Motos, Pepe: 347
ópera flamenca: 41, 300, 313
Original Gypsy Dances: 244
Pavón, Pastora: (see: Peines, La Niña de los)
Pavón, Tomás: 154
Peines, La Niña de los: 42, 53, 54, 114, 115, 142-154, 157, 207, 300, 391

Pelao, El: 189, 209, 213, 232, 234, 236, 290
Pericón de Cádiz: 207, 321
peteneras: 149-152
Pinto, Pepe: 154
Pohren, Donn E.: 369
politics and flamenco: 182
Primo de Rivera, General: 184, 185
Puebla, La Niña de la: 133
Queen of the Gypsies: 338
Quica, La: 53, 57, 82
Ramos, Carlos: 35, 301
Reyes, Goyo: 312, 316, 342
Ricardo, Niño: 38, 118, 155-158, 207, 300, 391
Ritmos Amaya: 337, 367, 372
Rodríguez, Salud: 44, 116
rondeñas: 35, 339
Rosario and Antonio: 216, 224, 240, 278, 299, 306, 318
Ruiz, Gabriel: 58, 59, 61, 189, 195, 198
rumba: 113
Sabicas: 113; photo, 128; early life, 130-135, 158; recording, 159, 161; solo playing, 159, 161; meets Carmen Amaya, 162; Buenos Aires, 220-222; New York, 239, 245, 249, 252, 254, 264, 272; *Panama Hattie,* 255; Hollywood Bowl, 274; *Follow the Boys,* 279; romance with Carmen, 285; Mexico, 286; New York (1955), 331; *Queen of the Gypsies,* 338; *Flamenco! Carmen Amaya,* 343; leaves Carmen, 343; epilogue, 388.
Sacromonte, El: 45, 181, 365
Sánchez Mejías, Ignacio: 74, 84, 86, 116, 124, 126, 167, 171
Serneta, La: 144
Sevilla, Anita: 83, 187, 222, 275
sevillanas: 148

siguiriyas: 118; danced for the first time, 195-196
Spanish Civil War: 186, 205
tablaos: El Guajiro, 314, 357
Talve, Clarissa: 329, 342
tangos: 115, 116
Tanguera, La: 43, 59
tarantos: 117, 249, 341
Tarantos, Los: 363, 369
Teetor, Charles: 271
Tena, Lucero: 332
tientos: 115
Torre, Manuel: 41, 115-128, 154
Triana, Antonio: early life, 86; meets Carmen, 167; also, 169, 190, 192, 206, 207, 225-228, 230, 246, 254, 263, 267, 272, 273, 274, 277, 283, 391
Triana, Felipe de: 20, 42
Triana, Fernando de: 131, 146, 176
Triana, Luisa: 192, 206, 227, 283, 286, 299
Trini, La: 144
Vallejo, Manuel: 39, 42, 53, 300
varieté: 19
Vedrines, Carlos: 41, 53
Verdeal, Carlos: 37, 192
vidalita: 112
Villa Rosa (Barcelona): 42
Villa Rosa (Madrid): 33, 321
Villarino, Jerónimo: 92, 277
Yance, Luis: 37, 53, 54, 62, 86, 88
zambra: 47, 264
Zambra, La: 321
zapateado: 56